READINGS IN CHILD DEVELOPMENT AND PERSONALITY

UNDER THE EDITORSHIP OF

GARDNER MURPHY AND WAYNE H. HOLTZMAN

Readings

IN CHILD DEVELOPMENT

AND PERSONALITY

Paul Henry Mussen
UNIVERSITY OF CALIFORNIA, BERKELEY

John Janeway Conger
UNIVERSITY OF COLORADO MEDICAL CENTER

Jerome Kagan
HARVARD UNIVERSITY

Harper & Row, Publishers
NEW YORK, EVANSTON, AND LONDON

CONTENTS

Contents vii

Contents

PREFACE

Part of the excitement of studying child development stems from the fact that the field is undergoing a period of unprecedented growth. Able investigators are being attracted by the challenges of the field in increasing numbers. As research techniques grow more sophisticated, empirical knowledge expands, and new facts replace older opinions. New concepts and theories are proposed, and these, in turn, stimulate the search for further knowledge of growth and development, and the factors affecting them.

As a result, books written a decade ago often seem hopelessly out of date. The student's understanding of the field, and his interest in it, increase in depth and breadth if, in addition to textbook summaries of various theories and research findings, he is exposed to primary sources illustrating recent developments in the field.

The present volume of readings was designed to make readily available a set of essays and empirical papers, most of them written recently, representing current theory and knowledge in the field of child development. A relatively small number of articles is included but, in the editors' opinion, these reflect major problem areas of the field, fundamental theoretical concepts and issues, basic research methods, and some of the most important research findings. A wide variety of topics is included: genetic and constitutional factors in development, critical periods, effects of infantile experience, dynamics of socialization during the preschool and early school years, relationships between personality and intelligence, problems of identity in adolescence, cognitive styles, and delinquency.

The editors regard human growth as a continuous process and they view the development of personality and behavior as the result of continuing interactions between the organism and its psychological, social, and physical environment. Consequently, the sections of the book are arranged according to successive stages of development, and most of the articles emphasize antecedent-consequent relationships. The editors' introductions to the sections, describing the major substantive and theoretical issues characterizing each stage of development, provide a general context for the illustrative articles presented.

We gratefully acknowledge our indebtedness to the authors and publishers who granted us permission to reprint their articles in this volume. They are given credit in the footnotes at the beginning of each selection. Dr. Douglas

Kenny offered us many valuable criticisms and suggestions about the selection of articles. We also wish to thank Miss Audrey Smolin and Mrs. Doris Simpson who prepared the manuscript for publication.

P. H. M.
J. J. C.
J. K.

SECTION I BIOLOGICAL FACTORS
IN DEVELOPMENT: THE EARLY YEARS

The development of the child's behavior, wishes, and values is the outcome of complex and continuous interactions between biologically determined forces and his physical, psychological, and social environment. There are many biological factors that may strongly condition the individual's reactions to his environment and, consequently, his social learning and personality development. Among these are genetically determined endowments and capabilities, degree of physical and neurological maturity, and state of health or disease. Birth injury, neurological defect, glandular malfunctioning, or disease often create profound and enduring disturbances in growth and psychological development.

The first paper in this section by Professor Anne Anastasi of Fordham University demonstrates how heredity and environmental factors interact in the formation of behavior and characteristics. The findings of a number of important studies on the relationship between heredity and behavior are reviewed and briefly summarized. Some genetic factors appear to be direct determinants

1

of physical characteristics, behavior, or psychological attributes. In other cases, genetic factors operate more indirectly. Environmental forces may modify or condition the impact of the hereditary factors. The genes cannot function unless various aspects of the environment play their necessary roles. On the other hand, the influence of environmental factors is subject to certain limitations. For example, how the individual reacts to environmental forces will be affected to some extent by certain of his innate, genetically based characteristics.

An individual's intelligence, as measured by intelligence tests, is determined by both hereditary and experiential variables. On the basis of her analysis of the resemblances between adopted children's IQs and those of their true and foster parents, Dr. Marjorie Honzik of the University of California's Institute of Human Development concluded that genetic factors set the limits of the individual's mental capacity. Her work is reported in the second article of this section.

Recent research indicates that there are *critical periods* in the development of certain body organs and of physiological and psychological functions. Interference with, or disruption of, the growth process at such periods may result in permanent deficiencies or malfunctions. The occurrence of this critical period depends upon the state of the organism's physical, neurological, neuromuscular, and sensory maturation. The third article, by Dr. John P. Scott of Jackson Memorial Laboratory, is a report of some interesting observations and experiments on critical periods in the development of social behavior in puppies. Puppies that are isolated from others between the ages of 3 and 7 weeks become timid and fearful of both dogs and people. Social isolation at other periods does not have these marked effects. There are probably similar critical periods in human development, but much more research is required to establish their existence, to specify their modes of operation, and to describe their effects.

The next two articles, one by Professor Anthony Davids and his colleagues at Brown University, and the other by the University of Wisconsin's Professor Frances Graham and her co-workers, should be regarded as a "set." The first, which deals with prenatal environmental factors, shows that women who are emotionally upset and anxious during pregnancy are more likely to have difficulties in labor and delivery. Graham and her colleagues present evidence that birth trauma, such as oxygen deprivation or injury during delivery, may lead to deficiencies in neonatal sensory functioning and motor responses.

The newborn's sensory and response capabilities—generally considered to be innate or "built into" the organism—have been the foci of a vast amount of research. As more sensitive and precise techniques of experimentation, observation, and measurement have been developed, more complete and detailed descriptions of neonatal behavior have become available. The final article of this section by Robert Fantz of Western Reserve University reports some recent ingenious experiments with humans and animals demonstrating that very young infants are capable of perceiving and differentiating complex patterns of stimuli.

Another biological, genetically controlled variable, rate of physical maturing, may indirectly influence the adolescent's personality development, motivations, and self-concepts. Evidence of this may be found in the study by Paul Mussen and Mary Cover Jones, presented in Section VI of this volume. This article could have been appropriately included in Section I.

HEREDITY, ENVIRONMENT, AND THE QUESTION "HOW?"[1]

Anne Anastasi
FORDHAM UNIVERSITY

TWO OR THREE DECADES AGO, the so-called heredity-environment question was the center of lively controversy. Today, on the other hand, many psychologists look upon it as a dead issue. It is now generally conceded that both hereditary and environmental factors enter into all behavior. The reacting organism is a product of its genes and its past environment, while present environment provides the immediate stimulus for current behavior. To be sure, it can be argued that, although a given trait may result from the combined influence of hereditary and environmental factors, a specific difference in this trait between individuals or between groups may be traceable to either hereditary or environmental factors alone. The design of most traditional investigations undertaken to identify such factors, however, has been such as to yield inconclusive answers. The same set of data has frequently led to opposite conclusions in the hands of psychologists with different orientations.

Nor have efforts to determine the proportional contribution of hereditary and environmental factors to observed individual differences in given traits met with any greater success. Apart from difficulties in controlling conditions, such investigations have usually been based upon the implicit assumption that hereditary and environmental factors combine in an additive fashion. Both geneticists and psychologists have repeatedly demonstrated, however, that a more tenable hypothesis is that of interaction (15, 22, 28, 40). In other words, the nature and extent of the influence of each type of factor depend upon the contribution of the

[1] Address of the President, Division of General Psychology, American Psychological Association, September 4, 1957.

Reprinted from *Psychological Review* (1958), **65** (4), 197–208, by permission of the author and the American Psychological Association.

other. Thus the proportional contribution of heredity to the variance of a given trait, rather than being a constant, will vary under different environmental conditions. Similarly, under different hereditary conditions, the relative contribution of environment will differ. Studies designed to estimate the proportional contribution of heredity and environment, however, have rarely included measures of such interaction. The only possible conclusion from such research would thus seem to be that both heredity and environment contribute to all behavior traits and that the extent of their respective contributions cannot be specified for any trait. Small wonder that some psychologists regard the heredity-environment question as unworthy of further consideration!

But is this really all we can find out about the operation of heredity and environment in the etiology of behavior? Perhaps we have simply been asking the wrong questions. The traditional questions about heredity and environment may be intrinsically unanswerable. Psychologists began by asking *which* type of factor, hereditary or environmental, is responsible for individual differences in a given trait. Later, they tried to discover *how much* of the variance was attributable to heredity and how much to environment. It is the primary contention of this paper that a more fruitful approach is to be found in the question *"How?"* There is still much to be learned about the specific modus operandi of hereditary and environmental factors in the development of behavioral differences. And there are several current lines of research which offer promising techniques for answering the question "How?"

VARIETY OF INTERACTION MECHANISMS

Hereditary Factors

If we examine some of the specific ways in which hereditary factors may influence behavior, we cannot fail but be impressed by their wide diversity. At one extreme, we find such conditions as phenylpyruvic amentia and amaurotic idiocy. In these cases, certain essential physical prerequisites for normal intellectual development are lacking as a result of hereditary metabolic disorders. In our present state of knowledge, there is no environmental factor which can completely counteract this hereditary deficit. The individual will be mentally defective, regardless of the type of environmental conditions under which he is reared.

A somewhat different situation is illustrated by hereditary deafness, which may lead to intellectual retardation through interference with normal social interaction, language development, and schooling. In such a case, however, the hereditary handicap can be offset by appropriate adaptations of training procedures. It has been said, in fact, that the degree of intellectual backwardness of the deaf is an index of the state of development of special instructional facilities. As the latter improve, the intellectual retardation associated with deafness is correspondingly reduced.

A third example is provided by inherited susceptibility to certain physical diseases, with consequent protracted ill health. If environmental conditions are such that illness does in fact develop, a number of different behavioral effects may follow. Intellectually, the individual may be handicapped by his inability to attend school regularly. On the other hand, depending upon age of onset, home conditions, parental status, and similar factors, poor health may have the effect of concentrating the individual's energies upon intellectual pursuits. The curtailment of participation in athletics and social functions may serve to strengthen interest in reading and other sedentary activities. Concomitant circumstances would also determine the influence of such illness upon personality development. And it is well known that the latter effects could run the gamut from a deepening of human sympathy to psychiatric breakdown.

Finally, heredity may influence behavior through the mechanism of social stereotypes. A wide variety of inherited physical characteristics have served as visible cues for identifying such stereotypes. These cues thus lead to behavioral restrictions or opportunities and—at a more subtle level—to social attitudes and expectancies. All of these influences eventually leave their mark upon his abilities and inabilities, his emotional reactions, goals, ambitions, and outlook on life.

The geneticist Dobzhansky illustrates this type of mechanism by means of a dramatic hypothetical situation. He points out that if there were a culture in which the carriers of blood group AB were considered aristocrats, and those of blood group O laborers, then the blood-group genes would become important hereditary determiners of behavior (12, p. 147). Obviously the association between blood group and behavior would be specific to that culture. But such specificity is an essential property of the causal mechanism under consideration.

More realistic examples are not hard to find. The most familiar instances occur in connection with constitutional types, sex, and race. Sex and skin pigmentation obviously depend upon heredity. General body build is strongly influenced by hereditary components, although also susceptible to environmental modification. That all these physical characteristics may exert a pronounced effect upon behavior within a given culture is well known. It is equally apparent, of course, that in different cultures the behavioral correlates of such hereditary physical traits may be quite unlike. A specific physical cue may be completely unrelated to individual differences in psychological traits in one culture, while closely correlated with them in another. Or it may be associated with totally dissimilar behavior characteristics in two different cultures.

It might be objected that some of the illustrations which have been cited do not properly exemplify the operation of hereditary mechanisms in behavior development since hereditary factors enter only indirectly into the behavior in question. Closer examination, however, shows this distinction to be untenable. First it may be noted that the influence of heredity upon behavior is always indirect. No psychological trait is ever inherited as such. All we can ever say directly from behavioral observations is that a given trait shows evidence of being influenced by certain "inheritable unknowns." This merely defines a problem for genetic research; it does not provide a causal explanation. Unlike the blood groups, which are close to the level of primary gene products, psychological traits are related to genes by highly indirect and devious routes. Even the mental deficiency associated with phenylketonuria is several steps removed from the chemically defective genes that represent its hereditary basis. Moreover, hereditary influences cannot be dichotomized into the more direct and the less direct. Rather do they represent a whole "continuum of indirectness," along which are found all degrees of remoteness of causal links. The examples already cited illustrate a few of the points on this continuum.

It should be noted that as we proceed along the continuum of indirectness, the range of variation of possible outcomes of hereditary factors expands rapidly. At each step in the causal chain, there is fresh opportunity for interaction with other hereditary factors as well as with environmental factors. And since each interaction in turn determines the direction of subsequent interactions, there is an ever-widening network of possible outcomes. If we visualize a simple sequential grid with only two alternatives at each point, it is obvious that there are two possible outcomes in the one-stage situation, four outcomes at the second stage, eight at the third, and so on in geometric progression. The actual situation is undoubtedly much more complex, since there will usually be more than two alternatives at any one point.

In the case of the blood groups, the relation to specific genes is so close that no other concomitant hereditary or environmental conditions can alter the outcome. If the organism survives at all, it will have the blood group determined by its genes. Among psychological traits, on the other hand, some variation in outcome is always possible as a result of concurrent circumstances. Even in cases of phenylketonuria, intellectual development will exhibit some relationship with the type of care and training available to the individual. That behavioral outcomes show progressive diversification as we proceed along the continuum of indirectness is brought out by the other examples which were cited. Chronic illness *can* lead to scholarly renown or to intellectual immaturity; a mesomorphic physique *can* be a contributing factor in juvenile delinquency or in the attainment of a college presidency! Published data on Sheldon somatotypes provide some support for both of the latter outcomes.

Parenthetically, it may be noted that geneticists have sometimes used the term "norm of reaction" to designate the range of variation of possible outcomes of gene properties (cf. *13*, p. 161). Thus heredity sets the "norm" or limits within which environmental differences determine the eventual outcome. In the case of some traits, such as blood groups or eye color, this norm is much narrower than in the case of other traits. Owing to the rather different psychological connotations of both the words "norm" and "reaction," however, it seems less confusing to speak of the "range of variation" in this context.

A large portion of the continuum of hereditary influences which we have described coincides with the domain of somatopsychological relations, as defined by Barker *et al.* (*6*). Under this heading, Barker includes "variations in physique that affect the psychological situation of a person by influencing the effectiveness of his body as a tool for actions or by serving as a stimulus to himself or others" (*6*, p. 1). Relatively direct neurological influences on behavior, which have been the traditional concern of physiological psychology, are excluded from this definition, Barker being primarily concerned with what he calls the "social psychology of physique." Of the examples cited in the present paper, deafness, severe illness, and the physical characteristics associated with social stereotypes would meet the specifications of somatopsychological factors.

The somatic factors to which Barker refers, however, are not limited to those of hereditary origin. Bodily conditions attributable to environmental causes operate in the same sorts of somatopsychological relations as those traceable to heredity. In fact, heredity-environment distinctions play a minor part in Barker's approach.

Environmental Factors

Organic. Turning now to an analysis of the role of environmental factors in behavior, we find the same etiological mechanisms which were observed in the case of hereditary factors. First, however, we must differentiate between two classes of environmental influences: (a) those producing organic effects which may in turn influence behavior and (b) those serving as direct stimuli for psychological reactions. The former may be illustrated by food intake or by exposure to bacterial infection; the latter, by tribal initiation ceremonies or by a course in algebra. There are no completely satisfactory names by which to designate these two classes of influences. In an earlier paper by Anastasi and Foley (4), the terms "structural" and "functional" were employed. However, "organic" and "behavioral" have the advantage of greater familiarity in this context and may be less open to misinterpretation. Accordingly, these terms will be used in the present paper.

Like hereditary factors, environmental influences of an organic nature can also be ordered along a continuum of indirectness with regard to their relation to behavior. This continuum closely parallels that of hereditary factors. One end is typified by such conditions as mental deficiency resulting from cerebral birth injury or from prenatal nutritional inadequacies. A more indirect etiological mechanism is illustrated by severe motor disorder—as in certain cases of cerebral palsy—*without* accompanying injury to higher neurological centers. In such instances, intellectual retardation may occur as an indirect result of the motor handicap, through the curtailment of educational and social activities. Obviously this causal mechanism corresponds closely to that of hereditary deafness cited earlier in the paper.

Finally, we may consider an environmental parallel to the previously discussed social stereotypes which were mediated by hereditary physical cues. Let us suppose that a young woman with mousy brown hair becomes transformed into a dazzling golden blonde through environmental techniques currently available in our culture. It is highly probable that this metamorphosis will alter, not only the reactions of her associates toward her, but also her own self-concept and subsequent behavior. The effects could range all the way from a rise in social poise to a drop in clerical accuracy!

Among the examples of environmentally determined organic influences which have been described, all but the first two fit Barker's definition of somatopsychological factors. With the exception of birth injuries and nutritional deficiencies, all fall within the social psychology of physique. Nevertheless, the individual factors exhibit wide diversity in their specific modus operandi—a diversity which has important practical as well as theoretical implications.

Behavioral. The second major class of environmental factors—the behavioral as contrasted to the organic—are by definition direct influences. The immediate effect of such environmental factors is always a behavioral change. To be sure, some of the initial behavioral effects may themselves indirectly affect the individual's later behavior. But this relationship can perhaps be best conceptualized in terms of breadth and permanence of effects. Thus it could be said that we are now dealing, not with a continuum of indirectness, as in the case of hereditary and organic-environmental factors, but rather with a continuum of breadth.

Social class membership may serve as an illustration of a relatively broad, pervasive, and enduring environmental factor. Its influence upon behavior development may operate through many channels. Thus social level may determine the range and nature of intellectual stimulation provided by home and community through books, music, art, play activities, and the like. Even more far-reaching may be the effects upon interests and motivation, as illustrated by the desire to perform abstract intellectual tasks, to surpass others in competitive situations, to succeed in school, or to gain social approval. Emotional and social traits may likewise be influenced by the nature of interpersonal relations characterizing homes at different socioeconomic levels. Somewhat more restricted in scope than social class, although still exerting a relatively broad influence, is amount of formal schooling which the individual is able to obtain.

A factor which may be wide or narrow in its effects, depending upon concomitant circumstances, is language handicap. Thus the bilingualism of an adult who moves to a foreign country with inadequate mastery of the new language represents a relatively limited handicap which can be readily overcome in most cases. At most, the difficulty is one of communication. On the other hand, some kinds of bilingualism in childhood may exert a retarding influence upon intellectual development and may, under certain conditions, affect personality development adversely (2, 5, 10). A common pattern is that the child speaks one language at home and another in school, so that his knowledge of each language is limited to certain types of situations. Inadequate facility with the language of the school interferes with the acquisition of basic concepts, intellectual skills, and information. The frustration engendered by scholastic difficulties may in turn lead to discouragement and general dislike of school. Such reactions can be found, for example, among a number of Puerto Rican children in New York City schools (3). In the case of certain groups, moreover, the child's foreign language background may be perceived by himself and his associates as a symbol of minority group status and may thereby augment any emotional maladjustment arising from such status (34).

A highly restricted environmental influence is to be found in the opportunity to acquire specific items of information occurring in a particular intelligence test. The fact that such opportunities may vary with culture, social class, or individual experiential background is at the basis of the test user's concern with the problem of coaching and with "culture-free" or "culture-fair" tests (cf. 1, 2). If the advantage or disadvantage which such experiential differences confer upon certain individuals is strictly confined to performance on the given test, it will obviously reduce the validity of the test and should be eliminated.

In this connection, however, it is essential to know the breadth of the environmental influence in question. A fallacy inherent in many attempts to develop culture-fair tests is that the breadth of cultural differentials is not taken into account. Failure to consider breadth of effect likewise characterizes certain discussions of coaching. If, in coaching a student for a college admission test, we can improve his knowledge of verbal concepts and his reading comprehension, he will be better equipped to succeed in college courses. His performance level will thus be raised, not only on the test, but also on the criterion which the test is intended to predict. To try to devise a test which is not susceptible to such coaching would merely reduce the effectiveness of the test. Similarly, efforts to rule out cultural differentials from test items so as to make them equally "fair" to subjects in different social classes or in different cultures may merely limit the usefulness of the test, since the same cultural differentials may operate within the broader area of behavior which the test is designed to sample.

METHODOLOGICAL APPROACHES

The examples considered so far should suffice to highlight the wide variety of ways in which hereditary and environmental factors may interact in the course of behavior development. There is clearly a need for identifying explicitly the etiological mechanism whereby any given hereditary or environmental condition ultimately leads to a behavioral characteristic—in other words, the "how" of heredity and environment. Accordingly, we may now take a quick look at some promising methodological approaches to the question "how."

Within the past decade, an increasing number of studies have been designed to trace the connection between specific factors in the hereditary backgrounds or in the reactional biographies of individuals and their observed behavioral characteristics. There has been a definite shift away from the predominantly descriptive and correlational approach of the earlier decades toward more deliberate attempts to verify explanatory hypotheses. Similarly, the cataloguing of group differences in psychological traits has been giving way gradually to research on *changes* in group characteristics following altered conditions.

Among recent methodological developments, we have chosen seven as being particularly relevant to the analysis of etiological mechanisms. The first represents an extension of selective breeding investigations to permit the identification of specific hereditary conditions underlying the observed behavioral differences. When early selective breeding investigations such as those of Tryon (36) on rats indicated that "maze learning ability" was inherited, we were still a long way from knowing what was actually being transmitted by the genes. It was obviously not "maze learning ability" as such. Twenty—or even ten—years ago, some psychologists would have suggested that it was probably general intelligence. And a few might even have drawn a parallel with the inheritance of human intelligence.

But today investigators have been asking: Just what makes one group of rats learn mazes more quickly than the other? Is it differences in motivation, emotionality, speed of running, general activity level? If so, are these behavioral characteristics in turn dependent upon group differences in glandular development, body weight, brain size, biochemical factors, or some other organic conditions? A number of recent and ongoing investigations indicate that attempts are being made to trace, at least part of the way, the steps whereby certain chemical properties of the genes may ultimately lead to specified behavior characteristics.

An example of such a study is provided by Searle's (31) follow-up of Tryon's research. Working with the strains of maze-bright and maze-dull rats developed by Tryon, Searle demonstrated that the two strains differed in a number of emotional and motivational factors, rather than in ability. Thus the strain differences were traced one step further, although many links still remain to be found between maze learning and genes. A promising methodological development within the same general area is to be found in the recent research of Hirsch and Tryon (18). Utilizing a specially devised technique for measuring individual differences in behavior among lower organisms, these investigators launched a series of studies on selective breeding for behavioral characteristics in the fruit fly, *Drosophilia*. Such research can capitalize on the mass of available genetic knowledge regarding the morphology of *Drosophilia,* as well as on other advantages of using such an organism in genetic studies.

Further evidence of current interest in the specific hereditary factors which influence behavior is to be found in an extensive research program in progress at the Jackson Memorial Laboratory, under the direction of Scott and Fuller (30). In general, the project is concerned with the be-havioral characteristics of various breeds and cross-breeds of dogs. Analyses of some of the data gathered to date again suggest that "dif-ferences in performance are produced by differences in emotional, moti-vational, and peripheral processes, and that genetically caused differ-ences in central processes may be either slight or nonexistent" (29, p. 225). In other parts of the same project, breed differences in physiological characteristics, which may in turn be related to behavioral differences, have been established.

A second line of attack is the exploration of possible relationships between behavioral characteristics and physiological variables which may in turn be traceable to hereditary factors. Research on EEG, au-tonomic balance, metabolic processes, and biochemical factors illustrates this approach. A lucid demonstration of the process of tracing a psycho-logical condition to genetic factors is provided by the identification and subsequent investigation of phenylpyruvic amentia. In this case, the causal chain from defective gene, through metabolic disorder and con-sequent cerebral malfunctioning, to feeblemindedness and other overt symptoms can be described step by step (cf. 32; 33, pp. 389–391). Also relevant are the recent researches on neurological and biochemical cor-relates of schizophrenia (9). Owing to inadequate methodological con-trols, however, most of the findings of the latter studies must be regarded as tentative (19).

Prenatal environmental factors provide a third avenue of fruitful in-vestigation. Especially noteworthy is the recent work of Pasamanick and his associates (27), which demonstrated a tie-up between socioeconomic level, complications of pregnancy and parturition, and psychological dis-orders of the offspring. In a series of studies on large samples of whites and Negroes in Baltimore, these investigators showed that various pre-natal and paranatal disorders are significantly related to the occurrence of mental defect and psychiatric disorders in the child. An important source of such irregularities in the process of childbearing and birth is to be found in deficiencies of maternal diet and in other conditions associated with low socioeconomic status. An analysis of the data did in fact reveal a much higher frequency of all such medical complications in lower than in higher socioeconomic levels, and a higher frequency among Negroes than among whites.

Direct evidence of the influence of prenatal nutritional factors upon subsequent intellectual development is to be found in a recent, well controlled experiment by Harrell *et al.* (16). The subjects were pregnant women in low-income groups whose normal diets were generally quite deficient. A dietary supplement was administered to some of these women during pregnancy and lactation, while an equated control group received placebos. When tested at the ages of three and four years, the offspring of the experimental group obtained a significantly higher mean IQ than did the offspring of the controls.

Mention should also be made of animal experiments on the effects of such factors as prenatal radiation and neonatal asphyxia upon cerebral anomalies as well as upon subsequent behavior development. These experimental studies merge imperceptibly into the fourth approach to be considered, namely, the investigation of the influence of early experience upon the eventual behavioral characteristics of animals. Research in this area has been accumulating at a rapid rate. In 1954, Beach and Jaynes (8) surveyed this literature for the *Psychological Bulletin,* listing over 130 references. Several new studies have appeared since that date (e.g., 14, 21, 24, 25, 35). The variety of factors covered ranges from the type and quantity of available food to the extent of contact with human culture. A large number of experiments have been concerned with various forms of sensory deprivation and with diminished opportunities for motor exercise. Effects have been observed in many kinds of animals and in almost all aspects of behavior, including perceptual responses, motor activity, learning, emotionality, and social reactions.

In their review, Beach and Jaynes pointed out that research in this area has been stimulated by at least four distinct theoretical interests. Some studies were motivated by the traditional concern with the relative contribution of maturation and learning to behavior development. Others were designed in an effort to test certain psychoanalytic theories regarding infantile experiences, as illustrated by studies which limited the feeding responses of young animals. A third relevant influence is to be found in the work of the European biologist Lorenz (23) on early social stimulation of birds, and in particular on the special type of learning for which the term "imprinting" has been coined. A relatively large number of recent studies have centered around Hebb's (17) theory regarding the importance of early perceptual experiences upon subsequent performance in learning situations. All this research represents a rapidly growing and promising attack on the modus operandi of specific environmental factors.

The human counterpart of these animal studies may be found in the comparative investigation of child-rearing practices in different cultures and subcultures. This represents the fifth approach in our list. An outstanding example of such a study is that by Whiting and Child (38), published in 1953. Utilizing data on 75 primitive societies from the Cross-Cultural Files of the Yale Institute of Human Relations, these investigators set out to test a number of hypotheses regarding the relationships between child-rearing practices and personality development. This analysis was followed up by field observations in five cultures, the results of which have not yet been reported (cf. 37).

Within our own culture, similar surveys have been concerned with the diverse psychological environments provided by different social classes (11). Of particular interest are the study by Williams and Scott (39) on the association between socioeconomic level, permissiveness, and motor development among Negro children, and the exploratory research by Milner (26) on the relationship between reading readiness in first-grade children and patterns of parent-child interaction. Milner found that upon school entrance the lower-class child seems to lack chiefly two advantages enjoyed by the middle-class child. The first is described as "a warm positive family atmosphere or adult-relationship pattern which is more and more being recognized as a motivational prerequisite of any kind of adult-controlled learning." The lower-class children in Milner's study perceived adults as predominantly hostile. The second advantage is an extensive opportunity to interact verbally with adults in the family. The latter point is illustrated by parental attitudes toward mealtime conversation, lower-class parents tending to inhibit and discourage such conversation, while middle-class parents encourage it.

Most traditional studies on child-rearing practices have been designed in terms of a psychoanalytic orientation. There is need for more data pertaining to other types of hypotheses. Findings such as those of Milner on opportunities for verbalization and the resulting effects upon reading readiness represent a step in this direction. Another possible source of future data is the application of the intensive observational techniques of psychological ecology developed by Barker and Wright (7) to widely diverse socioeconomic groups.

A sixth major approach involves research on the previously cited somatopsychological relationships (6). To date, little direct information is available on the precise operation of this class of factors in psychological development. The multiplicity of ways in which physical traits—whether hereditary or environmental in origin—may influence behavior thus offers a relatively unexplored field for future study.

The seventh and final approach to be considered represents an adaptation of traditional twin studies. From the standpoint of the question "How?" there is need for closer coordination between the usual data on twin resemblance and observations of the family interactions of twins. Available data already suggests, for example, that closeness of contact and extent of environmental similarity are greater in the case of monozygotic than in the case of dizygotic twins (cf. 2). Information on the social reactions of twins toward each other and the specialization of roles is likewise of interest (2). Especially useful would be longitudinal studies of twins, beginning in early infancy and following the subjects through school age. The operation of differential environmental pressures, the development of specialized roles, and other environmental influences could thus be more clearly identified and correlated with intellectual and personality changes in the growing twins.

Parenthetically, I should like to add a remark about the traditional applications of the twin method, in which persons in different degrees of hereditary and environmental relationships to each other are simply compared for behavioral similarity. In these studies, attention has been focused principally upon the amount of resemblance of monozygotic as contrasted to dizygotic twins. Yet such a comparison is particularly difficult to interpret because of the many subtle differences in the environmental situations of the two types of twins. A more fruitful comparison would seem to be that between dizygotic twins and siblings, for whom the hereditary similarity is known to be the same.

In Kallmann's monumental research on psychiatric disorders among twins (20), for example, one of the most convincing bits of evidence for the operation of hereditary factors in schizophrenia is the fact that the degrees of concordance for dizygotic twins and for siblings were practically identical. In contrast, it will be recalled that in intelligence test scores dizygotic twins resemble each other much more closely than do siblings—a finding which reveals the influence of environmental factors in intellectual development.

SUMMARY

The heredity-environment problem is still very much alive. Its viability is assured by the gradual replacement of the questions, "Which one?" and "How much?" by the more basic and appropriate question, "How?" Hereditary influences—as well as environmental factors of an organic nature—vary along a "continuum of indirectness." The more indirect their connection with behavior, the wider will be the range of variation of possible outcomes. One extreme of the continuum of indirectness may be illustrated by brain damage leading to mental deficiency; the other extreme, by physical characteristics associated with social stereotypes. Examples of factors falling at intermediate points include deafness, physical diseases, and motor disorders. Those environmental factors which act directly upon behavior can be ordered along a continuum of breadth or permanence of effect, as exemplified by social class membership, amount of formal schooling, language handicap, and familiarity with specific test items.

Several current lines of research offer promising techniques for exploring the modus operandi of hereditary and environmental factors. Outstanding among them are investigations of: (a) hereditary conditions which underlie behavioral differences between selectively bred groups of animals; (b) relations between physiological variables and individual differences in behavior, especially in the case of pathological deviation; (c) role of prenatal physiological factors in behavior development; (d) influence of early experience upon eventual behavioral characteristics; (e) cultural differences in child-rearing practices in relation to intellectual and emotional development; (f) mechanisms of somatopsychological relationships; and (g) psychological development of twins from infancy to maturity, together with observations of their social environment. Such approaches are extremely varied with regard to subjects employed, nature of psychological functions studied, and specific experimental procedures followed. But it is just such heterogeneity of methodology that is demanded by the wide diversity of ways in which hereditary and environmental factors interact in behavior development.

REFERENCES

1. Anastasi, Anne. *Psychological testing.* New York: Macmillan, 1954.
2. Anastasi, Anne. *Differential psychology.* (3rd ed.) New York: Macmillan, 1958.
3. Anastasi, Anne, & Cordova, F. A. Some effects of bilingualism upon the intelligence test performance of Puerto Rican children in New York City. *J. educ. Psychol.*, 1953, **44**, 1–19.

4. Anastasi, Anne, & Foley, J. P., Jr. A proposed reorientation in the heredity-environment controversy. *Psychol. Rev.*, 1948, **55**, 239–249.

5. Arsenian, B. Bilingualism in the postwar world. *Psychol. Bull.*, 1945, **42**, 65–86.

6. Barker, R. G., Wright, Beatrice A., Myerson, L., & Gonick, Mollie R. Adjustment to physical handicap and illness: a survey of the social psychology of physique and disability. *Soc. Sci. Res. Coun. Bull.*, 1953, No. 55 (rev.).

7. Barker, R. G., & Wright, H. F. *Midwest and its children: the psychological ecology of an American town.* Evanston, Ill.: Row, Peterson, 1955.

8. Beach, F. A., & Jaynes, J. Effects of early experience upon the behavior of animals. *Psychol. Bull.*, 1954, **51**, 239–263.

9. Brackbill, G. A. Studies of brain dysfunction in schizophrenia. *Psychol. Bull.*, 1956, **53**, 210–226.

10. Darcy, Natalie T. A review of the literature on the effects of bilingualism upon the measurement of intelligence. *J. genet. Psychol.*, 1953, **82**, 21–57.

11. Davis, A., & Havighurst, R. J. Social class and color differences in child rearing. *Amer. sociol. Rev.*, 1946, **11**, 698–710.

12. Dobzhansky, T. The genetic nature of differences among men. In S. Pearsons (Ed.) *Evolutionary thought in America.* New Haven: Yale University Press, 1950. Pp. 86–155.

13. Dobzhansky, T. Heredity, environment, and evolution. *Science,* 1950, **111**, 161–166.

14. Forgus, R. H. The effect of early perceptual learning on the behavioral organization of adult rats. *J. comp. physiol. Psychol.*, 1954, **47**, 331–336.

15. Haldane, J. B. S. *Heredity and politics.* New York: Norton, 1938.

16. Harrell, Ruth F., Woodyard, Ella, & Gates, A. I. *The effect of mothers' diets on the intelligence of the offspring.* New York: Bur. Publ., Teach. Coll., Columbia Univer., 1955.

17. Hebb, D. O. *The organization of behavior.* New York: Wiley, 1949.

18. Hirsch, J. & Tryon, R. C. Mass screening and reliable individual measurement in the experimental behavior genetics of lower organisms. *Psychol. Bull.*, 1956, **124**, 429–430.

19. Horwitt, M. K. Fact and artifact in the biology of schizophrenia. *Science,* 1956, **53**, 429–430.

20. Kallman, F. J. *Heredity in health and mental disorder; principles of psychiatric genetics in the light of comparative twin studies.* New York: Norton, 1953.

21. King, J. A., & Gurney, Nancy L. Effect of early social experience on adult aggressive behavior in C57BL10 mice. *J. comp. physiol. Psychol.*, 1954, **47**, 326–330.

22. Loevinger, Jane. On the proportional contributions of differences in nature and in nurture to differences in intelligence. *Psychol. Bull.*, 1943, **40**, 725–756.

23. Lorenz, K. Der Kumpan in der Umwelt des Vogels, Der Artgenosse als auslosendes Moment sozialer Verhaltungsweisen. *J. Orn., Lpz.,* 1935, **83**, 137–213; 289–413.

24. Luchins, A. S., & Forgus, R. H. The effect of differential postweaning environment on the rigidity of an animal's behavior. *J. genet. Psychol.*, 1955, **86**, 51–58.
25. Melzack, R. The genesis of emotional behavior: an experimental study of the dog. *J. comp. physiol. Psychol.*, 1954, **47**, 166–168.
26. Milner, Esther A. A study of the relationships between reading readiness in grade one school children and patterns of parent-child interaction. *Child Develpm.*, 1951, **22**, 95–112.
27. Pasamanick, B., Knobloch, Hilda, & Lilienfeld, A. M. Socioeconomic status and some precursors of neuropsychiatric disorder. *Amer. J. Orthopsychiat.*, 1956, **26**, 594–601.
28. Schwesinger, Gladys C. *Heredity and environment.* New York: Macmillan, 1933.
29. Scott, J. P., & Charles, Margaret S. Some problems of heredity and social behavior. *J. genet. Psychol.*, 1953, **48**, 209–230.
30. Scott, J. P., & Fuller, J. L. Research on genetics and social behavior at the Roscoe B. Jackson Memorial Laboratory, 1946–1951—a progress report. *J. Hered.*, 1951, **42**, 191–197.
31. Searle, L. V. The organization of hereditary maze-brightness and maze-dullness. *Genet. psychol. Monogr.*, 1949, **39**, 279–325.
32. Snyder, L. H. The genetic approach to human individuality. *Sci. Mon., N.Y.*, 1949, **68**, 165–171.
33. Snyder, L. H., & David, P. R. *The principles of heredity.* (5th ed.) Boston: Heath, 1957.
34. Spoerl, Dorothy T. Bilinguality and emotional adjustment. *J. abnorm. soc. Psychol.*, 1943, **38**, 37–57.
35. Thompson, W. R., & Melzack, R. Early environment. *Sci. Amer.*, 1956, **194** (1), 38–42.
36. Tryon, R. C. Genetic differences in maze-learning ability in rats. *Yearb. nat. Soc. Stud. Educ.*, 1940, **39**, Part I, 111–119.
37. Whiting, J. W. M. *et al.* Field guide for a study of socialization in five societies. Cambridge, Mass.: Harvard Univ., 1954 (mimeo.).
38. Whiting, J. W. M., & Child, I. L. *Child training and personality: a cross-cultural study.* New Haven: Yale University Press, 1953.
39. Williams, Judith R., & Scott, R. B. Growth and development of Negro infants: IV. Motor development and its relationship to child rearing practices in two groups of Negro infants. *Child Develpm.*, 1953, **24**, 103–121.
40. Woodworth, R. S. Heredity and environment: a critical survey of recently published material on twins and foster children. *Soc. Sci. Res. Coun. Bull.*, 1941, No. 47.

DEVELOPMENTAL STUDIES OF PARENT-CHILD RESEMBLANCE IN INTELLIGENCE[1]

Marjorie P. Honzik
UNIVERSITY OF CALIFORNIA INSTITUTE OF HUMAN
DEVELOPMENT

A NUMBER OF DEVELOPMENTAL studies have reported that the mental test scores of children under two years have little or no relationship to parental ability as measured by the number of years of schooling, ratings of intelligence, or test scores (1, 2, 6). When these same children are re-tested at later ages, their mental test scores are found to be significantly correlated with parental ability. A crucial question is the extent to which these age changes in relationship are due to environmental factors, or to intrinsic differences in the patterns of mental growth. One way in which this increasing resemblance can be evaluated is by comparing the age changes in the correlations which occur among children reared by their own parents in contrast to those reared apart from their parents.

In this report we shall compare the age changes in relationship for two distinct groups, each of over 100 children, who were tested at various ages between 21 months and 16 years; and then contrast this trend with that reported by Skodak and Skeels for 100 adopted children who were tested four times between their second and fourteenth year (6).

In the Guidance Study at the University of California Institute of Child Welfare, a sample of 252 children who were representative of those born in Berkeley during an 18-month period were divided into equivalent subsamples called the "Guidance" and "Control" groups. This division of the main sample was made on the basis of certain socioeconomic variables before the mental testing program was begun (5). The children

[1] Acknowledgment is due Harold E. Jones and John P. McKee for their helpful suggestions and to the U.S. Public Health Service for clerical and statistical assistance.

Reprinted from *Child Development* (June, 1957), 28 (2), 215–228, by permission of the author and the Society for Research in Child Development.

in the two groups were first brought to the Institute for mental tests at the age of 21 months. The tests used at this age level and at the subsequent testings during the preschool years were the California Preschool Schedules (see Table 1). Beginning at six years, the 1916 Stanford Revision of the Binet Scale was the test used, with a shift to the 1937 Revision at age eight. The parents were not given intelligence tests but the number of years of schooling is known for both parents. In addition, in the Guidance group, ratings (on a seven-point scale) of the mothers' intelligence were made when the children were between 3½ and 4½ years by staff members who had had many hours of discussion with the mothers.[2] The correlation between these ratings of the moth-

TABLE 1. *Correlations of the Children's Mental Test Scores with the Mother's Education and Ratings of Her Intelligence (G = Guidance Group; C = Control Group)*

								Relation of the Children's Mental Test Scores X
Age in Years	Mental Test Given Children	Number of Cases			Mother's Education			Ratings of Mother's Intelligence
		G	C	G + C	G	C	G + C	G
					r	r	r	r
1¾	Calif. Preschool	117	117	234	.13	00	.06	.11
2	Calif. Preschool	113	—	113	.07	—	.07	.08
2½	Calif. Preschool	114	—	114	.10	—	.10	.06
3	Calif. Preschool	116	113	229	.10	.08	.09	.17
3½	Calif. Preschool	107	108	215	.27a	.25a	.26a	.39a
4	Calif. Preschool	105	106	211	.22b	.25a	.23a	.38a
5	Calif. Preschool	104	106	210	.45a	.25a	.35a	.53a
6	Stanf.-Binet (1916 rev.)	109	102	211	.27a	.37a	.32a	.40a
7	Stanf.-Binet (1916 rev.)	104	104	208	.35a	.33a	.33a	.51a
8	Stanf., Form L	100	98	198	.34a	.32a	.33a	.54a
10	Stanf., Form L or M	105	92	197	.33a	.34a	.34a	.52a
12 or 13	Stanf., Form L or M	98	94	192	.38a	.38a	.38a	.54a
14 or 15	Stanf., Form L or M	90	78	168	.39a	.30a	.35a	.59a

[a] Significant at the 1 percent level.
[b] Significant at the 5 percent level.

[2] Ratings used were an average of these ratings made independently for each mother by a psychiatric social worker and Dr. Jean W. Macfarlane, Director of the Guidance Study. The ratings were made without reference to the mental test scores of the children who were tested on the then new California Preschool Scales. These scales were scored in final form several years after the parental ratings were assigned.

ers' intelligence and the number of years of schooling of the mothers is +.73. In fact, in this study all measures which reflect the ability of the parents were intercorrelated to about the same extent (socioeconomic status correlates with both mothers' and fathers' schooling +.73; mothers' and fathers' schooling correlate +.74). The relationship between these indices of parental ability and the children's mental test scores was reported earlier for the age period 21 months to 8 years (2).

The correlation between the education of the mothers and the children's mental test scores at 21 months was negligible but between 3 and 3½ years, the relationship became significant (see Table 1). To check the validity of this age trend, correlations were computed separately for the two subsamples of the total Guidance Study sample. The results of this comparison are shown in Table 1 and Figure 1. The finding that

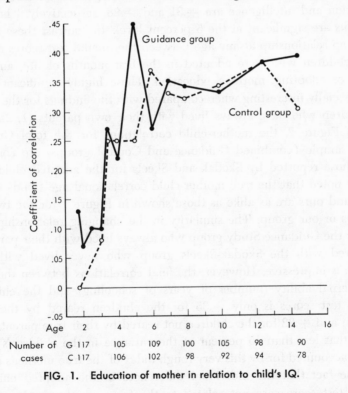

FIG. 1.   Education of mother in relation to child's IQ.

these subsamples exhibit essentially the same age changes in relationship suggests that the trend is a valid one and would be duplicated in comparable developmental studies; in fact, Bayley (1) has reported a similar trend in the Berkeley Growth Study.

In a study of 100 adopted children, Skodak and Skeels report that adopted children whose true mothers tested quite low in intelligence earned mental test scores which were substantially higher than those of their mothers (6). In addition, these authors report the relation of various indices of ability of the true mothers to the mental test scores of their children at four successive age levels. It is these correlations which interest us and which we wish to compare with the relationships obtained in the Guidance Study for children reared by their own mothers.

Regardless of the index used (IQ or number of years of schooling), Skodak and Skeels found that the correlation between the *true* mother's ability and her child's mental test scores at approximately two years of age is insignificant. By the time the adopted children reached four years on the average, the correlations between their IQs and the true mothers' education and intelligence are +.31 and +.28, respectively. These correlations are significant at the 5 percent level. In contrast these authors found no relationship at any age between the mental test scores of these same children who were adopted in the first months of life, and their *foster,* or adopting, mothers' education. These highly significant results are especially interesting when compared with the findings for the groups of children who have always lived with their own parents (1, 2).

In Figure 2, the mother-child correlations for the total Guidance Study sample (combined Guidance and Control groups) are compared with those reported by Skodak and Skeels for the adopted children. It will be noted that the true mother-child correlational age trends in their study and ours are as alike as those shown in Figure 1 for the two subsamples of our group. The similarity in the changing relationships with age for the Guidance Study group who always lived with their parents as compared with the Skodak-Skeels group who never lived with their parents is impressive. However, the final correlations between the index of maternal ability (number of years of schooling) and the children's mental test scores is only +.35 for the children reared by their true parents; and +.32 for the children not reared by their true parents, indicating that less than 15 percent of the variance in the children's scores can be accounted for by this very rough index of the true mother's ability.

The fact that the individual differences in the adopted children's mental test scores are not related to the foster mothers' education at any age is also shown in Figure 2. This finding is surprising since the average IQ of the adopted children at 13½ years was 106, while the average IQ of their true mothers was reported as only 86. A regression upward toward the mean is to be expected but not beyond the mean.

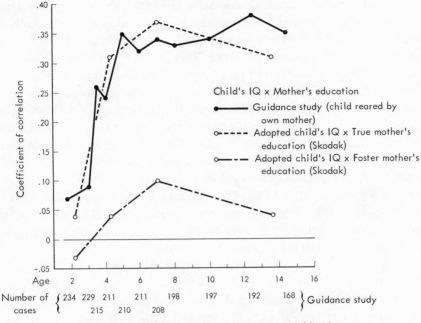

FIG. 2. Education of mother in relation to child's IQ.

Our interpretation of these findings is that the educational level of the true mother roughly indicates her intellectual capacity and this capacity is at least somewhat determined by genetic factors which she, in turn, transmits to her children. The difference in the level of ability of the adopted children and their true mothers may be due in part to systematic undermeasurement of the true mothers' intelligence and in part to the generally favorable environment provided by the foster families. It is conceivable, and it seems to us probable, that in this sample certain unmeasured family variables such as the affection and emotional support given the foster children were as important as purely intellectual stimulation in nurturing the mental growth and performance of these foster children.[3]

A better indication of the age changes in the mother-child resemblance would probably have been obtained if optimal test scores had been available for the mothers in these two studies. In the Skodak-Skeels investigation, 63 of the mothers were given individual mental tests but

---

[3] The importance of various nonintellectual environmental factors to the mental test scores of the children in the Guidance Study will be presented later in a report entitled "Mental Growth in Relation to Intellective and Nonintellective Parental Variables."

these mothers were tested shortly after the babies' births "usually after the mother had decided to release the baby for adoption." The authors note that "these IQs were consistent with other evidence of the mental adequacy of the mothers" and the "tests were never given when the mother was ill or obviously upset," but it is unlikely that these IQs reflect the optimum performance of which these mothers might have been capable under more favorable conditions. However, even these IQs showed age trends in relationship to the mental test scores of the children which were similar but tended to run a little higher than those obtained for the mothers' education. The mother-child correlations in the Guidance Study are higher when based on ratings of the mother's intelligence than when education is used as an index of the mother's ability (Table 1). They are, in the former instance, comparable with the correlation of .49 reported by Jones in a study in which testing procedures for both parents and children were carefully controlled (4).

In Figure 3, the age change in mother-child resemblance in intelligence reported by Skodak and Skeels for 63 of the adopted children is compared with the findings for the Guidance group where the measure of maternal intelligence was an averaged rating. The correlations obtained in the Guidance group are higher than those reported for the adopted children. This latter difference may be due to differential environmental stimulation by the more intelligent mothers in the Guidance group but there is also the likelihood in the Skodak-Skeels study of an unequal effect of stress on the mothers' IQs. These findings certainly suggest that the variations in the magnitude of the correlations depend somewhat on the sensitivity of the measures of maternal intelligence, but the question of whether the differences shown in Figure 3 are entirely attributable to differences in the validity of the measures of mothers' intelligence cannot be answered by these studies.

The correlations between the number of years of schooling of the father and the children's mental test scores at successive ages are reported for the Guidance and Control groups separately and combined in Table 2. Although there are a few coefficients in this table which appear too high or too low in relation to the trend (e.g., the correlations of +.40 at five years for the Guidance group and +.43 for the Control group at seven years), the age changes are similar to those found between the mental test scores of these children and the mothers' education. The relationship between the number of years of schooling of the father and the children's test scores is negligible at 21 months (+.07) and 3 years (+.11) but is significant at the 5 percent level at 3½ years (+.21) and

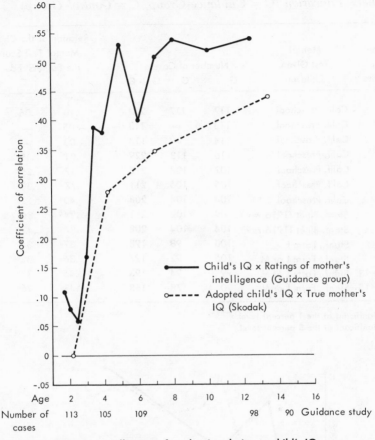

FIG. 3.   Intelligence of mother in relation to child's IQ.

reaches a high of +.40 at 7 years, thereafter ranging from +.34 to +.39. The trend of the age changes in relationship between the children's mental test scores and the fathers' schooling is similar in the two groups (Guidance and Control) in spite of the above mentioned inconsistencies. In Figure 4, the correlations for these two groups combined are compared with the findings for adopted children in relation to the education of their true fathers. The correlations between the mental test scores of the adopted children and the education of their true fathers were computed from the raw data presented by Skodak and Skeels (see Table 3). The impressive fact shown by Figure 4 is that the trend in relationships for the adopted children resembles so closely that found for the children reared by their own parents. Since the relationships obtained in the Guidance Study are no higher than those found for the

TABLE 2. *Correlations of the Children's Mental Test Scores with the Fathers' Education (G = Guidance Group, C = Control Group)*

Age in Years	Mental Test Given Children	Number of Cases			Relation of the Children's Mental Test Scores to the Fathers' Education		
		G	C	G + C	G	C	G + C
					r	r	r
1¾	Calif. Preschool	117	117	234	.10	.06	.07
2	Calif. Preschool	113	—	113	—.05	—	—.05
2½	Calif. Preschool	114	—	114	.03	—	.03
3	Calif. Preschool	116	113	229	.01	.19	.11
3½	Calif. Preschool	107	108	215	.17	.25[a]	.21[a]
4	Calif. Preschool	105	106	211	.17	.30[a]	.24[a]
5	Calif. Preschool	104	104	208	.40[a]	.19[b]	.29[a]
6	Stanf.-Binet (1916 rev.)	109	102	211	.24[b]	.36[a]	.30[a]
7	Stanf.-Binet (1916 rev.)	104	104	208	.37[a]	.43[a]	.40[a]
8	Stanf., Form L	100	98	198	.37[a]	.34[a]	.35[a]
10	Stanf., Form L or M	105	92	197	.36[a]	.32[a]	.34[a]
12 or 13	Stanf., Form L or M	99	94	193	.45[a]	.33[a]	.39[a]
14 or 15	Stanf., Form L or M	90	78	168	.48[a]	.26[a]	.37[a]

[a] Significant at the 1 percent level.
[b] Significant at the 5 percent level.

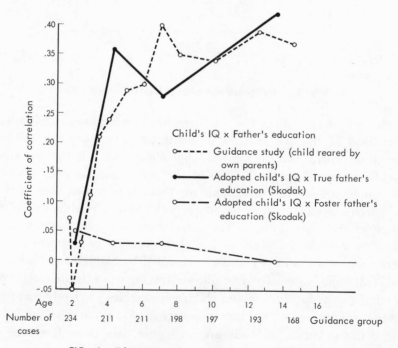

FIG. 4. Education of father in relation to child's IQ.

adopted children, we may infer that the more highly educated fathers do not offer differentially more stimulating environments to their children. This inference is confirmed by the findings for the foster fathers shown in Table 3.

TABLE 3. *Correlations Between the Children's Mental Test Scores and the Fathers' Education (Skodak-Skeels)*

Average Age of Adopted Children in Years	Mental Test Given Children	True Father's Education X Child's IQ N = 60	Foster Father's Education X Child's IQ N = 100
		r^a	r
2–2	Kuhlman or 1916 Stanford-Binet	+.03	+.05
4–3	Stanford-Binet (1916 rev.)	+.36[b]	+.03
7–1	Stanford-Binet (1916 rev.)	+.28[b]	+.03
13–6	Stanford, 1937 revision	+.42[b]	+.00

[a] These correlations were computed from the original data published by Skodak and Skeels (6).
[b] Significant at the 1 percent level.

INDIVIDUAL MENTAL GROWTH RECORDS

The mental growth patterns for individual children have been considered in relation to the parental ability. The method used was to convert both the children's mental test scores and the average of the number of years of schooling of the parents into standard scores, and then note the age level at which the child's mental test SD score reaches the parental SD score with respect to educational level. Using this technique, Bayley presents three cases from the Berkeley Growth Study in which the mental test SD scores of the children reaches the parents' relative educational level at ages 4, 8, and 16 years, respectively, after a period of scoring above or below the parental status (1). Inspection of individual mental growth records in the Guidance Study also suggests that there are marked differences in the ages at which the children's scores reached the parental level of ability, as indicated by their education. Twelve cases are shown in Figures 5, 6, 7.

In Figure 5, the mental test scores of four children of highly educated parents are shown. These children begin to resemble their parents in ability at ages 2½, 4, 8, and 18 years, as judged by the comparison of the standard mental test scores of the children and a standard score based on the averaged years of education of the two parents.

Figure 6 shows the low or decreasing IQs of children of parents of

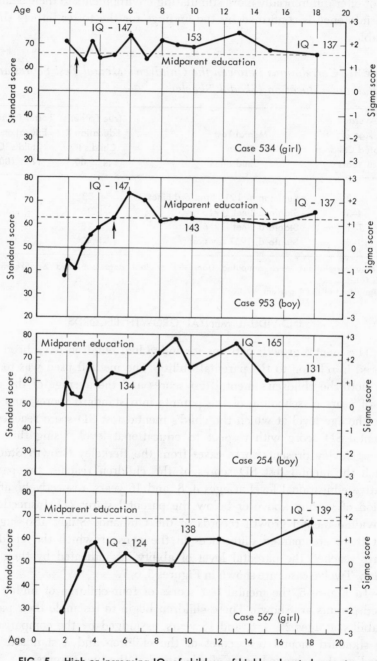

FIG. 5. High or increasing IQs of children of highly educated parents.

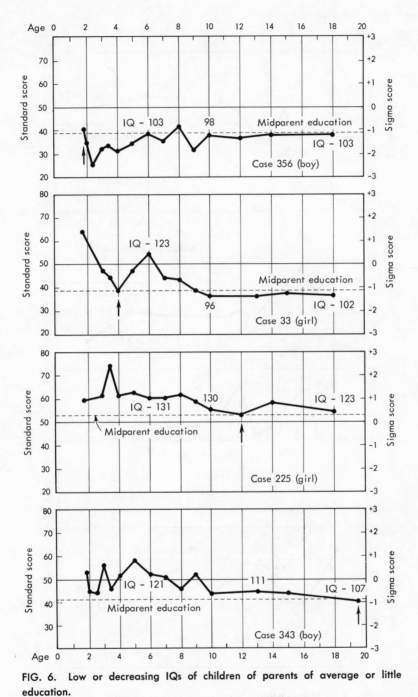

FIG. 6. Low or decreasing IQs of children of parents of average or little education.

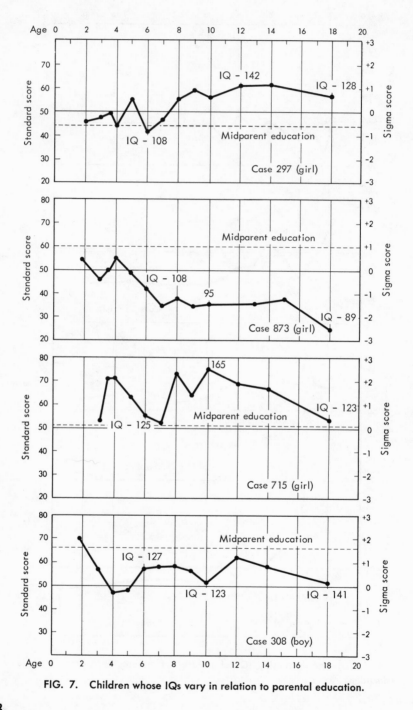

FIG. 7. Children whose IQs vary in relation to parental education.

average or less than average education. Here again, the children vary with respect to the age at which their mental scores are comparable with the educational level of their parents.

In Figure 7, the scores of four children whose IQs fluctuate markedly may be seen in relation to their parents' education level. At certain ages, the IQs of these children reach a status which is comparable with that of their parents and then deviate to a position which is substantially above or below that of the parents. Case 873 is an unusually shy, inhibited girl who was so withdrawn that she did not want to go to school. The mother of this girl said that she was less precocious than her other children so perhaps this decreasing IQ may be accounted for in part by emotional factors and in part by the fact that she has less capacity than would be expected in this family. Consideration of these cases suggests the great individuality in patterns of mental growth and that, although the trend is toward an increasing resemblance between parents and children, the patterning varies markedly.

SUMMARY AND CONCLUSIONS

The increasing parent-child resemblance in mental ability found for two groups of children reared by their own parents has been compared and found to be similar to that reported for a group of children reared from early infancy by foster parents (6). The ability measures used in both studies were, for the children, individually administered intelligence tests, and for the parents, the number of years of schooling; and additionally for the mother, test scores and ratings. The finding that the parent-child resemblance in ability follows the same age changes in the two studies, even though the true parents did not rear the children in the Skodak-Skeels group, suggests that the existing relationship is largely due to genetic factors which tend to become manifest in the child during the later preschool years. Although the group age trends in relationship for both the adopted and nonadopted children are similar, the extent of the relationship is of low predictive value. There were wide individual differences in the ages at which children achieved mental test standard scores which were comparable with their parents' standard scores.

The fact that the parent-child resemblance is no greater for children reared by their own parents and the further fact reported by Skodak-Skeels of no relationship between the children's mental test performance and the foster parents' ability suggest that the education of the parents per se is not an environmentally important factor and that the obtained parent-child correlations reflect individual differences which are largely genetically determined.

REFERENCES

1. Bayley, Nancy. Some increasing parent-child similarities during the growth of children. *J. educ. Psychol.*, 1954, **45**, 1–21.
2. Honzik, Marjorie P. Age changes in relationship between certain environmental variables and children's intelligence. *Yearb. nat. Soc. Stud. Educ.*, 1940, **39**, Part II, 185–205.
3. Honzik, Marjorie P., Macfarlane, Jean W., & Allen, Lucile. The stability of mental test performance between two and eighteen years. *J. exp. Educ.*, 1948, **17**, 309–324.
4. Jones, H. E. A first study of parent-child resemblance in intelligence. *Yearb. nat. Soc. Stud. Educ.*, 1928, **27**, Part I, 61–72.
5. Macfarlane, Jean W. Studies in child guidance. I. Methodology of data collection and organization. *Monogr. Soc. Res. Child Develpm.*, 1938, **3**, (6).
6. Skodak, Marie, & Skeels, H. M. A final follow-up study of one-hundred adopted children. *J. genet. Psychol.*, 1949, **75**, 85–125.

CRITICAL PERIODS IN THE DEVELOPMENT OF SOCIAL BEHAVIOR IN PUPPIES

J. P. Scott, Ph.D.

R. B. JACKSON MEMORIAL LABORATORY

As PART OF A PROGRAM for the study of heredity and social behavior in dogs, the author and his colleagues have made a thorough study of the development of social behavior in puppies, with the idea of finding out the times at which heredity was most likely to exert its effects. As we did so, we also observed that there were certain periods in which environmental factors were particularly likely to affect behavior. As a result we have, from time to time, reported evidence on what we have called the critical period hypothesis (16, 18). This idea is one which is basically related to certain clinical ideas concerning the effect of early experience on later mental health and behavioral adjustment. It is therefore important that it be clearly understood.

CRITICAL PERIOD HYPOTHESIS

What is the critical period hypothesis? In the first place it is in certain respects no longer a hypothesis but a well-established generalization which can be stated as follows: All highly social animals which have been so far studied show, early in life, a limited period in which the group of animals with which the individual will form positive social relationships is determined. To take a few of many examples, the slave-making ants raid the nests of other species for eggs and larvae. As the

From the Division of Behavior Studies, R. B. Jackson Memorial Laboratory, Bar Harbor, Maine. Presented at the Annual Meeting of the American Psychosomatic Society, May 5, 1957, Atlantic City, N.J. Reprinted from *Psychosomatic Medicine* (January-February, 1958), **20** (1), 42–54, by permission of the author and the American Psychosomatic Society. Copyright 1958, by the American Psychosomatic Society, Inc. Published by Hoeber Medical Division, Harper & Row, Inc.

captive ants grow up, they become attached to their captors and take care of their young, and no longer recognize their own species. The experiments of Lorenz (9) with the newly hatched greylag geese which quickly form a social bond with the first moving object they see, whether goose or human, have dramatized the findings of Heinroth and others that contact with the young birds in the proper stage of development establishes a strong social relationship regardless of the species concerned. Lambs that are taken at birth and raised on the bottle form social relations with people rather than other sheep, and become as a result quite unsheeplike in many respects (13). The dog is particularly interesting because the process of socialization with human beings is a normal part of its life as a domestic animal. Dogs are more closely attached to people than are many animals, and develop a relationship which is in many ways similar to the human parent-child relationship. Furthermore, the critical period for socialization in the dog does not begin at birth but approximately three weeks later (15).

The existence of critical periods for the process of primary socialization can therefore be taken as established. Other parts of the critical period hypothesis, namely, that there exist certain periods of sensitivity to psychological damage, still remain as hypotheses and need a great deal more experimental evidence before they are accepted.

The existence of critical periods of any sort implies certain subsidiary hypotheses. The first of these is that the critical period has a physical basis and results from the state of anatomical, psychological, and physiological development of the animal. The second is that hereditary variability between species will affect the course of development. We have found in a limited survey of different forms that such differences are great, and they do not consist simply of the condensation or elongation of a standard type of development. The order of developmental events may even be reversed in different species. It does look, and this is the third hypothesis, as if the social development of any particular species is strongly correlated with the social organization of the adult (14). For example, in dogs there is a close association between mother and puppies during the first 3 weeks in life. But since the permanent social relations of the puppy are formed after this period and at a time when the mother leaves the litter for long periods, the result is that the strongest relationships are formed with the litter mates. This relationship is in turn the basis of pack organization of adult dogs and wolves. A final hypothesis is that there should be genetic variability in the course of development *within a species,* which means that the time of onset of critical periods and their relative sensitivity should vary from individual to individual. This paper will be chiefly concerned with the evidence which we have been able to gather regarding the physical basis of the critical period for primary socialization in the puppy.

NORMAL DEVELOPMENT

I shall first describe the normal course of social development in the puppy. The newborn pup is a very immature animal, being both blind and deaf, and unable to move except in a slow crawl. Its movements are slow and shaky, and its reflexes sometimes occur seconds after stimulation. In spite of being deaf it whines loudly if cold or without food. Its chief needs appear to be warmth, milk, and elimination, and these are taken care of by reflex behavior. If moved away from the mother the puppy will crawl, usually in a circle, throwing the head from side to side. If it comes into contact with the mother it attempts to nurse. When it succeeds it pushes with its head and forepaws and also with the hind feet. In doing this it touches and so stimulates the other puppies in the litter. Any touch will initiate exploratory movements. The mother also frequently stimulates the puppies by nosing them and licking the genital and anal areas. This produces reflex elimination as well as stimulating the pups to exploratory movement and nursing.

This is the typical behavior of puppies in the *neonatal period*. No immediate change is observed in their behavior. They gradually grow somewhat stronger and quicker until the opening of the eyes, which typically occurs just before 2 weeks of age. This marks the beginning of the *transition period*, one of very rapid change and development. At its beginning the eyes open, and at its end the puppy gives a startled reaction to sound. It can walk instead of crawl, and can move backward as well as forward. Its first teeth appear, it takes solid food, and it begins to urinate and defecate without assistance by the end of the period, which typically occurs just before 3 weeks of age.

At approximately 3 weeks of age the puppy first begins to notice other individuals at a distance and shows evidence of conditioning and habit formation. This is the beginning of the period of *socialization*, in which its primary social relationships are formed. At almost the same time the mother begins to leave the puppies unattended, so that there is a tendency for the strongest relationships to be developed with the litter mates rather than the mother. During the next few weeks it is easy for the human observer to form a positive social relationship with the puppy. This period of primary socialization comes to an end somewhere around 7 to 10 weeks of age, which is the normal period of weaning. This does not mean that the puppies are self-sufficient with regard to food. Studies of wolves show that the pups are not able to hunt at all until 4 months of age, and are not really independent until 6 months of age (*10*). In the domestic dog, food is normally supplied by man, but in the wild state it is provided by the hunting parents. This period, which ends with the sexual maturity of the puppy, is called the *juvenile* period. In some of our domestic breeds estrus of the females occurs as early as 5 months, but in the ancestral wolves this does not happen until the end of the second year.

We can see that there might be several critical periods affecting the development of new social relations, that of primary socialization at 3 weeks, the time when sexual relations are established as a new generation of pups is born. We are here concerned primarily with the first of these periods, the period of primary socialization, because we can make the assumption that the end of the primary social relationships will strongly affect the degree of adaptation and adjustment in later relationships.

ANATOMICAL BASIS FOR SOCIAL BEHAVIOR

Function is of course related to form, and form in turn to the process of growth. Let us examine the anatomical changes which accompany changes in social behavior. In the young pups there are three sorts of external changes which are easy to follow, the eruption of the teeth, the opening of the eyes, and the opening of the external ear canal. The last is somewhat harder to follow and is probably less reliable than the other two.

All the following data are based on observations of purebred puppies reared under the standard conditions of our long-term experiment on genetics and social behavior (*17*). The total numbers differ slightly from table to table because complete information was not gathered on all animals in the early part of the experiment.

The first teeth to appear are the canines, followed shortly by the incisors, which all come in together except that the corresponding upper teeth come in before the lower. No animals show teeth at 2 weeks, nearly half have some teeth by 3 weeks, and nearly all have at least the upper canines through the gums by 4 weeks of age. An eruption of the teeth therefore coincides with the beginning of the period of socialization.

The teeth erupt the earliest in basenjis and beagles (Table 1), and wirehaired terriers are definitely slower than all the rest. The shelties are unusual in that the lower teeth develop relatively fast and, in certain animals, the lower canines actually appear before the upper.

TABLE 1. *Eruption of Upper Canine Teeth*

Breed	Number	2 Weeks	3 Weeks	4 Weeks
			Percent Erupted at	
Basenji	51	0	79	100
Beagle	54	0	74	100
Cocker spaniel	67	0	22	100
Sheltie	30	0	30	100
Wirehaired fox terrier	31	0	14	89
Total	233	0	47	99

The eyes typically open about 2 weeks of age or slightly before. Very few are partly open at 1 week, the majority are open at 2 weeks, and all animals have the eyes completely open by 3 weeks of age (Table 2). The opening of the eye is the first external sign of the transition

TABLE 2. *Opening of the Eye*

Breed	Number	1 Week	2 Weeks	3 Weeks
			Percent Completely Open at	
Basenji	43	0	65	100
Beagle	49	0	94	100
Cocker spaniel	51	2	94	100
Sheltie	25	0	31	100
Wirehaired fox terrier	27	0	11	100
Total	195	0.5	67[a]	100

[a] Average with equal weight for breeds = 59.

period. Eighty-five percent of the purebred puppies have the eyes partly open at 2 weeks, and we can estimate the average time at 13 days. There is, however, individual variability and differences between breeds. The eyes open earliest in cocker spaniels and beagles, a little later in basenjis, and much slower in shelties and wirehaired terriers.

The opening of the ears is a more prolonged process and comes a little later than that of the eyes. Over half the animals show the ears at least partly open at 2 weeks, and all are completely open at 4 weeks.

The differences between strains are not great. The shelties appear to be the most rapid, and the wirehaired terriers the slowest, with the other breeds being intermediate and showing only slight differences.

The variability of any of these events which can be precisely timed, such as the eruption of the teeth or opening of the eyes, has a range of approximately 1 week in normal animals. The wirehaired fox terriers appear to be definitely slower in all respects, but in the other breeds the speed of development is not correlated in the different traits. It looks as if there can be separate variability in any one of these characters. One might expect that the development of all the teeth would be correlated, but even here the shelties show a relatively more rapid development of teeth in the lower jaw than do the other strains.

FUNCTION OF THE SENSE ORGANS

Histological studies of the development of the puppy eye (1) indicate that the retina is not fully developed at the time of the opening of the eyes, nor even by 3 weeks of age (Table 3). However, it can be shown that the eye responds to light at a much earlier age. Some puppies

TABLE 3.   *Pupillary Reflex (Eye Open or Partly Open)*

		Percent of Animals Responding at			
Breed	Number	1 Week	2 Weeks	3 Weeks	4 Weeks
Basenji	42	0	57	98	100
Beagle	45	0	78	98	100
Cocker spaniel	51	0	88	100	100
Sheltie	26	0	38	96	100
Wirehaired fox terrier	24	0	13	83	100
Total	188[a]	0	62[b]	96	100

[a] Not observed in 8 additional animals: 1 basenji, 4 beagles, 3 terriers.
[b] Average weighted equally for breeds = 59 percent.

will give a winking reflex to light at birth, long before the eyes open. This appears to happen most frequently in those breeds which have red hair color and light skin pigment.

As soon as the eyes open and the pupil can be clearly seen we can demonstrate a pupillary reflex when a strong light is shown into the eye. At the same time the nystagmus reflex can also be observed. If the puppy's head is moved slowly sideways the eyes roll or flick back and forth. This, however, is probably a reflex controlled by the nonauditory portion of the acoustic nerve rather than by sight. Incidentally, puppies do not show nystagmus in reaction to a moving object or rotating cylinder held in front of them.

The above reflexes concerned with eye function appear early in development, but it is probable that these are responses to light and darkness, and that the capacity to perceive images is not developed until 4 or 5 weeks of age.

The onset of function in the ears is much more definite (Table 4). Only 1 percent of the puppies give a startle reaction to sound by 2 weeks of age, and 74 percent give a reaction at 3 weeks of age. We may therefore estimate that the average time is about 19.5 days. There is considerable genetic variability between the breeds, and the wirehaired terriers have the highest percentage of animals which give a definite startle reaction.

As with the eyes, there is no evidence that the puppies use their ears in finer ways at first. The tendency to startle to all sorts of loud sounds persists for a week or two.

All the puppies gave some reaction to odors at birth. They give

TABLE 4. *Animals Giving Startle Responses to Some Sort of Sound*

| | | Percent Responding at | | |
Breed	Number	2 Weeks	3 Weeks	4 Weeks
Basenji	43	0	72	100
Beagle	49	0	84	100
Cocker spaniel	57	2	61	100
Sheltie	24	0	62	100
Wirehaired fox terrier	27	4	92	100
Total	200	1	74	100

reliable avoidance reflexes to two substances, oil of anise and a proprietary drug used as a dog repellant, which is a compound related to citronella. Eighty-three percent of all puppies gave the avoidance response to the repellant, and a smaller number to oil of anise. Harman found that the parts of the brain connected with olfaction were unmyelinated at birth, and it is probable that these reactions to odor are largely connected with the sense of taste rather than true olfaction. In the human subject both substances can be detected in both the nose and throat. There is some observational evidence that hungry puppies react to the smell of milk in the neonatal stage, but we have no definite evidence on this point.

With regard to other senses, puppies definitely react to pain and touch at birth. The majority of all newborn animals give a "winking reflex" to touch and nearly all of them show this by 1 week of age (Table 5).

TABLE 5.   *Appearance of the "Wink Reflex" to Touch*

Breed	Number	Percent Responding By		
		Birth	1 Week	2 Weeks
Basenji	43	86	100	—
Beagle	49	96	98	100
Cocker spaniel	51	74	98	100
Sheltie	26	69	100	—
Wirehaired fox terrier	27	63	100	—
Total	196	80	99	100

In general, the function of the sense organs at birth is quite limited, but all senses are at least partially functional at approximately 3 weeks. Prior to the beginning of the period of socialization it is impossible for the animal to be stimulated by many environmental changes. Those stimuli which are effective are ones which set off the reflexes connected with eating and other vital processes. In effect, the very young puppy is insulated from many sorts of environmental stimulation.

DEVELOPMENT OF THE CENTRAL NERVOUS SYSTEM

Observation of puppies in the neonatal and transition stages gives no indication that the animals learn in the way that adults do. For example, a puppy placed on the scales may crawl to the edge and fall off. When he is put in the situation repeatedly he does the same thing time and again, with no improvement in adjustment.

The only change in behavior for some time after birth is that the puppies become somewhat faster and stronger in their simple behavioral reactions. Fuller *et al.* (5) found that the avoidance behavior of puppies could be easily conditioned to sounds shortly before 3 weeks of age. This could not be done previously, and the change in an individual animal's behavior occurred from one day to the next. This change is, of course, related to the development of the function of hearing, but no conditioning to other sensory stimuli could be obtained at earlier ages. Responses were given to taste and touch, but did not produce conditioning. James and Cannon (7) confirmed Fuller's results and found that the avoidance reaction to a mild electric shock is restricted to the part stimulated by 28 days of age, indicating that psychological development is still going on.

Harman (6) has made histological examination of the brains of young puppies and finds that the newborn brain is myelinated in very few places, those corresponding to the parts associated with the observed reflex patterns of behavior. This lack of myelination may account for the slow movements of the young puppies, as contrasted with their more rapid responses at later ages.

A measure of actual function of the developing nervous system was obtained by Charles and Fuller (3) by taking the EEG of puppy brains at different ages. At birth the puppy brain has almost no waves at all, and there is no differentiation between sleeping and waking states. At 3 weeks, corresponding to the other differences in behavior noted above, the sleeping and waking states are differentiated, and the amplitude of waves is increased. The adult form of the EEG is achieved at approximately 8 weeks of age, which is shortly after the earliest time at which mothers normally wean their pups.

Another measure of nervous development is the heart rate (Fig. 1). At first glance this might be considered a purely physiological response. However, the heart is actually a very sensitive indicator of both body activity and various kinds of emotions. As will be seen on the graph, the heart rate of the newborn puppies is very high and stays this way through the second week. Then it takes a very decided dip at from 3 to 6 weeks, coming back up to the early level around 7 weeks of age. Thereafter the heart rate slowly declines toward the adult level. These general changes seem to be independent of breed. The first change occurs at the beginning of socialization, and its end occurs at 7 weeks, coinciding approximately with the time of the adult EEG. We can suppose that this is the period when complete cortical connections are established with the hypothalamus. We can conclude that the period from 3 to 7 weeks is an especially sensitive one for emotional reactions, which corresponds to observation of overt behavior. We might also speculate that, since the cortex is not completely developed, emotional reactions during this time might be less permanently learned. On the other hand, they might be more disturbing because complete cortical

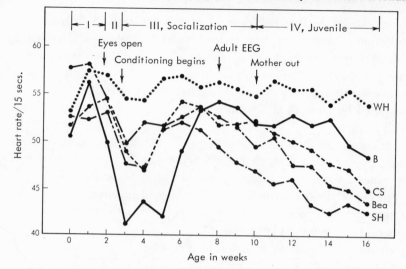

FIG. 1. Average heart rates at different periods in development. Note that all breeds show a lower rate during the early part of the period of socialization than they do either earlier or later. The heart rate change probably measures the puppy's emotional reaction to being picked up, and indicates unusual emotional sensitivity at this age.

control has not been established. We have here a fascinating field for further precise experiments on the effects of early experience.

The development of the nervous system and its associated psychological abilities goes through several stages. The puppy definitely does not come into the world with all its psychological abilities developed. They are, in fact, quite immature at birth and for the next 3 weeks. We would expect and have found (16) that it would be extremely difficult to produce psychological trauma upon very young puppies, and that any future effects on their behavior produced at this time would have to be made by physiological or anatomical injury.

These results raise the question of what the situation is in the human infant. Human development is obviously different from that of the puppy, but we have every indication that the neonatal human infant has a nervous system which is decidedly undeveloped. We need to know more about the origin of learning abilities in human infants before we can talk authoritatively about the effects of early experience. It is not too much to suggest that it would be contrary to the general law of biological adaptation to find that the nervous system was highly sensitive to psychological damage at such a period as birth. This, however, does not invalidate the possibility of anatomical birth injuries.

SOCIAL BEHAVIOR

The most obvious social behavior of young puppies is vocalization. This response is obviously related to various sorts of social contacts. The type of behavior involved is et-epimeletic, or calling for care and attention. In any situation in which the puppy is unable to adapt, the puppy substitutes this reaction for any attempt at adjustment on its own part. Newborn puppies whine repeatedly until they begin to nurse. Fredericson (4) has shown that, besides hunger, the sensation of cold is the stimulus most likely to produce whining. In addition, puppies will whine loudly if accidentally hurt. All these things can be alleviated by social contact.

During the early stages of development the number of whines made by the puppies while being weighed for a period of 1 minute was counted. In general the response decreases, so that by 4 weeks of age most of the puppies make no noise at all. The response is chiefly due to contact with the cold scales, and there is evidence of breed differences, the beagles reacting with relatively small numbers of noises.

During the period of socialization the puppies begin to whine in response to being placed in a strange environment no matter whether warm or cold. Fredericson (4) has shown that this response is considerably lessened if another puppy from the same litter is placed with it. We are now gathering data on the development of this response, and it appears that isolation in a strange environment always produces a stronger reaction than isolation in the home pen.

This brings up another experimental problem which has been scarcely touched. There is considerable evidence (21) that there is a process of primary "localization," in which a young animal becomes psychologically attached to a particular physical environment. There may be a critical period in development for this as well as for the analogous process of socialization.

DEVELOPMENTAL CHANGES IN EATING BEHAVIOR

General changes from sucking to eating solid food have already been described. Our most objective measurement of eating behavior is an indirect one. The gain in weight of the animal reflects the amount eaten. If we chart the weekly gains of puppies we find, as we might expect, that the rate of gain declines week by week. However, there is a definite change in the nature of this curve at 3 weeks of age. The curve before this time is entirely dependent upon the milk supply of the mother. Afterwards the puppy has the possibility of eating solid food, and we would expect that the decline in the growth would be less rapid as soon as solid food was available. However, there is probably a psychological factor involved also. Puppies pay no attention to solid food if they get plenty of milk from the mother, even beyond the age of 3 weeks. This was definitely the case in our F_2 hybrids which were fed by F_1 mothers having an abundance of milk, even in excess of what the pups could use. In their case also the rate of decline of growth was halted after 3 weeks, indicating that the animals were taking in more food (Fig. 2). We may conclude that because of their ability to be conditioned the animals now learn to eat, increasing their food motivation.

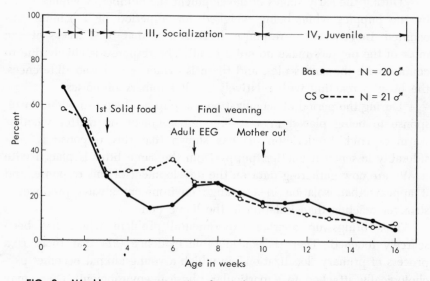

FIG. 2. Weekly percentage gain of weight in male cocker spaniel and basenji pups. Note the change in the slope of the curve at 3 weeks. This reflects both the taking of solid food and increased food motivation resulting from learning and habit formation. The difference between the two breeds reflects a genetic difference in palatability of the food supplied.

This idea is supported by observations on hand-fed puppies. During the neonatal stage they are quite difficult to feed by ordinary means. It is hard to get them to take a nursing bottle, and they have a tendency to stop before the stomach is filled. They can be laboriously fed by a dropper, but the easiest and most practical way to insure adequate feeding is to inject milk into the stomach through a tube. The explanation is that natural feeding is stimulated by specific primary stimuli or releasers which activate certain reflexes and simple patterns of behavior. Puppies become more active and more responsive to external stimuli if hungry, but hunger has little relation to the amount of food taken.

During the transition period, between 2 and 3 weeks, the pups are much more easy to feed. They will readily take a bottle and, if placed near a dish, they can clumsily lap the food. However, they will not take adequate amounts if the dish of warm milk is simply left with them. They still have to be stimulated by fresh food and handling several times a day in order to be properly nourished.

By contrast, puppies older than 3 weeks of age are relatively easy to feed, particularly because a supply of food can be left with them and they will continue to eat adequate amounts.

We can draw several conclusions from these observations. One is that puppies cannot be satisfactorily fed on a demand schedule before 3 weeks of age. Maternal care, together with the reflex behavior of the puppies, will provide adequate nutrition, but the puppy has not yet become a self-regulating organism with regard to eating. He needs external stimulation. Later on, when the ability to form associations and habits is developed, the hunger mechanisms, together with motivation to eat produced by learning, are sufficient to regulate the eating of the puppy in a satisfactory way. This, of course, poses certain questions regarding the reasons back of the necessity for handling human infants, a problem which has been raised by Spitz (20), Ribble (11), and others.

FEEDING AND SOCIALIZATION

The simplest theory of primary socialization is that this relationship is built up through the association of food with a particular individual, and that the relationship can develop further based on this original bond. Brodbeck (2) tested this by rearing cocker spaniel puppies which were mechanically fed, and comparing their behavior with that of puppies fed by hand. In both cases the experimenter spent an equal amount of time playing with the pups. The result was that the pups which had never been fed by people still showed strong attraction to the experimenter. This indicates that feeding is not the only element in the formation of a social bond.

On various occasions we have observed puppies which through some accident to the mother or deficiency in her milk supply were underfed. Young pups that are well-fed are fat and lethargic. In contrast, the underfed animals are active, show more interest in people, and seem to show an earlier expression of many behavior traits than do the normal ones. An opportunity to check this finding occurred recently in connection with an experiment of John A. King, in which he fed two groups of basenji puppies by hand twice a day during the period of socialization. One group was given as much as they could eat, and food was left in the dish so that they could eat later. The other group was given considerably less and their weight was much lower. Both groups were given a handling test which measures responses of the puppy to a human handler.

In puppies raised in a different situation in which most of the food comes from the mother but in which there is considerable handling from 5 weeks on, there is a big decline of the timidity score between 5 and 7 weeks, which may be taken as a measure of the process of socialization. In the experimental pups whose contacts with people were started at 4 weeks and confined to feeding, the timidity score at 5 weeks averaged very nearly as low as the other animals at 7 weeks. The average score stayed slightly higher in subsequent weeks than the controls, but not significantly so. At an early age, and using a genetic type of animal susceptible to the development of timidity, animals which are totally dependent for food show a greater degree of socialization than those only partially dependent.

Another obvious result was that there was a differentiation between the reaction to the person who did the feeding and another person who did not. This difference appeared more strongly as the pups grew older. All this indicates that the process of feeding does contribute importantly to social relationships but does not constitute the whole process.

The difference between the hungry and nonhungry animals was not as great as had been anticipated. There was a great deal of individual variability in behavior. However, hungry animals did show a consistently great proportion of investigation and food begging in their responses than did the controls.

SUCKING FRUSTRATION

Levy's experiment on puppies (8) indicated that the canine equivalent of thumb-sucking could be produced by sucking frustration. Levy's experiment extended over a relatively long period in the development of the puppy, including the transition period and the early part of the period of socialization. Because of the importance of sucking in early development and its disappearance later, there should be a limited period in which this effect could be produced.

Ross, Fisher, and King (12) experimented with this possibility using the technique of sudden weaning, after which the pups could obtain food only by lapping or eating solid food. The experiment was done on a group of 34 experimental and 24 control animals. None of the experimental puppies developed spontaneous body sucking, but they did show an increased tendency to suck a finger of the experimenter. When this was analyzed in relation to age of the puppy, it was found that all the puppies weaned between the ages of 10 and 18 days showed more finger sucking than the controls. After this date many experimental animals were as low as the controls, although there were some indications of smaller effects. There were no effects at all by the time the animals were 5 weeks of age.

We can draw two conclusions. One is that there is an obvious change in the puppies' behavior with regard to sucking at the beginning of the period of socialization. Up to this time a puppy deprived of its mother will readily suck objects which are put into its mouth. After this point it shows very little tendency to suck. The simplest explanation is that the power to discriminate between objects which give nourishment and those which do not has been developed.

The other conclusion is that the simple and sudden deprivation of the opportunity to nurse does not by itself produce the neurotic form of body sucking. Whether there is a critical period for this latter phenomenon is yet to be determined.

HEREDITARY VARIABILITY

As can be seen in Table 6, there is considerable evidence that hereditary variability in development exists, both between individuals

TABLE 6. *Estimated Developmental Ages in Days for Significant Events*

| Breed | Mean and Standard Deviation | | |
	Eyes Completely Open	Ears Startle to Sound	Teeth Eruption, Upper Canines
Basenji	13.1	19.6	18.6
Beagle	11.0	18.7	19.1
Cocker spaniel	11.0±1.9	20.2±2.9	23.3
Sheltie	15.2	20.3	22.6
Wirehaired fox terrier	16.9	17.8±2.2	24.3±3.0
Total	13.0±2.3	19.5±2.3	20.8±2.9

and between breeds. For example, cocker spaniels are the first to open their eyes, are slow to develop the startle response to sound, and are intermediate between the other breeds with regard to the development of teeth. The wirehaired terriers were the slowest to develop in every trait observed except the startle reaction to sound, in which they are the fastest. There is every indication that the different sense organs and anatomical characteristics vary in the speed of development independently of each other. There is no one highly correlated pattern of development which is slowed down or speeded up as a unit.

Assuming that the age of onset of each developmental event falls into a normal curve, we can estimate the average time and variability of each event. As seen by Table 6, there is approximately 3 days' difference between the fastest and slowest breeds. Eighty-six percent of all animals should fall within a range of 1 week. If anything, these estimates of variability are probably too great, since they are based on the 1 percent or so of animals which are as much as a week away from the normal.

The species as a whole shows a developmental pattern which is not departed from except in cases of gross abnormality. Events occur in the general order described in the early part of this paper, so that we can speak of definite periods of development. We can set the beginning of the transition period at 13 days with a normal range of 3 or 4 days on either side. Similarly, we can place the beginning of the period of socialization at approximately 19.5 days with a similar range of variability. This means that when experimental procedures are employed in which time is the experimental variable, close attention must be paid to the breed and the state of individual development. Two litters of puppies of exactly the same chronological age could give completely different results.

CONCLUSIONS

At the beginning of this paper I stated that there is a definite critical period for the process of socialization, and that it must rest on a physical basis. The data which I have just presented show that there is a definite physical basis in the dog, and that there are two important points where sudden changes occur. One of these is the point just before 3 weeks, where there are changes in the ability to be conditioned, in the EEG, in the emotional responses indicated by the heart rate, in the ability to hear, and in the growth rate and method of nutrition. The other point at 7 to 8 weeks is so far defined only by the adult EEG and the change in emotional reaction measured by the heart rate. Final weaning sometimes occurs as early as this date.

To summarize, the puppy before 3 weeks of age is highly insulated from its environment by the immature state of development of the sense organs, by the lack of ability for conditioning, and by maternal care. From 3 to 7 weeks the puppy is in an extremely interesting stage in which its sense organs and cerebral cortex are not yet completely developed but in which it has extremely sensitive emotional reactions and is capable of making associations. This is the time when primary socialization normally takes place and during which it is easiest for a dog owner to establish a strong social bond. These facts provide us with an experimental opportunity to analyze some of the theories of the effects of early experience on later social adjustment and mental health.

Comparing these with results on human babies, we see that we need more fundamental facts about human development. We know a great deal about babies from birth until 10 days of age. After this time mothers and babies leave the hospital and disappear into the home where there is little opportunity for scientific study. Facts and information are very scarce until about the age of 2 years when the babies begin to emerge from the home and appear in nursery school. It is precisely this period in which we are most likely to find the period corresponding to the primary period of socialization in the dog, if it exists. As I mentioned above, one of the most important basic facts yet to be adequately described is the development of simple learning ability in young infants.

One of the biggest problems in predicting human development is the element of individual variability in behavior. The study of development in the different dog breeds, where we should get the maximum possible variability in development, gives us some hint as to what we might expect in human beings. There is considerable individual variability, and variability between dog strains. However, the timing does not vary a great deal in terms of the length of the period of development. The changes at 3 weeks of age in puppies appear to take place within a week for all animals. If we assume that the life span of a dog is one sixth that of a human, we might expect a human range of variability of 6 weeks. Actually, the possible range in early development is probably considerably less than this.

The existence of a critical period for primary socialization is so widespread in the animal kingdom that there is every reason for suspecting that a similar period exists in human development. If so, we are faced with a number of questions:

1.   When? In other animals, the critical period may occur immediately after birth or hatching, or fairly late in development, as it does in the puppy. The human infant is somewhat more mature than a puppy at birth, but far less so than a lamb. We would expect that the critical period would not begin immediately after birth, and the evidence that we have indicates that it may begin as early as a month or 6 weeks, or as late as 5 or 6 months. However, any social relationship depends on the behavior of two individuals, and the period immediately after birth may be a critical one for the mother, although the evidence from adoptions indicates that mothers can form a strong social relationship at other times.

2.   How long? The period of primary socialization certainly lasts as long as the period of complete dependency on the mother, up to 1½ or 2 years, and possibly even longer.

3.   By what means? The positive behavioral mechanisms which establish primary social relationships, such as feeding, contact, handling, and the like, are difficult to understand without experimental data. Likewise, we would expect to find negative mechanisms which prevent the socialization of infants to strangers, such as the anxiety or fear reaction to strangers described by Spitz (19). Their understanding would be immensely important as a means for bringing about a better identification with other human beings, and a broader range of tolerance.

4.   Why? This brings us down to the primary data in this paper, and raises the question of the physical basis of critical periods in the human infant. As I have indicated above, animal experiments indicate the type of thing we should look for: the development of sensory and motor organs, the development of the central nervous system, and the power of simple learning, the development of social behavior patterns, and the development of individual hereditary differences. We have much information on the first two, and far less on the rest. It is this kind of evidence which is the easiest to get on human subjects, and without this firm foundation we shall never be on safe ground.

Seen in this light, our study on the dog provides the opportunity for the experimental analysis of environmental and hereditary influence on an undeveloped nervous system. The dog is an animal which is capable of forming a type of social relationship with people very similar to the human parent-child relationship. We should be able to find out whether early emotional experiences produce lasting effects. Without evidence, it is just as logical to suppose that an immature nervous system would be less severely affected. It will take a long time and will be a laborious and expensive job to obtain the needed facts, but we should eventually be able to bring the phenomena of early social experience out of the realm of conjecture into that of established scientific fact.

SUMMARY

1. The existence of a critical period for the establishment of primary social relationships is a well-established phenomenon in social animals. This paper has dealt with the physical and hereditary basis of the critical period in the dog.
2. Normal social development in the puppy can be divided into several periods based on changes in social relationships. Several of these may be critical, but the most important is that of primary socialization, beginning about 3 weeks of age.
3. The beginning of this period is accompanied by certain anatomical changes: the eruption of the teeth and the opening of the ears. Eyes open at an earlier date.
4. Its beginning is also closely associated with the appearance of the function of the ears. The senses of touch and taste (including tasting gases) are present at birth. The eye is sensitive to light before it opens, but not completely functional until some time after.
5. Changes in the heart rate appear which correspond to changes in the EEG and ability to be conditioned.
6. At 3 weeks there is a change in the rate of growth, which may be attributed to both additional food and to a psychological change in food motivation.
7. Experimental evidence indicates that feeding is an important factor in socialization, but not the only factor.
8. There is a marked change in the finger-sucking response of weaned puppies at an age corresponding to the beginning of the critical period.
9. Hereditary variability of the exact time of onset of the critical period exists both between individuals and between breeds. However, the functional variability appears to be smaller than that in the accompanying anatomical changes.
10. In the period immediately following birth the puppy is strongly protected from psychological influences. During the critical period it becomes highly sensitive, at a time when the sense organs and nervous system are still not completely developed. The exact effects of experience during this time are still to be determined.
11. These data suggest facts which must be ascertained in order to establish the existence and duration of a similar critical period in human infants. They also suggest ways in which important clinical theories can be experimentally tested.

REFERENCES

1. Blume, D. A study of the eye of the dog. In preparation.
2. Brodbeck, A. J. An exploratory study on the acquisition of dependency behavior in puppies. *Bull. ecol. Soc. Am.*, 1954, **35**, 73.
3. Charles, M. S., & Fuller, J. L. Developmental study of the electroencephalogram of the dog. *Electroencephalog. & clin. Neurophysiol.*, 1956, **8**, 645.
4. Fredericson, E. Perceptual homeostasis and distress vocalization in puppies. *J. Person.*, 1952, **20**, 472.
5. Fuller, J. L., Easler, C. A., & Banks, E. M. Formation of conditioned avoidance responses in young puppies. *Am. J. Physiol.*, 1950, **3**, 462.
6. Harman, P. J. Private communication.
7. James, W. T., & Cannon, D. J. Conditioned avoiding responses in puppies. *Am. J. Physiol.*, 1952, **168**, 251.
8. Levy, D. M. Experiments on the sucking reflex and social behavior of dogs. *Am. J. Orthopsychiat.*, 1934, **4**, 203.
9. Lorenz, K. Der Kumpan in der Umvelt des Vogels. *J. Ornithol.*, 1935, **83**, 137.
10. Murie, A. *The wolves of Mt. McKinley.* Washington, D.C., G.P.O., 1944.
11. Ribble, M. A. Infantile experience in relation to personality development. In J. M. Hunt (Ed.) *Personality and the behavior disorders.* New York: Ronald Press, 1944.
12. Ross, S., Fisher, A., & King, D. The effect of early enforced weaning on sucking behavior of puppies. In preparation.
13. Scott, J. P. Social behavior, organization and leadership in a small flock of domestic sheep. *Comp. Psychol. Monogr.*, 1945, **18**, 1.
14. Scott, J. P. The relationships between developmental change and social organization among mammals. *Anat. Rec.*, 1951, **111**, 73.
15. Scott, J. P. The process of socialization in higher animals. In *Interrelations between the social environment and psychiatric disorders.* New York: Milbank Mem. Fund, 1953.
16. Scott, J. P., Fredericson, E., & Fuller, J. L. Experimental exploration of the critical period hypothesis. *J. Person.*, 1951, **1**, 162.
17. Scott, J. P., & Fuller, J. L. Manual of dog testing techniques. Bar Harbor, Maine: Jackson Laboratory, 1950.
18. Scott, J. P., & Marston, M. V. Critical periods affecting the development of normal and maladjustive social behavior of puppies. *J. genet. Psychol.*, 1960, **77**, 25.
19. Spitz, R. A. Anxiety in infancy: a study of its manifestations in the first year of life. *Int. J. Psychoanal.*, 1950, **21**, 1.
20. Spitz, R. A. The psychogenic diseases in infancy. *Psychoanalyt. Study Child*, 1951, **6**, 255.
21. Thorpe, W. H. *Learning and instinct in animals.* London: Methuen, 1956.

Anxiety, Pregnancy, and Childbirth Abnormalities[1]

Anthony Davids, Spencer DeVault, and
Max Talmadge
BROWN UNIVERSITY AND EMMA PENDLETON BRADLEY
HOSPITAL

SINCE THE DEVELOPMENT of a rather simple instrument for assessing manifest anxiety (4), there has been an epidemic of psychological studies concerned with the role of anxiety in a wide range of experimental situations. Here, we will not attempt to survey this vast literature. We wish merely to point out that these studies of anxiety have been conducted mainly in laboratory and academic research settings, and little use has been made of the instrument in clinical or "real life" situations. . . .

It seems, then, that the Manifest Anxiety Scale has demonstrated utility as a research instrument and has generated considerable interesting research. However, since most personality theorists place great emphasis on anxiety as a motivating factor in life adjustment, and since it is a well established fact that anxiety plays a crucial role in the formation of psychopathology, it seems worthwhile to conduct further research on the clinical utility of this objective instrument for assessing manifest anxiety.

At present, there appears to be increasing research interest in the effects of anxiety and stress on the psychological course of pregnancy

[1] This study was made possible by a research grant, B–2356, from the National Institute of Neurological Diseases and Blindness, United States Public Health Service, awarded to the Brown University Institute for Research in the Health Sciences. The present report stems from an ancillary study to the National Collaborative Project, conducted locally at the Providence Lying-In Hospital, which is investigating perinatal factors in child development. We wish to express our appreciation to Glidden Brooks, who is Director of the Research Institute at Brown University, for facilitating this study. Also, we are indebted to the clinic staff of the Providence Lying-In Hospital for their cooperation and assistance.

Abridged from *Journal of Consulting Psychology* (1961), **25** (1), 74–77, by permission of the author and the American Psychological Association.

and the influence that emotional turmoil during pregnancy may have on the subsequent adjustment of the offspring. In a study of physical and mental handicaps following disturbed pregnancy, Stott (3) suggested that prenatal influences were to blame. In studying a group of mentally defective children, he found that in a large proportion of the cases there had been marked emotional stress during pregnancy, as a result of family conflicts and personal unhappiness. In a recently reported study of the influence of prenatal maternal anxiety on emotionality in rats, Thompson (5) tested and confirmed the hypothesis that "emotional trauma undergone by female rats during pregnancy can affect the emotional characteristics of the offspring."

The plan of the research program from which the present report derives is to use a variety of psychological procedures to study emotional factors in pregnant women. This report, however, is concerned specifically with findings obtained from the MAS [Manifest Anxiety Scale] administered to a group of women during pregnancy and readministered soon after delivery of their children.

METHOD

The subjects of this investigation were 48 pregnant women who were studied at the clinic of the Providence Lying-in Hospital. They are a representative sample of a larger group of women who were studied in the course of a pilot study conducted by a team of medical and scientific investigators who were engaged in a collaborative project on perinatal factors in child development. The women were seen for individual psychological testing during the course of a routine visit to the clinic, which in most cases was at approximately the seventh month of pregnancy. Of the group of 48 women, 20 returned for a routine physical checkup at approximately 6 weeks following childbirth, while the other 28 women failed to return for this scheduled hospital visit. The 20 patients who were seen twice will be labeled Group I, and the 28 women who were seen only during pregnancy constitute Group II.

In the course of the large scale investigation, voluminous data were gathered for each patient. As part of the assessment, they were administered a comprehensive battery of psychological tests. Included in this assessment procedure was the 50-item MAS, which is the focus of the present report. In Group I, the MAS was administered both during and following pregnancy, while in Group II it was administered only during pregnancy. On the basis of the official hospital records, it was possible to classify each patient's delivery room record as "normal" or as indicating some "abnormality or complication." In Group I, there were 13 patients in the normal category and 7 patients in the abnormal category. In Group II, the subdivisions were 12 normal deliveries and 16 with abnormalities or complications.

The patients in both groups were of "normal" intelligence. As measured by the Wechsler-Bellevue Intelligence Scale, the mean IQ in Group I was 101 and the mean IQ in Group II was 95. Moreover, in both groups the mean age was 25 years and ranged from 17 to 40 years. Thus, although no attempt was made to match the patients in the two groups, it happened that the groups were of very similar age and IQ, and in regard to these two variables it seems probable that they are representative of pregnant women who are being studied at various clinics throughout the country.

RESULTS AND DISCUSSION

Now let us consider the findings from the MAS. In Group I, on the first testing, the normal subgroup obtained a mean manifest anxiety score of 16.5, which is significantly lower ($t = 2.19$, $p = .05$) than the mean of 23.5 in the abnormal subgroup. Examination of the ranges of the manifest anxiety scores in the two subgroups further evidences the greater anxiety in the abnormal group, with their scores ranging from 14 to 37, as compared with scores ranging from 8 to 26 in the normal group. Thus, both the mean scores and the spread of the individual scores reveal the abnormal delivery group to have been relatively high on manifest anxiety according to their own avowal of feelings and symptoms during pregnancy. In analyzing the results from the second testing of the patients in Group I, it is noteworthy that the level of manifest anxiety decreased in both subgroups following pregnancy, with a mean of 15 in the normal subgroup and a mean of 18.3 in the abnormal subgroup. Although the group that experienced difficult deliveries continued to score higher on manifest anxiety than did the group who had normal delivery room experiences, the nonsignificant difference ($t = .70$) was not as pronounced as it was when the women were in a state of pregnancy.

The findings in regard to manifest anxiety in Group II were remarkably similar to those obtained in Group I. In this second group of patients, the mean MAS score in the normal subgroup was 16, which is significantly lower ($t = 2.39$, $p = .05$) than the mean score of 23.6 in the abnormal subgroup. Again, the range of MAS scores from 4 to 30 in the normal subgroup was noticeably lower than the range from 12 to 38 in the abnormal subgroup. Thus, in both samples studied in this research, it was found that women who were later to experience complications in delivery or were to give birth to children with abnormalities tended to report a relatively high amount of disturbing anxiety while they were pregnant.

In considering these findings, it should be emphasized that at present we have no information regarding the causes or reasons underlying the higher MAS scores in the abnormal subgroup. One possibility is that the obstetricians may have anticipated abnormalities or complications and may have conveyed this information to the patients. However, this possibility does not seem too likely, as for the majority of these patients the psychological assessment was conducted during their first visit to the clinic. That is, these women did not have private obstetricians who followed their medical progress throughout the pregnancy, but were being seen for their first medical examination at a rather late stage of their pregnancy. Future examination of sociological, medical, and past history data on these clinic patients may provide some understanding of causative factors, and greater understanding in this regard may well come from comparisons of clinic and private patients. One other point that should be made at this time, however, is that there was no difference between the two subgroups in regard to the number of patients for whom this was the first delivery. The mean number of previous pregnancies and previous deliveries was practically identical in the normal and abnormal subgroups.

It is also interesting to note that the mean MAS scores of about 16, obtained in the normal subgroups both during and after pregnancy, are very similar to the mean MAS scores obtained previously in relatively large samples of female college undergraduates (1, 4). The present findings suggest, therefore, that, as a group, pregnant women who will later experience normal childbirth do not differ from normal nonpregnant college females in the avowal of manifest anxiety, but pregnant women who are likely to experience childbirth abnormalities later are significantly higher on manifest anxiety than are other groups of pregnant and nonpregnant women.

The results of this preliminary study, which should be regarded as tentative and in need of further independent confirmation, are quite encouraging. In addition to demonstrating the utility of the MAS in this clinical setting, the positive findings obtained with this objective instrument suggest that even more fruitful results may be obtained through use of projective techniques designed to uncover indices of emotional factors operating at deeper levels in the personality. It is hoped that the intensive program of investigation we have embarked upon will eventually lead to greater psychological understanding of complex relations between maternal psychodynamics during pregnancy and the process of child development.

SUMMARY

The purpose of this research was to compare measures of manifest anxiety obtained during pregnancy and following childbirth, and to relate these anxiety measures to delivery room experiences. In two independent samples of clinic patients, women who were later to experience complications in the delivery room or were to give birth to children with abnormalities obtained significantly higher manifest scores during pregnancy than did women who later had "normal" delivery room records. The results obtained from retesting one of the samples shortly after childbirth showed decreased levels of manifest anxiety both in patients who had undergone normal childbirth and those who had experienced complications or abnormalities. Manifest anxiety scores were still relatively higher in this latter subgroup, but the difference was no longer significant. It was concluded that these findings demonstrate the clinical utility of the Manifest Anxiety Scale, and also suggest that utilization of projective methods in future research may lead to greater psychological understanding of the role of emotional factors in pregnancy and childbirth.

REFERENCES

1. Smith, W., Powell, Elizabeth K., & Ross, R. Manifest anxiety and food aversions. *J. abnorm. soc. Psychol.*, 1955, **50**, 101–104.
2. Spence, K. W., & Taylor, Janet A. The relation of the conditioned response strength to anxiety in normal, neurotic, and psychotic subjects. *J. exp. Psychol.*, 1953, **45**, 265–272.
3. Stott, D. H. Physical and mental handicaps following a disturbed pregnancy. *Lancet*, 1957, **1**, 1006–1012.
4. Taylor, Janet A. A personality scale of manifest anxiety. *J. abnorm. soc. Psychol.*, 1953, **48**, 285–290.
5. Thompson, W. R. Influence of prenatal maternal anxiety on emotionality in young rats. *Science*, 1957, **125**, 698–699.

BEHAVIORAL DIFFERENCES BETWEEN NORMAL AND TRAUMATIZED NEWBORNS[1]

Frances G. Graham
UNIVERSITY OF WISCONSIN

Ruth G. Matarazzo
UNIVERSITY OF OREGON

Bettye M. Caldwell
SYRACUSE UNIVERSITY

WHILE THE DESIRABILITY of considering the infant's response to trauma may be readily acknowledged, it is necessary to develop a satisfactory method of measuring newborn behavior before this variable can be introduced into experimental work. The present paper reports our efforts to do this. We have spoken of measuring "response" or "behavior," but this is an amorphous categorization which may be variously defined. For our present purpose, we are interested in measuring any response in the behavioral repertoire of the neonate which may be related to the kinds of trauma and the kinds of consequence which may be the result of birth injury. More specifically, we set as our goal the measurement of behavior which would differentiate a group of infants who were "normal" from those who might be candidates for "brain injury." We were interested primarily in differences between normal and abnormal or traumatized infants and not in variability among normal infants.

[1] This investigation is part of a long-term project being carried out in collaboration with Drs. Alexis F. Hartmann and Miriam M. Pennoyer. The work was initiated by a four-month grant from the Frances Israel Fund of the Noshin Rachmonioth Society of St. Louis, Mo. From November 1, 1953 to October 31, 1954 it was supported by the Children's Research Foundation, St. Louis, Missouri, and since November 1, 1954 by a research grant B685 from the National Institute of Neurological Diseases and Blindness, of the National Institutes of Health, Public Health Service.

Abridged and reprinted from *Psychological Monograph* (1956), **70** (5), 427–428, by permission of the authors and the American Psychological Association.

Five procedures were eventually developed—measures of pain threshold, maturational level, visual response, and ratings of irritability and muscle tension. It is the purpose of this and the following paper to report in detail the methods and their standardization and degree of differentiating power. These five tests constitute a measure of neonatal response now being emphasized in a second study as a basis for prediction of subsequent development.

TEST PROCEDURES

In selecting these particular procedures, we were guided by a number of considerations. The primary one was that the test should differentiate normal from traumatized Ss and that the range of possible variation should be sufficiently great so that differences would not be minimized by a low ceiling. A second consideration was the desirability of making measurement objective and reliable. We did, however, prefer to explore relatively subjective measures giving promise of validity rather than concentrate attention on developing precision of measurement in an area where the worth of measuring at all remained to be established.

It was also necessary to take into account special difficulties arising from the nature of the Ss and the hospital setting. In the infant, for example, the momentary internal state is a factor which may obscure the effect of other determinants of behavior if allowance is not made for it. In general, we attempted to solve this by maintaining a constant state between waking and sleeping. . . .

The infant also presents special difficulty in that his repertoire of response is limited and that there seem to be few clear-cut stimulus-response connections.

A great deal has already been said about generalized mass movements as characteristic of the newborn. Whether he characteristically indulges in generalized or in specialized movements, it is unquestionably difficult in many cases to determine whether movements occurring after application of a stimulus are "responses" or are spontaneous. One of our major tasks, therefore, was to discover responses which did show a specific relationship to a stimulus and to set up rules for unequivocally identifying the response.

Changes in behavior during the newborn period are very rapid, and behavior characteristic of Day 1 may not be present to the same degree on Day 2. Either the age of infants must be held constant to the day, or the relationship between age and the particular test measure must be empirically determined. In order to obtain maximum differences we

wanted to examine infants on the first day. Yet the most severely traumatized Ss, the most likely to show marked differences, often could not be
tested for several days. Holding the day of testing constant, therefore,
meant either sacrificing the sensitivity gained from testing on Day 1 or
sacrificing the Ss most severely traumatized. Rather than make either of
these sacrifices, we carried out the more time-consuming method of obtaining age norms. . . .

The most seriously limiting factor was the relatively few abnormal
Ss available. In the well-run modern obstetrical hospital, the percentage
of babies who suffer severe birth injury is only 1 to 3 percent. This meant
that an immediate check on the validity of a measure could not be made
but had to wait until a sufficiently large number of traumatized Ss had
accumulated. Probably the major effect of this was only to threaten the
experimenters' morale, but it also meant that once a test procedure
had been adopted and given to any appreciable number of abnormals,
changes which might have improved the procedure were not made since
they entailed too great a loss of difficult-to-replace data. It was because
of this scarcity of traumatized Ss that we also included infants with mild
or questionable injury rather than using more widely separated criterion
groups. . . .

Pain Threshold

A determination of pain threshold was employed for a number of
reasons. Both pediatric and psychological examinations of the newborn
have concentrated on motor ability and have neglected sensory functioning. Yet impairment of sensory functioning has been a useful sign of
brain damage in the adult. . . . We selected pain as the sensory area on
which to concentrate precise measurement, after preliminary experimentation revealed various practical difficulties in the other areas. One
major advantage of using pain was that a specific, discrete response could
be obtained which was relatively easy to differentiate from spontaneous
movement. Another consideration was the possibility that sensitivity to
pain has not reached a maximum at birth. If so, pain thresholds might
prove a relatively sensitive indicator of brain damage, since many lines
of investigation have suggested that functions which are not well established are especially susceptible to impairment. . . .

Our general procedure was to determine the stimulus intensity necessary
to elicit a specified response within a specified time. . . . The apparatus (an
electronic stimulator) delivers shocks whose intensity, duration, and frequency
can be varied within the stimulating range for skin and peripheral nerves. For
the present work, duration and frequency were held constant so that the shock

consisted of a two-second impulse at a frequency of 14 per second which could be varied in intensity from 50 to 530 volts. . . .

The infant was stimulated while lying on his back with the legs in the usual flexed position. The indifferent electrode, covered with moist gauze, was placed in the center of the back against the skin, and the shirt tied so that it remained in position. A circular area, approximately ¾ inches in diameter, just below the knees of both legs, was treated with vaseline. These areas were stimulated alternately by a silver ball electrode of 1 mm. diameter. An effort was made to avoid stimulating the same spot successively, especially if the skin reddened. There was, apparently, sufficient spread of stimulation so that differences in spot sensitivity did not introduce undue variable error.

The specific response required was a movement of the stimulated leg or the foot of that leg, with or without other bodily movement. . . .

Maturation Scale

A maturation scale was devised on the basis of items reported in previous studies (1, 2, 4, 5), and adapted to the needs of the present study and the nature of the present age-groups. The primary criterion for inclusion of an item was that it should reflect changes with age, in this case, differences between one-day-old prematures and one-day-old full term infants or between one-day and five-day-old full terms. A few items were included which did not differentiate well on the basis of age because preliminary work suggested that they might differentiate the traumatized infant. Other criteria used were that the scale as a whole should survey the total repertoire of behavior not covered in other tests of the battery, that the items should include little subjectivity in scoring, that the total time of administration be about fifteen minutes, and that it not require any elaborate equipment.

The scale consists of nine items, which receive varying credits depending upon the level of the response. If more than one kind of response occurs, the infant is given credit for the higher-scoring response. The general distinction between low-scoring and high-scoring responses is between generalized, mass movements and more specialized, stimulus-oriented responses. The maximum possible score is twenty-one.

The nine items used are labeled and described briefly as follows:

1. reaction in prone position (turning and lifting the head);
2. crawling (alternating movement of the leg simulating crawling);
3. pushing feet in response to gentle pressure exerted against the feet;
4. auditory reaction (movement or any change in behavior in response to sound of rattle and bell);
5. response to stimulus of cotton lightly placed so that it covers the nostrils and touches the upper lip (credit given for head, mouth, and coordinated arm movement);

6. response to piece of cellophane lightly held so that it covers nostrils and mouth;
7. resistance (percentage of time during which infant responds to stimuli of items 5 and 6);
8. vigor (rating of rate and extent of movement in items 5 and 6);
9. grasp (measure of strength of infant's pull of rubber-covered objects placed in his palm).

Vision Scale

The general procedure we followed, that of observing and categorizing the response to a moving stimulus, is similar to the procedure used by Gesell (3) and adopted by other designers of infant tests. . . .

The stimulus is presented with the infant in a supine position. Either the examiner's hand, a bell, or a metal tape measure 1⅜ inches in diameter was used. . . .

The newborn usually does not turn head and eyes toward a stimulus at the periphery. Fixation is limited to a relatively narrow range directly in front of the eyes, an area which is determined by the tonic-neck reflex. Stimuli are therefore initially presented in this area. The experimenter observes the direction in which one or both eyes appear to be turned and places the stimulus in line with the eyes. He then moves it slowly toward and away from the infant, since the distance from the eyes at which an object can be fixated is also limited, varying from about 3 inches to 12 inches (3, p. 191). . . .

After preliminary efforts to locate the position which is optimal for fixation, there are presented a number of trials in which the stimulus is moved slowly upward from the line of regard, or in either horizontal direction for as great a distance as the infant's eyes will follow. Each trial is begun with the stimulus in the place of regard. Visual items are scored both for the type of response which can be elicited and for ease of elicitation. As many trials may be given as are necessary to arrive at these judgments. . . .

Several aspects of the visual response are considered in making a classification: (a) presence or absence of a kind of response (such as fixation or pursuit); (b) the ease of eliciting the response; (c) the direction of eye movement (horizontal or vertical); (d) the distance the eye moves. . . .

Irritability and Muscle-Tension Ratings

In pediatric discussions of the brain-injured newborn, there are frequent references to such symptoms as a high-pitched and feeble cry, excessive irritability, muscular rigidity or flaccidity, and poor muscle tonus. We attempted to provide a crude quantification of these character-istics by means of two ratings—a rating of irritability and one of muscle tension or tone. The ratings are based on observations of the infant while other tests are being administered, and on a few simple supplementary procedures. . . .

Irritability Rating. Irritability as used here is similar to the concept of physiological irritability—how sensitive the infant is to stimulation and not how loudly and lustily he cries. . . .

A three-point scale, with numerical values of 0, 1, and 2, was provided for the rating of irritability. It was decided in advance that the zero point should represent the behavior of a normal infant, the endpoint (value 2.0) the extreme and easily identified form of behavior seen in a grossly abnormal infant, and the midpoint (value 1.0) a "just-perceptible" form of abnormal behavior. . . .

Muscle Tension Rating. The Muscle Tension Rating was designed to measure deviations in the direction of either increased flaccidity (lessened muscle tone) or increased rigidity. However, only amount of deviation and not direction was considered in statistical treatment of the data. Five submeasures were employed in making the rating. . . .

The five submeasures required rating the following: (1) nature (flexed or extended) of the supine position which the legs assumed spon-taneously; (2) resistance to limb displacement; (3) change in muscle tone in response to being pulled to sitting posture; (4) amount of spontaneous activity; and (5) frequency of trembling of body parts and the stimuli evoking this response. . . .

At the end of examination, the overall rating on muscle tension was made. A five-point scale, with numerical values from -2 to $+2$, was de-signed for the rating. The zero point represented the behavior of a nor-mal infant and the endpoints (values -2 and $+2$) the extremes of flaccidity and rigidity, respectively, as seen in a grossly abnormal infant. The -1 and $+1$ points represented a "just perceptible" form of abnormal behavior. . . .

SUBJECTS

Our subjects (Ss) were full term infants born on the inpatient service of the St. Louis Maternity Hospital during the period from July, 1953, through October, 1955. . . .[2]

[2] The writers are indebted to the authorities of the St. Louis Maternity Hospital and to the obstetricians and pediatricians who provided the opportunity for carrying out the study. We should like to express special gratitude for the cooperation of the nursing staff and especially of Miss Margaret Weber.

The traumatized group was composed of almost the total population of traumatized infants born during the course of the study, with the exclusion of infants who were overlooked, and of a few infants whom we could not obtain permission to examine. We were informed by the pediatric staff of all infants who, either at birth or subsequently, might be classified as abnormal. Infants were tested, if possible, within 24 hours after birth or as soon after that as their condition permitted. Only infants 7 days old or younger are included in the study.

The kinds and degree of trauma present in the abnormal group are shown in Table 1. A pediatrician experienced in the neonatal field made the classification without the knowledge of psychological test results. . . .

TABLE 1.   *Classification of Traumatized Subjects According to Kind and Degree of Trauma*

| Kind of Trauma | Degree of Trauma | | |
	Mild	Moderate	Severe
Anoxia	21	26	11
Mechanical trauma	0	0	3
Infections or diseases[a]	3	12	5
Total N	24	38	19

[a] Erythroblastosis fetalis, hypoglycemia, meningitis.

The normal group was composed of infants without prenatal, perinatal, or postnatal complications. Cases were not included where there was maternal bleeding during pregnancy or serious maternal illnesses such as rubella, diabetes, hypertension, etc. Perinatal circumstances were considered satisfactory when delivery was spontaneous or by low forceps, respiration and cry were established in a few seconds, and the infant was active. Infants were not tested on the day of circumcision or with elevated temperatures. Sufficient numbers were tested on each of the first five days of life so that the effect of age could be either statistically weighted or controlled by pairing normal with traumatized Ss.

PROCEDURE

The Ss were examined in a hospital room maintained in the same manner as the regular nursery. No soundproofing was available in this room. Whenever extraneous noises were sufficiently loud to startle an S, test procedures were repeated. Examinations were carried out between

10:15 A.M. and 3:00 P.M. with most Ss seen during the morning. As pointed out previously, the number and kind of tests given varied during the course of the study. For those Ss who were tested with the final battery, the pain threshold was obtained first. Vision tests were given whenever the infant opened his eyes, and the maturation and tension scale items were given in whatever order best maintained the infant in a satisfactory state. Irritability was rated at the end of the examination. . . .

RESULTS

Differences Between Normal and Traumatized Groups

Mean difference. Table 2 shows the size of the groups, the variables on which they were equated by pairing, the mean scores of the two groups, the statistic used in estimating probabilities, and the probability

TABLE 2. *Comparison of Normal and Traumatized Groups on Five Tests*

Test	N	Variables Controlled	Mean Scores	Comparison Statistic	p
Pain threshold					
normal	55	age	165	t test	.01
traumatized	55		270		
Maturation scale					
normal	28	age, race	13.0	F test	.05
traumatized	28		10.6		
Vision scale					
normal	37	age, race	6.8	t test	.01
traumatized	37		4.2		
Irritability					
normal	91	—	.12	chi-square	.01
traumatized	29		.61		
Tension					
normal	103	—	.08	chi-square	.01
traumatized	29		.48		

that differences between groups are due to chance. The means are included on all five measures, although they were, of course, not used when chi-square was the comparison statistic. On all tests the performance of the traumatized groups was significantly poorer than that of the normal groups.

Shape of the distributions. In the preceding section, evidence was

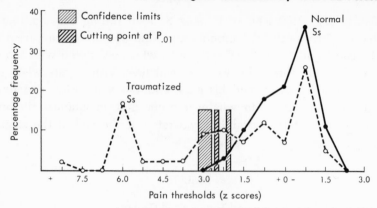

FIG. 1. Pain thresholds (in standard score form) of normal and traumatized subjects.

presented that the normal and traumatized groups differed significantly, but nothing was said about the shape of the distributions. Figure 1 shows the distribution of pain thresholds in the two groups. Percentage frequency rather than frequency is plotted on the ordinate to equate the size of the groups. Standard scores are plotted on the abscissa so that thresholds of individuals tested on different days could be combined. Since the standard score transformation is a linear transformation, the shape of the curve is altered only to the extent that the distributions of the several days show differences in skewness. Standard scores of traumatized Ss are based on the normal group.

The graph shows a skewed distribution in the normal group, the skewness probably reflecting the effect of a lower limit to the pain threshold. Thresholds of the traumatized group on the other hand, cover a much wider range and do not appear to fall into any type of unimodal distribution. Unless it is assumed that the considerable variability has distorted what would otherwise be a unimodal distribution, we must assume a bi- or multimodal distribution. Since the tendency to bimodality is also present in each of the three subsamples of mild, moderate, and severely traumatized infants, the hypothesis of bimodality is strengthened.

If thresholds of traumatized Ss are not unimodally distributed, what does this signify? It can only mean that pain sensitivity is not affected in a unitary fashion under conditions of trauma. More than one factor must be present. It is possible that the presence of a new factor is due to the greater intensity of stimulation used with some of the traumatized Ss, rather than to the trauma per se. This would be the case if other sense modalities were activated when a certain intensity of stimulation is reached. It is tempting, however, to speculate that the new factor is related to brain functioning. Is there a threshold for impairment of brain functioning such that on one side of the threshold, the same factors determining pain sensitivity in normal brains are operating while, once beyond the threshold, sensitivity is determined by changed condition of the brain? It is idle to speculate on the brain physiology which might be involved; there are many physiological phenomena which show this all-or-none character. . . .

Graphic distributions of the other four tests are not presented. Interpretation of them is complicated by the fact that scoring was empirically determined on the basis of observation by the authors, and changes in the scoring system would, of course, change the character of the distributions. The distribution of Maturation and Vision Scale scores was similar to that for Pain Threshold in both normal and traumatized groups. On the Irritability and Tension ratings, the normal groups show a heavy concentration of scores receiving a 0 rating with a rapid falling off of the curve. There is little tendency for frequencies to pile up at the tail as in a J curve. The traumatized groups, however, do show an increased frequency of higher ratings as well as a wider range.

Cutting Points and Normative Data

In order to identify those Ss among whom we expect to find later evidence of brain damage, it is desirable to establish a cutting point. . . . The cutting point selected was at the extreme of the normal distribution,

TABLE 3. *Percentage of Subjects Identified as Abnormal by Scores Below the Cutting Point on the Day of Poorest Performance*

Test	Normal	Total Traumatized	Mild Trauma	Moderate Trauma	Severe Trauma
Maturation scale	0	25	(33)[a]	12	57
Pain	1	42	43	30	(50)
Vision scale	1	41	(17)	31	60
Irritability	1	28	(33)	8	46
Tension	3	34	(33)	23	46
Any one or more tests	4	51	46	37	84

[a] Percentages in parentheses are based on an N of less than ten.

that point below which only 1 percent of the normal population would fall. . . . Table 3 shows the percentage of Ss who score on the abnormal side of the cutting point on any one or more tests and on each test separately. When Ss were retested, the poorest performance has been taken as the score on a test. These data are supplied for the normal and traumatized groups and for the three subsamples of traumatized Ss. Pain thresholds and the Vision Scale are superior, but all tests identify some Ss as abnormal. The percentage identified as abnormal appears to increase with the degree of trauma and, if scores on all tests are considered, is statistically significant at the .01 level when tested by chi-square.

DISCUSSION

The group of tests we have used samples much of the repertoire of an infant's response to his environment. All of the responses are relatively simple, but they represent a substantial portion of the most complicated behavior which an infant of this age can show. How complicated is such behavior? With the exception of the two rating scales, the tests can be described as measuring sensorimotor ability, i.e., (a) the capacity to respond at all to various kinds of sensory stimuli, and (b) the extent to which the response is specific to a particular stimulus. The ratings of irritability and of muscular tension provide two more dimensions along which all responses of an infant, both spontaneous and elicited, may be described. We should like to know whether measuring such behavior gives any information about either past or future development. . . .

The present work is not primarily concerned with predicting the relative superiority of "normal" individuals, but rather in determining whether external trauma has caused brain injury. We did find that a considerable percentage of traumatized infants show impaired functioning as compared with nontraumatized newborns, and that such impairment is related to clinical judgments of severity of trauma. But will measures of impairment of a newborn predict the extent of later impairment? The question cannot be answered at the present time. One can say only that it seems reasonable to assume that the greater the present trauma, the greater the likelihood that some cells will suffer irreversible damage.

SUMMARY

Five test procedures were administered to 265 infants without prenatal, perinatal, or postnatal complications, and to 81 infants suffering from anoxia, mechanical birth injury, or diseases or infections associated with brain damage. The traumatized newborns composed nearly the total population of such infants born at the St. Louis Maternity Hospital during a two-year period.

The five tests consist of a Pain Threshold Test, a Maturation Scale, a Vision Scale, an Irritability Rating and a Muscle Tension Rating. Reliability of the procedures was variously measured by split-half correlation, test-retest agreement, and interscorer agreement as applicable. All of the tests appeared to be satisfactorily reliable. A sample of 109 test scores obtained without knowledge of Ss' classification did not differ significantly from those obtained under the usual conditions of partial knowledge.

Norms have been presented for each test, with separate norms provided for each of the first five days of life and for Negro and white Ss where these variables were related to performance. Older Ss were found to be more sensitive than younger on the Pain Threshold Test and to perform better on the Maturation and Vision Scales. Negro Ss were superior to whites on both the Maturation and Vision Scales, but there was no race difference on the other tests. Private-clinic status and sex of the S did not measurably affect performance. There was no practice or learning effect from retesting when age was held constant.

Normal and traumatized groups, paired for relevant variables, obtained significantly different scores on all tests. When a cutting point at the poorer extreme of the normal distribution was selected, all tests identified some traumatized Ss as abnormal while false positives ranged only from 1 to 3 percent. The percentage identified as abnormal increased with seriousness, as rated by pediatric judges, of the trauma.

REFERENCES

1. Cattell, Psyche. *The measurement of intelligence of infants and young children.* New York: Psychological Corp., 1940.
2. Gesell, A., & Armatruda, Catherine. *Developmental diagnosis.* New York: Hoeber, 1941.
3. Gesell, A., Ilg, Frances L., & Bullis, G. D. *Vision, its development in infant and child.* New York: Hoeber, 1949.
4. Gilliland, A. R. *The northwestern intelligence tests.* Boston: Houghton Mifflin, 1951.
5. Griffiths, Ruth. *The abilities of babies.* New York: McGraw-Hill, 1954.

THE ORIGIN OF FORM PERCEPTION

Robert L. Fantz

WESTERN RESERVE UNIVERSITY

LONG BEFORE AN INFANT can explore his surroundings with hands and feet he is busy exploring it with his eyes. What goes on in the infant's mind as he stares, blinks, looks this way and that? Does he sense only a chaotic patchwork of color and brightness or does he perceive and differentiate among distinctive forms? The question has always fascinated philosophers and scientists, for it bears on the nature and origin of knowledge. At issue is the perennial question of nature v. nurture. On the one side is the nativist who believes that the infant has a wide range of innate visual capacities and predilections, which have evolved in animals over millions of years, and that these give a primitive order and meaning to the world from the "first look." On the other side is the extreme empiricist who holds that the infant learns to see and to use what he sees only by trial and error or association, starting, as John Locke put it, with a mind like a blank slate.

It has long been known that very young infants can see light, color, and movement. But it is often argued that they cannot respond to such stimuli as shape, pattern, size, or solidity; in short, that they cannot perceive form. This position is the last stronghold of the empiricist, and it has been a hard one to attack. How is one to know what an infant sees? My colleagues and I have recently developed an experimental method of finding out. We have already disposed of the basic question, that of whether babies can perceive form at all. They can, at least to some degree, although it appears that neither the view of the simple nativist nor that of the simple empiricist tells the whole story. Now we are investigating the further question of how and when infants use their capacity

Reprinted by permission from *Scientific American* (May, 1961). Copyright © 1961 by *Scientific American, Inc.* All rights reserved.

to perceive form to confer order and meaning on their environment.

The technique grew out of studies with lower animals, which are of importance in themselves. They were undertaken in 1951 at the University of Chicago with newly hatched chicks. Paradoxically, chicks can "tell" more directly what they see than higher animals can. Soon after they break out of the shell they go about the business of finding things to peck at and eat. Their purposeful, visually dominated behavior is ideally suited for observation and experiment.

We presented the chicks with a number of small objects of different shapes. Each object was enclosed in a clear plastic container to eliminate the possible influence of touch, smell, or taste, but this did not prevent the chicks from pecking at preferred forms for hours on end. An electrical circuit attached to each container recorded the number of pecks at it.

FIG. 1. Pattern preference of newly hatched chicks is studied by recording their pecks at each of a number of different shapes in plastic containers set into the wall of a test box. Reprinted with permission. Copyright © 1953, 1961 by Scientific American, Inc. All rights reserved.

More than 1,000 chicks were tested on some 100 objects. To exclude any opportunity for learning, the chicks were hatched in darkness and tested on their first exposure to light, before they had had any experience with real food. Presented with eight objects of graded angularity, from a sphere to a pyramid, the subjects pecked 10 times oftener at the sphere than they did at the pyramid. Among the flat forms, circles were preferred to triangles regardless of comparative size; among circles, those of ⅛-inch diameter drew the most attention. In a test of the effect of three-dimensionality the chicks consistently selected a sphere over a flat disk.

The results provided conclusive evidence that the chick has an innate ability to perceive shape, three-dimensionality, and size. Furthermore, the chick uses the ability in a "meaningful" way by selecting, without learning, those objects most likely to be edible: round, three-dimensional shapes about the size of grain or seeds. Other birds exhibit similar visual

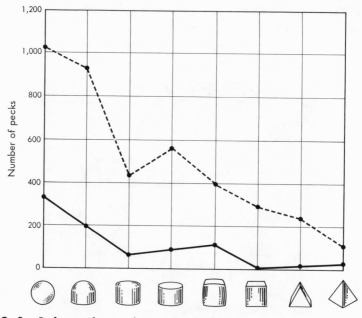

FIG. 2.   Preference for roundness is shown by this record of total pecks by 112 chicks' first 10 minutes (*black line*) and first 40 minutes (*dash line*) of visual experience. Reprinted with permission. Copyright © 1953, 1961 by Scientific American, Inc. All rights reserved.

capacity. For example, N. Tinbergen of the University of Oxford (6) found selective pecking by newly hatched herring gulls. These chicks prefer shapes resembling that of the bill of the parent bird from which they are fed.

Of course, what holds true for birds does not necessarily apply to human beings. The inherent capacity for form perception that has developed in birds may have been lost somewhere along the evolutionary branch leading to the primates, unlikely as it seems. Or, more plausibly, the primate infant may require a period of postnatal development to reach the level of function of the comparatively precocious chick.

When we set out to determine the visual abilities of helpless infants, the only indicator we could find was the activity of the eyes themselves. If an infant consistently turns its gaze toward some forms more often than toward others, it must be able to perceive form. Working on this premise, we developed a visual-interest test, using as our first subjects infant chimpanzees at the Yerkes Laboratories of Primate Biology in Orange Park, Florida.

A young chimpanzee lay on its back in a comfortable crib inside a "looking chamber" of uniform color and illumination. We attached to the ceiling of the chamber pairs of test objects, slightly separated from each other. They were exposed to view, alternately at right and left, in a series of short periods. Through a peephole in the ceiling we could see tiny images of the objects mirrored in the subjects' eyes. When the image of one of the objects was at the center of the eye, over the pupil, we knew the chimpanzee was looking directly at it. The experimenter recorded on an electric timer the amount of attention given each target. The results were then analyzed to determine their statistical significance. Our first subject was a five-month-old chimpanzee. Later we followed a chimpanzee from birth, keeping it in darkness except during the tests. In both cases we found a definite preference for certain objects, indicating an inborn ability to distinguish among them.

Turning to human infants, we made no major change in our procedure except that we did not tamper with their everyday environment. The experiments did not disturb the infants but they did demand great patience of the investigators. Human infants are more rapidly bored than chimpanzees and they tend to go to sleep.

In the first experiment we tested 30 infants, aged 1 to 15 weeks, at weekly intervals. Four pairs of test patterns were presented in random sequence. In decreasing order of complexity they were: horizontal stripes and a bull's-eye design, a checkerboard and two sizes of plain square, a cross and a circle, and two identical triangles. The total time spent looking at the various pairs differed sharply, the more complex pairs drawing the greater attention. Moreover, the relative attractiveness of the two members of a pair depended on the presence of a pattern difference. There were strong preferences between stripes and bull's-eye and between checkerboard and square. Neither the cross and circle nor the two triangles aroused a significant differential interest. The differential response to pattern was shown at all ages tested, indicating that it was not the result of a learning process. The direction of preference between stripes and bull's-eye, on the other hand, changed at 2 months of age, due either to learning or to maturation.

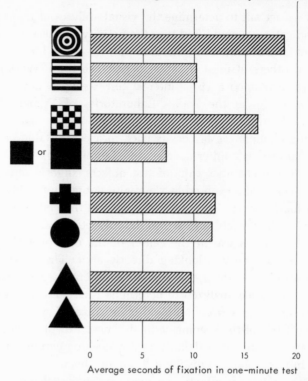

FIG. 3.   Interest in form was proved by infants' reactions to various pairs of
patterns (*left*) presented together. (The small and large plain squares were used
alternately.) The more complex pairs received the most attention, and within
each of these pairs differential interest was based on pattern differences. These
results are for 22 infants in 10 weekly tests. Reprinted with permission. Copyright © 1953, 1961 by Scientific American, Inc. All rights reserved.

Later we learned that a Swiss pediatrician, F. Stirnimann, had obtained similar results with still younger infants. He held cards up to the
eyes of infants 1 to 14 days old and found that patterned cards were of
more interest than those with plain colors.

Clearly some degree of form perception is innate. This, however,
does not dispose of the role of physiological growth or of learning in the
further development of visual behavior. Accordingly we turned our attention to the influence of these factors.

By demonstrating the existence of form perception in very young
infants we had already disproved the widely held notion that they are
anatomically incapable of seeing anything but blobs of light and dark.
Nevertheless, it seems to be true that the eye, the visual nerve-pathways

and the visual part of the brain are poorly developed at birth. If this is so, then the acuteness of vision—the ability to distinguish detail in patterns—should increase as the infant matures.

To measure the change in visual acuity we presented infants in the looking chamber with a series of patterns composed of black and white stripes, each pattern paired with a gray square of equal brightness. The width of the stripes was decreased in graded steps from one pattern to the next. Since we already knew that infants tend to look longer and more frequently at a patterned object than at a plain one, the width of the stripes of the finest pattern that was preferred to gray would provide an index to visual acuity. In this modified version the visual-interest test again solved the difficulties involved in getting infants to reveal what they see.

The width of the finest stripes that could be distinguished turned out to decrease steadily with increasing age during the first half-year of life. By 6 months babies could see stripes 1/64 inch wide at a distance of 10 inches—a visual angle of five minutes of arc, or 1/12 degree. (The adult standard is one minute of arc.) Even when still less than a month old, infants were able to perceive ⅛-inch stripes at 10 inches, corresponding to a visual angle of a little less than one degree. This is poor perform-

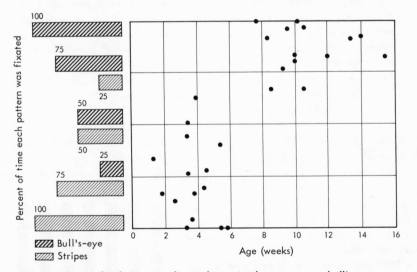

FIG. 4. Reversal of interest from the striped pattern to bull's-eye was apparent at 2 months of age. Each dot is for a single infant's first test session. It shows the time spent looking at the bull's-eye and at the stripes as a percent of the time spent looking at both. Reprinted with permission. Copyright © 1953, 1961 by Scientific American, Inc. All rights reserved.

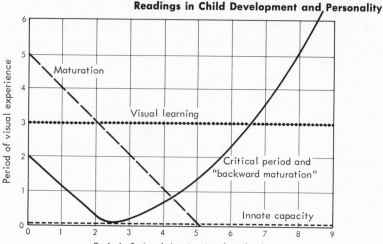

FIG. 5. Hypothetical results that might be expected if any one developmental factor operated alone is plotted. The horizontal axis shows the period of rearing without visual experience; the vertical axis, the time subsequently required in the light until a given response is shown. Units of time are arbitrary. If innate capacity alone were effective, the response would always come without any experience (*short-dash line*). If maturation were necessary, the response would not be shown before a certain age, in this case five units regardless of deprivation (*long-dash line*). If learning alone were operative, the required amount of experience would be constant (*dot line*). Actually, tests with chicks and monkey infants suggest the result shown by the solid black curve: after a short period of maturation, a "critical period" is reached when innate capacity can be manifested; more deprivation brings on "backward maturation," in which more and more experience is required before a response is shown. Reprinted with permission. Copyright © 1953, 1961 by Scientific American, Inc. All rights reserved.

ance compared to that of an adult, but it is a far cry from a complete lack of ability to perceive pattern.

The effects of maturation on visual acuity are relatively clear and

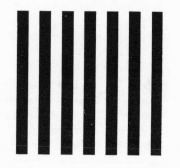

FIG. 6. Visual accuity was tested with these stripes: ⅛, ¹⁄₁₆, ¹⁄₃₂, and ¹⁄₆₄ of an inch wide. Each pattern was displayed with a gray square of equal brightness 10 inches from the infants' eyes. The finest pattern, consistently preferred to gray, showed how narrow a stripe the infant could perceive. Infants under a month old could see the ⅛-inch stripes and the 6-month-olds could see ¹⁄₆₄-inch stripes. Reprinted with permission. Copyright © 1953, 1961 by Scientific American, Inc. All rights reserved.

not too hard to measure. The problem of learning is more subtle. Other investigators have shown that depriving animals of patterned visual stimuli for a period after birth impairs their later visual performance especially in form perception (5). Learned behavior is particularly vulnerable, but even innate responses are affected. For example, chicks kept in darkness for several weeks after hatching lose the ability to peck at food.

Research is now under way at Western Reserve University on this perplexing problem. We have raised monkeys in darkness for periods varying from 1 to 11 weeks. In general, the longer the period of deprivation, the poorer the performance when the animals were finally exposed to light and the more time they required to achieve normal responses. When first brought into the light, the older monkeys bumped into things, fell off tables, could not locate objects visually—for all practical purposes they were blind. It sometimes took weeks for them to "learn to see."

Monkeys kept a shorter time in the dark usually showed good spatial orientation in a few hours or days. Moreover, they showed normal interest in patterned objects, whereas the animals deprived of light for longer periods seemed more interested in color, brightness, and size.

These results cannot be explained by innate capacity, maturtation, or learning alone. If form perception were wholly innate, it would be evident without experience at any age, and visual deprivation would have no effect. If maturation were the controlling factor, younger infant animals would be inferior rather than superior to older ones with or without visual experience. If form perception were entirely learned, the same period of experience would be required regardless of age and length of deprivation.

Instead there appears to be a complex interplay of innate ability, maturation, and learning in the molding of visual behavior, operating in this manner: there is a critical age for the development of a given visual

response when the visual, mental and motor capacities are ready to be used and under normal circumstances will be used together. At that time the animal will either show the response without experience or will learn it readily. If the response is not "imprinted" at the critical age for want of visual stimulus, development proceeds abnormally, without the visual component. Presented with the stimulus later on, the animal learns to respond, if it responds at all, only with extensive experience and training. This explanation, if verified by further studies, would help to reconcile the conflicting claims of the nativist and the empiricist on the origin of visual perception.

To return to human infants, the work described so far does not answer the second question posed earlier in this article: whether or not the infant's innate capacity for form perception introduces a measure of order and meaning into what would otherwise be a chaotic jumble of sensations. An active selection process is necessary to sort out these sensations and make use of them in behavior. In the case of chicks such a process is apparent in the selection of forms likely to be edible.

In the world of the infant, people have an importance that is perhaps comparable to the importance of grain in the chick's world. Facial pattern is the most distinctive aspect of a person, the most reliable for distinguishing a human being from other objects, and for identifying him. So a face-like pattern might be expected to bring out selective perception in an infant if anything could.

We tested infants with three flat objects the size and shape of a head. On one we painted a stylized face in black on a pink background, on the second we rearranged the features in a scrambled pattern, and on the third we painted a solid patch of black at one end with an area equal to that covered by all the features. We made the features large enough to be perceived by the youngest baby, so acuity of vision was not a factor. The three objects, paired in all possible combinations, were shown to 49 infants from 4 days to 6 months old.

The results were about the same for all age levels: the infants looked mostly at the "real" face, somewhat less often at the scrambled face, and largely ignored the control pattern. The degree of preference for the "real" face to the other one was not large, but it was consistent among individual infants, especially the younger ones. The experiment suggested that there is an unlearned, primitive meaning in the form perception of infants as well as of chicks.

Further support for the idea was obtained when we offered our infant subjects a choice between a solid sphere and a flat circle of the same

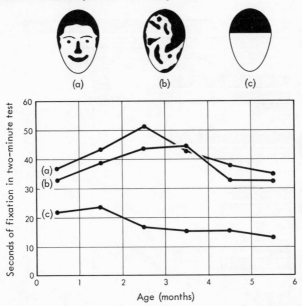

FIG. 7. Adaptive significance of form perception was indicated by the preference that infants showed for a "real" face (a) over a scrambled face (b), and
for both over a control (c). The results charted here show the average time
scores for infants at various ages when presented with the three face-shaped
objects paired in all the possible combinations. Reprinted with permission. Copyright © 1953, 1961 by Scientific American, Inc. All rights reserved.

diameter. When the texture and shading clearly differentiated the sphere
from the circle—in other words, when there was a noticeable difference
in pattern—the solid form was the more interesting to infants from one
to six months old. This unlearned selection of a pattern associated with
a solid object gives the infant a basis for perceiving depth.

The last experiment to be considered is a dramatic demonstration
of the interest in pattern in comparison to color and brightness. This
time there were six test objects: flat disks, six inches in diameter. Three
were patterned—a face, a bull's-eye and a patch of printed matter. Three
were plain—red, fluorescent yellow, and white. We presented them
against a blue background, one at a time in varied sequence, and timed
the length of the first glance at each.

The face pattern was overwhelmingly the most interesting, followed
by the printing and the bull's-eye. The three brightly colored plain
circles trailed far behind and received no first choices. There was no
indication that the interest in pattern was secondary or acquired.

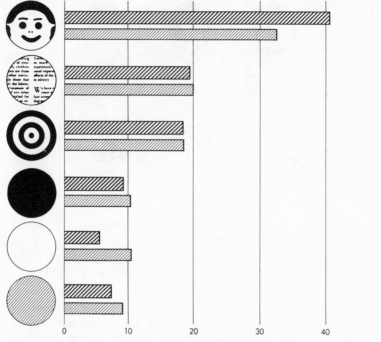

FIG. 8.   Importance of pattern rather than color or brightness was illustrated by the response of infants to a face, a piece of printed matter, a bull's-eye, and plain red, white, and yellow disks. Even the youngest infants preferred patterns. Black bars show the results for infants from two to three months old; gray bars, for infants more than three months old. Reprinted with permission. Copyright © 1953, 1961 by Scientific American, Inc. All rights reserved.

What makes patterns so intrinsically interesting to young infants? It seems to me that the answer must lie in the uses of vision for the child and adult.

One of these functions is the recognition of objects under various conditions. The color and brightness of objects change with illumination; retinal size changes with distance; outline changes with point of view; binocular depth perception is helpful only at short range. But the pattern of an object—the texture, the arrangement of details, the complexity of contours—can be relied on for identification under diverse conditions.

A good example is social perception. As noted earlier, the general configuration of a face identifies a human being to an infant. At a later age a specific person is recognized primarily by more precise perception of facial pattern. Still later, subtle details of facial expression tell the child whether a person is happy or sad, pleased or displeased, friendly or unfriendly.

Another important function of vision is to provide orientation in space. For this purpose James J. Gibson of Cornell University has shown clearly the importance of a specific type of pattern: surface texture. For example, texture indicates a solid surface, whereas untextured light usually indicates air or water. Gradual changes in texture show whether a surface is vertical or horizontal or oblique, flat or curved or angular— and therefore indicate whether it can be walked on, walked around or climbed over. Discontinuities in texture mark the edges of objects and abrupt changes in surfaces.

From these few examples there can be no question of the importance of visual pattern in everyday life. It is therefore reasonable to suppose that the early interest of infants in form and pattern in general, as well as in particular kinds of pattern, play an important role in the development of behavior by focusing attention on stimuli that will later have adaptive significance.

Further research is necessary to pin down this and other implications more concretely, but the results to date do require the rejection of the view that the newborn infant or animal must start from scratch to learn to see and to organize patterned stimulation. Lowly chicks as well as lofty primates perceive and respond to form without experience if given the oportunity at the appropriate stage of development. Innate knowledge of the environment is demonstrated by the preference of newly hatched chicks for forms likely to be edible and by the interest of young infants in kinds of form that will later aid in object recognition, social responsiveness, and spatial orientation. This primitive knowledge provides a foundation for the vast accumulation of knowledge through experience.

REFERENCES

1. Beach, F. A., & Jaynes, J. Effects of early experience upon the behavior of animals. *Psychol. Bull.*, 1954, **51** (3), 239–263.
2. Fantz, R. L. Form preferences in newly hatched chicks. *J. comp. & physiol. Psychol.*, 1957, **50** (5), 422–430.
3. Fantz, R. L. Pattern vision in young infants. *Psychol. Rec.*, 1958, **8**, 43–47.
4. Gibson, J. J. *The perception of the visual world*. Boston: Houghton Mifflin, 1950.
5. Riesen, A. H. Arrested vision. *Sci. Amer.*, July, 1950.

6. Tinbergen, N., & Perdeck, A. C. On the stimulus situation releasing the begging response in the newly hatched herring gull chick. *Behavior,* 1950, 3, Part I. Pp. 1–39.

7. Tinbergen, N. The evolution of behavior in gulls. *Sci. Amer.,* December, 1960.

SECTION ▐▐ EARLY INFANT-ENVIRONMENT INTERACTION

During the first year of life, the infant's physical maturation continues at a very rapid pace, and with dramatic results. At the same time, birth brings with it an enormous increase in the range of environmental stimuli to which the infant may be exposed. The developing child's behavior is a complex function of a continuing interaction between these two sets of forces: his unfolding biological nature, influenced in turn by his genetic inheritance, and his expanding experience with the world about him.

It is important to emphasize that the effects of this interaction upon the child's development are neither random nor haphazard, but are guided by definite principles. These principles are the laws of learning. What an infant learns in a particular situation, or indeed whether he learns anything at all, will depend on his needs, biological or psychological; his ability to attend to and differentiate among environmental stimuli; and his capacity for making responses, ranging from gross bodily movements to the most complex, differentiated, and specific thoughts, feelings, and motor acts. Learning will also depend on the kinds of environmental stimuli to which the infant is exposed, and on the consequences to which his responses lead.

In general, responses to stimuli which lead to satisfaction (i.e., reward or reinforcement) of an unresolved need, whether biological or psychological in nature, tend to be learned. Conversely, responses which produce no such reinforcement, or which actually lead to an aggravation of the need and a further departure from a homeostatic state, tend not to be learned—or if already learned, tend to be unlearned.

Thus, in the experiment reported in Dorothy Marquis' article, it was demonstrated that hungry infants will learn to respond to the sound of a buzzer preceding feeding with responses (e.g., mouth-opening, sucking) that are associated with a reduction in hunger, while at the same time tending to eliminate irrelevant or incompatible responses (e.g., general activity, crying). Apparently, infants are capable of relatively simple kinds of learning, such as adjusting to a feeding schedule, very early in life.

More complex types of learning, such as learning a language or memorizing a poem, must obviously await further biological maturation and the establishment of a number of basic skills which serve as "building blocks" for learning the very complex responses involved in gaining verbal proficiency. However, the first steps in language development may begin very early, and environmental factors may play a crucial role in determining the rate at which they are acquired. It has been found, for example, that babies under 6 months of age living in unstimulating orphanage environments are often retarded both in frequency of vocalizations and number and types of sounds. Conversely, during the second half of the first year infants raised in middle-class homes show more frequent and varied sounds than children of working-class families. This finding suggests that middle-class mothers may do more vocalizing to their infants which, in turn, may stimulate the child's vocal expression.

In their article on social conditioning of vocalizations in infants, Rheingold, Gewirtz, and Ross demonstrate that rewarding the 3-month-old child's utterances by smiling and touching his abdomen after each sound leads to an increase in the amount of infant vocalization. Apparently the young child's verbal behavior can be modified through experience, and can be increased or decreased, depending on the amount of social stimulation his vocalizations receive.

Primary and learned needs. The kinds of unresolved needs which may serve as the motivational basis for the infant's learning fall into two general categories: *innate* (or *primary*) and *learned.* The former category is illustrated by Marquis' study, and includes a variety of needs—for food, water, warmth, oxygen—which are basically biological in character and which, in many cases, require gratification if the organism is to survive. The latter category includes many of the child's most important needs: security, recognition, love from his mother. There is nothing innate about such needs, for they must in themselves be learned.

Thus, the child's need for love from his mother may develop out of her role in satisfying many of his basic biological needs: through feeding him when he is hungry or thirsty, changing him when he is cold and wet, and putting him to bed when he is tired. We still have much to learn, however, about the exact nature of all of the infant's needs, and hence about the relative importance of the mother's behavior in satisfying them. Harlow and Zimmermann in the ingenious experiments on newborn monkeys reported here, have made an important contribution in this area by indicating that there is a strong need, apparently innate, for tactile stimulation, and that one of the most important functions of the mother is to provide this sort of "contact comfort." These findings with animals lend experimental support to the contention of a number of psychologists and psychiatrists, such as Margaret Ribble, that physical contact between mother and infant is innately gratifying or rewarding.

Once a learned need has developed, it can itself serve as the motivational basis for learning new response sequences, in the same fashion as primary needs. Furthermore, failure of the environment to provide satisfaction for a learned need once it has developed can lead to serious disruptions of adaptive behavior. In one of the articles included in this section, Bowlby describes how healthy children, separated from their mothers by institutionalization or hospitalization, may go through a series of adaptational crises, including protest, despair, and finally a kind of hollow detachment. It is interesting to note that these phenomena were observed most often in cases where a strong love for the mother had already developed, and hence where separation from her produced a state of need-deprivation. In cases where there was little attachment to the mother to begin with, similar evidences of protest were not manifested.

One other topic merits comment here. We have already noted that responses which lead to the satisfaction (reinforcement) of an existing need tend to be learned. However, a major unresolved scientific issue at the present time concerns the nature of reinforcement. It has long been observed in a variety of experiments that both animals and people will learn responses that lead to the satisfaction of acute thirst or hunger, to a lessening of physical pain, or to reductions in fear or anxiety.

It may be noted that in each of the above instances, the animal or person approached the situation in a state of intense stimulation—whether from the pangs of hunger or thirst, or the stimulation of pain receptors, as in the case of electric shock or severe burn—and made a response to reduce or eliminate the intense stimulation. On the basis of such observations, a number of psychological theorists were led to postulate that *when a response leads to a reduction in intense stimulation, it tends to be learned.* Stated in somewhat different fashion, they have been led to conclude that a motivation involves an increase in stimulation, and that a reinforcement involves a decrease in stimulation.

There appears to be little question that reduction in intense stimulation plays an important role in many kinds of learning. However, an increasing amount of empirical evidence is accumulating which suggests that there are also many situations in which increases in stimulation, rather than decreases, are reinforcing and lead to learning. In his article, J. McVicker Hunt, a psychologist at the University of Illinois, discusses a number of these investigations and the problems they raise for a theory of reinforcement. In attempting to resolve these problems, Hunt develops the hypothesis that organisms, including infants, seek not only to reduce heightened states of unpleasant stimulation, but also to achieve what Hebb calls an *optimal level of activation* below which, in Hunt's view, *increases* in stimulation are reinforcing and lead to learning, and above which *decreases* are reinforcing.

In his article, Hunt also attacks the common notion that fear and anxiety, which play such a crucial role in determining the development of behavior, are *always* the "result of traumatic experiences of helplessness in the face of homeostatic need or painful external stimulation." He supports the contention of Donald Hebb in the second article of this section that fear may also be aroused when a stimulus pattern contains both familiar and unfamiliar elements. For example, Hebb found that chimpanzees show fear reactions when presented with a plaster cast of a chimpanzee head. The head is a familiar stimulus element, but the absence of the attached body makes this stimulus incongruous and the animal behaves as if it were afraid.

If Hebb's hypothesis is valid, a completely novel stimulus should elicit less fear than one which has some familiar elements embedded in a generally unfamiliar context. That is, as children mature they learn certain rules about the world, and build up definite images or expectations about the environment. They expect that animals will have four feet, that birds will have wings, that snow will be white, and so on. Consequently, if a child's expectations of what he will see, hear, smell, or feel are seriously contradicted, he may become anxious and seek to find some response which will solve the problem of incongruity, thus reducing his anxiety.

As these articles make clear, we still have much to learn about the principles and conditions governing the early interactions between the infant and his environment. At the same time, however, there are few areas in which so many exciting and original investigations are presently being undertaken at all levels—physiological and psychological—and involving both humans and animals. It is probably also fair to state that few areas show as much promise of yielding findings of critical importance for our knowledge of development and for the future welfare of man.

Can Conditioned

RESPONSES BE ESTABLISHED IN

THE NEWBORN INFANT?[1]

Dorothy Postle Marquis

UNIVERSITY OF MICHIGAN

THE PROBLEM

THE PRESENT PROBLEM was undertaken to investigate the contention made by the Pavlovian school of Russian psychologists and physiologists that the formation of conditioned responses in newborn infants is impossible because the cerebral cortex of the human infant functions only very incompletely the first few months after birth.

Most neurologists agree that the cerebral cortex of the newborn infant functions very imperfectly, if at all. Various investigators (Pavlov, Krasnogorski, Bechterew, and Lang and Olmsted) have failed to establish conditioned responses in infants under 5 months of age and in decerebrate animals, and have attributed their failure to the incomplete functioning of the cortex of their subjects. Pavlov (8) asserts that no new nervous connections can be formed except in the cerebral hemispheres.

One very important issue, however, seems to have been overlooked by these investigators. It is evident that when the cerebral cortex has reached functional maturity, it is the "dominant part" or the "pace setter" of the central nervous system (3). On the other hand, is it not logical to assume that before the cortex has reached its full development,

[1] From the Psychological Laboratories of the Ohio State University. Recommended by Albert P. Weiss and received for publication by Carl Murchison of the Editorial Board, August 25, 1930. The present paper is a brief summary of a dissertation for the doctor's degree, "Habit Formation in the Newborn Infant," a detailed account of which is available at the Graduate School of Ohio State University. The experiment was performed under the direction of Dr. A. P. Weiss.

Reprinted from *Journal of Genetic Psychology* (Dec., 1931), 39 (4), 479–492, by permission of the author and publisher.

the lower centers (thalamus, midbrain, medulla, etc.,) serve even more important functions than they do at a later time when the inhibitory action of the cortex dominates them? It is a well-established neurological fact that in the human infant at birth, the midbrain, which in the adult is a highly important correlation center for the reflexes of sight, hearing, and touch, is completely myelinated and apparently fully functional. Tracts to and from the red nucleus of the midbrain are also completely developed at birth. In the medulla oblongata there are present at birth important relay centers which regulate sucking, respiration, digestion, and secretion. Moreover, the thalamus, which in adults acts as a relatively complex correlation center for all impulses coming into the cortex, has at the time of birth reached a fairly high degree of functional maturity. Can we asume that the cortex possesses some mysterious function of power qualitatively different from any other part of the nervous system, so that it is only by means of *its* function that a response to one stimulus is replaced by a surrogate response? This seems improbable, since it is largely in the *amount* of its correlating tissue that the cortex differs from the other parts of the nervous system.

If the last conclusion is sound, then it should be possible to set up conditioned responses in the newborn human infant by means of the subcortical correlation centers, whose functions are the more complete before the inhibitory influence of the cortex has developed, *provided* we select reactions which are relatively well integrated at this stage of biological development. For our experimental work, in accordance with the principles above, as the unconditioned response, the feeding reactions of the infant (sucking, mouth-opening, and quieting, etc.) to a food stimulus (milk from the nursing bottle) were chosen. The conditioned stimulus was the sound of a buzzer. In these stimuli there are represented an auditory and a tactual-and-gustatory stimulus, and probably secretory and kinesthetic stimuli, all of whose impulses possess subcortical correlation centers. The specific experimental problem was to ascertain whether, after a sufficient number of pairings of buzzer and bottle, the buzzer alone would lead to feeding reactions.

METHOD

Ten subjects were used in this experiment, all newborn children of clinical maternity patients at the Ohio State University Hospital. Three Negro infants were used, two girls and one boy, and seven white infants, four girls and three boys. The plan of the experiment was never to permit the infants, from the first time they were fed, to feed without the bottle being immediately preceded or accompanied by the sound of the buzzer. The infants are fed six times each day. Instead of being taken to the mothers for nursing, the subjects of this experiment were brought one at a time into the experimental room and were fed from the bottle, milk which had been pumped from their own mothers' breasts. The period of experimentation extended from the first time the infants were fed (24 hours after birth) to the tenth day of life.

The specific experimental procedure after the infants were brought into the experimental room was as follows:

1.   The infant was placed on a stabilimeter[2] in a small compartment, the temperature and lighting of which were kept fairly constant, and remained there with no experimental stimulation for a period varying from 1 to 5 minutes (control period).
2.   At the end of this time the experimenter stepped inside the curtain of the compartment, carefully noted and recorded the infant's reactions for a few seconds, then rang the buzzer for 5 seconds.
3.   As soon as possible after the end of the buzzer, the bottle was inserted in the infant's mouth and the buzzer rung for 5 seconds more after the infant started sucking.
4.   At various times while the infant was sucking, the buzzer was sounded for periods of 5 seconds.
5.   During each experimental period the bottle was removed from the infant's mouth from 2 to 5 times, to prevent too quick consumption of milk. Each time the bottle was replaced in the infant's mouth, it was preceded by the buzzer in the manner described above.

Record of the infant's reactions during the experiment was kept in two ways—through the experimenter's recorded observations, and through the polygraph record. The polygraph record furnished (a) a continuous record of the infant's movements by means of registration of the stabilimeter movements; (b) a record of sucking movements by means of pneumatic recording through a balloon-type capsule fastened under the infant's chin and a Marey tambour; (c) a time record including time of stimulation and other events during the control period. The experimenter's protocols included a detailed record of the specific reactions made by the infant for a few seconds before each buzzer, and the reactions after the buzzer began to sound, as well as the reactions at other times during the experimental period.

[2] For details of the experimental cabinet refer to (10).

Two experiments served as control for the results. The first was a test in the control periods of the last day or last two days of each infant's experiment to see whether other stimuli would elicit reactions similar to those after the buzzer. As a visual stimulus, a flashlight was projected into the infant's eyes. As an auditory stimulus, a fall hammer striking the end of a tin can was used. As a second control experiment, four subjects of the same age as the experimental group were stimulated by the buzzer at feeding times without being permitted to feed immediately afterwards. The latter experiment was carried out throughout a nine-day period for each infant.

RESULTS

General. The following are the results of this experiment for eight infants. The results of the first two subjects of the experiment are omitted since the method of recording was not uniform with that of the others. Their reactions, in general, however, are not essentially different from those of other infants.

1. Seven of the eight infants, after a period of 3 to 6 days, began to show significant changes of reaction following the buzzer. Certain reactions began to increase, others to decrease.

2. The reactions following the buzzer on the first few days with all infants were predominantly an increase in general activity or crying, no change in general activity or crying, or an occasional decrease of general activity.

3. The reactions following the buzzer which increased were sucking, mouth-opening, and cessation of general activity and crying. All of these reactions are directly related to foodtaking.

4. The reactions following the buzzer which decreased were general activity and crying—reactions which are not usually concomitants of the foodtaking response.

5. Reactions preceding the buzzer showed few significant changes throughout the experiment. In four instances mouth-opening preceding the buzzer increased on the seventh and eighth days of the experiments. This was interpreted as a possible indication that the whole experimental situation might be taking on the properties of conditioned stimuli.

6. Sucking without an object in the mouth very rarely occurred before the buzzer sounded.

7. The infants showed great individual differences in the onset of the change of reaction after the buzzer, in the degree of the change, and in the suddenness with which the change occurred.

8. Increase in mouth-opening and decrease in crying after the buzzer, in most infants, started on the fourth day, while increase in sucking and general activity began, in most instances, on the fifth day.

9. With one exception, the seven infants who showed an increased number of foodtaking reactions *after* the buzzer, showed least increase when they were quiet and asleep *before* the buzzer sounded.

10. One infant failed to show increase in foodtaking reactions following the buzzer. This infant's physiological condition was poor, he never seemed hungry, and was not as responsive generally to stimuli as the other infants. This infant, all through the experiment, showed either no significant change of activity when the buzzer sounded, or increase in general activity and crying.

11. In the first control experiment where the infants were stimulated during the control periods on the last or the last two days of the experiment by the flashlight and by the hammer striking the can, they never responded by any foodtaking reactions. Usually there was no change in general activity and crying or there was increased general activity and crying.

12. In the second control experiment, in which four additional infants were stimulated by the buzzer at feeding times without ever feeding immediately afterward, the infants in the majority of cases showed increase in general activity and crying after the buzzer throughout the nine-day period.

RESULTS OF INDIVIDUAL INFANTS

1. *Infant Rn (white, female).* Infant Rn was the "brightest" of all the subjects. She was unusually alert to all stimuli and reached the highest percentage in number of feeding reactions after the buzzer. The changes in her reactions after the buzzer were as follows: *Sucking* reactions increased from 0 on the first two days to an average of 74 percent frequency[3] on the seventh, eighth, and ninth days. *Mouth-opening* increased from 0 on the first day to 75 percent on the last day. *Cessation of crying* increased from 0 on the first two days to 100 percent on the sixth, seventh, eighth, and ninth days; and *cessation of general bodily activity* from 0 on the first four days to 100 percent on the seventh and eighth days. *General activity* after the buzzer decreased from 92 percent on the first day to 0 on the last day, and *crying* from 46 percent on the first day to 0 on the last four days. Instances when Rn remained *quiet and awake*

---

[3] As compared with frequency of the buzzer stimulations.

after the buzzer decreased from an average of 26 percent on the first two days to 0 on the last two days. There were no significant differences in the number of conditioned responses, whether the infant was quiet and awake, quiet and asleep, or active and awake before the buzzer sounded. In the control experiment she never responded to the light or sound by any feeding reaction.

2. *Infant Cb (white, female).* The change in the Cb infant's reactions to the buzzer proceeding in the following manner. *Sucking* increased from 0 on the first four days to an average of 42 percent on the last two days. *Mouth-opening* after the buzzer showed a significant predominance over mouth-opening before the buzzer from the second day, and a predominance over mouth-closing after the buzzer from the fourth day on. *Cessation of crying* increased from 0 on the first three days to 100 percent on the sixth, seventh, and eighth days. *Cessation or significant decrease of general activity* showed an increase from 0 on the first three days to 100 percent on the last two days. *General activity* after the buzzer decreased from 62 percent on the first day to 0 on the last two days, and crying from an average of 17 percent on the first three days to 0 on the last three days. General activity and crying before the buzzer remained about the same throughout the experiment. When the infant was quiet and asleep before the buzzer, she seldom made "feeding responses" to the buzzer.

3. *Infant Cla (white, female).* Foodtaking responses at the sound of the buzzer began in the Cla infant on the fourth day, after approximately 140 to 150 pairings of buzzer and bottle. *Sucking* after the buzzer increased from 0 on the first four days to an average of 30 percent on the last three days. *Mouth-opening* increased from 0 on the first day to 62 percent on the last day. *Cessation of general bodily activity* increased from 0 on the first day to 100 percent on the last day; and *crying,* from 0 on the first day to 100 percent from the fourth day on. *General bodily activity* decreased from 67 percent on the first day to 0 on the last day, and *crying* from 17 percent on the first day to 0 on the last five days. General activity before the buzzer showed no significant change throughout the experiment. Crying before the buzzer varied, but showed no consistent tendency to increase or decrease in the course of the experiment. Fewer "feeding reactions" after the buzzer occurred when the infant was quiet and asleep before the buzzer sounded. No feeding reactions occurred to the stimuli in the control experiment.

4. *Infant Car (Negro, female).* Change of reaction following the buzzer began with the Car infant on the fourth day of the experiment

after 125 to 130 pairings of buzzer and bottle. *Sucking* increased from 0 on the first day to 53 percent on the last day. *Mouth-opening* increased from 20 percent on the first day to 35 percent on the sixth day, then decreased as sucking increased. *Cessation of crying* increased from an average of 17 percent on the second and third days to an average of 95 percent on the last two days; *cessation of general activity* from 0 on the first four days to 100 percent on the last two days. Crying before the buzzer increased from 0 on the first day to 53 percent on the last day, while general bodily activity before the buzzer increased from 0 on the first day to 47 percent on the last day. The infant showed more feeding reactions after the buzzer when she was active and awake than when she was quiet and awake or quiet and asleep. No feeding reactions occurred to the control stimuli on the last two days of the experiment.

5. *Infant Mar (Negro, female).* The change in the reactions to the buzzer was less pronounced in the Mar infant than in most others. The increase in reactions after the buzzer was as follows: *Sucking* increased from 0 on the first four days to 41 percent, 24 percent, and 23 percent, respectively, on the seventh, eighth, and ninth days; *cessation of general activity* from 0 on the first two days to an average of 56 percent on the last two days. *Mouth-opening* after the buzzer showed an increase over mouth-opening before the buzzer from the fifth day, with one exception on the seventh day. *General activity* after the buzzer showed a slight decrease from an average of 26 percent on the first three days to 19 percent for the last three days, while general activity before the buzzer increased on the last three days, crying after the buzzer decreased from 17 percent on the first day to 0 on the last three days. The instances when the infant remained quiet and awake after the buzzer decreased significantly from the fifth day. Highest frequency of feeding reactions after the buzzer occurred when the infant was active and awake before the buzzer. No feeding reactions occurred to the control stimuli on the last day of the experiment.

6. *Infant Lld (Negro, male).* With Lld infant the change of reactions following the buzzer occurred in the following fashion: *Sucking* increased irregularly from 0 on the first three days to 32 percent on the fourth day, 73 percent on the sixth day, and an average of 40 percent on the last three days. *Mouth-opening* increased irregularly from 11 percent on the first day to 46 percent on the last day. *Cessation of general activity* increased from 0 on the first two days to 50 percent on the third and fourth days and 100 percent on the next three days. On the last two days it decreased to an average of 76 percent. General activity before the

buzzer increased from an average of 35 percent on the first three days to 63 percent on the last three days, while general activity after the buzzer showed a corresponding decrease from 34 percent to 14 percent. *Crying* before the buzzer remained about the same throughout the experiment; crying after the buzzer decreased from 22 percent on the first day to 0 on the second day, never increasing to more than 6 percent on any day thereafter. The percentage of feeding reactions after the buzzer was highest when the infant was active and awake before the buzzer. In the control experiment the Lld infant responded 3 times (once to the light and once to the sound) in 24 stimulations, by slight quieting of general activity and crying.

7. *Infant Mont* (*white, male*). The changes in the Mont infant's responses to the buzzer occurred in the following manner. Sucking never attained a very high percentage of frequency. However, it increased from 0 on the first two days to 6 percent on the third day, and 33 percent on the seventh and ninth days. *Mouth-opening* after the buzzer was less than mouth-opening before the buzzer on the first day, equal to it on the second day, and exceeded it from the third day on. A very great increase in mouth-opening after the buzzer occurred on the fourth day when the percentage rose from 6 percent on the third day to 65 percent on the fourth. *Crying* after the buzzer exceeded crying before the buzzer on the second day. On the third day cessation of crying reached 100 percent, and in almost every case after this crying stopped as soon as the buzzer sounded. *Cessation of general activity* after the buzzer showed a steady increase from 12 percent on the first day to 100 percent on the sixth day and 89 percent, 90 percent and 82 percent, respectively, on the last three days. Although general activity before the buzzer showed no significant change throughout the experiment, general activity after the buzzer decreased from an average of 67 percent on the first two days to an average of 14 percent on the last two days. There was little difference in the percentage of feeding reactions after the buzzer whether the infant before the buzzer was quiet, active, or asleep. In the control experiment, the infant reacted to the sound twice out of 24 stimulations by cessation of crying.

8. *Infant Zim* (*white, male*). The Zim infant was an infant whose physiological condition was very poor. He showed no conditioned reactions to the buzzer. *General activity and crying* after the buzzer exceeded general activity and crying before the buzzer throughout the experiment. In only one instance did *sucking* ever occur after the buzzer. *Mouth-opening* after the buzzer slightly exceeded mouth-opening before

the buzzer after the third day, but its highest frequency was only 20 percent, on the seventh day.

The curves of Figure 1 present graphically the composite results of the seven infants who showed conditioned foodtaking response to the buzzer.

Since the combined averages of all infants, such as those shown in Figure 1, obscure individual differences, Figure 2 showing the results of infants Rn and Mar is presented to show an instance of a high percentage of conditioning and an instance of a much lower percentage of conditioning.

RESULTS OF SECOND CONTROL EXPERIMENT

In the second control experiment, in which four infants were stimulated by the buzzer at feeding times without ever being permitted to feed immediately afterward, practically no "feeding reactions" ever occurred after the buzzer. Their occurrence after the buzzer was not more frequent than their occurrence before the buzzer. For every infant the most frequent reactions to the buzzer were increased general activity and increased head-movement. No significant change in the infants' reactions after the buzzer was evident on any day of the experiment. The results of this check experiment were therefore negative.

CONCLUSIONS

1. A conditioned response of foodtaking reactions to the sound of a buzzer was established in seven out of eight newborn infants during the first ten days of life.

2. Since present neurological evidence indicates that the cerebral cortex of the newborn infant functions only very incompletely the first few months after birth, we may infer that *conditioned responses can be formed* in *newborn infants, at least, by subcortical correlation.* The type of responses included in the conditioned foodtaking reactions to the buzzer indicates that the midbrain, and especially the red nucleus, was important as a controlling mechanism.

3. The foodtaking response in the newborn infant includes a wide variety of reactions.

4. The results of this experiment bear out, in general, Pavlov's contention that an alert state of the subject is favorable to the formation of conditioned responses, since in most cases a higher frequency of

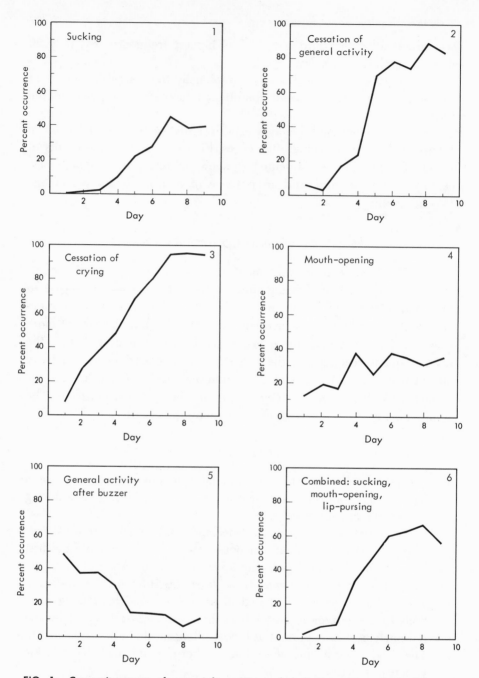

FIG. 1. Composite curves of seven infants (Zim excluded). Percentage of the different conditioning indices. Sucking is differentiated from mouth-opening and closing by including more lip-pursing and more tongue movement. Cessation of general activity means a sudden cessation of kicking, squirming, etc., as soon as the buzzer sounds. Cessation of crying means sudden stopping of crying at the sound of the buzzer. Mouth-opening (4) and combined: sucking, mouth-opening, and lip-pursing (5) include only those respective mouth-movement components which were not occurring before the buzzer sounded. Suck-

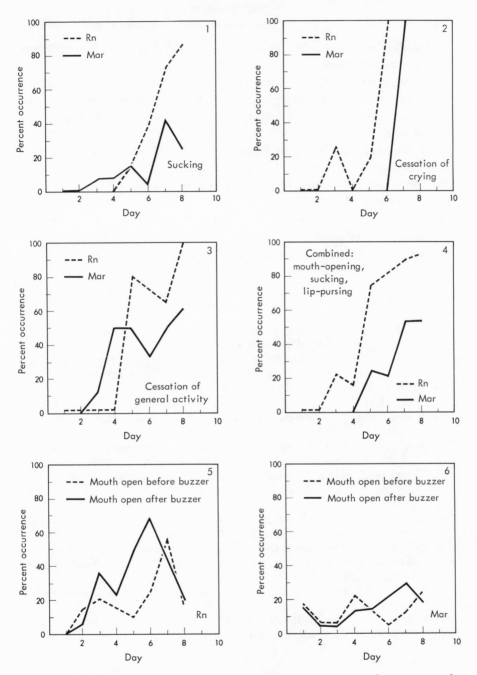

FIG. 2. Reactions after buzzer of infants Rn and Mar. A comparison of an instance of high percentage and one of low percentage of conditioning.

ing, mouth-opening, and lip-pursing combined includes the percentage of times when one or any combination of these occurred at the sound of the buzzer. Percentage of occurrence is derived by dividing the number of times each specific reaction occurred at the sound of the buzzer by the number of pairings of bottle and buzzer on each day.

feeding reactions after the buzzer occurred when the infants were active and awake.

5. The contention that a good physiological condition of the subject is necessary to the development of conditioned responses finds support in the case of the Zim infant, who showed no conditioning to the buzzer.

6. Individual differences in learning ability are present even at this early age.

7. Systematic training of human infants along social and hygienic lines can be started at birth.

8. Since habit formation may begin so early, the sharp lines drawn by some writers in their classifications of some acts as instinctive and some acts as learned must be viewed with some hesitation.

REFERENCES

1. Bechterew, W. Uber die Erregbarkeit der Grosshirnrinde neugeborener Thiere. *Neur. Zentralbl.*, 1895, **17**, 148–150.

2. Bechterew, W. Objektive Psychologie oder Psychoreflexologie. Die Lehre von den Assoziationsreflexen. Leipzig: Teubner, 1913, viii, 468.

3. Child, C. M. Physiological foundations of behavior. New York: Holt, 1924, xii, 330.

4. Krasnogorski, N. Uber die Bedingungsreflexe im Kindesalter. *Jahrb. f. Kinderhk.*, 1909, **69**, 1–24.

5. Krasnogorski, N. Uber die Grundmechanismen der Arbeit in der Gross-hirnrinde bei Kindern. *Jahrb. f. Kinderhk.* 1913, **78**, 373–398.

6. Krasnogorski, N. Die letzten Fortschritte in der Methodik der Erforschung der bedingten Reflexe an Kindern. *Jahrb. f. Kinderhk.*, 1926, **114**, 255–268.

7. Lang, J. M., & Olmsted, J. M. D. Conditioned reflexes and pathways in the spinal cord. *Amer. J. Physiol.*, 1923, **65**, 603–611.

8. Pavlov, I. P. Conditioned reflexes: an investigation of the physiological activity of the cerebral cortex. (G. V. Anrep, Trans.) London: Oxford Univ. Press, 1927, xv, 430.

9. Pavlov, I. P. Certain problems in the physiology of the cerebral hemispheres. *Proc. Roy. Soc. Lond.*, 1928, **103** (B), 97–108.

10. Pratt, K. C., Nelson, A. K., Sun, K. H. The behavior of the newborn infant. *Ohio State Univ. Stud., Contrib. Psychol.*, 1930 (10), xiii, 237.

Social Conditioning

of Vocalizations in the Infant

Harriet L. Rheingold, Jacob L. Gewirtz, and
Helen W. Ross

NATIONAL INSTITUTES OF HEALTH

BY THREE MONTHS OF AGE the infant gives a well-defined social response
to the appearance of adults. He looks at them intently, smiles, becomes
active, and vocalizes. This behavior is repeated again and again in sequence. Adults often respond to these acts of the infant; they may only
look at the child, but they may also smile to him, touch or caress him,
or vocalize in return. Frequently one observes "answering" social and,
in particular, vocal play between mother and child. The adults' responses may therefore play an important part in maintaining and developing social responsiveness in the child (10). The principles of operant
conditioning (11) suggest that some of these adult responses, functioning as reinforcers, may affect the development of the child's social behavior (2). Thus, smiling in the infant has been shown to respond to conditioning (1).

The present study was an attempt to condition vocalizations in infants. Vocalizations were selected for study because they seem to provide an index of the whole social response (10). The reinforcing stimulus
was a complex of social acts which resembled those an attentive adult
might naturally make when a child vocalizes. If temporal contiguity between the infant's vocalization and the reinforcing stimulus, which follows it, brings about an increase in the vocalizations, conditioning may
be said to have occurred. The possibility that the reinforcing stimulus
may also have functioned as an arouser of vocalizations will be considered. In any case, the results of the study should provide further understanding about the development of social responsiveness, as well as of
speech.

Reprinted from the *Journal of Comparative and Physiological Psychology* (1959),
52, pp. 68–73, by permission of the authors and the American Psychological Association.

METHOD

Two parallel experiments were carried out in sequence. In the first, 11 babies (Ss) were studied, with one experimenter (E) and one observer-recorder (0), both women. In the second, 10 other Ss and one S from Experiment I were studied with the E and O of the first experiment exchanging roles. An experiment was composed of three successive units in each of which three or four Ss were studied at one time.

Subjects

The Ss were 21 infants, all residents almost from birth in the same institution. (We are grateful to Sister Thecla and the staff of St. Ann's Infant Asylum, Washington, D.C., for their generous cooperation.) Their median age was 3.0 months; three-quarters of them were no more than three days older or younger than the median. In each experiment six Ss were male, five were female. Age was the main criterion for selection. Four possible Ss were rejected: one seemed immature, two had a very high rate of vocalizing during the first baseline measure, and one was markedly fussy.

The institution offers excellent care and, as is characteristic of institutions, there are multiple caretakers. In general, the Ss were well developed, healthy, alert, and socially responsive. The Es asked for no modifications in the usual caretaking routines. The caretakers knew that the Es were observing the development of social behavior, but they did not know the details of the experiment. The caretakers' usual behavior toward the Ss appeared not to be modified by the conditions of the experiment.

Experimental Conditions

Baseline. In Experimental days 1 and 2 (first and second Baseline days) E leaned over the crib with her face about 15 inches above S's and looked at him with an expressionless face, while O tallied vocalizations, out of S's sight. The E moved her head as necessary to remain in S's line of vision, a condition which obtained throughout the experiments.

Conditioning. During Experimental days 3 and 4 (first and second Conditioning days), E again leaned over the crib with an expressionless face except that when S vocalized, E made an immediate response and then resumed the expressionless face until the next vocalization. The response, or *reinforcing stimulus*, consisted of three acts executed by E simultaneously, quickly, and smoothly. They wore a broad smile, three "tsk" sounds, and a light touch applied to the infant's abdomen with thumb and fingers of the hand opposed. No more than a second of time was required to administer the reinforcer.

At the beginning of the conditioning periods each vocalization was reinforced. Sometimes, as the rate of vocalizing increased, only every second, and later, every third, vocalization was reinforced. In Experiment I, 72 percent of the reinforcers occurred after *each* vocalization; in Experiment II, 94 percent. Less frequent reinforcing seemed to depress the rate, at least initially, and because of the rather severe time restrictions, was abandoned altogether by the end of the study.

Extinction. Experimental days 5 and 6 (first and second Extinction days) were the same as days 1 and 2; E leaned over the crib with an expressionless face and made no response to S's vocalizations.

The Vocal Response

Every discrete, voiced sound produced by S was counted as a *vocalization.* A number of other sounds characteristically made by very young infants, e.g., straining sounds and coughs, and the whistles, squeaks, and snorts of noisy breathing, were not counted as vocalizations. Sounds falling under the categories of protests, fusses, and cries (see Emotional Behavior) were recorded separately. No attempt was made to record the phonetic characteristics of any of the sounds or their duration.

Observer agreement. Agreement between two Os on the number of vocalizations produced by Ss in 3-minute periods was high. Counts for 27 periods, using 13 different Ss yielded a median percentage agreement of 96 (range 67 to 100). About half of these reliability measures were obtained at the Ss' cribs, and the rest from tape recordings made during the experiment. These two techniques yielded similar percentages of observer agreement.

The unit of measurement. The unit for statistical analysis was the number of vocalizations an S gave in a 3-minute period. The counts were recorded by half-minutes and these were summed to give the score for the 3-minute period. After a rest period of 2 minutes, in which both E and O walked away from the baby's crib, another 3-minute count was made. After a second rest period a third count was made.

In each day nine such 3-minute counts were planned, distributed thus: one block of three in the first part of the morning, the second block of three in the late morning, and the third block of three after the midday meal. The minimum amount of time between blocks was 10 minutes, although usually an hour or more elapsed.

Actually, nine periods of observations were obtained during only 80 percent of the 132 subject-days (22 Ss × 6 experimental days). Since three or four Ss were studied at a time, it was not always possible to find nine periods in a day when each was awake, alert, and content. Further, because the experiments were carried out in the nursery which the Ss shared with 12 other infants, the presence and activities of these other babies, and of the caretakers in carrying out their routines, sometimes made it impossible to obtain the desired number of periods.

Emotional Behavior

A number of responses which seemed to be "emotional" were recorded during the observation periods. These were: "protests," discrete sounds of a whining nature; "fusses," a series of sounds separated by a catch in the voice, whimpering; "cries," continuous loud, wailing sounds; "persistent looking away from E," rolling of the head from side to side or staring to one side or the other of E; and "marked hand activity," hand play, finger sucking, or face or head rubbing. The last two activities seemed to be attempts to avoid E. Measures of observer-agreement in the recording of these responses were not made.

Each of these responses was given a credit of one for each half-minute in which it occurred. From the sum for each S a mean score was obtained for each experimental day.

RESULTS

Similarity Between Experiments

Figure 1 presents the means of both experiments for the six experimental days. Each point represents the mean of 11 individual means. It was expected that the effect of the experimental conditions would be similar from experiment to experiment, but the extent to which the slopes of the curves would be congruent was not predicted.

The amount of similarity between the two experiments was estimated by an analysis of variance (Table 1), using Lindquist's Type VI design (5). The analysis reveals no evidence of a difference between experiments. Further, no source of variation involving experiments is significant. (The difference between the two experiments in second Extinction day means is not significant; it suggests, however, that the less frequent reinforcement in Experiment I may have made the behavior more resistant to extinction.)

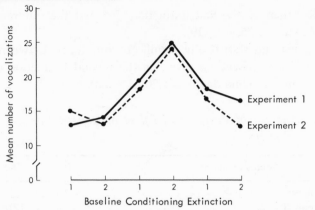

FIG. 1. Consecutive experimental days. Mean number of vocalizations on consecutive experimental days.

Three conclusions may be drawn from such close agreement in the results of two parallel experiments, each using different Ss and different Es: first, we are dealing with some relatively stable characteristics of 3-month-old infants; second, the results may be accepted with confidence; and third, the results of the separate experiments may be pooled for all remaining analyses.

Effect of Experimental Conditions

Table 1 shows that there was a difference in the effect of the three 2-day experimental conditions ($p < .001$), and, also, in the effect of successive days within conditions ($p < .001$). These effects were assessed by t tests (for paired data) on the amount of change from one day to another in the mean number of vocalizations given by individual Ss. The error term was derived only from the scores for the two days being compared. The tests on the pooled sample (21 df) show that:

1. There was no statistically significant difference in the mean number of vocalizations given in a 3-minute period from the first to the second Baseline day ($t = 0.87, p > .30$).
2. The mean number of vocalizations increased from the second Baseline day to the first Conditioning day ($t = 2.69, p < .01$).
3. A further increase occurred from the first to the second Conditioning day ($t = 3.61, p < .001$).
4. On the first Extinction day, vocalizations decreased ($t = 3.19, p < .0025$).
5. The mean number of vocalizations on the second Extinction day was

smaller than on the first Extinction day, but the difference was not reliable ($t = 1.35$, $p < .10$).

6. There was no statistically significant difference between the mean number of vocalizations given on the second Extinction day and on the second Baseline day ($t = 1.20$, $p > .20$).

TABLE 1. *Analysis of Variance of Effect of Consecutive Experimental Days*

Source of Variation	DF	MS	F
Between subjects	21		
experiments (1 vs. 2)	1	1218	0.03
error	20	45322	
Within subjects	110		
conditions (Baseline vs. Conditioning vs. Extinction)	2	71243(1)[a]	10.63[b]
days within conditions (1 vs. 2)	1	4205(2)[a]	1.88
conditions × days	2	22917(3)[a]	9.24[b]
days × experiments	1	1738(2)[a]	0.78
conditions × experiments	2	2031(1)[a]	0.30
conditions × days × experiments	2	866(3)[a]	0.35
error 1	40	6703	
error 2	20	2233	
error 3	40	2481	

[a] Number in parentheses refers to the error term used. The terms were not pooled because of statistically significant differences among them.
[b] Significant at .001 level.

The test between Baseline days and between Baseline and Extinction days were two-sided tests; the others were one-sided.

If final days within conditions are compared, the differences are more marked: the mean for the second Conditioning day is higher than that of the second Baseline day at $p < .0005$ ($t = 4.80$), and the second Extinction day mean is lower than the second Conditioning day mean at $p < .0005$ ($t = 4.08$). Similar differences occur between the means of experimental conditions, obtained by averaging the first- and second-day results for each condition.

Amount of Change in Number of Vocalizations

The treatment effects have been found reliable. It seems in order, therefore, to present the means of vocalizations for each day and to calculate the amount of change produced by the experimental conditions. Under baseline conditions the 3-month-old infants gave about 13 to 14 vocalizations in a 3-minute period. Individual differences were wide and ranged from 3 to 37 vocalizations. Using the social reinforcer for one day raised the rate to 18 vocalizations, an increase of 39 percent. A second day of conditioning elevated the rate to 25, a further increase of 34 percent. In all, conditioning brought about an increase of 86 percent. Removing the reinforcer depressed the rate to 17 during the first and to 15 during the second day, the latter approaching very closely the level of baseline performance.

Emotional Behavior

Emotional behavior, while striking when it occurred, was observed infrequently. The largest mean for any day in both experiments was 3.0, the smallest was 1.9. The order of the means by experimental days was identical in the two experiments. It was: first Extinction day, second Extinction day, second Baseline day, second Conditioning day, first Conditioning day, and first Baseline day. The greater number of emotional responses during Extinction agrees with the findings of others (e.g., *1, 11, 12*). Because the responses labeled emotional occurred so infrequently and because observer-agreement measures were not made, no further statistical analysis seemed warranted.

Additional Findings

Performance of successive groups. It will be recalled that in any one experimental week the Ss were studied in groups of three or four. Inspection of the results suggests that in each successive group of each experiment an increasing number of Ss conformed to expectation, showing an increase in vocalizations during Conditioning and a decrease during Extinction. The Es apparently became more adept in executing the reinforcer as each experiment progressed.

Performance of individual subjects. Although differences between experimental conditions have been demonstrated for the Ss as a group, the performance of individual Ss is of interest. Of the 22 Ss, 19 showed an increase in vocalizations under Conditioning. For 14 of these 19 the increase was significant at the .05 level, according to the Mann-Whitney Test (*6*). Under Extinction, 16 of the 22 Ss showed some decrease, and for 10 of these 16 the decrease was significant at the .05 level.

Three Ss departed widely from the group pattern. For two, not only did the Conditioning depress the rate of vocalizing, but Extinction restored it to its Baseline rate. The first chewed her thumb more during Conditioning than before or after. The second strained (in an apparent effort to defecate) during Conditioning whenever anyone, E or the nurse, leaned over his crib. Both activities precluded vocalizing. Both babies were very active, and it is possible, therefore, that in the very first Conditioning period E may have inadvertently reinforced these activities. For the third S, in Experiment I the experimental conditions appeared not to affect the frequency of vocalizations. Developmental immaturity seemed the most likely reason, for two weeks later he was studied again in Experiment II (the only S to be used in both experiments) with satisfactory results.

Effect of Baseline performance upon Conditioning. The Ss tended to maintain their relative positions under Baseline and Conditioning. The rank-order coefficient of correlation (R) was .66, $p < .0005$. Further, the amount of gain under Conditioning was not correlated with original position ($R = .24, p > .05$).

Sex differences. The 12 male Ss gave slightly more vocalizations during Baseline and gained more under Conditioning than the 10 female Ss, but the differences were not reliable.

DISCUSSION

The results of these experiments suggest that:

1. Infants' vocal behavior in a social situation can be brought under experimental control; that is, it appears to be conditionable.
2. A social event composed of an everyday complex of acts, performed by an adult who is not a caretaker, can function as a reinforcing stimulus.
3. The incidence of such behavior can be very quickly modified in as young an organism as the 3-month-old infant.

Alternative Explanation

The question raised in the introduction may now be considered. Did the reinforcing stimulus function as an arouser of vocalizations? Would infants have vocalized more often because of the stimulation it provided, even if it had *not* been made contingent upon the infant's behavior? Or, did some part of the reinforcing stimulus (say, the smile) act as a social "releaser"? The findings appear to be compatible with the conclusion that conditioning occurred: The rate of vocalizing continued to rise on the second day of Conditioning; the rate did not fall to the Baseline level on the first day of Extinction; it continued to fall on the second day of Extinction; and Ss with low Baseline rates of vocalizing gained under Conditioning, although for them there was often a relatively long time interval (30 seconds or more) between the reinforcing stimulus and the occurrence of the next vocalization. Still, the decisive answer to the question must await an experiment in which the reinforcing stimulus is administered with equal frequency, but never directly after the infant vocalizes.

Nature of the Reinforcer

The results seem to show that some everyday behavior of adults can function as a reinforcing stimulus for an infant. One would like to know from what sources its reinforcing properties arise. In the simplest case, the smiles, sounds, and caresses of adults may be reinforcing only because they provide a change in stimulation. Further information on this matter could be obtained by working with the separate parts of the reinforcing stimulus, one by one; by substituting for them lights or sounds dispensed by a machine; or by using a reinforcer of a less "affectionate" nature than the one used here appears to be. On the other hand, even for the 3-month-old infant the smiles, sounds, and caresses of the adults may function as conditioned reinforcers because of their past association with caretaking acts.

It is possible that the Ss of this study, living in an institution, may have had a less rich experience with adults. Institutional babies were used as Ss only because they were more readily available, because more of them could be studied at one time, and because the complicating variable of differences in maternal care could be bypassed. They did not appear however to be "starved" for attention or affection. Indeed, the attendants were often observed responding to babies when they vocalized. While it is possible that mothers would respond more often, in the absence of a comparative study we believe that infants in general would respond as these infants did.

Relation of Results to Theories of Speech

Since this study was limited to the vocalizing of infants in a social situation, attempts to reconcile the results with theories which account for all classes of prelinguistic utterances (babbling is a class frequently mentioned) cannot be complete. Thus, nothing in the findings of this study is incompatible with, for example, Holt's theory (3) that the sound which the child hears himself make has reinforcing properties; with Lewis' theory (4) that the adult's speech calls forth the infant's speech (a kind of imitation); or with Piaget's theory (9) that vocalizing is perpetuated for its own sake by the processes of assimilation and accommodation. These may be labeled circular theories, for they do not postulate the necessity for any class of events prior to the moment when the infant responds to his own or another's vocalization. The theories of Miller and Dollard (7) and of Mowrer (8), on the other hand, are based upon the infant's associating the gratification of his needs and the accompanying vocalizations of the caretaker. Again, the results do not contradict this possibility.

The present study, however, does demonstrate the operation of still another principle: that the speech of the infant, if only in a social situation, can be modified by a response from the environment which is contingent upon his vocalizing. Hence, what happens *after* the infant vocalizes has been shown to be important.

Significance of Results

On the basis of the results of these experiments it is seen that responses of adults which do not involve caretaking can affect the vocalizing of the young in a social setting. If the results can be extended to life situations, then mothers might be able to increase or decrease the vocal output of their children by the responses they make when the children vocalize. Other kinds of social behavior in addition to vocalizing behavior should respond similarly to conditioning. Brackbill (1) has shown that smiling in the 4-month-old infant may be increased when followed by a social response from an adult. It is likely that still other kinds of social behavior in babies, such as showing an interest in people, reaching out to them or turning away, perhaps even fear of the stranger, may also be affected by the responses adults make to them.

SUMMARY

Infants often vocalize as part of the response they give to the appearance of an adult. The central question of this study is: Can the frequency of vocalizing be increased if the adult makes a social response contingent upon it?

The Ss were 21 normal infants, 3 months of age, living in an institution. Eleven of them were studied in Experiment I with one E; 10 different Ss and one S from Experiment I were studied in Experiment II with a different E.

During the first and second Baseline days E leaned over S with an expressionless face, and the number of vocalizations was tallied. During the next two days, the first and second Conditioning days, E reinforced vocalizations by simultaneously smiling, clucking, and touching S's abdomen. During the last two days, the first and second Extinction days, E returned to Baseline conditions.

The results indicated that: (a) there was no difference between Experiments, (b) Conditioning raised the rate of vocalizing above the Baseline level, (c) while Extinction lowered it until it approached the Baseline level.

The results suggest that the social vocalizing of infants, and, more generally, their social responsiveness may be modified by the responses adults make to them.

REFERENCES

1. Brackbill, Y. Extinction of the smiling response in infants as a function of reinforcement schedule. *Child Develpm.*, 1958, **29**, 115–124.
2. Gewirtz, J. L. A program of research on the dimensions and antecedents of emotional dependence. *Child Develpm.*, 1956, **27**, 205–221.
3. Holt, E. B. *Animal drive.* London: Williams & Norgate, 1931.
4. Lewis, M. M. *Infant speech: a study of the beginnings of language.* (2nd ed.) New York: Humanities Press, 1951.
5. Lindquist, E. F. *Design and analysis of experiments in psychology and education.* Boston: Houghton Mifflin, 1953.
6. Mann, H. B., & Whitney, D. R. On a test of whether one or two random variables is stochastically larger than the other. *Ann. Math. Statist.*, 1947, **18**, 50–60.
7. Miller, N. E., & Dollard, J. *Social learning and imitation.* New Haven: Yale Univer. Press, 1941.
8. Mowrer, O. H. *Learning theory and personality dynamics.* New York: Ronald, 1950.
9. Piaget, J. *The origins of intelligence in children.* New York: Int. Univer. Press, 1952.
10. Rheingold, H. L. The modification of social responsiveness in institutional babies. *Monogr. Soc. Res. Child Develpm.*, 1956, **21**, No. 63, (Whole No. 2).
11. Skinner, B. F. *Science and human behavior.* New York: Macmillan, 1953.
12. Verplanck, W. S. The control of the content of conversation: Reinforcement of statements of opinion. *J. abnorm. soc. Psychol.*, 1955, **51**, 668–676.

AFFECTIONAL RESPONSES
IN THE INFANT MONKEY

Harry F. Harlow and Robert R. Zimmermann
UNIVERSITY OF WISCONSIN

INVESTIGATORS FROM DIVERSE behavioral fields have long recognized the strong attachment of the neonatal and infantile animal to its mother. Although this affectional behavior has been commonly observed, there is, outside the field of ethology, scant experimental evidence permitting identification of the factors critical to the formation of this bond. Lorenz (16) and others have stressed the importance of innate visual and auditory mechanisms which, through the process of imprinting, give rise to persisting following responses in the infant bird and fish. Imprinting behavior has been demonstrated successfully in a variety of avian species under controlled laboratory conditions, and this phenomenon has been investigated systematically in order to identify those variables which contribute to its development and maintenance (see, for example, Hinde, Thorpe, and Vince (12), Fabricius (7), Hess (11), Jaynes (13), and Moltz and Rosenblum (17)). These studies represent the largest body of existent experimental evidence measuring the tie between infant and mother. At the mammalian level there is little or no systematic experimental evidence of this nature.

Observations on monkeys by Carpenter (5), Nolte (18), and Zuckermann (22) and on chimpanzees by Kohler (15) and by Yerkes and Tomilin (21) show that monkey and chimpanzee infants develop strong ties to their mothers and that these affectional attachments may persist for years. It is, of course, common knowledge that human infants form strong and persistent ties to their mothers.

Although students from diverse scientific fields recognize this abiding attachment, there is considerable disagreement about the nature of

Reprinted from *Science* (1959), **130**, (3373), 421–432, by permission of the authors and the American Association for the Advancement of Science.

its development and its fundamental underlying mechanisms. A common theory among psychologists, sociologists, and anthropologists is that of learning based on drive reduction. This theory proposes that the infant's attachment to the mother results from the association of the mother's face and form with the alleviation of certain primary drive states, particularly hunger and thirst. Thus, through learning, affection becomes a self-supporting, derived drive (6). Psychoanalysts, on the other hand, have stressed the importance of various innate needs, such as a need to suck and orally possess the breast (12), or needs relating to contact, movement, temperature (19), and clinging to the mother (2).

The paucity of experimental evidence concerning the development of affectional responses has led these theorists to derive their basic hypotheses from deductions and intuitions based on observation and analysis of adult verbal reports. As a result, the available observational evidence is often forced into a preconceived theoretical framework. An exception to the above generalization is seen in the recent attempt by Bowlby (2) to analyze and integrate the available observational and experimental evidence derived from both human and subhuman infants. Bowlby has concluded that a theory of component instinctual responses, species specific, can best account for the infant's tie to the mother. He suggests that the species-specific responses for human beings (some of these responses are not strictly limited to human beings) include contact, clinging, sucking, crying, smiling, and following. He further emphasizes that these responses are manifested independently of primary drive reduction in human and subhuman infants.

The absence of experimental data which would allow a critical evaluation of any theory of affectional development can be attributed to several causes. The use of human infants as subjects has serious limitations, since it is not feasible to employ all the experimental controls which would permit a completely adequate analysis of the proposed variables. In addition, the limited response repertoire of the human neonate severely restricts the number of discrete or precise response categories that can be measured until a considerable age has been attained. Thus, critical variables go unmeasured and become lost or confounded among the complex physiological, psychological, and cultural factors which influence the developing human infant.

Moreover, the use of common laboratory animals also has serious limitations, for most of these animals have behavioral repertoires very different from those of the human being, and in many species these systems mature so rapidly that it is difficult to measure and assess their orderly development. On the other hand, subhuman primates, including the macaque monkey, are born at a state of maturity which makes it possible to begin precise measurements within the first few days of life. Furthermore, their postnatal maturational rate is slow enough to permit precise assessment of affectional variables and development.

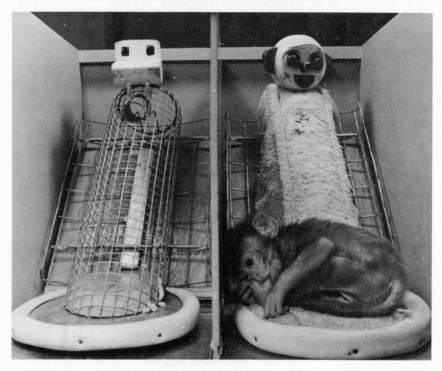

FIG. 1.   Wire and cloth mother surrogates.

Over a 3-year period prior to the beginning of the research program reported here (23), some 60 infant macaque monkeys were separated from their mothers 6 to 12 hours after birth and raised at the primate laboratory of the University of Wisconsin. The success of the procedures developed to care for these neonates was demonstrated by the low mortality and by a gain in weight which was approximately 25 percent greater than that of infants raised by their own mothers. All credit for the success of this program belongs to van Wagenen (20), who had described the essential procedures in detail.

These first 3 years were spent in devising measures to assess the multiple capabilities of the neonatal and infantile monkey. The studies which resulted have revealed that the development of perception, learning, manipulation, exploration, frustration, and timidity in the macaque monkey follows a course and sequence which is very similar to that in the human infant. The basic differences between the two species appear to be the advanced postnatal maturational status and the subsequent more rapid growth of the infant macaque. Probably the most important similarities between the two, in relation to the problem of affectional development, are characteristic responses that have been associated with, and are considered basic to, affection; these include nursing, clinging, and visual and auditory exploration.

In the course of raising these infants we observed that they all showed a strong attachment to the cheesecloth blankets which were used to cover the wire floors of their cages. Removal of these cloth blankets resulted in violent emotional behavior. These responses were not short-lived; indeed, the emotional disturbance lasted several days, as was indicated by the infant's refusal to work on the standard learning tests that were being conducted at the time. Similar observations had already been made by Foley (8) and by van Wagenen (20), who stressed the importance of adequate contact responses to the very survival of the neonatal macaque. Such observations suggested to us that contact was a true affectional variable and that it should be possible to trace and measure the development and importance of these responses. Indeed there seemed to be every reason to believe that one could manipulate all variables which have been considered critical to the development of the infant's attachment to a mother, or mother surrogate.

To attain control over maternal variables, we took the calculated risk of constructing and using inanimate mother surrogates rather than real mothers. The cloth mother that we used was a cylinder of wood covered with a sheath of terry cloth (24), and the wire mother was a hardware-cloth cylinder. Initially, sponge rubber was placed underneath the terry cloth sheath of the cloth mother surrogate, and a light bulb behind each mother surrogate provided radiant heat. For reasons of sanitation and safety these two factors were eliminated in construction of the standard mothers, with no observable effect on the behavior of the infants. The two mothers were attached at a 45-degree angle to aluminum bases and were given different faces to assure uniqueness in the various test situations (Figure 1). Bottle holders were installed in the upper middle part of the bodies to permit nursing. The mother was designed on the basis of previous experience with infant monkeys, which suggested that nursing in an upright or inclined position with something for the infant to clasp facilitated successful nursing and resulted in healthier infants (see 20). Thus, both mothers provided the basic known requirements for adequate nursing, but the cloth mother provided an additional variable of contact comfort. That both of these surrogate mothers provided adequate nursing support is shown by the fact that the total ingestion of formula and the weight gain was normal for all infants fed on the surrogate mothers. The only consistent difference between the groups lay in the softer stools of the infants fed on the wire mother.

DEVELOPMENT OF AFFECTIONAL RESPONSES

The initial experiments on the development of affectional responses have already been reported (9) but will be briefly reviewed here, since subsequent experiments were derived from them. In the initial experiments, designed to evaluate the role of nursing on the development of affection, a cloth mother and a wire mother were placed in different cubicles attached to the infant's living cage. Eight newborn monkeys were placed in individual cages with the surrogates; for four infant monkeys the cloth mother lactated and the wire mother did not, and for the other four this condition was reversed.

The infants lived with their mother surrogates for a minimum of 165 days, and during this time they were tested in a variety of situations designed to measure the development of affectional responsiveness. Differential affectional responsiveness was initially measured in terms of mean hours per day spent on the cloth and on the wire mothers under two conditions of feeding, as shown in Figure 2. Infants fed on the cloth mother and on the wire mother have highly similar scores after a short adaptation period (Figure 3), and over a 165-day period both groups show a distinct preference for the cloth mother. The persistence of the differential responsiveness to the mothers for both groups of infants is evident, and the overall differences between the groups fall short of statistical significance.

These data make it obvious that contact comfort is a variable of critical importance in the development of affectional responsiveness to the surrogate mother, and that nursing appears to play a negligible role. With increasing age and opportunity to learn, an infant fed from a lactating wire mother does not become more responsive to her, as would be predicted from a derived-drive theory, but instead becomes increasingly more responsive to its nonlactating cloth mother. These findings are at

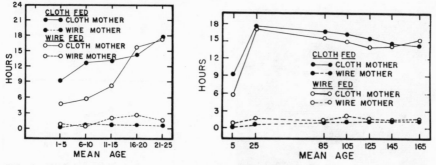

FIG. 2.   Time spent on cloth and wire mother surrogates. Short term.

FIG. 3.   Time spent on cloth and wire mother surrogates. Long term.

complete variance with a drive-reduction theory of affectional development.

The amount of time spent on the mother does not necessarily indicate an affectional attachment. It could merely reflect the fact that the cloth mother is a more comfortable sleeping platform or a more adequate source of warmth for the infant. However, three of the four infants nursed by the cloth mother and one of the four nursed by the wire mother left a gauze-covered heating pad that was on the floor of their cages during the first 14 days of life to spend up to 18 hours a day on the cloth mother. This suggests that differential heating or warmth is not a critical variable within the controlled temperature range of the laboratory.

Other tests demonstrate that the cloth mother is more than a convenient nest; indeed, they show that a bond develops between infant and cloth-mother surrogate that is almost unbelievably similar to the bond established between human mother and child. One highly definitive test measured the selective maternal responsiveness of the monkey infants under conditions of distress or fear.

Various fear-producing stimuli, such as the moving toy bear illustrated in Figure 4, were presented to the infants in their home cages. The data on differential responses under both feeding conditions are given in Figure 5. It is apparent that the cloth mother was highly preferred to the wire mother, and it is a fact that these differences were unrelated to feeding conditions—that is, nursing on the cloth or on the wire mother. Above and beyond these objective data are observations on the form of the infants' responses in this situation. In spite of their abject terror, the infant monkeys, after reaching the cloth mother and rubbing their bodies about hers, rapidly come to lose their fear of the frightening

FIG. 4. Typical fear stimulus.

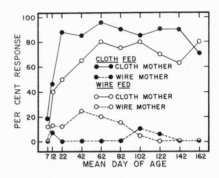

FIG. 5. Home cage fear. First response dual-fed raised. Differential responsiveness in fear tests.

stimuli. Indeed, within a minute or two most of the babies were visually exploring the very thing which so shortly before had seemed an object of evil. The bravest of the babies would actually leave the mother and approach the fearful monsters, under, of course, the protective gaze of their mothers.

These data are highly similar, in terms of differential responsiveness, to the time scores previously mentioned and indicate the overwhelming importance of contact comfort. The results are so striking as to suggest that the primary function of nursing may be that of insuring frequent and intimate contact between mother and infant, thus facilitating the localization of the source of contact comfort. This interpretation finds some support in the test discussed above. In both situations the infants nursed by the cloth mother developed consistent responsiveness to the soft mother earlier in testing than did the infants nursed by the wire mother, and during this transient period the latter group was slightly more responsive to the wire mother than the former group. However, these early differences shortly disappeared.

Additional data have been obtained from two groups of four monkeys each of which was raised with a single mother placed in a cubicle attached to the living-cage. Four of the infants were presented with a lactating wire mother and the other four were presented with a nonlactating cloth mother. The latter group was hand-fed from small nursing bottles for the first 30 days of life and then weaned to a cup. The development of responsiveness to the mothers was studied for 165 days; after this the individual mothers were removed from the cages and testing was continued to determine the strength and persistence of the affectional responses.

Figure 6 presents the mean time per day spent on the respective mothers over the 165-day test period, and Figure 7 shows the percentage of responses to the mothers when a fear-producing stimulus was introduced into the home cage. These tests indicate that both groups of infants developed responsiveness to their mother surrogates. However, these measures did not reveal the differences in behavior that were displayed in the reactions to the mothers when the fear stimuli were presented. The infants raised on the cloth mother would rush to the mother and cling tightly to her. Following this initial response these infants would relax and either begin to manipulate the mother or turn to gaze at the feared object without the slightest sign of apprehension. The infants raised on the wire mother, on the other hand, rushed away from the feared object toward their mother but did not cling to or embrace her. Instead, they would either clutch themselves and rock and vocalize for the remainder of the test or rub against the side of the cubicle. Contact with the cubicle or the mother did not reduce the emotionality produced by the introduction of the fear stimulus. These differences are revealed in emotionality scores, for behavior such as vocalization, crouching, rocking, and sucking, recorded during the test. Figure 8 shows the mean emotionality index for test sessions for the two experimental groups, the dual-mother groups, and a comparable control group raised under

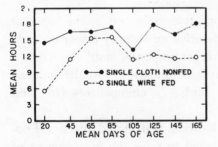

FIG. 6. Time spent on cloth and wire, single mother surrogates.

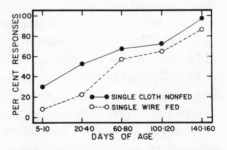

FIG. 7. Home cage fear. Withdrawal to single surrogate mothers in fear tests.

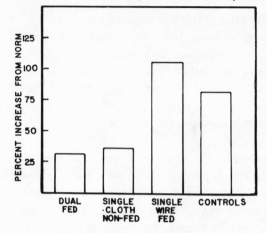

FIG. 8. Home cage fear. Change in emotionality index in fear tests: total emotion score, increase from norm-mechanical stimuli.

standard laboratory conditions. As can be seen, the infants raised with the single wire mother have the highest emotionality scores of all the groups, and the infants raised with the single cloth mother or with a cloth and wire mother have the lowest scores. It appears that the responses made by infants raised only with a wire mother were more in the nature of simple flight responses to the fear stimulus and that the presence of the mother surrogate had little effect in alleviating the fear.

During our initial experiments with the dual-mother conditions, responsiveness to the lactating wire mother in the fear tests decreased with age and opportunity to learn, while responsiveness to the nonlactating cloth mother increased. However, there was some indication of a slight increase in frequency of response to the wire mother for the first 30 to 60 days (see Figure 5). These data suggest the possible hypothesis that nursing facilitated the contact of infant and mother during the early developmental periods.

The interpretation of all fear testing is complicated by the fact that all or most "fear" stimuli evoke many positive exploratory responses early in life and do not consistently evoke flight responses until the monkey is 40 to 50 days of age. Similar delayed maturation of visually induced fear responses has been reported for birds (7), chimpanzees (10), and human infants (14).

Because of apparent interactions between fearful and affectional developmental variables, a test was designed to trace the development of approach and avoidance responses in these infants. This test, described as

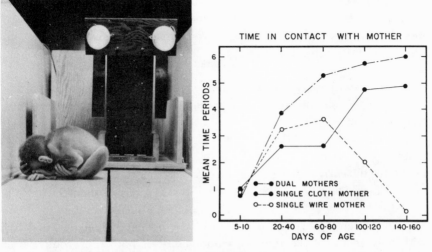

FIG. 9. Response to the fear stimulus in the straight-alley test.

FIG. 10. Responsiveness to mother surrogates in the straight-alley tests.

the straight-alley test, was conducted in a wooden alley 8-feet long and 2-feet wide. One end of the alley contained a movable tray upon which appropriate stimuli were placed. The other end of the alley contained a box for hiding. Each test began with the monkey in a start box 1 foot in front of the hiding box; thus, the animal could maintain his original position, approach the stimulus tray as it moved toward him, or flee into the hiding box. The infants were presented with five stimuli in the course of five successive days. The stimuli included a standard cloth mother, a standard wire mother, a yellow cloth mother with the head removed, a blank tray, and a large black fear stimulus, shown in Figure 9. The infants were tested at 5, 10, and 20 days of age, respectively, and then at 20-day intervals up to 160 days. Figure 10 shows the mean number of 15-second time periods spent in contact with the appropriate mother during the 90-second tests for the two single-mother groups, and the responses to the cloth mother by four infants from the dual-mother group.

During the first 80 days of testing, all the groups showed an increase in response to the respective mother surrogates. The infants fed on the single wire mother, however, reached peak responsiveness at this age and then showed a consistent decline, followed by an actual avoidance of the wire mother. During test sessions 140 to 160, only one contact was made with the wire mother, and three of the four infants ran into the hiding box almost immediately and remained there for the entire test session. On the other hand, all of the infants raised with a cloth mother, whether or not they were nursed by her, showed a progressive increase in time spent in contact with their cloth mothers until approaches and contacts during the test sessions approached maximum scores.

The development of the response of flight from the wire mother by the group fed on the single wire mother is, of course, completely contrary to a derived-drive theory of affectional development.

A comparison of this group with the group raised with a cloth mother gives some support to the hypothesis that feeding or nursing facilitates the early development of responses to the mother but that without the factor of contact comfort, these positive responses are not maintained.

The differential responsiveness to the cloth mother of infants raised with both mothers, the reduced emotionality of both the groups raised with cloth mothers in the home-cage fear tests, and the development of approach responses in the straight-alley test indicate that the cloth mother provides a haven of safety and security for the frightened infant. The affectional response patterns found in the infant monkey are unlike tropistic or even complex reflex responses; they resemble instead the diverse and pervasive patterns of response to his mother exhibited by the human child in the complexity of situations involving child-mother relationships.

The role of the mother as a source of safety and security has been demonstrated experimentally for human infants by Arsenian (1). She placed children 11 to 30 months of age in a strange room containing toys and other play objects. Half of the children were accompanied into the room by a mother or a substitute mother (a familiar nursery attendant), while the other half entered the situation alone. The children in the first group (mother present) were much less emotional and participated much more fully in the play activity than those in the second group (mother absent). With repeated testing, the security score, a composite score of emotionality and play behavior, improved for the children who entered alone, but it still fell far below that for the children who were accompanied by their mothers. In subsequent tests, the children from the mother-present group were placed in the test room alone, and there was a drastic drop in the security scores. Contrariwise, the introduction of the mother raised the security scores of children in the other group.

We have performed a similar series of open-field experiments, comparing monkeys raised on mother surrogates with control monkeys raised in a wire cage containing a cheesecloth blanket from days 1 to 14 and no cloth blanket subsequently. The infants were introduced into the strange environment of the open field, which was a room measuring 6 by 6 by 6 feet, containing multiple stimuli known to elicit curiosity-manipulatory responses in baby monkeys. The infants raised with single mother surrogates were placed in this situation twice a week for 8 weeks, no mother surrogate being present during one of the weekly sessions and the appropriate mother surrogate (the kind which the experimental infant had always known) being present during the other sessions. Four infants raised with dual mother surrogates and four control infants were subjected to similar experimental sequences, the cloth mother being present on half of the occasions. The remaining four "dual-mother" infants were given repetitive tests to obtain information on the development of responsiveness to each of the dual mothers in this situation. A cloth blanket was always available as one of the stimuli throughout the sessions. It should be emphasized that the blanket could readily compete with the cloth mother as a contact stimulus, for it was standard laboratory procedure to wrap the infants in soft cloth whenever they were removed from their cages for testing, weighing and other required laboratory activities.

As soon as they were placed in the test room, the infants raised with cloth mothers rushed to their mother surrogate when she was present and clutched her tenaciously, a response so strong that it can only be adequately depicted by motion pictures. Then, as had been observed in the fear tests in the home cage, they rapidly relaxed, showed no sign of apprehension, and began to demonstrate unequivocal positive responses of manipulating and climbing on the mother. After several sessions, the infants began to use the mother surrogate as a base of operations, leaving her to explore and handle a stimulus and then returning to her before going to a new plaything. Some of the infants even brought the stimuli to the mother, as shown in Figure 11. The behavior of these infants changed radically in the absence of the mother. Emotional indices such as vocalization, crouching, rocking, and sucking increased sharply. Typical response patterns were either freezing in a crouched position, as illustrated in Figure 12, or running around the room on the hind feet, clutching themselves with their arms. Though no quantitative evidence is available, contact and manipulation of objects was frantic and of short duration, as opposed to the playful type of manipulation observed when the mother was present.

In the presence of the mother, the behavior of the infants raised

FIG. 11.   Subsequent response to cloth mother and stimulus in the open-field test.

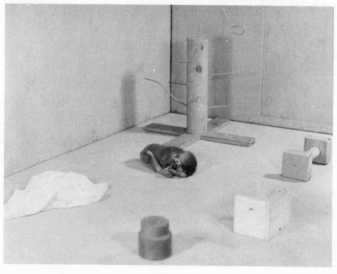

FIG. 12.   Response in the open-field test in the absence of the mother surrogate.

with the single wire mothers was both quantitatively and qualitatively different from that of the infants raised with cloth mothers. Not only did these infants spend little or no time contacting their mother surrogates but the presence of the mother did not reduce their emotionality. These

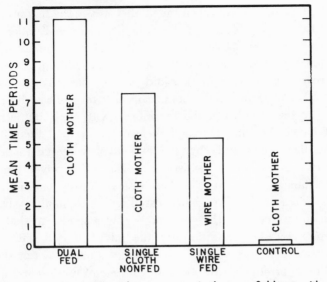

FIG. 13. Responsiveness to mother surrogates in the open-field test, with mean time periods in contact with mother.

differences are evident in the mean number of time periods spent in contact with the respective mothers, as shown in Figure 13, and the composite emotional index for the two stimulus conditions depicted in Figure 14. Although the infants raised with dual mothers spent considerably more time in contact with the cloth mother than did the infants raised with single cloth mothers, their emotional reactions to the presence and absence of the mother were highly similar, the composite emotional index be-

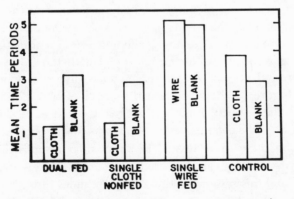

FIG. 14. Open field, composite emotionality index in testing with and without the mother surrogates.

ing reduced by almost half when the mother was in the test situation. The infants raised with wire mothers were highly emotional under both conditions and actually showed a slight, though nonsignificant, increase in emotionality when the mother was present. Although some of the infants reared by a wire mother did contact her, their behavior was similar to that observed in the home-cage fear tests. They did not clutch and cling to their mother as did the infants with cloth mothers; instead, they sat on her lap and clutched themselves, or held their heads and bodies in their arms and engaged in convulsive jerking and rocking movements similar to the autistic behavior of deprived and institutionalized human children. The lack of exploratory and manipulatory behavior on the part of the infants reared with wire mothers, both in the presence and absence of the wire mother, was similar to that observed in the mother-absent condition for the infants raised with the cloth mothers, and such contact with objects as was made was of short duration and of an erratic and frantic nature. None of the infants raised with single wire mothers displayed the persistent and aggressive play behavior that was typical of many of the infants that were raised with cloth mothers.

The four control infants, raised without a mother surrogate, had approximately the same emotionality scores when the mother was absent that the other infants had in the same condition, but the control subjects' emotionality scores were significantly higher in the presence of the mother surrogate than in her absence. This result is not surprising, since recent evidence indicates that the cloth mother with the highly ornamental face is an effective fear stimulus for monkeys that have not been raised with her.

Further illustration of differential responsiveness to the two mother surrogates is found in the results of a series of developmental tests in the open-field situation, given to the remaining four "dual-mother" infants. These infants were placed in the test room with the cloth mother, the wire mother, and no mother present on successive occasions at various age levels. Figure 15 shows the mean number of time periods spent in contact with the respective mothers for two trials at each age level, and Figure 16 reveals the composite emotion scores for the three stimulus conditions during these same tests. The differential responsiveness to the cloth and wire mothers, as measured by contact time, is evident by 20 days of age, and this systematic difference continues throughout 140 days of age. Only small differences in emotionality under the various conditions are evident during the first 85 days of age, although the presence of the cloth mother does result in slightly lower scores from the 45th day

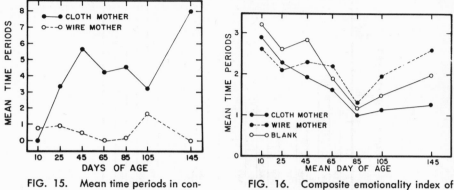

FIG. 15. Mean time periods in contact with mother of dual-fed raised.
Differential responsiveness in the
open-field test.

FIG. 16. Composite emotionality index of
dual-fed raised under three conditions in
the open-field test.

onward. However, at 105 and 145 days of age there is a considerable difference for the three conditions, the emotionality scores for the wire-
mother and blank conditions showing a sharp increase. The heightened
emotionality found under the wire-mother condition was mainly contributed by the two infants fed on the wire mother. The behavior of
these two infants in the presence of the wire mother was similar to the
behavior of the animals raised with a single wire mother. On the few
occasions when contact with the wire mother was made, the infants did
not attempt to cling to her; instead they would sit on her lap, clasp their
heads and bodies, and rock back and forth.

In 1953 Butler (3) demonstrated that mature monkeys enclosed in a
dimly lighted box would open and reopen a door for hours on end with
no other motivation than that of looking outside the box. He also demonstrated that rhesus monkeys showed selectivity in rate and frequency of
door-opening in response to stimuli of different degrees of attractiveness
(4). We have utilized this characteristic of response selectivity on the
part of the monkey to measure the strength of affectional responsiveness
of the babies raised with mother surrogates in an infant version of the
Butler box. The test sequence involves four repetitions of a test battery
in which the four stimuli of cloth mother, wire mother, infant monkey,
and empty box are presented for a 30-minute period on successive days.
The first four subjects raised with the dual mother surrogates and the
eight infants raised with single mother surrogates were given a test
sequence at 40 to 50 days of age, depending upon the availability of the
apparatus. The data obtained from the three experimental groups and a
comparable control group are presented in Figure 17. Both groups of

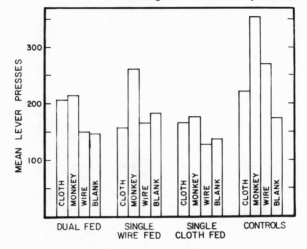

FIG. 17.   Differential responses to visual exploration.

infants raised with cloth mothers showed approximately equal responsiveness to the cloth mother and to another infant monkey, and no greater
responsiveness to the wire mother than to an empty box. Again, the results are independent of the kind of mother that lactated, cloth or wire.
The infants raised with only a wire mother and those in the control group
were more highly responsive to the monkey than to either of the mother
surrogates. Furthermore, the former group showed a higher frequency of
response to the empty box than to the wire mother.

In summary, the experimental analysis of the development of the
infant monkey's attachment to an inanimate mother surrogate demonstrates the overwhelming importance of the variable of soft body contact
that characterized the cloth mother, and this held true for the appearance, development, and maintenance of the infant-surrogate-mother tie.
The results also indicate that, without the factor of contact comfort, only
a weak attachment, if any, is formed. Finally, probably the most surprising finding is that nursing or feeding played either no role or a subordinate role in the development of affection as measured by contact
time, responsiveness to fear, responsiveness to strangeness, and motivation to seek and see. No evidence was found indicating that nursing
mediated the development of any of these responses, although there is
evidence indicating that feeding probably facilitated the early appearance
and increased the early strength of affectional responsiveness. Certainly
feeding, in contrast to contact comfort, is neither a necessary nor a sufficient condition for affectional development.

Retention of Affectional Responses

One of the outstanding characteristics of the infant's attachment to its mother is the persistence of the relationship over a period of years, even though the frequency of contact between infant and mother is reduced with increasing age. In order to test the persistence of the responsiveness of our "mother-surrogate" infants, the first four infant monkeys raised with dual mothers and all of the monkeys raised with single mothers were separated from their surrogates at 165 to 170 days of age. They were tested for affectional retention during the following 9 days, then at 30-day intervals during the following year. The results are of necessity incomplete, inasmuch as the entire mother-surrogate program was initiated less than 2 years ago, but enough evidence is available to indicate that the attachment formed to the cloth mother during the first 6 months of life is enduring and not easily forgotten.

Affectional retention as measured by the modified Butler box for the first 15 months of testing for four of the infants raised with two mothers is given in Figure 18. Although there is considerable variability in the

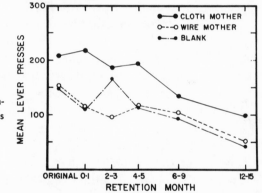

FIG. 18. Retention of differential visual-exploration responses by the dual fed.

total response frequency from session to session, there is a consistent difference in the number of responses to the cloth mother as contrasted with responses to either the wire mother or the empty box, and there is no consistent difference between responses to the wire mother and to the empty box. The effects of contact comfort versus feeding are dramatically demonstrated in this test by the monkeys raised with either single cloth or wire mothers. Figure 19 shows the frequency of response to the appropriate mother surrogate and to the blank box during the preseparation period and the first 90 days of retention testing. Removal of the mother resulted

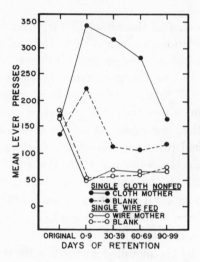

FIG. 19. Love machine. Retention of differential visual-exploration responses by single-surrogate infants.

in a doubling of the frequency of response to the cloth mother and more than tripled the difference between the responses to the cloth mother and those to the empty box for the infants that had lived with a single nonlactating cloth mother surrogate. The infants raised with a single lactating wire mother, on the other hand, not only failed to show any consistent preference for the wire mother but also showed a highly significant reduction in general level of responding. Although incomplete, the data from further retention testing indicate that the difference between these two groups persists for at least 5 months.

Affectional retention was also tested in the open field during the first 9 days after separation and then at 30-day intervals. Each test condition was run twice in each retention period. In the initial retention tests the behavior of the infants that had lived with cloth mothers differed slightly from that observed during the period preceding separation. These infants tended to spend more time in contact with the mother and less time exploring and manipulating the objects in the room. The behavior of the infants raised with single wire mothers, on the other hand, changed radically during the first retention sessions, and responses to the mother surrogate dropped almost to zero. Objective evidence for these differences is given in Figure 20, which reveals the mean number of time periods spent in contact with the respective mothers. During the first retention test session, the infants raised with a single wire mother showed almost no responses to the mother surrogate they had always known. Since the infants raised with both mothers were already approaching the maximum score in this measure, there was little room for improve-

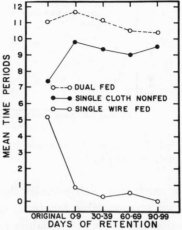

FIG. 20. Mean time periods in contact with mother surrogate compared with retention of responsiveness to mother in open-field tests.

ment. The infants raised with a single nonlactating cloth mother, however, showed a consistent and significant increase in this measure during the first 90 days of retention. Evidence for the persistence of this responsiveness is given by the fact that after 15 months' separation from their mothers, the infants that had lived with cloth mothers spent an average of 8.75 out of 12 possible time periods in contact with the cloth mother during the test. The incomplete data for retention testing of the infants raised with only a lactating wire mother, or a nonlactating cloth mother indicates that there is little or no change in the initial differences found between these two groups in this test over a period of 5 months. In the absence of the mother, the behavior of the infants raised with cloth mothers was similar in the initial retention tests to that during the preseparation tests, but with repeated testing they tended to show gradual adaptation to the open-field situation and, consequently, a reduction in their emotionality scores. Even with this overall reduction in emotionality, these infants had consistently lower emotionality scores when the mother was present.

At the time of initiating the retention tests, an additional condition was introduced into the open-field test: the surrogate mother was placed in the center of the room and covered with a clear plexiglas box. The animals raised with cloth mothers were initially disturbed and frustrated when their efforts to secure and contact the mother were blocked by the box. However, after several violent crashes into the plastic, the animals adapted to the situation and soon used the box as a place of orientation for exploratory and play behavior. In fact, several infants

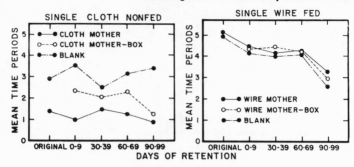

FIG. 21. Composite emotionality index under three conditions in the open-field retention tests.

were much more active under these conditions than they were when the mother was available for direct contact. A comparison of the composite emotionality index of the babies raised with a single cloth or wire mother under the three conditions of no mother, surrogate mother, and surrogate-mother-box is presented in Figure 21. The infants raised with a single cloth mother were consistently less emotional when they could contact the mother but also showed the effects of her visual presence, as their emotionality scores in the plastic box condition were definitely lower than their scores when the mother was absent. It appears that the infants gained considerable emotional security from the presence of the mother even though contact was denied.

In contrast, the animals raised with only lactating wire mothers did not show any significant or consistent trends during these retention sessions other than a general overall reduction of emotionality, which may be attributed to a general adaptation, the result of repeated testing.

Affectional retention has also been measured in the straight-alley test mentioned earlier. During the preseparation tests it was found that the infants that had only wire mothers developed a general avoidance response to all of the stimuli in this test when they were about 100 days of age and made few, if any, responses to the wire mother during the final test sessions. In contrast, all the infants raised with a cloth mother responded positively to her. Maternal separation did not significantly change the behavior of any of the groups. The babies raised with just wire mothers continued to flee into the hiding booth in the presence of the wire mother, while all of the infants raised with cloth mothers continued to respond positively to the cloth mother at approximately the same level as in the preseparation tests. The mean number of time periods spent in contact with the appropriate mother surrogates for the first 3 months of retention testing are given in Figure 22. There is little, if any, waning of responsiveness to the cloth mother during these 3 months. There appeared to be some loss of responsiveness to the mother in this situation after 5 to 6 months of separation, but the test was discontinued at that time as the infants had outgrown the apparatus.

The retention data from these multiple tests demonstrate clearly the importance of body contact for the future maintenance of affectional responses. Whereas several of the measures in the preseparation period suggested that the infants raised with only a wire mother might have developed a weak attachment to her, all responsiveness disappeared in the first few days after the mother was withdrawn from the living-cage. Infants that had had the opportunity of living with a cloth mother showed the opposite effect and either became more responsive to the cloth mother or continued to respond to her at the same level.

FIG. 22. Retention of responsiveness to mother surrogates in the straight-alley test.

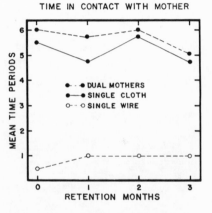

These data indicate that once an affectional bond is formed it is maintained for a very considerable length of time with little reinforcement of the contact-comfort variable. The limited data available for infants that have been separated from their mother surrogates for a year suggest that these affectional responses show resistance to extinction similar to the resistance previously demonstrated for learned fears and learned pain. Such data are in keeping with common observation of human behavior.

It is true, however, that the infants raised with cloth mothers exhibit some absolute decrease in responsiveness with time in all of our major test situations. Such results would be obtained even if there were no true decrease in the strength of the affectional bond, because of familiarization and adaptation resulting from repeated testing. Therefore, at the end of 1 year of retention testing, new tests were introduced into the experimental program.

Our first new test was a modification of the open-field situation, in which basic principles of the home-cage fear test were incorporated. This particular choice was made partly because the latter test had to be discontinued when the mother surrogates were removed from the home cages.

For the new experiment a Masonite floor marked off in 6- by 12-inch rectangles was placed in the open-field chamber. Both mother surrogates were placed in the test room opposite a plastic start-box. Three fear stimuli, selected to produce differing degrees of emotionality, were placed in the center of the room directly in front of the start-box in successive test sessions. Eight trials were run under each stimulus condition, and in half of the trials the most direct path to the cloth mother was blocked by a large plexiglas screen, illustrated in Figure 23. Thus, in these trials the infants were forced to approach and bypass the fear stimulus or the wire mother, or both, in order to reach the cloth mother. Following these 24 trials with the mothers present, one trial of each condition with both mothers absent was run, and this in turn was fol-

FIG. 23.   Typical response to mother in the modified open-field test.

lowed by two trials run under the most emotion-provoking condition: with a mechanical toy present and the direct path to the mother blocked.

We now have complete data for the first four infants raised with both a cloth and a wire mother. Even with this scanty information, the results are obvious. As would be predicted from our other measures, the emotionality scores for the three stimuli were significantly different and these same scores were increased greatly when the direct path to the mother was blocked. A highly significant preference was shown for the cloth mother under both conditions (direct and blocked path), although the presence of the block did increase the number of first responses to

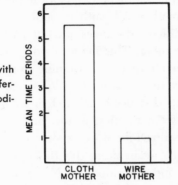

FIG. 24. Time in contact with mothers of the dual fed. Differential responsiveness in the modified open-field test.

the wire mother from 3 to 10 percent. In all cases this was a transient response and the infants subsequently ran on to the cloth mother and clung tightly to her. Objective evidence for this overwhelming preference is indicated in Figure 24, which shows the mean number of time periods spent in contact with the two mothers. After a number of trials, the infants would go first to the cloth mother and then, and only then, would go out to explore, manipulate, and even attack and destroy the fear stimuli. It was as if they believed that their mother would protect them, even at the cost of her life—little enough to ask in view of her condition.

The removal of the mother surrogates from the situation produced the predictable effect of doubling the emotionality index. In the absence of the mothers, the infants would often run to the plexiglas partition which formerly had blocked their path to the mother, or they would crouch in the corner behind the block where the mother normally would have been. The return of the mothers in the final two trials of the test in which the most emotion-evoking situation was presented resulted in behavior near the normal level, as measured by the emotionality index and contacts with the cloth mother.

Our second test of this series was designed to replace the straight-alley test described above and provide more quantifiable data on responsiveness to fear stimuli. The test was conducted in an alley 8-feet long and 2-feet wide. At one end of the alley and directly behind the monkeys' restraining chamber was a small stimulus chamber, which contained a fear object. Each trial was initiated by raising an opaque sliding door which exposed the fear stimulus. Beginning at a point 18 inches from the restraining chamber, the alley was divided lengthwise by a partition; this provided the infant with the choice of entering one of two alleys.

The effects of all mother combinations were measured; these combinations included no mothers, two cloth mothers, two wire mothers, and a cloth and wire mother. All mother conditions were counterbalanced by two distance conditions—distances of 24 and 78 inches, respectively, from the restraining chamber. This made it possible, for example, to provide the infant with the alternative of running to the cloth mother which was in close proximity to the fear stimulus or to the wire mother (or no mother) at a greater distance from the fear stimulus. Thus, it was possible to distinguish between running to the mother surrogate as an object of security, and generalized flight in response to a fear stimulus.

Again, the data available at this time are from the first four infants raised with cloth and wire mothers. Nevertheless, the evidence is quite conclusive. A highly significant preference is shown for the cloth mother as compared to the wire mother or to no mother, and this preference appears to be independent of the proximity of the mother to the fear stimulus. In the condition in which two cloth mothers are present, one 24 inches from the fear stimulus and the other 78 inches from it, there was a preference for the nearest mother, but the differences were not statistically significant. In two conditions in which no cloth mother was present and the infant had to choose between a wire mother and no mother, or between two empty chambers, the emotionality scores were almost twice those under the cloth-mother-present condition.

No differences were found in either of these tests that were related to previous conditions of feeding—that is, to whether the monkey had nursed on the cloth or on the wire mother.

The results of these two new tests, introduced after a full year's separation of mother surrogate and infant, are comparable to the results obtained during the preseparation period and the early retention testing. Preferential responses still favored the cloth as compared to the wire mother by as much as 85 to 90 percent, and the emotionality scores showed the typical 2:1 differential ratio with respect to mother-absent and mother-present conditions.

The researches presented here on the analysis of two affectional variables through the use of objective and observational techniques suggest a broad new field for the study of emotional development of infant animals. The analogous situations and results found in observations and study of human infants and of subprimates demonstrate the apparent face validity of our tests. The reliability of our observational techniques is indicated, for example, by the correlation coefficients computed for the composite emotional index in the open-field test. Four product-moment correlation coefficients, computed from four samples of 100 observations by five different pairs of independent observers over a period of more than a year, ranged from .87 to .89.

Additional Variables

Although the overwhelming importance of the contact variable has been clearly demonstrated in these experiments, there is reason to believe that other factors may contribute to the development of the affectional response pattern. We are currently conducting a series of new experiments to test some of these postulated variables.

For example, Bowlby (2) has suggested that one of the basic affectional variables in the primate order is not just contact but *clinging* contact. To test this hypothesis, four infant monkeys are being raised with the standard cloth mother and a flat inclined plane, tightly covered with the same type of cloth. Thus, both objects contain the variable of contact with the soft cloth, but the shape of the mother tends to maximize the clinging variable, while the broad flat shape of the plane tends to minimize it. The preliminary results for differences in responsiveness to the cloth mother and responsiveness to the inclined plane under conditions that produce stress or fear or visual exploration suggest that clinging as well as contact is an affectional variable of considerable importance.

Experiments now in progress on the role of rocking motion in the development of attachment indicate that this may be a variable of measurable importance. One group of infants is being raised on rocking and stationary mothers and a second group, on rocking and stationary inclined planes. Both groups of infants show a small but consistent preference for the rocking object, as measured in average hours spent on the two objects.

Preliminary results for these three groups in the open-field test give additional evidence concerning the variable of clinging comfort. These data revealed that the infants raised with a standard cloth mother were more responsive to their mothers than the infants raised with inclined planes were to the planes.

The discovery of three variables of measurable importance to the formation and retention of affection is not surprising, and it is reasonable to assume that others will be demonstrated. The data so far obtained experimentally are in excellent concordance with the affectional variables named by Bowlby (2). We are now planning a series of studies to assess the effects of consistency and inconsistency with respect to the mother surrogates in relation to the clinical concept of rejection. The effects of early, intermediate, and late maternal deprivation and the generalization of the infant–surrogate attachment in social development are also being investigated. Indeed, the strength and stability of the monkeys' affectional responses to a mother surrogate are such that it should be practical to determine the neurological and biochemical variables that underlie love.

REFERENCES

1. Arsenian, J. M. *J. abnorm. soc. Psychol.*, 1943, **38**, 225.
2. Bowlby, J. *Int. J. Psycho-anal.*, 1958, **39**, Part 5.
3. Butler, R. A. *J. comp. & physiol. Psychol.*, 1953, **45**, 95.
4. Butler, R. A. *J. exptl. Psychol.*, 1954, **48**, 19.
5. Carpenter, C. R. *Comp. psychol. Monogr.*, 1934, No. 10, 1.
6. Dollard, J., & Miller, N. E. *Personality and psychotherapy.* New York: Mc-Graw-Hill, 1950, 133; Mussen, P. H. & Conger, J. J. *Child development and personality.* New York: Harper & Row, 1956, 137–138.
7. Fabricius, E. *Acta Zool, Fennica*, 1951, **68**, 1.
8. Foley, Jr., J. P. *J. genet. Psychol.*, 1934, **45**, 39.
9. Harlow, H. F. *Am. Psychologist*, 1958, **13**, 673; Harlow, H. F., & Zimmermann, R. R. *Proc. Am. phil. Soc.*, 1958, **102**, 501.
10. Hebb, D. O. *The organization of behavior.* New York: Wiley, 1949, 241 ff.
11. Hess, E. H. *J. comp. & physiol. Psychol.*, in press.
12. Hinde, R. A., Thorpe, W. H., & Vince, M. A. *Behavior*, 1956, **9**, 214.
13. Jaynes, J. *J. comp. physiol. & Psychol.*, in press.
14. Jersild, A. T., & Holmes, F. B. *Child Develop. Monogr.*, 1935, No. 20, 356.
15. Kohler, W. *The mentality of apes.* New York: Humanities Press, 1951.
16. Lorenz, K. *Auk*, 1937, **54**, 245.
17. Moltz, H., & Rosenblum, L. *J. comp. physiol. & Psychol.*, 1958, **51**, 658.
18. Nolte, A. Z. *Tierpsychol.*, 1955, **12**, 77.
19. Ribble, M. A. *The rights of infants.* New York: Columbia Univ. Press.

20. van Wagenen, G. In E. J. Farris (Ed.), *The care and breeding of laboratory animals*. New York: Wiley, 1950, 1.

21. Yerkes R. M., & Tomilin, M. I. *J. comp. Psychol.*, 1935, **20**, 321.

22. Zuckerman, S. *Functional affinities of man, monkeys, and apes*. London: Harcourt Brace, 1933.

23. Support for the research presented in this article was provided through funds received from the graduate school of the University of Wisconsin; from grant M-772, National Institutes of Health; and from a Ford Foundation grant.

24. We no longer make the cloth mother out of a block of wood. The cloth mother's body is simply that of the wire mother, covered by a terry-cloth sheath.

SEPARATION ANXIETY[1]

John Bowlby
TAVISTOCK INSTITUTE, LONDON

OBSERVATIONS OF YOUNG CHILDREN

SINCE 1948 the Tavistock Child Development Research Unit has been concerned with recording the manifest responses which commonly occur when children between the ages of about 12 months and 4 years are removed from the mother figures to whom they are attached and remain with strangers. Preliminary papers and a scientific film have been published (13, 14, 64, 65, 67), and a comprehensive report by James Robertson and the writer is in preparation. In it we shall draw not only on Robertson's own observations and those of other workers reported in the scientific literature, notably those of Burlingham and Freud (17, 18), and Heinicke (42), but also on reports given us by mothers and nurses with firsthand experience of the problem. Since there is a high consensus in these reports, we regard it as firmly established empirically that all children of this age, except those who have already suffered considerable deprivation of maternal care, or are seriously ill, react to the experience with shock and anxiety. Our confidence in the validity of these observations is something we wish to emphasize since it is not uncommon for those whose theories lead to expectations of a different kind to cast doubt on them. In our view it is the theories which are mistaken, not the observations, and it is with the theoretical issues raised by these data that this paper is concerned.

It is evident, however, that the nature and dynamics of the responses to the rupture of a social bond cannot be understood until there is some understanding of the nature and dynamics of the bond itself. It was because of this that in a recently published paper (16) I discussed how best

[1] The paper, from which these excerpts are taken, appeared originally in the *International Journal of Psychoanalysis* (1960), **41**, 89–113. For a more detailed discussion of the relation of the author's investigations and theoretical formulations to those of others, the reader is referred to the original article. Footnotes have also been omitted for lack of space.

the nature of the young child's tie to his mother could be conceptualized. In it I advanced the view that instead of the tie being motivated by a secondary drive or one wholly based on orality, which are the most commonly held views today, it may be mediated by a number of instinctual response systems which are partially independent of one another and which wax and wane in activity at different periods of the infant's and young child's life. I suggested that much psychoanalytic theory, by concentrating attention too narrowly either on the meeting of "physiological" needs (e.g., for food and warmth) or on orality, may have led to the picture as a whole being seen out of perspective; and that other responses, particularly clinging and following which seem to reach their zenith in the second and third years, require far more attention than they have yet been given.

The reasons leading me to advance these views are clinical: traditional theory has seemed to me to account neither for the intense attachment of child to mother-figure which is so conspicuous in the later months of the first year and throughout the second and third years of life, nor for the dramatic responses to separation from her which are the rule in these years. A formulation, based on a theoretical framework stemming from modern instinct theory, has seemed to me more promising. It is the line of thought begun in the previous paper that I shall pursue further in this one.

First let us consider the data. Our observations concern healthy children of 15 to 30 months admitted to a hospital, perhaps for investigation or elective surgery, or to some other residential institution and there cared for in traditional ways. By traditional ways we mean that the child is handled by a succession of strange nurses, mainly students, who will variously bathe, feed, and change him. The nurses will be on shift duty, and often within a few weeks most will have moved to other departments. No matter how kind each may be in her fragment of care, there will be no nurse whom he can come to know or with whom he can enter into a stable relationship. He may see his mother for a short time each day, but it may be less often. In this context a child of 15 to 30 months who has had a normal relationship to his mother and has not previously been parted from her will commonly show a predictable sequence of behavior. This sequence can usefully be broken into three phases according to what attitude to his mother is dominant. We describe these phases as those of protest, despair, and detachment. Though in presenting them it is convenient to differentiate them sharply, it is to be understood that in reality each merges into the next, so that the child may be, for days or weeks, in a state of transition from, or alternation between, one phase and another.

The initial phase, that of *Protest*, may last from a few hours to a week or more. During it the young child appears acutely distressed at having lost his mother and seeks to recapture her by the full exercise of his limited resources. He will often cry loudly, shake his cot, throw himself about, and look eagerly towards any sight or sound which might prove to be his missing mother. All his behavior suggests strong expectation that she will return. Meantime he is apt to reject all alternative figures who offer to do things for him, though some children will cling desperately to a nurse.

During the phase of *Despair,* which succeeds protest, his preoccupation with his missing mother is still evident, though his behavior suggests increasing hopelessness. The active physical movements diminish or come to an end, and he may cry monotonously or intermittently. He is withdrawn and inactive, makes no demands on the environment, and appears to be in a state of deep mourning. This is a quiet stage, and sometimes, clearly erroneously, is presumed to indicate a diminution of distress.

Because the child shows more interest in his surroundings, the phase of *Detachment* which sooner or later succeeds protest and despair is often welcomed as a sign of recovery. He no longer rejects the nurses, accepts their care and the food and toys they bring, and may even smile and be sociable. This seems satisfactory. When his mother visits, however, it can be seen that all is not well, for there is a striking absence of the behavior characteristic of the strong attachment normal at this age. So far from greeting his mother he may seem hardly to know her; so far from clinging to her he may remain remote and apathetic; instead of tears there is a listless turning away. He seems to have lost all interest in her.

Should his stay in hospital or residential nursery be prolonged and should he, as is usual, have the experience of becoming transiently attached to a series of nurses each of whom leaves and so repeats for him the experience of the original loss of his mother, he will in time act as if neither mothering nor contact with humans had much significance for him. After a series of upsets at losing several mother-figures to whom in turn he has given some trust and affection, he will gradually commit himself less and less to succeeding figures and in time will stop altogether taking the risk of attaching himself to anyone. Instead he will become increasingly self-centered and, instead of directing his desires and feelings towards people, become preoccupied with material things such as sweets, toys, and food. A child living in an institution or hospital who has reached this state will no longer be upset when nurses change or leave. He will cease to show feelings when his parents come and go on visiting day; and it may cause them pain when they realize that, although he has an avid interest in the presents they bring, he has little interest in them as special people. He will appear cheerful and adapted to his unusual situation and apparently easy and unafraid of anyone. But this sociability is superficial: he appears no longer to care for anyone.

. . . I wish to emphasize that the behavior seen in the phases of Protest and Despair is not, as is sometimes alleged, confined to children whose relations to their mothers are already impaired. Though we have no large series of well-observed cases to quote, we are satisfied that there is clear evidence that it occurs in children whose previous relationships would be judged to have been anything between excellent and fairly unfavorable. It appears to be only in children whose relationships are already severely impaired, and who may therefore already be in a phase of Detachment, that such behavior is absent.

In examining the theoretical problems raised by these observations it is convenient to consider them with reference to these three phases of behavior. The phase of Protest raises the problem especially of separation anxiety; Despair that of grief and mourning; Detachment that of defense. Each of them is central to psychoanalytic theory and will therefore need detailed discussion—the first in this paper, the second and third in succeeding ones. The thesis to be advanced is that the three types of response —separation anxiety, grief and mourning, and defense—are phases of a single process and that when treated as such each illumines the other two.

• • •

[The hypothesis I shall be adopting is that] the anxiety is a primary response not reducible to other terms and due simply to the rupture of the attachment to his mother. I propose to call it the theory of *Primary Anxiety*. It is the counterpart to theories which account for the child's tie to his mother in terms of component instinctual responses. It has been advanced by James (49), Suttie (73), and Hermann (44), but has never been given much attention in analytic circles.

[The idea stems] from my hypothesis that the child is bound to his mother by a number of instinctual response systems, each of which is primary and which together have high survival value. Soon after birth, it is held, conditions of isolation tend to activate crying and a little later tend to activate both clinging and following also; until he is in close proximity to his familiar mother-figure these instinctual response systems do not cease motivating him. Pending this outcome, it is suggested, his subjective experience is that of primary anxiety; when he is close to her it is one of comfort.

Such anxiety is not to be conceived merely as a "signal" to warn against something worse (though it might subsequently come to have this function). Instead, it is thought of as an elemental experience and one which, if it reaches a certain degree of intensity, is linked directly with the onset of defense mechanisms. It is because of this, and because I wish to distinguish it sharply from states of anxiety dependent on foresight, that I have termed it Primary Anxiety.

Although I believe states of primary anxiety due to separation to be among the most frequent and pathogenic of such states, it is postulated that primary anxiety will arise in other circumstances also—perhaps whenever any instinctual response system is activated but not terminated. Primary anxiety due to separation seems likely, therefore, to be but one example of a common condition. It has, however, several special features. Not least of these is its specially close linkage in infants and young children to the experiences of fright and fear. When frightened, infants and young children look to their mother for security and if they fail to find her are doubly upset: both comfort and security are missing.

· · ·

While the theory of primary anxiety postulates that separation anxiety is itself an unlearned and biologically based anxiety, it is far from blind to the existence and pathogenic importance of anxieties which are dependent on learning and anticipation. In the human it seems useful to distinguish at least two main forms of anticipatory behavior—that based on primitive forms of learning, such as conditioning, and that based on memory organized by means of symbols. As soon as infants can be conditioned, which is very early, they can acquire a simple form of anticipatory behavior and, in so far as the events to which they are conditioned are disagreeable, such, for example, as pain, hunger, or lack of human contact, they may be supposed to experience anxiety. This I shall term *Conditioned Anxiety*. Cognitively, it is still rather a primitive form of anxiety and in many ways more closely resembles primary anxiety than the form next to be described. Later, when the infant develops his capacity for using symbols and can thereby construct a world of objects existing in time and space and interacting causally, he is able to develop some measure of true foresight. Should the foreseen events be of a kind he has learned are disagreeable, he will once again experience anxiety. This I shall term *Expectant Anxiety*. Once this level of psychic organization is reached many kinds of danger, real and imaginary, may be foreseen and responded to. For example, whatever may occur at more primitive levels, at this level both persecutory and depressive anxieties play a crucial role; for anything which leads the child to believe he either has destroyed or alienated his mother, or may do so, cannot fail to exacerbate his expectant anxiety of temporary or permanent separation.

. . .

INGREDIENTS OF SEPARATION ANXIETY

. . . According to the hypothesis advanced, separation anxiety is initially a form of primary anxiety, with or without the addition of fright, and . . . as the infant develops, anxiety based on learning comes to be added. . . . My confidence in it springs from my belief that it provides a better explanation of observations of infants and young children than do other hypotheses and is enhanced by the fact that it seems also to fit comparable observations of the young of other species. . . .

In very many species of bird and mammal, the young show signs of anxiety when removed from their parents. The "lost piping" of young ducklings who have become attached to and have temporarily lost a mother figure is a familiar example. The behavior of infant chimpanzees in such situations is well recorded.

. . .

Except for being less mobile, human infants during the second half of their first year seem to respond similarly to the lower primates. By this age they have become much more demanding of their mother's company. Often when she leaves the room they are upset and do their utmost to see that contact with her is resumed, either by crying or following her as best they can. Such protest behavior, I am postulating, is accompanied initially only by primary anxiety.

Later, in both humans and chimpanzees, conditioned and expectant anxiety develop as a result of learning. Their development in chimpanzees is, of course, well attested. Comparing Gua [a chimpanzee "adopted" and brought up in the home] with their son, who was 2½ months older than she, the Kelloggs (53) report: "Both subjects displayed what might be called anxious behavior (i.e., fretting and crying) if obvious preparations were being made by the grown-ups to leave the house. This led (in Gua) to an early understanding of the mechanism of door closing and a keen and continual observation of the doors in her vicinity. If she happened to be on one side of a doorway, and her friends on the other, the slightest movement of the door toward closing, whether produced by human hands or by the wind, would bring Gua rushing through the narrowing aperture, crying as she came." From this account, it seems clear, by a process of learning Gua was able to anticipate and so to avoid the danger of separation.

Similarly with human infants: it is signs that mother is going to leave them that come to evoke conditioned and expectant anxiety most commonly. At what period during the infant's first year the capacity for foresight develops is difficult to say. Experiment, however, should be easy. If Piaget's views are confirmed we should expect it to be present from about 9 months.

Not only do attachment behavior and anxiety responses appear similar in humans and other species, but the same is true of fright responses in the absence of the mother. In such circumstances the young of many species freeze.

It seems almost certain, in fact, that every child who has not been institutionalized develops during his first year a clear preference for one person, namely the person who cares for him and whom I am calling "mother," and this remains the case even though, in addition, he is likely to include a few others to whom he will turn as second best if mother is absent. It is because of this marked tendency to monotropy that we are capable of deep feelings; for to have a deep attachment to a person (or place, or thing) is to have taken them as the terminating object of our instinctual responses. It is probably when these responses include those mediating attachment and escape that there exists what Erikson (22) and others have described as "basic trust."

Unless this high degree of selectivity of the object terminating the response systems mediating attachment and escape behavior is understood, reactions to separation from loved objects will remain a closed book. This is where, on occasion, formulations stemming from the theory of secondary drive break down. So long as the caretaker ministers efficiently to the child's physiological needs, it is sometimes reasoned, the child has nothing to grumble about: and so he ought not to grumble. This outlook would be ridiculous were it not so tragic—both for the child and for the well-intentioned caretaker.

As presented here, separation anxiety is the inescapable corollary of attachment behavior—the other side of the coin. As soon as the instinctual response systems mediating such behavior have matured and, by a process of learning of a simple kind, become oriented towards any object whatsoever, the child will become prone to experience primary anxiety at separation from it. Plainly this formulation implies that there is a period early in the infant's life during which he is not prone to separation anxiety as a specific form of anxiety. This needs discussion.

In [a] previous paper I discussed the perceptual and cognitive aspects of the child's tie to his mother and pointed to the evidence that prior to about 6 months the infant's differentiation, as measured by his responsiveness, between familiar mother-figure and stranger is present but only evident on careful observation. After about 6 months, however, differential responses are very striking. In particular I refer to the recent work of Schaffer, who observed the responses of 25 healthy infants aged under 12 months to admission to hospital for elective surgery. Of those over 28 weeks of age, all but one fretted piteously, exhibiting all the struggling, restlessness, and crying with which we are familiar in rather older children. On the other hand, of those aged 28 weeks and under, all but two are reported to have accepted the new environment without protest or fretting; only an unwonted silence indicated their awareness of change. Similarly, infants in the two age groups exhibited very different responses both to visitors during the period of separation and also to their mothers on return home. Those over 28 weeks behaved negatively to strangers, but to their visiting mothers were demanding and clinging; those under 28 weeks, on the other hand, seemed hardly to differentiate between stranger and mother (though it was noticed that they became more vocal during their mother's visit). On return home those over 28 weeks clung tenaciously to their mother and cried and were distressed if left alone by her; those under this age showed no such behavior but instead appeared bewildered, scanning their surroundings with a blank expression (68, 69).

These observations, if confirmed, strongly suggest that separation anxiety on losing mother is not exhibited before about 28 weeks. As Schaffer points out, this is strikingly in keeping with a prediction made by Anthony (2) on the basis of Piaget's findings.

· · ·

CONCLUSION

[The hypothesis advanced to account for] separation anxiety is an immediate corollary of that advanced to account for the child's tie to his mother. In the earlier paper reasons were advanced why it was both legitimate and economical to conceive the child's tie as being the direct outcome of a number of instinctual response systems—crying, smiling, sucking, clinging, and following—which have become bred into the species as a result of their survival value. When they are activated and the mother-figure is available, attachment behavior follows. Similarly, as we have discussed in this paper, when they are activated and the mother-figure is temporarily not available, protest behavior and separation anxiety follow. This formulation not only has the merit of appearing to account for the facts, but is also simple. Furthermore, it brings separation anxiety into immediate relation to grief and mourning, which in this scheme are seen respectively as the subjective experience and the psychological processes which occur when the responses mediating attachment behavior are activated and the mother-figure is permanently unavailable, or at least believed to be so. A liability to experience separation anxiety and grief are thus the ineluctable risks of a love relationship, of caring for someone.

· · ·

REFERENCES

In most cases references to the works of Sigmund Freud are given in the text, wherever possible to the Standard Edition. S.E.=Standard Edition; C.P.= Collected Papers.
1. Abraham, K. Notes on the psycho-analytical investigation and treatment of manic-depressive insanity and allied conditions. In *Selected papers on psycho-analysis*. London: Hogarth, 1927.
2. Anthony, E. J. The significance of Jean Piaget for child psychiatry. *Brit. J. med. Psychol.*, 1956, **29**, 20–34.
3. Anthony, S. *The child's discovery of death*. London: Kegan Paul, 1940.
4. Balint, M. New beginning and the paranoid and the depressive syndromes. Reprinted in M. Balint, *Primary love and psycho-analytic technique*. London: Hogarth, 1953.
5. Basowitz, H. *et al. Anxiety and stress: an interdisciplinary study of a life situation*. New York: McGraw-Hill, 1955.
6. Bastock, M., Morris, D., & Moynihan, M. Some comments on conflict and thwarting in animals. *Behaviour*, 1953, **6**, 66–84.
7. Bender, L., & Yarnell, H. An observation nursery: a study of 250 children on the psychiatric division of Bellevue hospital. *Amer. J. Psychiat.*, 1941, **97**, 1158–1172.
8. Benedek, T. *Insight and personality adjustment: a study of the psychological effects of war*. New York: Ronald Press, 1946.
9. Bernfeld, S. *The psychology of the infant*. London: Kegan Paul, 1929.
10. Bowlby, J. The influence of early environment in the development of neurosis and neurotic character. *Int. J. Psycho-anal.*, 1940, **21**, 154–178.
11. Bowlby, J. Forty-four juvenile thieves: their characters and home life. *Int. J. Psycho-anal.*, 1944, **25**, 19–52, & 107–127.
12. Bowlby, J. *Maternal care and mental health. W.H.O. Monogr.*, No. 2., London: H.M.S.O., 1951.

13. Bowlby, J. Some pathological processes set in train by early mother-child separation. *J. ment. Sci.*, 1953, **99**, 265–272.
14. Bowlby, J. Psychopathological processes set in train by early mother-child separation. In *Proceedings of seventh conference on infancy and childhood*. New York: Jos. Macy, Jr., Fdn., 1953.
15. Bowlby, J. An ethological approach to research in child development. *Brit. J. med. Psychol.*, 1957, **30**, 230–240.
16. Bowlby, J. The nature of the child's tie to his mother. *Int. J. Psycho-anal.*, 1958, **39**, 350–373.
17. Burlingham, D. & Freud, Anna. *Young children in war time*. London: Allen and Unwin, 1942.
18. Burlingham, D. & Freud, Anna. *Infants without families*. London: Allen and Unwin, 1944.
19. Deutsch, H. Absence of grief. *Psychoanal. Quart.*, 1937, **6**, 12–22.
20. Dixon, J. J., De Monchaux, C., & Sandler, J. Patterns of anxiety: and analysis of social anxieties. *Brit. J. med. Psychol.*, 1957, **30**, 107.
21. Edelston, H. Separation anxiety in young children: a study of hospital cases. *Genet. psychol. Monogr.*, 1943, **28**, 3–95.
22. Erikson, E. H. *Childhood and society*. New York: Norton, 1950.
23. Fairbairn, W. R. D. A revised psychopathology of the psychoses and psychoneuroses. In *Psycho-analytic studies of the personality*. London: Tavistock, 1952.
24. Fairbairn, W. R. D. The war neuroses—their nature and significance. In *Psycho-analytic studies of the personality*. London: Tavistock, 1952.
25. Fairbairn, W. R. D. A synopsis of the development of the author's views regarding the structure of the personality. In *Psycho-analytic studies of the personality*. London: Tavistock, 1952.
26. Freud, Anna. The mutual influences in the development of ego and id. *Psychoanal. Study Child*, 1952, **7**, 42–50.
27. Freud, Anna. Some remarks on infant observation. *Psychonal. Study Child*, 1953, **8**, 9–19.
28. Freud, S. *Introductory lectures on psycho-analysis*. London: Allen and Unwin, 1922.
29. Freud, S. *Inhibitions, symptoms and anxiety*. London: Hogarth, 1936.
30. Freud, S. Female sexuality. In *Collected papers*, 1931, **5**.
31. Freud, S. *New introductory lectures on psycho-analysis*. London: Hogarth, 1933.
32. Gerard, R. W. Anxiety and tension. *Bull. N.Y. Acad. Med.*, (2nd Series), 1958, **34**, 429–444.
33. Goldfarb, W. Infant rearing and problem behavior. *Amer. J. Orthopsychiat.*, 1943, **13**, 249–265.
34. Goldstein, K. *The organism*. New York: American Book Co., 1939.
35. Greenacre, P. The predisposition to anxiety. In *Trauma, growth and personality*. New York: Norton, 1952.
36. Greenacre, P. The biological economy of birth. In *Trauma, growth, and personality*. New York: Norton, 1952.

37. Greenacre, P. Conscience in the psychopath. In *Trauma, growth, and personality*. New York: Norton, 1952.
38. Greenacre, P. *Trauma, growth and personality*. New York: Norton, 1952.
39. Harlow, H. F. The nature of love. *Amer. Psychologist*, 1958, **13**, 673–685.
40. Harlow, H. F., & Zimmermann, R. R. The development of affectional responses in infant monkeys. *Proc. Amer. philosophical Soc.*, 1958, **102**, 501–509.
41. Hayes, C. *The ape in our house*. New York: Harper, 1951.
42. Heinicke, C. M. Some effects of separating two-year-old children from their parents: a comparative study. *Human Relations*, 1956, **9**, 105–176.
43. Heinicke, C. M. The effects of separating two-year-old children from their parents: a comparative study. Paper read at the International Congress of Psychology, Brussels, 1957.
44. Hermann, I. Sich-Anklammern—Auf-Suche-Gehen. *Int. Zeitschr. für Psycho-Anal.*, 1936, **22**, 349–370.
45. Hinde, R. A. Factors governing the changes in strength of a partially inborn response. *Proc. Roy. Society, B*, 1954, **142**, 306–331.
46. Hinde, R. A. Changes in responsiveness to a constant stimulus. *Brit. J. Animal Behaviour*, 1954, **2**, 41–55.
47. Hug-Hellmuth, H. von. *A study of the mental life of the child*. Washington: Nervous and Mental Disease Pub. Co., 1919.
48. Isaacs, S. The nature and function of phantasy. In Melanie Klein *et al.*, *Developments in psycho-analysis*. London: Hogarth, 1952.
49. James, W. *A textbook of psychology*. New York: Holt, 1890.
49a. Johnson, A. M., Falstein, E. I., Szurek, S. A., & Svensden, M. School Phobia. *Amer. J. Orthopsychiat.*, 1941, **11**, 702–711.
50. Jones, E. The early development of female sexuality. In *Papers on psycho-analysis*. (5th ed.) London: Bailliere, 1948.
51. Jones, E. Fear, guilt and hate. In *Papers on psycho-analysis*. (5th ed.), London: Bailliere, 1948.
52. Jones, E. *Sigmund Freud: life and work*. Vol. 3. London: Hogarth, 1957.
53. Kellogg, W. N., & Kellogg, L. A. *The ape and the child*. New York: Whittlesey, 1933.
54. Klein, Melanie. *The psycho-analysis of children*. London: Hogarth, 1932.
54a. Klein, Melanie. On criminality. *Brit. J. med. Psychol.*, 1934, **14**, 312–315.
55. Klein, Melanie. A contribution to the psychogenesis of Manic-depressive states. In Melanie Klein *et al. Developments in psycho-analysis*. London: Hogarth, 1952.
56. Klein, Melanie & Riviere, Joan. *Love, hate and reparation*. (London: Hogarth, 1937.
56a. Kris, E. The recovery of childhood memories in psychonalysis. *Psychonal. Study Child*, **11**, 54–88.
57. Levy, D. Primary affect hunger. *Amer. J. Psychiat.*, 1937, **94**, 643–652.
58. Liddell, H. Some specific factors that modify tolerance for environmental stress. In *Life stress and bodily disease*. New York: Assoc. for Research in Nervous and Mental Disease, 1950.

59. Lorenz, K. Z. The comparative method in studying innate behaviour patterns. In *Physiological mechanisms in animal behaviour*. IV: Symposia of the society for experimental biology. London: Cambridge Univ. Press, 1950.

60. McDougall, W. *An outline of psychology*. London: Methuen, 1923.

61. Odier, C. *Anxiety and magic thinking*. New York: Int. Univ. Press, 1956.

62. Prugh, D., Staub, E. M., Sands, H. H., Kirschbaum, R. M., & Lenihan, E. A. Study of emotional reactions of children and families to hospitalization and illness. *Amer. J. Orthopsychiat.*, 1953, **23**, 70–106.

63. Rank, O. *The trauma of birth*. London: Kegan Paul, 1929.

64. Robertson, J. Film: A two-year-old goes to hospital. London: Tavistock Child Development Research Unit, 1953a.

65. Robertson, J. Some responses of young children to the loss of maternal care. *Nurs. Times*, April, 1953b, 382–386.

66. Robertson, J. Film: Going to hospital with mother. London: Tavistock Child Development Research Unit, 1958.

67. Robertson, J., & Bowlby, J. Responses of young children to separation from their mothers. *Courrier de la Centre Internationale de l'Enfance*, 1952, **2**, 131–142.

68. Schaffer, H. R. Objective observations of personality development in early infancy. *Brit. J. med. Psychol.*, 1958, **31**, 174–183.

69. Schaffer, H. R., & Callender, W. M. Psychological effects of hospitalization in infancy. *Pediatrics*, 1949, **24**, 528–539.

69a. Spitz, R. A. Anaclitic depression. *Psycho-Anal. Study Child*, 1946, **2**, 313–341.

70. Spitz, R. A. Anxiety in infancy: a study of its manifestations in the first year of life. *Int. J. Psycho-anal.*, 1950, **31**, 138–143.

71. Spitz, R. A. Aggression: its role in the establishment of object relations. In Ed. Loewenstein (Ed.), *Drives, affects and behaviour*. New York: Int. Univ. Press, 1953.

72. Stendler, C. B. Possible causes of overdependency in young children. *Child Develpm.*, 1954, **25**, 125–146.

73. Suttie, I. D. *The origins of love and hate*. London: Kegan Paul, 1935.

74. Thorpe, W. H. The concepts of learning and their relation to those of instinct. In *Physiological mechanisms in animal behaviour. Symposium IV of S. E. B.* London: Cambridge Univ. Press, 1950.

75. Winnicott, B. W. Psychoses and child care. In *Collected papers*. London: Tavistock, 1958.

76. Yerkes, R. M. *Chimpanzees: a laboratory colony*. New Haven: Yale Univ. Press, 1943.

77. Yerkes, R. M., & Yerkes, A. W. Nature and conditions of avoidance (fear) response in chimpanzees. *J. comp. Psychol.*, 1936, **21**, 53–66.

78. Zetzel, E. R. The concept of anxiety in relation to the development of psychoanalysis. *J. Amer. psychoanal. Assn.*, 1955, **3**, 369–388.

EXPERIENCE AND

THE DEVELOPMENT OF MOTIVATION:

SOME REINTERPRETATIONS[1]

J. McV. Hunt

DEPARTMENT OF PSYCHOLOGY, UNIVERSITY OF ILLINOIS

A RECENT ISSUE of the *Saturday Evening Post* carried a cartoon that some of you may have noted. It depicts a boy entering his house, perhaps from school, where his father is sitting with his paper. The boy appears to be fixing his father with an accusing glare. The punch line reads, "Somebody goofed, I'm improperly motivated."

This cartoon depicts the vantage point from which I have been examining what we think we know about the relation between experience and motivation. When a child's behavior fails to fit the standards somebody in our society holds for him, it is pretty well agreed among us who are supposed to be experts on human nature that "somebody goofed." And that somebody is usually considered to be a parent.

The question is: what is the proper formula? If one examines the accruing evidence relevant to what has been the dominant conception of the experiential sources of motivation, one can hardly escape the conclusion that this conceptual scheme needs some revisions. If we based our child-rearing entirely on our dominant theory of motivational development, we would probably goof as often and as badly as run-of-the-mill parents.

Today I wish, first, to remind you of three of the most basic and

[1] Earlier versions of this paper were read at the Eleventh Annual Institute in Psychiatry and Neurology of the Veterans Administration Hospital at North Little Rock, Arkansas, 27 February 1959, and at colloquia of the Department of Psychiatry at the Medical School of Colorado. The paper was prepared in connection with a survey of the implications of the work in behavioral science for childrearing which has been supported by the Russell Sage Foundation.

Reprinted from *Child Development* (1960), **31**, 489–504, by permission of the author and the Society of Research in Child Development.

general of the propositions in that theory of motivation which has been dominant for the past 30 to 40 years. These are propositions which, although stated in somewhat varied forms, have been shared by both psychoanalysts and academic behavior theorists. Secondly, I wish to cite evidence which calls these propositions into question, and thirdly, to suggest, tentatively, three new interpretative principles which appear to me to be congruent with a large number of facts and which have interesting implications.

Our conceptions of motivation have traditionally been concerned with three large questions: (a) Why does an organism or person become active? (b) Why does the organism or person act one way rather than another? and (c) How do you get the organism or person to change his behavior to something conceived to be more desirable or appropriate?

THE DOMINANT THEORY

Drive

According to our dominant theory, it is claimed, first of all, that "all behavior is motivated," and that the aim or function of every instinct, defense, action, or habit is to reduce or eliminate stimulation or excitation within the nervous system. It is not easy to state when this view was first presented. Signs of it appear in the seventh chapter of Freud's *Interpretation of Dreams* (15) in 1900, and the idea is full-blown in his paper entitled *Instincts and Their Vicissitudes* (17) in 1915. The idea also appears in Woodworth's *Dynamic Psychology* (68), published in 1918, where the term *drive* was first introduced into the glossary of American psychology. The idea was full-blown in Dashiell's *Fundamentals of Objective Psychology* (11) in 1928.

Although Freud (17) believed that the source of motivation lay outside the domain of psychology in physiology, American psychologists, untroubled by such limits to their domain, have gone on to answer the first question concerning what motivates organisms to become active by saying that they are *driven*. Organisms have been conceived to be driven, first by those so-called primary inner stimuli which arise from homeostatic imbalances or needs. With no shame whatsoever, psychologists have long cited the evidence from the work of such physiologists as Claude Bernard (5) and his successors, and especially of Walter B. Cannon (10), and also of the psychologist Curt Richter (59) to document this answer. Organisms are driven, second, by various forms of intense and painful external stimulation. It has been assumed that these two forms of stimulation arouse an inner state of excitement which has usually been called *drive*.

It is also assumed, as the proposition that "all behavior is motivated" implies, that the organism would be inactive unless driven by either inner or outer stimuli. Freud (*17*) has been highly explicit about this assumption, and the assumption lies implicitly behind the notion of conditioned or learned drive in behavior theory and behind the traumatic notion of anxiety in psychoanalysis. It is obvious, of course, that animals and people are sometimes active when it is hard to see how either homeostatic drive or painful external stimulation could be operative. It is then assumed that some of the weak, innocuous stimuli present must have been associated in the past with either painful stimuli or homeostatic needs. In such a way the weak stimuli which are present must have acquired the capacity to arouse the drive, often now called anxiety by psychologists as well as psychoanalysts, and it is such acquired or conditioned drive that is conceived to activate the organism.

Such conditioned drive or anxiety has been well demonstrated in the laboratory. Before World War II, Miller (*45, 46*) at Yale showed that rats which had been repeatedly shocked in a white box would, when later returned to the white box, make an effort to escape. Moreover, in the course of these efforts, they could be got to learn new skills such as that of turning a wheel to open a door. Rats which had not been shocked in the white box made no such efforts to escape. In another demonstration, Solomon and Wynne (*64*) have shown that dogs which have experienced a tone or a buzzer paired a few times with a subtetanizing shock will run away from that tone or buzzer for hundreds of trials, with the average reaction time of starting continuing to decrease through 600 such trials. In my own work (*31*) rats fed irregularly in infancy ate more than their littermate controls and sometimes (*32*) hoarded food in adulthood after a period without food. Here, as I conceived it, the cues of hunger were conditioned to intense hunger excitement during the infantile experience. In adulthood the conditioned hunger drive facilitated the rate of eating and, sometimes, hoarding.

Such work has demonstrated that this notion of conditioned drive or anxiety, which goes back to the work of Bechterev (*2*) and Watson and Raynor (*67*), has a solid basis in reality. But in what has been the dominant theory of motivation, as epitomized by Freud's (*18*) later traumatic theory of anxiety, and by the Hull (*30*) and Dollard-Miller (*13, 47*) theory of acquired drives, conditioning is conceived to be the only way in which an organism can become fearful of innocuous stimuli.

Habit

Habit has been the answer to the second question concerned with why an animal or person acts one way rather than another. The organism is controlled by the habits which have served to reduce drive in the past when that organism was in the presence of the inner and outer drive stimuli, and the cue stimuli impinging upon him at any given moment now. Under the term *habit,* I am including psychoanalytic modes, which have supposedly been fixated during infancy in the course of either too much gratification or too much frustration, and I am including also ego-defenses, or anxiety equivalents, and cathexes, as well as the instrumental responses and traits commonly investigated in psychological laboratories.

Changing behavior has been conceived to be a matter of motivating the organism with either punishment or homeostatic need to make the desired behavior which can then be reinforced by arranging for it to reduce the drive aroused by the punishment or the need. Although the conditions and conceptions of psychotherapy in the clinic differ considerably from the conditions and conceptions of the behavior theorist investigating learning in laboratory animals, in either case it is conceived that motivation is a necessity, and motivation means changing the emotional or drive conditions which are quite extrinsic to either the instrumental behavior or the cognitive, informational processes concerned.

This dominant theory has been a conceptual edifice of large dimensions and of considerable detail. It has provided a plausible account of both personality development and social motives. The experimental facts of homeostasis and of conditioned drive and fear are sound. Nevertheless, it has become more and more evident in the past 10 years that some of the basic assumptions of this dominant theoretical scheme and some of the explanatory extrapolations contradict facts and call for reinterpretation.

REINTERPRETATIONS

Is All Behavior Motivated?

The first of the assumptions to be called into question is the one that *all behavior is motivated* and that *organisms become inactive unless stimulated* by homeostatic need or painful stimulation or conditional stimuli for these. A large variety of observations contradict this assumption and imply spontaneous molar activity. Beach (*1*) has reviewed the observations of play in the young to show that playful activities are most likely to occur when either young animals or children are homeostatically satisfied and also comfortably warm. The very occurrence of either homeostatic need or strong external stimulation stops play and turns the young animal or child to activities calculated to relieve such stimulation. Berlyne (3, 4) has shown that well-fed and watered rats will explore areas new to them if given only the opportunity. Montgomery (49) moreover, has shown that hunger and thirst tend to limit the exploratory behavior of rats rather than facilitate it, and Montgomery and Monkman (50), as well as others, have shown that conditioned fear inhibits exploration. Harlow, Harlow, and Meyer (23) have demonstrated that well-fed monkeys will learn to unassemble a three-device puzzle with no other drive and "no other reward than the privilege of unassembling it." In another study Harlow (20) found two well-fed and well-watered monkeys worked repeatedly at unassembling a six-device puzzle for 10 continuous hours, and they were still showing what he characterized as enthusiasm for their work on the tenth hour of testing. From his observations of the human child, moreover, Piaget (55) remarks repeatedly on the enthusiastic and repeated performance of such emerging skills as the release of a toy, sitting up, standing, etc.

Such evidences of spontaneous behavior, which is unmotivated in the traditional sense, have led to the naming of such new motives as a curiosity drive by Berlyne (4), an exploratory drive by Montgomery (48), and exteroceptive and curiosity drives by Harlow (21). I would like to object that merely naming such drives explains nothing. If we continue, we shall be revisiting McDougall's (44) practice of postulating a separate drive for almost every variety of activity. Let us stop with noting that such observations do contradict our assumption that organisms will become inactive unless driven by homeostatic needs and painful stimuli, and give up this ancient Greek notion that living matter is inert substance to which motion must be imparted by extrinsic forces. We can then embrace the thermodynamic conception of living things as open systems of energy exchange which exhibit activity intrinsically and upon which stimuli have a modulating effect, but not an initiating effect.

This notion of activity being intrinsic in living tissue is receiving support from studies of organ systems as well as studies of molar organisms. The EEG, for example, shows that brain cells are continuously active (33, 58). In sleep the slow waves of large amplitude are taken to imply that large numbers of cells are firing synchronously, and the effect of waking and stimulation and exciting the brain-stem-reticular formation is to asynchronize this firing which shows in rapid waves of low magnitude (42).

Granit (19) points out that the spontaneous firing of retinal cells increases with dark adaptation and thereby functions to prevent the deafferentization of visual cortex with darkness. Twenty years ago, this spontaneous firing was considered, at worst, to be due to some failure of experimental control, or at best, noise in the channel of information. Recently, the Laceys (36) have found spontaneous fluctuations of sudomotor activity and cardiac activity which they also see as functioning in the control of the organism's relations with its environment. Especially intriguing is their notion that the carotid sinus mechanism functions as a feedback loop which participates in the directing of attention inward or outward by inhibiting or facilitating receptor inputs. But the point of mentioning these evidences of spontaneous activities of organ systems here is merely to help inter for good the notion that activity of living systems requires homeostatic need or painful external stimulation and to foster the idea that to live means to be active in some degree.

Reinforcement

This idea of activity being intrinsic in living organisms has implications for our conception of reinforcement. It makes it unnecessary to see all activity as a matter of either reducing or avoiding stimulation which is implied in the assumption that organisms become inactive unless stimulated. This is a second fundamental assumption of the dominant theory which has been shared by psychoanalysts and behavior theorists alike.

On the one hand, there is still a place for drive reduction. It is clear that under conditions of homeostatic need and painful stimulation, and perhaps under circumstances when the conditions of stimulation are changing with too great rapidity, both animals and persons learn techniques and strategies leading to gratification or reduction in external stimulation. The evidence that led Thorndike to formulate the "law of effect" is as convincing as ever. Moreover, in association with reductions of homeostatic need, animals and men may also learn cathexes or emotional attachments. The facts referred to are those highly familiar in secondary reinforcement (30, 54).

On the other hand, the facts implying that organisms show spontaneous molar activity also imply that, when animals and human beings have been living under conditions of low and unchanging stimulation for a time, increases of stimulation become reinforcing. Butler has shown that rhesus monkeys will learn quite complex discriminations with the only reward being a peek through a glass window (7) at the things in the next room or a few seconds of auditory experience (8). Berlyne (3) has shown that, the greater the variety of stimulation in an area which rats are permitted to explore, the longer they continue their explorations.

Especially important in this connection are the studies of human behavior under conditions of minimal variation in stimulation. I refer to the studies of perceptual isolation by Bexton, Heron, and Scott (6) at McGill and also the work of Lilly (41). At McGill, college students were paid 20 dollars a day to do nothing. They lay for 24 hours a day on a comfortable bed. The temperature was optimal and constant. Eyes, ears, and hands were shielded to minimize stimulus variation. Few subjects could endure more than two or three days of such conditions. They developed a desire for variation which was almost overwhelming.

While interpreting such facts in terms of a multiple set of drives for curiosity, exploration, or stimulation will get us only to a redescription of them, Hebb's (26) notion of an optimal level of activation—and, I would like to add, stimulus variation below which *increases* are reinforcing and above which *decreases* are reinforcing—is an integrative conception of fair magnitude. Moreover, the drive-reduction principle of reinforcement may be seen to be but half of this more general curvilinear principle.

But this is probably not the whole story. It looks as if there were, natively, both positive and negative forms of exciting stimulation. Sheffield, Roby, and Campbell (61) have argued that the reinforcing effect of eating is not a matter of reduction of the hunger drive but rather a matter of the positive value of the consummatory act of eating. Moreover, Sheffield, Wulff, and Backer (62) have shown that male rats will learn mazes to get to females in heat even when they are allowed only intromission but not allowed to continue coitus to the point of drive-reducing ejaculation. From the fact that Davis (12) and his collaborators at Indiana have shown that showing pictures of nude women to college males increases excitement as shown by increased palmar conductance and the arrest of EEG-alpha, it is clear that such stimulation is exciting rather than excitement-reducing. Young (69) has long emphasized the importance of the hedonic quality of experience for reinforcement, and he has shown that speed of running in rat subjects increases with the concentration of sucrose in the incentive drink.

The suggestion that the two forms of excitation, one positive and one negative, are built into organisms comes also from the work of Olds and Milner (53). Electrical stimulation of the septal area is positively reinforcing, but electrical stimulation of the brain-stem reticular formation is negatively reinforcing. Perhaps, it is not without significance that the septal area is part of the old olfactory brain which has been considered to have an especially important part in the mediation of sexual and consummatory behavior in mammals. At any rate, it looks as though certain types of stimulation may be positively reinforcing even though they be intense and exciting. This may mean that the curvilinear principle may be limited in its domain to strong stimulation via the exteroceptors when homeostatic needs are minimized.

The suggestion of innate, positive and negative exteroceptive stimulation comes secondly from recent work by Harlow (22). It has been customary to see an infant's cathexis or love for its mother developing as secondary reinforcement largely out of its feeding experiences. Freud (16), of course, contended that the pleasure from stimulation of the oral erogenous zone furnished the experiential basis for both pleasure-sucking and maternal attachment, a contention which contradicted his most definitive formulations of drive theory (17). The fact that an infant must suck for its nourishment, according to libido theory (16, p. 587), merely guaranteed discovery of the pleasures of oral stimulation. Behavior theorists have seen both sucking and love of mother as forms of secondary reinforcement deriving from the fact that the child satisfies its hunger by means of sucking the mother's breasts (51, pp. 137ff.). Harlow (22), however, has recently compared the degree of attachment of young monkeys to a wire mother-surrogate on which they nursed at a bottle with attachment to a padded and cloth-covered mother-surrogate on which they received nothing but the feel of softness. In terms of the amount of time spent on each of the two mother-surrogates, the monkeys showed more than 10 times the attachment to the soft-padded surrogate as to the wire surrogate. When various fear-evoking stimuli were presented to the baby monkeys in their cages, it was to the padded and cloth-covered surrogate that the frightened infant monkey turned, not to the wire surrogate on which it had been nursed. Harlow argues from these findings that it is the sensory quality of softness which gives the reinforcement. His study suggests, moreover, that it is important to investigate the capacity for various kinds of stimuli for positive and negative reinforcement in the very young. Pratt (57) cites a monograph by Canestrini (9) on the sensory life of the newborn for an observation that certain stimuli are associated with decreases in the rate of the heart rate, and are therefore pleasant, while others are associated with increases in heart rate and are unpleasant.[2] In view of the finding by Davis (12) and his collaborators that seeing a picture of a nude female results in reduction of the heart rate of male college students, it is possible that this physiological indicator may provide a technique for determining the direction of the reinforcing effect of stimuli in the newborn. At any rate, what is suggested is that McDougall's (44) old notion of natively positive and negative values for receptors inputs be reexamined.

Conditioned Fear and Anxiety

The third assumption that I wish to examine in the light of empirical evidence is the notion that fear and anxiety are *always* inculcated as a consequence of traumatic experiences of helplessness in the face of homeostatic need or painful external stimulation. Note that I am not denying that such conditioned fears do exist. I am only questioning the word *always* . . . are always inculcated as a consequence of traumatic experiences.

The first relevant studies go way back to the 1920 s. Harold and Mary Cover Jones (34) attempted to test the claims of Watson (66) and Watson and Raynor (67) concerning conditioned fears. They exposed their subjects of various ages, ranging from early infancy to adult, to a large but sluggish and harmless bull-snake. Fear of the snake was exceedingly common among adults, teenagers, and latency-age children, but it was absent in children below three years of age. It began to appear among children older than 3 and was typical of children 6 and older. From the fact that the fear appeared at a younger age in those of higher intelligence than those of lower intelligence, the Joneses argued that fear of snakes is a response which comes automatically into the developing child's repertoire through maturation. This remains as an alternative hypothesis to that of conditioned fear.

A study by Frances Holmes (29), which is seldom cited, calls both of these interpretations into question. Holmes compared the fearfulness of the children of lower-class background who were attending a day nursery, with the fearfulness of children of upper-class background who were attending a private nursery school. She got her fear scores by indicating that the child could get some attractive toys with which to play

---

[2] An examination of Canestrini's (9) monograph shows that Pratt was mistaken in stating that Canestrini remarked upon decreases in heart rate being associated with pleasure, but some of his published kymograph records do indicate decreases in heart rate. It may well be that heart rate could serve as an indicator of the emotional value of various sensory inputs and these might be tested for their reinforcement values. I am indebted to Dr. William Gerler for reading this monograph carefully to check my own impression of Canestrini's text.

by going into the dark room adjacent to the examining room, or by taking them off a chair situated beside that of a strange woman dressed in a large floppy black hat and a long gray coat, or by climbing along a plank some three feet off the floor. If the child started immediately for the toys, he got a score of one for that item. If he hesitated but ultimately went ahead on his own, he got a score of two. If he would go only if accompanied by the examiner, the score was three. If he refused to go at all, the score was four. There were seven such situations. The results show that the fear scores of the lower-class children averaged only about half the size of those for the upper-class children, and the fear scores for boys were lower than those for girls. Yet it would be the lower-class children who had experienced the more homeostatic need and painfully rough treatment than the upper-class children, and the boys had probably experienced more painful experiences than the little girls. That intelligence is not the factor is shown by the fact that the fear scores showed a correlation of only about $+.2$ with mental age, and the differences were still significant when intelligence was partialed out. Something besides either conditioned fear or the correlation between fear and intelligence is required to make these results comprehensible.

Recently, evidence even more contradictory to the notion of conditioned fears has been coming from the work of Seymour Levine. Levine, Chevalier, and Korchin (40) have compared the adult behavior of rats shocked and rats petted daily from birth to their 20th day with the adult behavior of rats left continuously in their nest with their mothers. When he started this work, Levine expected to find that the shocked animals would show traumatic effects of their shock experiences in heightened emotionality and damaged capacity to learn adaptive responses. On the contrary, the shocked animals, along with the handled animals gained weight faster than those left in the nest (37, 38, 39, 40). Byron Lindholm, working with the writer, has repeated and confirmed this finding. Moreover, Levine's shocked and handled animals both showed less emotionality than those left continuously in the nest with their mothers, i.e., less emotionality in the sense that they defecated and urinated less frequently when placed in a strange situation. Finally, the shocked and handled animals, which have appeared alike in all of these experiments, learned an avoidance response more rapidly and drank more readily after 18 hours without water than did the rats left in the nest with their mother.

Clearly these results on both human children and rats imply that fear and anxiety must sometimes have some other basis than that of being associated with painful stimulation. As many of you know, Hebb (24, 25) has formulated a radically different explanation of fear which may be termed either an incongruity or a dissonance theory.

The facts which suggested Hebb's conception came largely from observing chimpanzees being raised under controlled conditions at the Yerkes Laboratory. Fear, defined as withdrawal behavior in response to the appearance of some object, does not appear in young chimpanzees until they are approximately four months old. Then, the objects feared are familiar objects in unfamiliar guise. Fear of strangers is an example. This appears spontaneously to the first stranger seen, so it cannot be based on associating strangers with painful stimulation. Fear of strangers does not appear in chimpanzees—or in children, I might add—who have always been exposed to a large number of persons. While the avoidance response is unlearned, the familiar, expected aspects of objects must be learned. The young animal must have established as residues of his experience cortical firing patterns (or cognitive structures—whichever term you like) from which new receptor inputs can be incongruous. Consider the kinds of objects regularly feared. They are, for instance, the familiar keeper or experimenter in strange clothes, the experimenter in a Halloween mask, a plaster cast of a chimpanzee head (which lacks, of course, the familiarly attached body), an anesthetized chimpanzee infant (from which the familiar patterns of motion are absent). On the other hand, objects which have never entered into the young chimpanzee's life may be strange without evoking withdrawal. In other words, the feared object is one which excites receptors in a fashion which is incongruous with the central, sequential pattern of neural firing which has accrued as a residue of the chimpanzee or human infant's past experience. Until the central pattern has been learned, incongruous stimulation is impossible.

Such a conception can well account for Holmes' findings that lower-class children are less fearful than higher-class children and that boys are less fearful than girls even though both lower-class children and boys of nursery school age are likely to have had the wider experience with the sorts of situations used by Holmes to evoke fear. It may well be that being shocked and handled provides a variety of experience which leaves the rat pups which have been subjected to it less disturbed by such things as open fields and 18 hours without water, but these effects may ultimately be found to be a matter of still another mechanism. It is too early to say.

Taking seriously this incongruity-dissonance conception of the genesis of fear leads to interesting reinterpretations of a great many of the motivational phenomena of child development. Consider these few. In considering separation anxiety, the incongruity principle makes it necessary to puzzle about how the absence of mother could be the conditional stimulus for the traumatizing and helpless distress that has been supposed to have occurred in her absence. In considering fear of the dark, it also becomes unnecessary to puzzle about how the absence of light stimulation could so widely have been associated with painful stimulation. Multiple mothering need not be seen as a traumatizing experience in the light of this conception, but rather as an inoculation against social shyness and fear. The timidity of the overprotected child and the social shyness of the rural mountain people get an explanation which has been difficult in terms of the theory of conditioned fear.

MOTIVATION IN TERMS OF THE INCONGRUITY-DISSONANCE PRINCIPLE

This introduction of the incongruity-dissonance principle concludes the three reinterpretations I wish to present today, but I do wish to call your attention to the pervasive character of this incongruity-dissonance principle. It appears to have great explanation power which figures, in one guise or another, in several systematic theories besides that of Hebb, all of which have been characterized as nondynamic.

Hebb's (25) theorizing is physiological, at least in a verbal sense, in that he conceives the residues of past inputs to be stored in semiautonomous, reverberating cerebral circuits which he terms *cell assemblies*. These cell assemblies are the neural analogue of concepts, and they get sequentially integrated into what he calls *phase sequences*. The sequential organization in time provides for the subjective phenomenon of expectation. When markedly incongruous receptor inputs disrupt this sequential organization, behavior is changed and the process is felt as unpleasant emotion. Slight degrees of incongruity, which can readily be accommodated, lend interest and may provide attractive problems, but the larger ones are repelling and perhaps even devastating.

Piaget (55, 56) utilizes very much the same incongruity notion to account for the development of intelligence and concepts in human children. In his system, the child comes at birth with certain sensory-motor coordinations which he terms *schemata*. Variation in stimulus situations call for adaptive *accommodations* or changes in these schemata, which changes are *assimilated* or stored as residues. Piaget also finds limited incongruities between central schemata and receptor inputs to be interesting and facilitative of growth, but incongruities which extend beyond the child's capacity for accommodation instigate withdrawal or fear and even terror. In Piaget's theory the child's gestalt-like conceptions of reality (space, time, and number) are schemata which develop through a continuous process of accommodations and assimilations and become fixed or static only when the child's schemata come to correspond so well with reality that no further accommodations are required. Here agreement among people is dictated by reality.

Helson (27, 28) has called the residues of immediate past experience in the typical psychophysical experiment an *adaptation level*. Both he and McClelland (43) have seen affective arousal to be a matter of the size of the discrepancy between receptor inputs and the adaptation level. Small discrepancies may be attractively pleasant, large ones repellingly unpleasant. As an example, some of you will readily recall having experienced the affective startle that comes when you have been set to pick up what you thought was a full pail, only to find it empty.

Festinger (14) has recently written a book entitled *A Theory of Cognitive Dissonance* in which he shows that a discrepancy between belief about a situation and perception of that situation acts like a drive. The subject acts to reduce the *dissonance* by either withdrawing from the incredible situation or by changing his beliefs, and, not incidentally, he finds the dissonance highly unpleasant.

Rogers (60) has described the basis for anxiety as discrepancy between the "phenomenological field" and the perceived reality as represented by his two circles. Roger's phenomenological field, however, is not the perceptually-given phenomenal field of such German phenomenologists as Delthei and Husserl. It is rather the inferred storehouse of past experience and represented in the present by expectations, aspirations, self-concept, and the like. Thus, his conceptual scheme appears to fall within the domain of the incongruity-dissonance principle.

Kelly's (35) *Psychology of Personal Constructs* also makes central use of this principle. The term *personal constructs* refers to the ways in which individuals construe and anticipate events. These each person derives from the way in which he has experienced such events in the past. When a person's constructions fail to predict events, this is disturbing, even anxiety-producing, and it motivates some kind of change, but the change may take place in defenses against such change of constructs or in avoiding such events, or in the constructs themselves.

Perhaps, it is worth noting in closing that this incongruity-dissonance principle makes both motivation and reinforcement intrinsic to the organism's relations with its environment, intrinsic, if you will, to the organism's information-processing. It is as if the organism operated like an error-actuated, feedback system where the error is derived from discrepancy between receptor-inputs of the present and the residues of past experience which serve as the basis for anticipating the future. The dominant view of the past half century has seen both motivation and reinforcement as extrinsic to the information-processing. This has put a tremendous burden of responsibility for the management of affective motivation on parents, teachers, and all those in positions of authority and control. Visions of man completely controlled, as exemplified by George Orwell's *1984*, are conceivable only by assuming that the extrinsic motivating forces of homeostatic need and painful stimulation are completely dominant. In this light the terror of the baby chimp at seeing his keeper in a Halloween mask and the irritation of the believer when his beliefs are disconfirmed are perhaps symbols of hope. They may justify Abraham Lincoln's well-known dictum that "you can fool some of the people all the time, and all the people some of the time, but you cannot fool all the people all the time."

To return to the cartoon of the lad who was improperly motivated: Perhaps, the task of developing proper motivation is best seen, at least in nutshell form, as limiting the manipulation of extrinsic factors to that minimum of keeping homeostatic need and exteroceptive drive low, in favor of facilitating basic information-processing to maximize accurate anticipation of reality.

REFERENCES

1. Beach, F. A. Current concepts of play in animals. *Amer. Naturalist,* 1945, **79,** 523–541.
2. Bechterev, V. M. *La psychologie objective* (N. Kostyleff, Trans.). Paris: Alcan, 1913.
3. Berlyne, D. E. Novelty and curiosity as determinants of exploratory behavior. *Brit. J. Psychol.,* 1950, **41,** 68–80.
4. Berlyne, D. E. The arousal and satiation of perceptual curiosity in the rat. *J. comp. physiol. Psychol.,* 1955, **48,** 238–246.
5. Bernard, C. *Lecons sur les propriétés physiologiques et les alterations pathologiques des liquides de l'organisme.* Paris: Ballière, 1859. 2 vols.
6. Bexton, W. H., Heron, W., & Scott, T. H. Effects of decreased variation in the sensory environment. *Canad. J. Psychol.,* 1954, **8,** 70–76.
7. Butler, R. A. Discrimination learning by rhesus monkeys to visual-exploration motivation. *J. comp. physiol. Psychol.,* 1953, **46,** 95–98.
8. Butler, R. A. Discrimination learning by rhesus monkeys to auditory incentives. *J. comp. physiol. Psychol.,* 1957, **50,** 239–241.

9. Canestrini, S. Uber das Sinnesleben des Neugebornen. In Alzheimer, A., & Lewandowsky, M. (Eds.), *Monogr. Gesamt. Neurol. Psychiat.* (Heft 5), Berlin: Springer, 1913.

10. Cannon, W. B. *Bodily changes in pain, hunger, fear, and rage.* New York: Appleton-Century, 1915.

11. Dashiell, J. *Fundamentals of objective psychology.* Boston: Houghton Mifflin, 1928.

12. Davis, R. C., & Buchwald, A. M. An exploration of somatic response patterns: stimulus and sex differences. *J. comp. physiol. Psychol.*, 1957, **50**, 44–52.

13. Dollard, J., & Miller, N. E. *Personality and psychotherapy.* New York: McGraw-Hill, 1950.

14. Festinger, L. *A theory of cognitive dissonance.* Evanston, Ill.: Row, Peterson, 1957.

15. Freud, S. The interpretation of dreams (1900). In *The basic writings of Sigmund Freud* (A. A. Brill Trans.). New York: Modern Library, 1938. Pp. 179–548.

16. Freud, S. Three contributions to the theory of sex (1905). In *The basic writings of Sigmund Freud.* (A. A. Brill, Trans.). New York: Modern Library, 1938. Pp. 553–629.

17. Freud, S. Instincts and their vicissitudes (1915). In *Collected papers.* Vol. IV. London: Hogarth, 1950. Pp. 60–83.

18. Freud, S. *Inhibition, sympton, and anxiety* (1926). (Translated by H. A. Bunker as *The Problem of Anxiety.*) New York: Norton, 1936.

19. Granit, R. *Receptors and sensory perception.* New Haven: Yale Univer. Press, 1955.

20. Harlow, H. F. Learning and satiation of response in intrinsically motivated complex puzzle performance by monkeys. *J. comp. physiol. Psychol.*, 1950, **43**, 289–294.

21. Harlow, H. F. Motivation as a factor in the acquisition of new responses. In *Current theory and research in motivation: a symposium.* Lincoln: Univer. of Nebraska Press, 1953. Pp. 24–49.

22. Harlow, H. F. The nature of love. *Amer. Psychologist*, 1958, **13**, 673–685.

23. Harlow, H. F., Harlow, M. K., & Meyer D. R. Learning motivated by a manipulation Drive. *J. exp. Psychol.*, 1950, **40**, 228–234.

24. Hebb, D. O. On the nature of fear. *Psychol. Rev.*, 1946, **53**, 259–276.

25. Hebb, D. O. *The organization of behavior.* New York: Wiley, 1949.

26. Hebb, D. O. Drives and the CNS (conceptual nervous system). *Psychol. Rev.*, 1955, **62**, 243–254.

27. Helson, H. Adaptation-level as frame of reference for prediction of psychophysical data. *Amer. J. Psychol.*, 1947, **60**, 1–29.

28. Helson, H. Adaptation-level as a basis for a quantitative theory of frames of reference. *Psychol. Rev.*, 1948, **55**, 297–313.

29. Holmes, Frances B. An experimental study of the fears of young children. In A. T. Jersild & Frances B. Holmes. Children's fears. *Child Developm. Monogr.*, 1935, **20**, 167–296.

30. Hull, C. L. *Principles of behavior.* New York: Appleton-Century, 1943.

31. Hunt, J. McV. The effects of infant feeding-frustration upon adult hoarding in the albino rat. *J. abnorm. soc. Psychol.*, 1941, **36**, 338–360.
32. Hunt, J. McV., Schlosberg, H., Solomon, R. L., & Stellar, E. Studies on the effects of infantile experience on adult behavior in rats: I. Effects of infantile feeding frustration on adult hoarding. *J. comp. physiol. Psychol.*, 1947, **40**, 291–304.
33. Jasper, H. H. Electrical signs of cortical activity. *Psychol. Bull.*, 1937, **34**, 411–481.
34. Jones, H. E., & Jones, Mary C. A study of fear. *Child Educ.*, 1928, **5**, 136–143.
35. Kelly, G. A. *The psychology of personal constructs.* New York: Norton, 1955.
36. Lacey, J. I., & Lacey, Beatrice C. The relationship of resting autonomic activity to motor impulsivity. In *The brain and human behavior.* Baltimore: Williams & Wilkins, 1958. Pp. 144–209.
37. Levine, S. Infantile experience and consummatory behavior in adulthood. *J. comp. physiol. Psychol.*, 1957, **50**, 609–612.
38. Levine, S. Infantile experience and resistance to physical stress. *Science*, 1957, **126**, 405.
39. Levine, S. Noxious stimulation in infant and adult rats and consummatory behavior. *J. comp. physiol. Psychol.*, 1958, **51**, 230–233.
40. Levine, S., Chevalier, J. A., & Korchin, S. J. The effects of shock and handling in infancy on later avoidance learning. *J. Pers.*, 1956, **24**, 475–493.
41. Lilly, J. C. Mental effects of reduction of ordinary levels of physical stimuli on intact, healthy persons. *Psychiat. Res. Rep.*, 1956 (5), 1–9.
42. Lindsley, D. B. Psychophysiology and motivation. In M. R. Jones (Ed.), *Nebraska symposium on motivation.* Lincoln: Univer. of Nebraska Press, 1957. Pp. 44–105.
43. McClelland, D. C., Atkinson, J. W., Clark, R. A., & Lowell, E. L. *The achievement motive.* New York: Appleton-Century-Crofts, 1953.
44. McDougall, W. *An introduction to social psychology.* Boston: Luce, 1915.
45. Miller, N. E. An experimental investigation of acquired drives. *Psychol. Bull.*, 1941, **38**, 534–535.
46. Miller, N. E. Studies of fear as an acquirable drive: I. Fear as motivation and fear-reduction as reinforcement in the learning of new responses. *J. exp. Psychol.*, 1948, **38**, 89–101.
47. Miller, N. E., & Dollard, J. *Social learning and imitation.* New Haven: Yale Univer. Press, 1941.
48. Montgomery, K. C. The relation between exploratory behavior and spontaneous alternation in the white rat. *J. comp. physiol. Psychol.*, 1951, **44**, 582–589.
49. Montgomery, K. C. The effect of the hunger and thirst drives upon exploratory behavior. *J. comp. physiol. Psychol.*, 1953, **46**, 315–319.
50. Montgomery, K. C., & Monkman, J. A. The relation between fear and exploratory behavior. *J. comp. physiol. Psychol.*, 1955, **48**, 132–136.
51. Mussen, P. H., & Conger, J. J. *Child development and personality.* New York: Harper, 1956.

52. Olds, J. Physiological mechanisms of reward. In M. R. Jones (Ed.), *Nebraska symposium on motivation*. Lincoln: Univer. of Nebraska Press, 1955. Pp. 73–139.

53. Olds, J., & Milner, P. Positive reinforcement produced by electrical stimulation of septal area and other regions of the rat brain. *J. comp. physiol. Psychol.*, 1954, **47**, 419–427.

54. Pavlov, I. P. *Conditioned reflexes.* (G. V. Anrep, Trans.) Oxford: Oxford Univer. Press, 1927.

55. Piaget, J. *The origins of intelligence in children.* New York: International Universities Press, 1952.

56. Piaget, J. *The construction of reality in the child.* (Margaret Cook, Trans.) New York: Basic Books, 1954.

57. Pratt, K. C. The neonate. In L. Carmichael (Ed.), *Manual of child psychology.* (2nd. ed.) New York: Wiley, 1954. Pp. 215–291.

58. Prosser, C. L. Action potentials in the nervous system of the crayfish: I. Spontaneous impulses. *J. cell. comp. Physiol.*, 1934, **4**, 185–209.

59. Richter, C. P. Animal behavior and internal drives. *Quart. Rev. Biol.*, 1927, **2**, 307–343.

60. Rogers, C. R. *Client-centered therapy.* Boston: Houghton Mifflin, 1951.

61. Sheffield, F. D., Roby, T. B., & Campbell, B. A. Drive reduction versus consummatory behavior as determinants of reinforcement. *J. comp. physiol. Psychol.*, 1954, **47**, 349–355.

62. Sheffield, F. D., Wulff, J. J., & Backer, R. Reward value of copulation without sex drive reduction. *J. comp. physiol. Psychol.*, 1951, **44**, 3–8.

63. Solomon, R. L., & Brush, Elinor S. Experimentally derived conceptions of anxiety and aversion. In M. R. Jones (Ed.), *Nebraska symposium on motivation*. Lincoln: Univer. of Nebraska Press, 1956. Pp. 212–305.

64. Solomon, R. L., & Wynne, L. C. Traumatic avoidance learning: acquisition in normal dogs. *Psychol. Monogr.*, 1953, **67**, No. 4 (Whole No. 354).

65. Thorndike, E. L. *Educational psychology.* Vol. I, *The original nature of man;* Vol. II, *The psychology of learning.* New York: Teachers Coll., 1913.

66. Watson, J. B. *Psychological care of the infant and child.* New York: Norton, 1928.

67. Watson, J. B., & Raynor, Rosalie. Conditional reactions. *J. exp. Psychol.*, 1920, **3**, 1–4.

68. Woodworth, R. S. *Dynamic psychology.* New York: Columbia Univer. Press, 1918.

69. Young, P. T. The role of hedonic processes in motivation. In M. R. Jones (Ed.), *Nebraska symposium on motivation*. Lincoln: Univer. of Nebraska Press, 1955. Pp. 193–237.

ON THE NATURE OF FEAR

D. O. Hebb

MC GILL UNIVERSITY

IN THE COURSE of an experiment dealing with individual differences of behavior among chimpanzees, observations of fear were made which held an immediate interest. Besides extending the information concerning the causes of anthropoid fear which is provided by the work of Kohler (23), Jacobsen, Jacobsen and Yoshioka (17), Yerkes and Yerkes (42), Haslerud (10), McCulloch and Haslerud (31) and Hebb and Riesen (14), the new data brought up again the question of mechanism. Analysis of the behavior leads, in the present discussion, to a review of the whole problem and an attempt to formulate an hypothesis of the causes and nature of fear.

NATURE OF THE DATA

Validity and reliability. The validity of naming fear in chimpanzees, or recognizing something in animals which can be identified with fear in man, and the reliability of naming have been discussed elsewhere (13). There it was shown that the recognition of emotion in an animal is possible in the same way as in another human being. Fear named in an animal means either that there was actual avoidance of some object or place, or that the observer inferred from incidental behavior ("associated signs") that avoidance was imminent and likely to appear with further stimulation. When such inferences are made with confidence by experienced observers, it appears that they are valid and reliable, the criterion being the animal's subsequent behavior.

Definition of fear behavior. The symbol "W," for withdrawal, was recorded when the animal actually moved away from a test object in such a way as to show that he did not move by coincidence, but was re-

From the Yerkes Laboratories of Primate Biology. Reprinted from *Psychological Review* (1946), **53**, 259–276, by permission of the author and the American Psychological Association.

sponding to the test situation. The evidence was of several kinds: (1) when change of position of the test object produced a corresponding movement of the animal, maintaining his distance from it; (2) when the original movement was abrupt and coincided exactly with the appearance of the test object; (3) when there was coincident evidence of unusual excitation, such as erection of hair, screaming, threatening gestures directed at the test object, or continued orientation of gaze at the object, while moving directly away from it. On occasions one of these three forms of evidence alone, if exceptionally clear, might provide the basis for an entry of "W" in the record; usually, at least two were present before the entry was made. In many instances the experimenter was certain that an animal would be afraid to approach the test object, but did not record his opinion since the formal behavioral criteria were not met.

EXPERIMENTAL METHOD

The experimental procedures were part of a study of individual differences of emotionality and temperament, and not planned to meet the problem of defining the adequate stimulus to fear. Thus the range of test objects was limited, and the order in which they were presented does not permit an exact comparison of the excitatory value of each.

Test objects. The test objects were representations of animals, from reptile to man, varying considerably in completeness and verisimilitude. They fall in three classes: picture, primate, and nonprimate objects. It was not expected that the pictures would induce fear—they were used for another purpose—but they were presented in the same way as the other objects and consequently are useful as control material.

Primate objects. There were 9 objects representing primates. The responses to these are the main interest of the study.

1. An adult chimpanzee head, three-fifths life size, made of papier-mâché, and painted to appear reasonably lifelike.
2. An unclothed doll representing a human infant, one-half life size.
3. An infant chimpanzee's head and shoulders, nearly life size, modelled in wax and painted—about as lifelike as the adult chimpanzee head.
4. The cadaver of a chimpanzee infant, newborn, fixed in formalin.
5. A lifelike full-sized human head from a window-display dummy.
6. The skull of a 5-year-old chimpanzee, with movable jaw controlled by a string.
7. The roughly mounted skin of a spider monkey, with head and shoulders movable by means of string.

8. An unpainted plaster of Paris cast of the visage of an adult chim-
    panzee without the ears or the rest of the head, made from a death
    mask.
9. The cured and flexible hide of a 5-year-old chimpanzee, somewhat
    denuded of hair; the proportions of the skin about the head and face
    were distorted out of recognition, but the hands and feet were
    recognizable.

The pictures are not described in detail, since they are important
here only as 14 emotionally unexciting objects, presented in the same way
as the others.

Nonprimate objects varied greatly in verisimilitude, from a careful
replica of a snake to a bug which was a rectangular block of wood on
coiled-spring legs.

1. A dog's head and forequarters, of cloth, slipped over the hand and
    manipulated from inside with the fingers; this common toy is sur-
    prisingly lifelike in its movements.
2. A model of an imaginary white grub, 4 inches long, with long white
    legs.
3. A grub identical in proportions and color, one-third as large.
4. A rubber tube, ½ inch in diameter, 24 inches long, with a roughly
    carved wooden snake's head at one end; so mounted, with string in-
    side the tube, that it could be given a snakelike movement without
    apparent external agency.
5. A rectangular wooden bug, 6 inches long. It was capable of an
    oscillating movement, since it was mounted on six coiled-wire legs,
    and had oscillating antennae.
6. A grasshopper, a mechanical toy with moving legs.
7. A similar turtle.
8. A rubber dog, 3½ inches high.
9. A brightly colored cloth dog, 7 inches high.
10. A painted wax replica of a coiled 24-inch snake.

Procedure. Test objects were presented to the animals while they
were in their own living cages. The animal or pair of animals was first
brought to the front of the cage by an offer of a small amount of food.
The hinged top and front of the presentation box (which was wheeled
from cage to cage) was then lifted, exposing one test object to the chimpanzee. At the end of 15 seconds the test object was set in motion if it
had movable parts; if not, it was moved forward about 6 inches nearer

the animal. The presentation box was closed at the end of another 15 seconds; total exposure was thus 30 seconds. The box had three compartments, and three objects were shown in succession on each experimental period, once or twice a week. The objects were shown to all animals in the same order with the same time intervals.

EXPERIMENTAL RESULTS

With a fixed order of presentation to all subjects, there is a probability that the serial position of a test object will affect the degree of response to it, either by negative adaptation or cumulative effect. There were marked indications that such effects occurred. Some animals apparently learned that the test objects, at first terrifying, would not move out of the presentation box; others began to show fear in the later trials before the box was opened at all.

The total number of animals making fear responses to any object, therefore, is not a wholly satisfactory index of its relative effectiveness in provoking fear. However, there is evidence that the amount of such error is limited. In each group of three objects one or more pictures were included. The number of avoidance responses was consistently low for these pictures, while remaining high for objects, such as dog or snake, known from the work of others (Yerkes, Haslerud) to be fear provoking. This means that transfer or generalization effects were limited. Also there was no sign of a steady increase or decrease of fear responses as the experiment progressed. The animals' responses were highly selective. Preliminary observations, and tests made after the completion of the experiment, also make it clear that such objects as a head without the body attached are in themselves capable of eliciting panic, and that the number of fear responses to human or chimpanzee head, recorded experimentally, is not due to an association of these test objects with the others.

Table 1 presents the number of fear responses to each test object, separating primate, pictorial and nonprimate objects. The table gives the order of presentation and also shows which three objects were grouped together for each test period. It is assumed, partly on the basis of evidence not presented here, that what particular pictures were used is irrelevant and that the number of animals avoiding the pictures is an index of the "spread" of fear from exciting to neutral objects. From a total of 30 animals the mean number making fear responses to each primate test object was 9.6; to pictures, 0.9; to nonprimate objects, 6.7. These scores, it must be remembered, are the number of actual overt

TABLE 1. *Number of Animals (From a Total of 30) Making Fear Responses to Primate Test Objects, Pictures, and Nonprimate Objects*

		Primate		Picture	Nonprimate	
Test	I	Adult ape head	7	0	dog head (M)*	10
	II	Doll	4	1	large grub	3
	III	Infant ape head	3	2	rubber tube (M)	3
	IV	Infant	1	1	wood-wire bug (M)	3
	V	—		0	mechanical grasshopper (M)	4
	VI	Human head	12	1	rubber dog	5
	VII	Skull (M)	24	0	—	
		Monkey (M)	16			
	VIII	—		4	small grub	2
	IX	Cast of ape visage	14	4	mechanical turtle (M)	8
	X	Ape hide	5	0	cloth dog	8
	XI	—		0	—	
				0		
				0		
				0	Cast of snake	21
	Total		86	13		67
	Mean		9.6	0.9		6.7

* (M) Indicates that the object was put in motion during the presentation period.

withdrawals which met the criteria set up in advance for a definable fear response. They take no account of signs of fear which were peculiar to an individual animal. Also, they are the number of such responses made while animal and test object were separated by a stout wire mesh. Tests in other circumstances show a higher percentage of avoidance, and show also that the relative effectiveness of two objects as causes of fear may vary somewhat according to the mode of presentation. In the conditions of the experiment, the following are the most effective stimuli, in descending order: *skull* (with moving jaw); painted wax *snake; monkey* (with moving head); plaster cast of *chimpanzee visage;* and *human head.* Least exciting are, in ascending order: chimpanzee infant; small wax grub; infant chimpanzee head; large wax grub; moving rubber tube (snake); and moving wood-and-wire bug.

SUPPLEMENTARY OBSERVATIONS

The chimpanzee's fear of toy animals and snakes is of course well known (23, 42). The data which are new and which were the occasion of this report are those showing that the chimpanzee is excited by, and avoids, parts of chimpanzee or human bodies. It was evident that such a conclusion had important implications, and that further observations would be desirable as a control of the data. Control observations, accordingly, were made after the formal experiment was completed. Their purpose was to discover whether some peculiarity of the actual experimental objects, or some detail of procedure, might have been the true cause of fear; or whether the behavior falls into a more general class related to the common human avoidance of a mutilated face and of dead bodies.

Preliminary experiments had already shown that all the adult chimpanzees were excited at the first sight of a chimpanzee head modelled in clay and carried in the hand from cage to cage. A majority showed avoidance, which was outright panic in five or six of the thirty subjects. In the supplementary observations an unpainted plaster cast of the clay model, and also an actual head from a dead chimpanzee, produced definite avoidance.

With different presentations the results were essentially the same, although intensity of response varied, in part with adaptation to sight of so many similar objects. Avoidance was observed when a head was carried by hand; when it was exposed by removing a cloth or opening a box; and when the head was first put in the chimpanzee's cage and the animal admitted afterward. In another observation the head was placed behind a small ledge, so that the actual termination of the neck was not visible (although the chimpanzee "knew" from familiarity with the cage in which the test was made that there was no space large enough for a body beneath the head). The chimpanzee was then admitted from a detaining inner room from which none of the preparations could be seen. A marked fear response occurred immediately, before the lapse of enough time to make the unresponsiveness of the head abnormal. Thus lack of movement in the test object did not determine the fear, nor yet an actual perception of the termination of the neck.

A painted human eye and eyebrow (sawn from a plaster manikin's head) produced marked avoidance.

Finally, observations were made with anesthetized chimpanzees as stimulus objects. Four adults were shown an anesthetized infant, two years old, carried by two members of the staff. The infant was recovering from nembutal, and made some spontaneous movements of an arm and hand. Three of the four adults were very excited and one at least afraid, in spite of the fact that they had often seen young chimpanzees being carried by the staff. A more deeply anesthetized adult was taken on a low, flat, two-wheeled barrow up to the cages of nine of the adults. Definite fear was shown by six, aggression (possibly related to fear) by two others, and the remaining animal was almost certainly afraid but remained at a distance without showing definable avoidance.

The fear evoked by a detached face or head in the formal experiment, therefore, was not a product of some uncontrolled detail of procedure or of the construction of the test objects. Any of a number of related stimuli have the same effect, in a number of situations.

From the data it appears that *either* lack of responsiveness in a whole animal, *or* an evident lack of a body when the head or part of the head is seen, can determine the fear. The first conclusion depends on the observations with anesthetized animals as stimuli. The second follows from the fact that avoidance of an isolated head was immediate and certainly was not delayed long enough for an unusual unresponsiveness, as such, to have become apparent before fear occurred.

SPONTANEITY OF THE FEAR

The fears observed must also have been spontaneous,[1] and not conditioned by some association of the test objects with a more primitive source of fear such as pain. This is shown by the following considerations.

There are two ways in which fear of a detached head or an anesthetized animal could be due to learning. Fear might occur (1) because the subjects recognized part of a whole which they had learned to fear in the past, or (2) because of an earlier association of a class of objects (detached heads, abnormally unresponsive chimpanzees) with a more primitive cause of fear.

1. The first explanation can be ruled out. The dummy human head represented an ordinary young man whom the adults of the colony might have teased or injured, as they often tend to do with strangers whose general appearance is similar to that of members of the laboratory staff, but whom they would not have feared. The cast of a face was a faithful replica of the chimpanzee Lita's, made from a death mask. She had died not long before the experiment began, and certainly would not have been a source of fear to any of the other chimpanzees with cage wire intervening, as in the conditions of the experiment. The anesthetized in-

[1] The term "spontaneous" is used here to mean that the fear is not built up by association, as a learned response. The term is not synonymous with "innate" since there are definite factors of past experience involved. . . .

fant in his normal state would not have been feared by an adult; and
the anesthetized adult who was used as a stimulus object was Don, who
is dominated by almost all of the other adults of the colony. The test object which aroused fear therefore did not do so because it was recognized
as part of a whole which in its normal completeness would have caused
the response.

2. The second possibility to be examined is that an association had
been formed earlier between the class of stimulus objects and some
event such as pain, loud noise, or a fall. For animals born in the bush and
captured when their mothers were killed this was a real possibility. But
nine of the adolescent and adult subjects of the experiment were born
and reared in captivity and definitely had no opportunity to make such
associations. None of these had seen a detached human or chimpanzee
head; a few of them had seen a dead chimpanzee, but no more primitive cause of fear would be associated with the sight. The nine animals
who are known not to have such associations showed on the average
rather more frequent and stronger avoidance than the remaining twenty-
one animals.

These facts require the conclusion that the fears discussed are spontaneous. Further support for the conclusion is found in the behavior of
human beings.

HUMAN AVOIDANCE OF MUTILATED AND DEAD BODIES

Human emotional responses to the dead and to such things as the
sight of a major operation or of a badly mutilated face cannot reasonably
be attributed to conditioning. The responses tend to be strongest on the
first experience, which eliminates direct conditioning as an explanation
and requires the supporting assumption of a preliminary verbal conditioning which forms the whole basis of the response. But if avoidance
were so readily established, with no innate tendency toward fear of the
conditioned stimulus itself, one could easily keep children from playing
in dangerous places or train adults to drive automobiles carefully—by
verbal instruction alone. This is the essence of Valentine's (39) brilliant
criticism of Watsonian theory and my rejection of the explanation by
conditioning rests upon his argument. What he did was to show how easy
it is to condition fear of some things, how hard with others, and thus
demonstrated the existence of emotional susceptibilities which are the
basis of spontaneous and almost spontaneous fears.

Watson's (40) theory of fear has rightly had a profound effect upon psychological thought, and a radical departure from his ideas is not easily accepted. Yet the present situation is that the theory has been demolished, with no good substitute in sight. Jones and Jones' (22) experiment on the human fear of snakes constituted a strong and radical attack on Watson's theory. The evidence adduced by Valentine (39) reinforced the attack with evidence from a variety of fears. He has shown that there is a wide range of situations, not easily defined or classified, which have some tendency to evoke human fear. Finally, Hebb and Riesen (14) have shown the existence of a spontaneous fear of strangers in infant chimpanzees, where the customary appeal to the subject's unknown past experience is impossible and the explanation by conditioning ruled out.

Watson's work, consequently, provides no more than a starting point in determining the causes of fear and gives no reason to reject the conclusion that human fear of dead or mutilated bodies is spontaneous. The conclusion is also not affected by the fact that an almost complete adaptation to such stimuli is possible, nor by the fact that some persons may not have an emotional disturbance at their first sight of an operation, autopsy, or dissection. It has sometimes been assumed that if a fear is not general it must have been learned by those who do have it: that an innate fear should be found in all persons. This argument of course is quite invalid in view of the existence of individual genetic differences, and it has been seen that some of the chimpanzee fears discussed in this paper are not found in all animals and yet cannot be ascribed to learning.

The evidence, therefore, is that both in man and in chimpanzee there occur spontaneous fears of mutilated and unresponsive bodies. The chimpanzee knows nothing of anesthesia, has no abstract conception of death, and presumably may confuse a model of a head and the real thing. Considering the intellectual differences between the species and the extent to which man's behavior is influenced by speech, one must say that human and chimpanzee fear susceptibilities, with dismembered or inert bodies as stimulus objects, are remarkably similar. In this fact there is further support for the idea that such fears are spontaneous and not associative or conditioned.

So that this conclusion will be seen in the proper perspective, the reader is reminded that the importance of learning is not minimized. There are essential factors of past experience in the fears which have been discussed; and the hypothesis which is to be presented lays a good deal of emphasis on learning as an element in the development of any fear.

CENTRAL VERSUS SENSORY FACTORS DETERMINING FEAR

The first step in an analysis of fear is a better definition of the problem and of its relation to other psychological investigations.

It should be specified that the problem is not simply that of the subcortical motor integration of fear behavior. The earlier studies of Bard (2) had the effect of concentrating attention on the hypothalamus, but it is now evident that more must be taken into account. The analysis by Lashley (24) and Masserman (32) has limited the emotional functions of the diencephalon to a motor integration. More recently, Bard (3) has described rage in a cat lacking *only* the hypothalamic region which he formerly considered to be essential to emotional activity. In view also of the marked differences of the stimuli which are effective in each case, and the absence of "after-discharge" in the decorticate preparation, it is evident that the processes of normal and decorticate emotions cannot be equated. Fear behavior has been demonstrated by Bard in the decorticate cat, but only with auditory stimuli. An essential problem remains in understanding cortico-subcortical interaction and the important role of perception in the fear responses of the normal animal.

The evidence presented has shown that the chimpanzee's fear of a detached head is in some way related to the physical lack of an attached body or of movement or both. But our real interest is not in the physical properties of the stimulus object but in the way they act on the organism. The first question to be asked concerns the existence of a sensory control of the response: can one find any property of the sensory excitation which in itself determines the occurrence and form of the response?

The answer seems to be no. In the first place, the physical lack in the stimulus object cannot be equated with a sensory lack by saying that the sight of a head without the normally associated sight of a body causes fear, for the statement would not be true. When a chimpanzee sees a man's head only, without movement and with the rest of the man's body out of sight behind a door, he is not afraid. There are certainly sensory cues which distinguish the two situations (i.e., detached head *vs.* attached head with body hidden) but I have not been able to find any generalization that distinguishes the purely sensory[2] event which causes fear from the one which does not. In the second place, it has been shown that the fears are spontaneous. If they were also sensorily determined, it

---

[2] "Sensory" in the present discussion is defined as referring to activity, in afferent structures, which is directly determined by environmental events; roughly, activity in the receptor organ and afferent tracts, up to and including the corresponding sensory projection area.

would follow that there are innate connections from the sensory cells, excited in seeing any chimpanzee or human head, to the motor centers determining avoidance; or in a more gestalt formulation, that the dynamic properties of every such sensory excitation have an innately selective action on those particular motor centers. It would follow further that this sensori-motor relationship is consistently inhibited and nonfunctional throughout the animal's lifetime, no matter how many times he sees a human or chimpanzee head, unless by chance the head has been cut off from its owner. The improbability of such ideas is evident. They seem to be a product of the assumption (quite reasonable in itself) that the form of a response is fully determined by the sensory event that precipitates it: since a physical lack in the stimulus object cannot excite receptor cells, the assumption means that the part of the stimulus object which is present is an adequate excitant of fear, and, since the whole object does not cause fear, that the part which is missing is normally an inhibitor or in some way prevents an innately determined response to the other part. Such reasoning will be found to lead rapidly to absurdities. Doubt is then cast on the original assumption, and the alternative conclusion is indicated that the determinant of certain strongly marked anthropoid fears is not any property of the sensory excitation alone but may have to be sought in some interaction of sensory events with other cerebral processes.

This argument depends on the accuracy of the analysis which has been made of the stimulating conditions in which fear of dismembered or inert bodies is observed. Other interpretations are possible, but seem either to beg the question or to amount to the same thing. (One might say, for example, that it is strangeness or mysteriousness that produces fear of a decapitated head and of an inert chimpanzee being carried by human beings. Actually, reference to strangeness only strengthens the preceding argument, as we shall see in a moment.) Nevertheless, it would be unwise to depend too strongly on the evidence of behavior into which so many complicating factors of experience may enter. Let us turn to fear of strangers (*14*) and of sudden noise (*8*). The theoretical interpretation suggested by fear of a dismembered body gains decisive support from these other observations and in turn makes their theoretical significance clearer.

The growing chimpanzee is persistently afraid of strange persons, objects and places, although the response is not always predictable in the individual case. Hebb and Riesen (*14*) have shown that the fear of strangers by chimpanzee infants is spontaneous and cannot be accounted

for as a conditioned response. Also, a slight change of clothing may produce fear of a familiar attendant who was not feared before. To assume
that the form of the response on seeing something strange is controlled
alone by some property of the sensory event is to assume that *any* visual
excitation is primarily a cause of fear and that other responses are sub-
stituted merely by repetition of the stimulation. Fear of strangers would
mean that the visual excitation from any human or chimpanzee face
(strange chimpanzees are feared as much as strange men) or any pattern
of clothing is an innately adequate excitant of fear; for any pattern whatever may be strange, depending on accidents of experience. The idea
seems absurd in itself, and is definitely contradicted by observations of
the behavior of an infant chimpanzee blindfolded from birth to the age
of four months, when the avoidance of strangers by normal animals is
beginning (Nissen).[3] In Senden's (35) comprehensive review of the literature on persons born blind and given their sight after infancy, there
is no mention of fear aroused by the first visual form-perception; and
Dennis (7) explicitly denies that fear occurs in these persons. Fear of a
strange person is, therefore, not determined by a particular property of the
sensory excitation, but by some discrepancy of the pattern from those
which have been frequently experienced by the subject—by a complex
relationship, that is, of the sensory event to preexistent cerebral processes.

A similar meaning lies in the fact noted by English (8) that a noise
must be sudden to cause fear. When auditory intensity is built up gradually, the response is hard to elicit. The same is true of loss of support. An
unexpected drop is the one that causes fear, not one for which preparation
has been made verbally or by playful swinging of infant subjects. Jones
(21) has shown that unexpectedness is an essential feature of a number
of fear-provoking situations. In all such fears the major determinant cannot be the afferent excitation alone but involves a relationship of that
excitation to concurrent cerebral activity.

These facts actually raise no new theoretical issue. Their effect is
to sharpen the definition of a problem which has been formulated in various ways by other writers. That both sensory and central processes are
involved in the control of behavior and must be distinguished for theoretical purposes is implied by the concept of "operants" (Skinner, 37) and of
"stimulus trace" (Hull, 16) no less than by the "expectancy" of Cowles
and Nissen (6), Mowrer (34) and Hilgard and Marquis (15). It is the
real problem of attention and of the selectivity of response to the several

[3] Personal communication from Dr. H. W. Nissen. The experiment was not an
investigation of emotional behavior, and detailed records on this point were not
kept. But it is known with certainty that there was no avoidance evoked by the
chimpanzee's first visual perception of human beings.

properties of a sensory event (Leeper, 27; Lashley, 26). The problem is made explicit by Hilgard and Marquis's "central process which seems relatively independent of afferent stimuli," Beach's (4) "central excitatory mechanism," and Morgan's (33) "central motive state." Every serious attempt in recent years to analyze the neural mechanisms of the more complex forms of behavior has found the need of distinguishing, as more or less independent factors, sensory and central states or processes; in other words, of denying that the direction of transmission of a sensory excitation is determined by the properties of that excitation alone, even when the stable changes of learning have been taken into account. This is thoroughly consistent also with modern electro-physiology. All parts of the brain are continuously active and there are reasons for believing that the activity may be self-maintaining, and even self-initiating (1, 18, 29, 30, 41). An afferent excitation does *not* arouse inactive tissue, but modifies an activity already in existence. The conclusion, therefore, that there are nonsensory factors in the determination of certain fears agrees with existing theory.

It must be added that the conclusion is not necessarily trivial. Current opinion recognizes the necessity of postulating central determinants of behavior but it has done so reluctantly, always with reference to a single, rather narrow aspect of behavioral theory, and apparently without recognizing how generally the necessity has actually cropped up in psychological analysis. The preceding discussion may do no more than suggest a change of emphasis, but the change is one which, as I shall try to show, has a considerable effect on theory. Besides drawing attention to facts of behavior which are usually forgotten, it reveals some order in the facts and makes possible a coherent hypothesis of the nature of fear.

DEVELOPMENT OF AN HYPOTHESIS

Avoidance of strangers provides a possible starting point for a theory of the nature of fear. An essential feature of the stimulating conditions is the divergence of the object avoided from a familiar group of objects, while still having enough of their properties to fall within the same class. It is a most important fact that the fear or shyness does not develop at first vision, as the already cited data of Nissen, Senden (35), and Dennis (7) have shown. Common experience indicates also that the fear is minimized or absent if the growing infant has always been exposed to sight of a large number of persons. It is therefore dependent on the fact that certain perceptions have become habitual, a limited number of central neural reactions to the sight of human beings having been established with great specificity by repeated experience. The idea that there are such habits of perception was developed by Gibson (9) and further supported by later studies of the effect of set upon perception (5, 27, 43). A number of facts relating to the development of intelligence, and its changes with advancing age, have the same import (11, pp. 286, 289). From this point of view, it might be proposed that fear occurs when an object is seen which is like familiar objects in enough respects to arouse habitual processes of perception, but in other respects arouses incompatible processes.

Such a treatment of the fear of strangers would amount to an interference, incongruity, or conflict theory. It might subsume fear of mutilated bodies as well, by classifying them as strange objects, and could be extended to cover fears due to pain and sudden loud noise, which obviously tend to disrupt concurrent psychological processes. But farther than this such a conflict theory will not go. There might be some difficulty in applying it even to the fear of strange objects, when the strangeness is apparently due to incompleteness in a familiar object (as with the chimpanzee's fear of a detached head); and conflict cannot account for causes of fear such as darkness (39) in which a sensory deficit is the effective condition, or nutritional disturbance (38).

Moreover, a fundamental question would remain as to the meaning of "conflict," and why an incompatibility between two perceptions should produce the incoordinations of emotional behavior. This is the crucial question, and in trying to answer it I believe we can find the possibility of a more comprehensive hypothesis, according to which conflict is only one of several ways in which a true source of fear occurs. If two perceptual processes, which cannot coexist, cannot even alternate without producing gross disturbances of behavior (which is what the conflict notion implies), ordinary unemotional behavior must depend on an essential temporal integration in cerebral processes, and fear may be a direct result of their disorganization. Let us ask what such ideas would involve.

It has already been seen that sensory and central processes contribute separately to the control of behavior. For convenience, let us designate the specific pattern of cellular activity throughout the thalamo-cortical system, at any one moment, as a "phase." Behavior is directly correlated with a phase sequence which is temporally organized (4), in part by the inherent properties of the system (the constitutional factor) and in part by the time relations of various afferent excitations in the past (the factor of experience). The spatial organization of each phase, the actual anatomical pattern of cells which are active at any moment, would be affected by the present afferent excitation also. Subjectively, the phase sequence would be identified with the train of thought and perception. Now each phase is determined by a neural interaction, between the preceding phase and the concurrent afferent excitations. Lorente De Nó's (29) discussion of the dynamics of neural action shows that two or more simultaneous neural events might reinforce each other's effects and contribute to a single, determinate pattern of subsequent cerebral activity; or on the contrary might be indeterminate, in the sense that slight changes of timing and intensity could lead to marked and sudden fluctuations of pattern. A phase sequence, that is, could be stable or unstable, and one can assume that vacillating, unpredictable, and incoordinated behavior is the expression of unstable cerebral activity. Also, the effect of learning in general is to increase the predictability and coordination of behavior. The element of learning in emotional behavior will be discussed more specifically, but in the meantime we may speak of the cerebral processes controlling predictable, coordinated behavior as "organized," and recognize the tendency of learning to establish and maintain cerebral organization.

Disorganization could occur in several ways, some of which may be called conflict. (1) A sensory event might disrupt the concurrent phase sequence. The event might be one whose facilitation has been integrated into other phase sequences, and disruptive only because it is "unexpected." If so the disruption would be brief, another well-organized phase sequence would be promptly established, and one would speak of the subject as having only been "startled." The disruption would be brief but it would occur; a well-organized phase could not be set up instantaneously, independent of facilitation from the preceding phase. On the other hand, the sensory event might fail to set up another organized sequence, and so initiate a prolonged disturbance; or might, like loud noise, and especially pain, tend persistently to break down cerebral organization. (2) Simultaneous sensory events might have facilitations which are enough unlike to make the following phase sequence unstable, even though each event separately might be capable of integration with the concurrent phase. Evidently (1) and (2) would be modes of conflict, one sensory-central, the other sensory-sensory.[4] But disorganization might also

---

[4] Logically, another category of "central-central" conflict would be possible, which might have some meaning with regard to emotional disturbances and anxiety arising from a conflict of ideas or beliefs. Such a concept might be applied to fear of socialism or of catholics and emotional disturbances due to such purely intellectual ideas as those of Galileo or Darwin.

result (3) from the absence of a usually present sensory process. Cerebral organization involves learning. If a sensory activity A has always been present during adaptation to a sensory event B, facilitation from A would necessarily affect the final pattern of cellular activities which constitutes the adaptation to B, and might be essential to it. If so, B in the absence of A could again produce behavioral disturbance (if B without A occurs often enough, however, another adaptation would be established). Finally (4) metabolic and structural changes in the central nervous system could obviously be a source of disorganization, by changing the time relations between the activities of individual cells, apart from any unusual conflict or sensory deficiency.

Attention must now be turned to the way in which cerebral processes tend to maintain their organization, in order to round out the picture of fear behavior. Whatever else may be true of it, avoidance certainly averts or minimizes disruptive stimulation. When we distinguish between the disruption and the processes tending to avert it, and assume that the degree of disruption may vary, we obtain the valuable result of seeing how a single mechanism of fear could on different occasions produce perfectly coordinated flight, a less coordinated avoidance accompanied by trembling and so on, startle, or the paralysis of terror: When cerebral disruption is extreme, it might presumably prevent any coordinated action, even flight.

It seems evident that the so-to-speak homeostatic processes which maintain the dynamic equilibrium of unemotional behavior are to a great extent processes of learning, operating in either of two ways. On the one hand there is negative adaptation to strange objects, which implies that a sensory-central conflict may be banished by an effect of learning on the central organization alone. The sensory event remains the same, yet disturbance disappears. With still further exposure, the formerly strange object may become not merely tolerated but "liked" and "pleasant," which is to say that the originally disturbing sensory event now actively supports cerebral integration.

On the other hand, learning may contribute to this integration indirectly, by reinforcing a mode of behavior (avoidance) which minimizes or removes the disturbing sensation. The incoordinations of emotional behavior, its most characteristic feature, are unlearned; they are apt to be most marked on the first occasion on which they are aroused by any particular stimulus. But the coordinated element of the behavior tends to become more prominent on repetition of the stimulus and to increase, while the unlearned incoordination is decreasing. It thus appears that the coordinated avoidance which occurs in fear behavior of normal animals is mainly learned.

There is indeed a primitive innate avoidance (manifested e.g., in the flexion reflex of Sherrington's (36) spinal animals, and the cowering of Bard's (3) decerebrate cats), but the avoidance which operates most efficiently to maintain coordinated effector activity is acquired. In the normal mammal at least, simple avoidance appears as a conditioned response to cues which in the past have preceded a disruptive stimulation. When a disruptive event is sudden and without warning the response is never an uncomplicated avoidance, a smooth and economical cooperation of effector organs, but involves startle, trembling, sweating, vocalization, and so on. The optimum toward which behavior tends, with repetition of such disturbances, is a response (to premonitory cues) which completely averts the disturbing sensory event. At this final stage of learning, avoidance is fully effective in maintaining integrated cerebral action, and no emotional component is left in the behavior. Thus avoidance without fear occurs. In the avoidance that does involve fear the learning process is not complete or premonitory cues have not been available, and the belated avoidance appears side by side with the excess of effector activity that justifies the inference of cerebral disorganization.

The reciprocal relationship of learning to the disruption of integrated behavior is most simply illustrated by an adult's unemotional avoidance of a hot stove which as an infant he may once have feared. Another illustration is provided by observation of adult chimpanzees where the course of learning in a very unusual social situation could be followed from its beginning. The experimenter, disguised with a grotesque false face and a change of clothing, approached each animal's cage wearing heavy gloves and acted the part of a very aggressive individual, instead of the cautious role one ordinarily takes with the chimpanzee. The results suggested an interpretation similar to that of Bridges (cited by Jones, 21) who concluded that an infant's fear develops out of primitive undifferentiated excitement. The first response by a number of animals was a generalized excitement and marked autonomic activity. An animal might be "friendly" and viciously aggressive, almost in the same breath, or show erection of hair and scream and yet solicit petting. Attack, flight, and the friendly pattern alternated unpredictably. As the stimulus was repeated over a 5-week period, the autonomic activity decreased and one or other of the various patterns dominated. Eventually each animal's behavior became predictable, but it appeared often to be a matter of chance whether the original disturbance would develop into fear, aggression or (less often) friendliness. When avoidance became dominant, the animal would move back out of reach while the experimenter was still distant, with a marked decrease of the excessive effector activity. Learning was clearly involved. We shall also see that the possibility, suggested by this example, that the learning may take more than one form, has a bearing on the theoretical relation of fear to other emotional patterns.

The hypothesis implicitly developed in this discussion can now be made explicit. The immediate source of fear is a disruption of a coordination, principally acquired in the timing of cellular activities in the cerebrum. The disruption may be due to conflict, sensory deficit or constitutional change. With disruption there at once occur processes tending to restore the integration of cerebral activities; in fear these include either liminal or subliminal (13) activation of processes determining avoidance. Optimally, avoidance tends toward completely averting the cerebral disruption, and at this stage avoidance without fear would be said to occur.

CLASSIFICATION OF SPECIFIC FEARS

The value and limitations of the hypothesis will be clearer if we next see how it would be related to specific causes of fear.

1. *Fears due to "conflict."* Here may be included fears induced by pain, loud noise, dead or mutilated bodies, and strange persons and animals. Pain and loud noise appear to have a primitive disrupting action, not psychologically analyzable nor dependent on any previous experience. To this extent fear of such things is in a special class. It is also noteworthy that there is little adaptation to the repetition of pain and sudden intense noise except in very special conditions (28).

Fear of the strange and of dead and mutilated bodies is included under the heading of conflict on the assumption that strange objects arouse incompatible perceptual and intellectual processes. If it should be concluded however that the effective condition is a perceptual deficit, fear of the strange should be included in the following category (2). Finally, fear of snakes and certain small mammals may belong either in this or the following category. Although some basis for including them in the present category might be proposed it would be much too speculative, and it is best to let such fears stand for the present as not fully accounted for.

2. *Fears due to sensory deficit.* Loss of support, darkness and solitude, as causes of fear, have in common an absence of customary stimulation.

Proprioceptive and pressure stimulation due to maintained position in space is practically always present, and it is plausible to suppose that the afferent excitation from these sources would have an essential part in maintaining experientially organized, or habitual, modes of cerebral action. With loss of support, however, the proprioception accompanying maintenance of posture against gravity, and exteroception from the surfaces on which the body's weight rests, are decreased or abolished. Redistribution of blood presure and changes of position of the viscera would no doubt also lead to positive stimulation, but it seems unlikely that this is an effective cause of fear in the infant. In the adult, of course, such stimulation would have become conditioned by experience. (If it should be true that positive visceral stimulation is the main cause of fear in an infant dropped for the first time, the fear should be classed in the preceding category 1, as one of those aroused by an unaccustomed stimulation.)

Fears induced by darkness and solitude (39) do not occur with time relations such that the emotional excitation can be attributed to the positive visual activity of the "off-effect." The response appears to be genuine reaction to deficit (25), intelligible only on the assumption of the present discussion that a "response" need have no direct *sensory* excitant. The violent attempts of the growing chimpanzee to avoid isolation, even in full daylight, seem to require a quite similar interpretation. Kohler (23) has shown that the effective condition here is the social deprivation, as such. Just as a few patterns of postural stimulation are a practically constant feature of the afferent influx to the brain, and visual stimulation during waking hours, so social perceptions are frequent (though intermittent) and might be expected to become an integral element in the organization of cerebral action patterns. It is important to note that this would be a function of experience, and that no fear of darkness or of being alone should be expected in the subject who has only infrequently experienced anything else. Such a subject would develop a different cerebral organization, in which the perceptions referred to would play no essential part. It is also implied that in early infancy neither darkness nor isolation would have any emotional effect; and that as psychological development continues the patterns of cerebral action might, toward maturity, become so stable as to be relatively independent of any particular set of perceptions. Some adults, or most adults in a particular culture, might have no fear of darkness and isolation.

3. *Constitutional disturbances and maturation.* Spies *et al.* (38) have provided exceptionally clear evidence that the psychotic fears so frequently found in pellegra are, in some instances at least, directly due

to nutritional disturbance (see also Jolliffe, 20). When the psychosis is acute (before irreversible neural damage has been done), fear of friends and relatives and of hallucinatory creatures may clear up dramatically upon administration of nicotinic acid. The patient regains insight rapidly, can recall his fears clearly, but also is puzzled at the lack of any incident that might have caused them. Controls made to exactly define the action of nicotinic acid rule out psychological influence as essential either to the mental illness or its cure. Such fears must be regarded as originating in a disturbance of the metabolism of the individual cell, changing (for example) the timing of its detonation cycle and thus its relationship to the activity of other cells. In other words, metabolic changes would have disrupted the orderly sequence of cerebral events which is postulated here as the basis of normal unemotional behavior.

It is also evident that endocrine factors might at times produce a similar effect, partly accounting for the increased shyness and emotional instability of adolescence. The gonadal hormones must be supposed to have a selective action on certain central neural cells (4, 25) changing their properties of excitability and thus disrupting to a greater or less degree the neural organizations into which those cells have entered. With the passage of time reorganization would occur and shyness would decrease.

I do not of course suggest that constitutional changes are the only cause of shyness, or even the main cause. In its most pronounced form it must be thought of simply as an avoidance of strangers; and the next most important factor, after the sight of a strange person, may well be the fact that as the child matures others begin to behave toward him in a different way, according to his age. The child is confronted by "strange" behavior, and situations which are strange to him. Thus shyness can be treated mainly as avoidance of the strange. It is not impossible however that structural and endocrine changes may also play a part in the emotional instabilities of youth. One thinks of maturation as slow and gradual; but there is actually little evidence on this point, and spurts of growth might well make a significant modification of cerebral organizations established by earlier experience. In general terms, such an approach makes intelligible the sporadic appearance of the "imaginative, subjective, or anticipatory fears" classified as such by Jersild and Holmes (19). The fears referred to by Jersild and Holmes are markedly subject to maturation during a period of rapid and irregular growth, and when one observes them in the growing child it is characteristically hard to discover any sufficient cause in experience.

THE RELATIONSHIP OF FEAR TO RAGE
AND OTHER STATES

Fear and rage are notoriously related, and it is impossible to frame any statement of the causes of rage (12) which would not on some points comprise causes of fear as well. The question, whether there is in fact any definite distinction, has been raised elsewhere (13). The hypothesis developed here suggests a kinship between the two emotions which may be put as follows.

The fundamental source of either emotion is of the same kind, a disruption of coordinated cerebral activity. Flight and aggression are two different modes of reaction tending to restore the dynamic equilibrium, or stability, of cerebral processes. The question may be left open at present whether there are different kinds of disturbance, one kind leading to rage, the other to fear. It seems almost certain that such a difference exists between extremes, but with no clear dichotomy; for in some situations, as I have suggested above, it appears to be a matter of chance whether aggression or flight will dominate behavior. Each of these modes of response tends to restore integrated cerebral action, one by modifying the disturbing source of stimulation, the other by removing the animal from it.

Fawning would be another mode of reaction which would tend to modify disruptive stimulation (by placating the source). It is evident also that the hypothesis of this paper opens a wide field of speculation concerning a number of socially and clinically familiar conditions, such as shame, grief, chronic depression and so on. To deal with these varied emotional disturbances the first step would be to classify the source of disturbance as modifiable by the subject's responses, or unmodifiable; and to further to classify the modifiable according to the mode of overt reaction which would be effective. Thus shame or grief would arise from unmodifiable conditions; fear primarily from situations which are (or appear to the subject to be) modifiable by retreat; and so on. Finally, neurosis and some forms of psychosis would be regarded as a chronic condition of cerebral disorganization which according to the hypothesis might be initiated either by severe and prolonged conflict, or by a metabolic disturbance.

It would be idle at present to carry speculation farther, but it has been worthwhile observing that a theoretical relationship of fear to other emotional patterns is provided. If the proposed hypothesis is on the right track, the details of the relationship will become evident when more is known of the physiology of the cerebrum.

CONCLUSIONS

The conclusions of this paper may be put as follows:

1.   Anthropoid fears of inert, mutilated, or dismembered bodies are spontaneous: that is to say, although experience of a certain kind is a prerequisite and learning is definitely involved, the avoidance of such objects is not built up by association with a more primitive cause of fear.

2.   These and a number of other fears are evidently not determined by a sensory event alone, and the behavior is not intelligible except on the assumption that its control is a joint product of sensory and "autonomous" central processes. Consequently no amount of analysis of the stimulating conditions alone can be expected to elucidate the nature of fear, or to lead to any useful generalization concerning its causes.

3.   An adequate hypothesis of the nature of fear cannot be framed in psychological terms alone, but must utilize physiological concepts of cerebral action. No common psychological ground can be discovered for all the various causes of fear. What is there in common, for example, between the characteristically high level of the auditory and low level of visual stimulation which induces fear in children? Or between fear of strangers, which decreases, and fear induced by pain, which tends to increase, with repetition?

The hypothesis developed here has made a considerable synthesis of formerly unrelated facts, although it remains vague on some crucial points. It proposes in brief that fear originates in the disruption of temporally and spatially organized cerebral activities; that fear is distinct from other emotions by the nature of the processes tending to restore cerebral equilibrium (that is, *via* flight); and classifies the sources of fear as involving (1) conflict, (2) sensory deficit, or (3) constitutional change. By distinguishing between processes which break down and those which restore physiological organization in the cerebrum, the variability of fear behavior is accounted for.

The conceptions of neurophysiological action on which this is based were developed originally as an approach to other problems. . . . When this is done, and the neurophysiological implications are made explicit, it may appear that a basis has been laid at last for an adequate theory of emotion and motivation—something which is lacking in psychology at present.

REFERENCES

1. Adrian, E. D. Electrical activity of the nervous system. *Arch. neurol. Psychiatr.*, 1934, **32**, 1125–1136.
2. Bard, P. On emotional expression after decortication with some remarks on certain theoretical views. *Psychol. Rev.*, 1934, **41**, 309–329.
3. Bard, P. Neural mechanisms in emotional and sexual behavior. *Psychosom. Med.*, 1942, **4**, 171–172.
4. Beach, F. A. Analysis of factors involved in the arousal, maintenance and manifestation of sexual excitement in male animals. *Psychosom. Med.*, 1942, **4**, 173–198.
5. Charmichael, L., Hogan, H. P., & Walter, A. A. An experimental study of the effect of language on the reproduction of visually perceived form. *J. exp. Psychol.*, 1932, **15**, 73–86.
6. Cowles, J. T., & Nissen, H. W. Reward-expectancy in delayed responses of chimpanzees. *J. comp. Psychol.*, 1937, **24**, 345–358.
7. Dennis, W. Congenital cataract and unlearned behavior. *J. genet. Psychol.*, 1934, **44**, 340–350.
8. English, H. B. Three cases of the "conditioned fear response." *J. abnorm. soc. Psychol.*, 1929, **24**, 221–225.
9. Gibson, J. J. The reproduction of visually perceived forms. *J. exp. Psychol.*, 1929, **12**, 1–39.
10. Haslerud, G. M. The effect of movement of stimulus objects upon avoidance reactions in chimpanzees. *J. comp. Psychol.*, 1938, **25**, 507–528.
11. Hebb, D. O. The effect of early and late brain injury on test scores, and the nature of normal adult intelligence. *Proc. Amer. phil. Soc.*, 1942, **85**, 275–292.
12. Hebb, D. O. The forms and conditions of chimpanzee anger. *Bull. Canad. psychol. Assoc.*, 1945, **5**, 32–35.
13. Hebb, D. O. Emotion in man and animal: an analysis of the intuitive processes of recognition. *Psychol. Rev.*, 1946, **53**, 88–106.
14. Hebb, D. O., & Riesen, A. H. The genesis of irrational fears. *Bull. Canad. psychol. Assoc.*, 1943, **3**, 49–50.
15. Hilgard, E. R., & Marquis, D. G. *Conditioning and learning*. New York: Appleton-Century, 1940.
16. Hull, C. L. *Principles of behavior: an introduction to behavior theory.* New York: Appleton-Century, 1943.
17. Jacobsen, C. F., Jacobsen, M. M., & Yoshioka, J. G. Development of an infant chimpanzee during her first year. *Comp. Psychol., Monog.*, 1932, **9**, 1–94.
18. Jasper, H. H. Electrical signs of cortical activity. *Psychol. Bull.*, 1937, **34**, 411–481.
19. Jersild, A. T., & Holmes, F. B. *Children's fears.* New York: Teachers College Bureau of Publications, 1935.
20. Jolliffe, N. The neuropsychiatric manifestations of vitamin deficiencies. *J. Mt. Sinai Hosp.*, 1942, **8**, 658–667.

21. Jones, M. C. Emotional development. In C. Murchison (Ed.), *A handbook of child psychology.* (2nd ed.) Worcester, Mass.: Clark Univ. Press, 1933. Pp. 271–302.

22. Jones, H. E., & Jones, M. C. A study of fear. *Childhood Educ.,* 1928, **5,** 136–143.

23. Kohler, W. *The mentality of apes.* New York: Harcourt, Brace, 1925.

24. Lashley, K. S. The thalamus and emotion. *Psychol. Rev.,* 1938, **45,** 42–61.

25. Lashley, K. S. Experimental analysis of instinctive behavior. *Psychol. Rev.,* 1938, **45,** 445–471.

26. Lashley, K. S. An examination of the "continuity theory" as applied to discrimination learning. *J. gen. Psychol.,* 1942, **26,** 241–265.

27. Leeper, R. A study of a neglected portion of the field of learning: the development of sensory organization. *J. genet. Psychol.,* 1935, **46,** 41–75.

28. Liddell, H. S. Animal behavior studies bearing on the problem of pain. *Psychosom. Med.,* 1944, **6,** 261–263.

29. Lorente De Nó, R. Transmission of impulses through cranial motor nuclei. *J. Neurophysiol.,* 1939, **2,** 402–464.

30. Lorente De Nó, R. Cerebral cortex: architecture. In J. F. Fulton (Ed.), *Physiology of the nervous system.* (2nd ed.) New York: Oxford Univ. Press, 1943. Pp. 274–301.

31. McCulloch, T. L., & Haslerud, G. M. Affective responses of an infant chimpanzee reared in isolation from its kind. *J. comp. Psychol.,* 1939, **28,** 437–445.

32. Masserman, J. H. The hypothalamus in psychiatry. *Amer. J. Psychiatr.,* 1942, **98,** 633–637.

33. Morgan, C. T. *Physiological psychology.* New York: McGraw-Hill, 1943.

34. Mowrer, O. H. Preparatory set (expectancy)—a determinant in motivation and learning. *Psychol. Rev.,* 1938, **45,** 62–91.

35. Senden, M. v. *Raum- und Gestaltauffassung bei operierten Blindgeborenen vor und nach der Operation.* Leipzig: Barth, 1932.

36. Sherrington, C. S. *Integrative action of the nervous system.* New York: Scribner's, 1906.

37. Skinner, B. F. *The behavior of organisms: an experimental analysis.* New York: Appleton-Century, 1938.

38. Spies, T. D., Aring, C. D., Gelperin, J., & Bean, W. B. The mental symptoms of pellagra: their relief with nicotinic acid. *Amer. J. med. Sci.,* 1938, **196,** 461–475.

39. Valentine, C. W. The innate bases of fear. *J. genet. Psychol.,* 1930, **37,** 394–419.

40. Watson, J. B. *Behaviorism.* New York: Norton, 1924.

41. Weiss, P. Autonomous versus reflexogenous activity of the central nervous system. *Proc. Amer. phil. Soc.,* 1941, **84,** 53–64.

42. Yerkes, R. M., & Yerkes, A. W. Nature and conditions of avoidance (fear) response in chimpanzee. *J. comp. Psychol.,* 1936, **21,** 53–66.

43. Zangwill, O. L. A study of the significance of attitude in recognition. *Brit. J. Psychol.,* 1937, **28,** 12–17.

SECTION III SOCIALIZATION:

THE PRESCHOOL YEARS

If he is to live a reasonably well-adjusted life, the individual must acquire many of the behavior patterns and characteristics that are appropriate and acceptable for his sex, family, social class, ethnic, and religious groups. The process of acquiring these characteristics, called socialization, begins very early in the child's life and is determined by the nature of his interaction with others. His first social learning occurs at home, as a result of his experiences with members of his family, particularly his mother. The mother's ways of taking care of the young infant's needs may have immediate and long-term impacts on his behavior and psychological well-being. Many child psychologists have studied the consequences of different kinds of specific child-rearing techniques, such as feeding or toilet-training, on the child's personality. Others have focused their research efforts on the effects of broadly-defined maternal or familial attitudes, atmospheres, or practices with the child (e.g., permissiveness or strictness, warmth or coldness, democracy or authoritarianism).

The first article in this section is part of an extensive study of child-rearing practices and their consequences by Sears, Maccoby, and Levin. The selection included here reports the findings on different kinds of toilet training techniques, the baby's responses to them, and the relationships between these and the child's behavior and adjustment during the preschool years. The investigators find that severe toilet training, involving punishment or pressure, may be a source of emotional disturbance during the second year. Severely trained children, especially those with cold or rejecting mothers, tend to become aggressive and irritable and have difficulties in bladder and bowel control.

The child's socialization is accomplished, to a large extent, by means of direct rewards or reinforcements—by parents and others—for appropriate, acceptable responses. Behavior that is inappropriate or disapproved is likely to be punished, or at least not rewarded, and, as a result, becomes "extinguished." However, part of the child's socialization is accomplished by means of his identification with his parents or other models. A child is said to be identified with a model such as a parent, when he believes he shares attributes with the model —when the child feels similar to the model. This feeling of similarity may be increased through the child's adoption of the model's behaviors, attitudes, and ideals. Since the models chosen (parents, older siblings, teachers) generally are carriers and exemplars of culturally approved behavior patterns, the child's identification with them contributes enormously to the process of his socialization.

The second article of this section, by Professor Kagan of Harvard, focuses on the motives underlying identification. The author hypothesizes that the child identifies with the parent because he perceives many differences between his own and his parents' abilities, powers, rights, and privileges. By identifying with his parents, the child begins to feel that he, too, has some mastery of the environment.

The third article, by Mussen and Rutherford, summarizes several other hypotheses about bases of identification and reports the findings of a study of sex-typing (the acquisition of interests and behavior appropriate to one's own sex). These researchers found that appropriate sex-typing, one of the major consequences of identification with the parent of the same sex, is related to feelings of affection, warmth, and respect for that parent.

The final paper in the section, by Bandura and Huston, provides an experimental demonstration that warm, nurturant, and rewarding interaction between the child and a model elicits behavior imitative of that model's. The results are entirely consistent with the findings of the Mussen and Rutherford study on parental warmth in relation to sex-typing, reported in the previous article.

TOILET TRAINING

Robert R. Sears, Eleanor E. Maccoby, and
Harry Levin
STANFORD UNIVERSITY AND CORNELL UNIVERSITY

. . . TOILET TRAINING IN AMERICAN CULTURE involves several problems for both mother and child. As with weaning, these derive fundamentally from the necessity of the child's changing from an infantile way of behaving to a way more suitable for adults. He must unlearn as well as learn. At birth, a baby is endowed with two sphincter reflexes for elimination that are as efficient for their purposes as the sucking reflex is for its. When sufficient urine or fecal matter has accumulated in the bladder or bowel, the sphincter muscles relax suddenly and the waste matter is expelled. In the early months of life, a child wets and has bowel movements according to a relatively unimpeded physiological rhythm, the timing being at first somewhat related to his periods of food and liquid intake. This is a highly satisfactory mechanism from the standpoint of the baby's internal economy, though it is not very considerate of the external household economy.

This is no problem to the child, however. He is diapered, and the only discomfort associated with toileting occurs if his skin becomes irritated or he develops a gastrointestinal upset that produces gas pains. The sphincter releases appear to relieve tension and to provide a pleasurable sort of relaxation. The changing of diapers is often rewarding, too, since the mother gives the child affection and attention while changing him, and his genital area is stimulated in the process of cleaning.

But the next step involves some learning. The child must gain voluntary control over his sphincters. He must learn to recognize the internal signals that warn of an impending movement. Then he must discover how to hold in until he is ready to let go. Voluntary control is

Abridged and reprinted by permission from Chapter Four, "Toilet Training," *Patterns of Child Rearing*. New York: Harper & Row, 1957, 102–137.

partly a matter of inhibition—stopping the action—and partly the positive act of releasing inhibition and even adding some impetus by "pushing" or "trying." The gaining of voluntary control over both holding-in and letting-go is a slow process at best, especially in the child under a year. The capacity to develop control undoubtedly undergoes considerable physiological maturation, too, although the exact nature of the maturational changes *independent of the influence of learning* is not known.

Along with voluntary control, the child must learn to signal his mother. Until he is able to undo his own clothes, she must be available to help. She has to be quick, at first, because his inhibition is not very strong. Gradually he develops a characteristic grunt, or call, and often some special and highly personal wordlike sound to indicate that he needs to go. When he can walk, he must learn to go to the toilet himself, but of course he cannot attend to his own needs fully when walking begins, for he cannot yet unbutton his clothes nor wipe himself properly. These final steps must be learned at a later date.

Toilet training can be considered complete when the child has learned to inhibit elimination at will, over fairly long periods of time. But every mother knows how difficult this is for a child when he is playing some distance from home or is occupied in an engrossing game; even at 7 or 8 years of age he may overestimate his capacity for delay and not get home in time. Families who have taken young children for long automobile trips know well that a child's capacity for delay is very limited at first, and develops but slowly to the adult levels. . . .

Besides these actual controls, there are two important attitudes and manners the child must learn in connection with toilet behavior. One of these is cleanliness. He must keep himself and his clothes from being soiled in the process of elimination. Not only must his waste matter go into the proper place—the potty—but afterwards he must make sure that he himself is wiped clean and that no spots or odors cling to him. For many children, the stress placed on cleanliness in this connection is their first contact with the cleanliness concept. Freud, probably rightly, saw in this experience the foundation pattern on which were laid down many future learnings about the importance of being clean and neat and orderly. It is certainly clear, as many observers have noted, that most children's attitudes of disgust toward the texture, color, and odor of feces develop only after considerable association with a mother who expresses these attitudes herself.

The other attitudinal matter that goes along with toilet training has to do with modesty. Since elimination requires exposure of the genital area, the taboos connected with sex in general, and with modesty in particular, influence the manner in which toileting may be performed. If a high premium is placed on modesty, elimination must be done in strictest privacy. Quite definite rules are often established in this respect, and children must learn just how much public reference may be made to toilet functions and who may be with him when he eliminates. In some families, for example, a child may not run out of the bathroom for help with the buttoning-up if guests or children of the opposite sex are present. The stringency of such rules varies with the age of the child, of course, and with special circumstances, such as illness or the unavailability of private toilet facilities.

In our interviewing, we found it difficult to keep the topics of sex training and toilet training separate. The questions were separate but the mothers' answers were not. When we were discussing modesty standards, mothers would describe their efforts to train their children not to urinate outdoors. Or when we were discussing toilet training, the question of maintaining privacy in the bathroom would come up. This problem had its origin in the mother's desire to teach modesty, but it had implications for toilet training too. In some societies children learn about the adult manner of elimination by accompanying an adult and watching him. While this practice is not unknown in the United States, it is relatively rare in such urban areas as that in which we made this study. Generally speaking, modesty taboos prevent American children from learning their toilet habits in the way they learn many other pre-scribed forms of behavior—by imitation.

If we may summarize the process of toilet training briefly, then, it goes like this. The baby has reflexes that enable him to expel waste products whenever there is sufficient accumulation. These reflexes must be brought under voluntary control, so that he can choose an acceptable time and place for eliminating. The act must be performed both cleanly and modestly.

In the present chapter we will report on two significant aspects of the training process. One of these is the age at which training occurred, and the other, the method by which it was accomplished. . . . We can also report findings concerning the effects of certain practices on the children, and we can say something about the personality characteristics of the mothers who chose various methods of training.

AGE OF TRAINING

Toilet training begins when the mother first puts the child on a potty with the intention of catching a bowel movement. A generation ago, mothers were rather generally advised to start this process as early as possible. There was a gradual recognition, however, that infants do not easily learn the inhibitory control required, and they do not, in the first few months of life, seem to get the idea of signaling. If, in the absence of understanding what they are supposed to do, they are punished for their failures, the learning process is likely to be thoroughly disrupted, and the family's dispositions along with it. More recent advice to mothers, therefore, has been to wait until the child is old enough to understand what he is supposed to do. Dr. Spock has suggested that 7 to 9 months is the earliest reasonable time (the baby cannot sit up alone steadily before then), and urges the latter half of the second year as the best period.

Evidently the great majority of the mothers in our group were in a stage of transition between old and new—or maybe the laundry problem was just too much in these maidless days. Whatever the reasons, nearly half of these mothers began bowel training before the child was 9 months old.

For the group as a whole (see Table 1), the average age at the

TABLE 1. *Ages at Beginning of and at Completion of Bowel Training*

Age in Months	Percent at Beginning	Percent at Completion
Under 5	6	0
5–9	41	8
10–14	30	25
15–19	10	24
20–24	5	23
25–29	1	4
30–34	1	6
After 34	1	5
Not ascertained	5	5
Total	100	100

beginning of training was about 11 months, and at the completion, about 18 months, so that the time required to complete bowel training to the point where accidents were very rare was about 7 months. There were very great differences among families in the time required, however. For some, according to the mothers, the task was finished within a few weeks, while for others it took as much as a year and a half.

As was the case with weaning, the total time required to complete bowel training was less when it was begun late. . . . When mothers began bowel training before the child was 5 months old, nearly 10 months were required for training, on the average. But when training was begun very late (at 20 months or later), only about 5 months were required. It is clear, then, that the later toilet training was begun, the quicker the child learned.

Amount of emotional upset. One measure of the satisfactoriness of any training process is the amount of emotional upset it creates. . . . The change from infantile to more mature ways of behaving represents something of a frustration for a child. This discomfort is sufficient, in some children, to produce a noticeable expression of dislike and rebellion. In the case of toilet training, this may involve a breakdown of partially attained success at inhibiting free elimination. It is often accompanied, too, by irritability and crying when the mother attempts to persuade the child to go to the toilet.

Because of the evident maturation that occurs in children's physiological functioning during the first two years of life, the question must be raised as to whether there is any special time at which training can begin that will elicit less expression of discomfort than other times. One might suppose that, in general, the more mature a child is, the more easily he could learn the new tasks required of him.

We have found no clear evidence for this supposition, however. In our interview, we did not address a specific question to the mothers concerning the extent of the child's upset during toilet training. However, we talked at length with the mothers about toilet training in general and 181 mothers volunteered enough information about their children's emotional reactions to toilet training that we were able to rate those children on our five-point-scale of *amount of emotional upset.* If we use what information we have, we must acknowledge that there is no simple relationship between the age of beginning bowel training and tolerance for training. Table 2 shows that upsets were least common when bowel training was begun between five and fourteen months of age; they were somewhat more frequent when training was begun either very early or in the 15- to 19-month range. Evidently the early-middle period is a more comfortable one for the child.

These percentage differences look large, but the statistical tests applied to the data show that there must have been other factors of much greater importance than age that influenced the amount of upset. . . . In the next section we will describe the variety of methods the mothers used, judging them in terms of severity, and then examine

TABLE 2.   *Age at Beginning of Bowel Training: Relationship to Amount of Emotional Upset*

	Age at Beginning of Bowel Training				
	Under 5 Months	5–9 Months	10–14 Months	15–19 Months	20 Months or More
Percentage of children showing emotional disturbance[a]	35	18	29	44	19
Number of cases	23	154	113	39	31
			$p = .05$ (F)		

[a] The percentages in this table are based upon the entire group of mothers, whether they discussed the amount of the child's upset or not. The figures therefore show the percentage of mothers who volunteered that their children were upset during toilet training, in the absence of a direct question about the matter. . . .

that dimension as another possible determinant of the quickness of learning and the amount of emotional upset that accompanied it.

METHODS OF TRAINING

A bit of cross-cultural perspective is helpful when one examines methods of toilet training. The American penchant for elaborate bathroom aids and facilities, complex clothing, and regular household schedules provides a setting with a good deal of rigidity so far as child training is concerned. We have a highly specialized environment. It sets fairly narrow limits within which variation in training techniques is possible. There are even limits within which the severity of training may vary. Other cultures provide quite different limits, not only with respect to the strictness of the standards they commonly maintain, but also in the physical and social aspects of the environment in which training occurs.

Differences in the surroundings and manner of life of a people influence toilet activities considerably. A nomadic tribe can simply move to another site if its area becomes too contaminated, but a group with stationary residence must be more careful about its toileting places. The availability of an abundant water supply permits the use of washable diapers, but whether washable or disposable, diapers create their own special problems. So does their lack. If the climate is tropical, and the baby is not diapered, a mother's first concern is to avoid being soiled herself when she is holding the child. She must recognize when he is about to eliminate, and hold him away from her or set him on the ground. Either that, or she must wash herself off.

Ecology does not account for all the differences among societies, however. In some, where diapers are not used, the mother who does not act quickly enough calmly cleans herself and the child without reprisals; in others the child is severely punished (from as early as 6 months of age on) for soiling the adult caretaker. When the undiapered child begins to walk, the mother's problem is much the same as for a child who is being taught to go without its diapers—she must teach him where he may go for elimination, and clean up after him if he makes mistakes.

Nevertheless, with all the fancy appurtenances of modern America, and all the limitations on training methods they create, probably no two mothers ever went about the training process in exactly the same way. If we may judge from our interviews, there are differences in belief about the proper age to start, about whether the child should stay on the potty if he does not go immediately, whether he should be talked to while he is waiting, whether he should be punished for accidents, and many other matters.

Underlying these differences there was a basic procedure common to most of the mothers, however. The baby's rhythm of bowel movements was noted, and the mother always tried to get him to the toilet in time for each one. She would use some standard word to describe toileting, and would use it repeatedly as he had his movement. Then she would smile and express approval. As the training continued, she would encourage the child's spontaneous use of this word. Ultimately he would learn to signal his need, and after that would have only very rare accidents. Then the mother would consider her job done.

This skeleton description leaves a lot of leeway for individual differences among the mothers. How often did she take the child to the bathroom? How long did she leave him there if he did not have a movement immediately? How did she handle the situation if he had an accident after he had begun to understand what was expected of him? Some of the alternatives are worth description.

A few mothers did not attempt to teach the child explicitly about bowel control; they allowed him to "train himself." For example:

I.   When did you start bowel training with Jim?
M.   I didn't. I did it with the other two, and it took a lot out of them and a lot out of me. So I said: "With this one, he'll do whatever he pleases." And it worked out beautifully.
I.   Just how did it work out?

M. There again, by example. He has a sister who is just a year older than he is. I noticed that whenever she went and came out, he would go in, too.

I. How old was he when he started this?

M. He was completely trained by the time he was 2, or slightly over.

I. How long would you say it took him to be trained? When did you start?

M. I didn't start. He sorta made up his own sound for whatever he wanted to do; what it was, now, I don't remember.

This mother's procedure was unusual among our group of mothers, however. More commonly, they would put a child on the toilet or a potty at regular intervals. . . . Some went through long months of putting the child on the toilet regularly, without establishing dependable habits, and then found he suddenly seemed "ready" to learn:

M. I started him on the doctor's advice, and he was about 7 months old. He was very unhappy, so I spoke to the pediatrician the next time he came, and he told me I was wasting my time, that he was too small, and to wait until he was 10 months; and I did, and at 10 months it was a totally different reaction. He was fine from that day on, he was no trouble at all after that.

Punishment was another thing on which mothers differed. Some mothers said they did not scold or punish their children for toilet "accidents." Some others, however, applied some degree of pressure, usually in an attempt to prevent accidents after training was nearly complete. Here are the replies, made by four mothers to the question "What did you do about it when he (or she) had accidents after he was mostly trained?"

A

M. I would reprimand her and scold her, and if that didn't work, I'd give her a few little slaps on her behind.

B

M. I would make a big issue of it, and most children don't like to be dirty. He was that way, and it made things easier for me. The minute it happened, and he was all dirty, I would make a big issue of it: "It's an awful thing, look at your clothes; and, oh what an awful thing for a boy to do! If the other boys knew about it . . ." and of course, that worked. Sometimes he would be outside playing and he just didn't give himself time to make it. And of course he would really be ashamed when you kept just bringing up the fact that his clothes and everything were all dirty. That really helped him clear the whole situation up.

C

M. At the time, I sort of put up with it, until I realized that he realized he shouldn't do it. I'd say he was all of maybe 14 months or so, and walking, before I really spanked him for having accidents. I mean, there comes a time when they act very shy, and you know that they've done wrong things.

D

M. Let me see now, she was about 14 months when she was fully broken.

I. Did it go pretty well then?

M. Yes, except lots of times she would do it in her pants. I would just tell her that if she did I would just wipe her face with it. So she decided she was going to go to the bathroom. It was a very good thing to put it under her nose a little bit, and tell her the next time she did it in her pants, she was going to get it in the face; and she didn't like the smell of it, so she learned.

SEVERITY OF TRAINING

The next question to be considered is the severity with which toilet training was accomplished. As was mentioned earlier, punishment introduced into the training procedure can be disruptive, not only of the new toilet habits, but of the disposition in general. In order to study these effects, we had to have some quantitative measure of severity. To this end a five-point scale was constructed. The scale-point definitions are shown in Table 3. The raters took into account everything the mother

TABLE 3. *Severity of Toilet Training*

	Percent
1. Not at all severe. Child more or less trained himself. Not his fault when he has accidents; they are considered natural. No punishment or scolding.	10
2. Slight pressure. Mild disapproval for some late accidents; mother makes some efforts to show child where, when, and how to go to toilet.	10
3. Moderate pressure. Scolding for some late deviations; fairly frequent toileting.	29
4. Fairly severe training. Child scolded fairly often; mother clearly shows disapproval. Child may be left on toilet for fairly lengthy periods.	16
5. Very severe training. Child punished severely for deviations; mother angry and emotional over them.	2
Not ascertained	1
Total	100

said about the way she handled toilet training *except* the age at which training was begun and the nature of the child's reaction to it. Raters were instructed to consider only what the mother did in relation to toilet training.

If we may judge from the number of interviews that were rated at each of the points on the scale, the prevailing mode of training was not very severe. The great majority of mothers used practically no punishment, though there was some scolding for accidents. Only about a fifth of the mothers reported definite punishments or emphatic, repeated scoldings. In spite of the tremendous material emphasis on bathrooms attributed to American culture, there was not a desperate severity in the training of children to use them. Many other cultures, some that even lack outhouses, begin their training earlier and are more severe in their punishment of deviations.

Personality Qualities of Severe Mothers

Before examining the effects of severe toilet training on the children, we may note what other dimensions of the mothers' personalities were correlated with this one. Rarely does any measured quality stand alone. One gets the impression, when looking at the intercorrelations among a number of rated dimensions, that several scales may be measuring different facets of the same thing. What child-rearing dimensions are associated with severity of toilet training?

This scale proved to be related to quite a number of other child-rearing practices. Most of the correlation coefficients are quite small, but the clusters seem meaningful in terms of deeper patterns of personality qualities.

The mothers who were *more severe* also:

1. Placed high demands for conformance to adult standards with respect to:
   a. table manners $(r = .21)$
   b. neatness and orderliness $(r = .19)$
   c. care of house and furniture $(r = .19)$
   d. being quiet $(r = .18)$
   e. doing well in school $(r = .16)$.
2. Used tangible forms of punishment:
   a. physical punishment $(r = .29)$
   b. deprivation of privileges $(r = .13)$
   c. avoided use of reasoning with child $(r = -.23)$.
3. Did not tolerate disobedience or aggression toward themselves:
   a. low permissiveness for aggression toward parents $(r = -.27)$
   b. high standards of obedience $(r = .15)$
   c. punished aggression expressed toward parents $(r = .14)$.
4. Were nonpermissive about the child's sex behavior:
   a. modesty $(r = -.31)$

    b.   masturbation $(r = -.25)$

    c.   social sex play $(r = -.25)$.

5. Had high child-rearing anxiety $(r = .20)$ and lacked warmth or esteem toward:

    a.   herself $(r = -.16)$

    b.   husband $(r = -.15)$

    c.   infant $(r = -.12)$

    d.   child $(r = -.30)$.

. . . We get the impression of a rather pervasive quality of strictness in the mothers who were most severe in their toilet training. They seem to have been seeking to achieve more mature standards of conduct at a faster pace than the other mothers. They had more tendency to drive rather than to lead their children, and they used a more punitive kind of discipline. They also felt more anxiety about their ability to bring up their children; possibly their strictness was in some sense an attempt to overcome whatever feelings of inadequacy they had. . . .

This rather wide range of associated practices and attitudes makes it difficult to separate out the effects of severity of toilet training itself, independently of these other factors. However, in this next section, we will examine its apparent influence on the amount of emotional upset the child suffered, as well as on the duration of training required. . . .

Effects of Severity

The mothers who put a good deal of pressure on their children during toilet training (scolding and punishing for deviations, taking them to the toilet frequently, etc.) did not succeed in completing the training any sooner than the mothers who employed more gentle methods. They did succeed, however, in producing a lot of emotional upset over the matter. As Table 4 shows, over half of the most severely trained children showed some disturbance, while not more than a sixth of the least severely trained showed it $(p < .01; r = .47)$.

The relationship of severe training to the child's emotional upset is significant, of course, but other interpretations of the findings must be considered. The children who most commonly showed disturbance during toilet training tended to be the ones whose training was completed relatively late. Since they had late bowel accidents, and wet their beds after most children had stopped, there were more occasions on which their mothers might be tempted to be angry and punitive. Thus, it might be the child's slowness in training (accompanied by emotional resistance)

TABLE 4. *Severity of Toilet Training: Relationship to Amount of Emotional Upset*

	Severity of Toilet Training			
	Not at All Severe	Slight Pressure	Moderate Pressure	Quite Severe
Percent of children showing emotional disturbance[a]	17	11	26	55
Number of cases	54	117	129	75
		$p < .01$ $(r = .47)$		

[a] These percentages are based upon the entire group of mothers interviewed, whether or not they discussed the amount of the child's disturbance. The figures show the proportion of mothers who volunteered that their children were upset during toilet training, in the absence of a direct question on the subject. . . .

which brought out severe treatment from the mother, not the other way around.

However, if we examine only those cases in which training was very slow, we find that the general principle holds up just as well as it does with the children who learned more rapidly. So, whatever else may contribute to emotional upset, there is little question but that severity of training is an important source of disturbance.

One word of caution must be added about the actual size of the differences in Table 4, however. When raters rated the severity of toilet training in a given family, they were told not to take into account the child's reactions. This may not always have been possible. There may have been cases in which this type of contamination could not have been avoided, instances in which a given training procedure seemed more severe simply by virtue of the fact that it upset the child. These two ratings, therefore, probably have less independence than one might wish.

These various findings present a reasonably clear picture of the effects of the age at which training was begun and of the severity with which it was performed. The later it started, the quicker it was finished. Punishment and scolding did not speed it in the slightest. So far as emotional upset over training was concerned, however, a relatively late start (15 to 19 months) produced as much disturbance as a very early one: the optimum periods appear to have been sometime between the sixth and ninth or tenth months, or after twenty months.

We can turn now to a different kind of question. Did other aspects of the mother's personality, besides the toilet-training methods themselves, influence the child's reaction to that training? There are two main clusters of measures that can be examined.

The first comprises those scales that were related to the mother's affectional relationship to the child. These were the dimensions described as contributing to the measurement of . . . the *warmth* factor. We reasoned that if the mother's punishment was an expression of an underlying hostility or rejection, we might expect it to be more upsetting to the child than punishment which occurred in a context of emotional security. In a sense, the child punished by a hostile mother was in double jeopardy: there was the physical pain of the punishment, plus the anxiety produced by the loss of love implied in the mother's manner while punishing. To the child of the cold and hostile mother, punishment may have meant, "I don't like *you*," while to the child of the warm mother, it may have meant "I don't like *what you did.*"

This reasoning led us to expect that severe toilet training would be more anxiety provoking, and hence more upsetting, for the children of cold mothers than for the children of warm mothers. This proved to be true, as Table 5 shows. Severe training produced far more upset than

TABLE 5. *Percentage of Children Who Showed Emotional Upset Over Toilet Training, in Relation to Severity of Toilet Training and Warmth of the Mother*

Severity of Toilet Training	Mother Warm	Mother Relatively Cold	Horizontal Differences
Mild toilet training	21	11	n.s.
	(112)[a]	(101)	
Severe toilet training	23	48	$p = .01$
	(48)	(98)	
Vertical differences	n.s.	$p = .01$	

[a] Figures in parentheses are number of cases.

mild training in the children of relatively cold mothers, but it had no differential effect whatsoever on the children of warm mothers. This finding requires us to qualify the generalization made before, that severity of training produced emotional upset. The statement can now be amended and made more precise: *severe toilet training increased the amount of upset in children whose mothers were relatively cold and undemonstrative.*

Parenthetically, it is interesting to note here that the mother's coldness per se did not serve to upset the child. It had to be manifested overtly, through severe training practice, before it produced disturbance in this particular sphere of behavior.

The second cluster of measures that need consideration as possible sources of upset are the scales that had to do with training demands and restrictions placed on the child with respect to several areas of social development. One might suppose that if a child were subjected to a number of frustrations, and not allowed to express his resentment directly, he would express it by showing resistance in the toilet-training process. This hypothesis is not borne out by our findings, however. The child's emotional upset during toilet training was *not* related to the severity of restrictions or achievement demands to which he was subjected. That is, children who were required to be quiet, mannerly, and obedient, and who had a strictly-enforced bedtime were no more likely to show emotional upset during toilet training than children of whom less was expected. Furthermore, emotional reactions to toilet training did not seem to be related to the amount the child was spanked, nor to whether his parents had allowed him to express feelings of anger toward them.

These findings are interesting in two respects. First, they emphasize that single-variable relationships between child-rearing practices and child-behavior must be scrutinized with some care before they are accepted as general principles. Simple cause-and-effect relations are probably not common in this area of science. Second, the "factors" derived from factor analysis have proved to be less important as antecedents, at least of the one aspect of child behavior we have called *upset,* than the specific child-rearing practices which we have examined. Neither the *permissiveness-strictness* factor nor the *warmth* factor appears to have been the main determiner of emotional upset during toilet training, if we may judge from the fact that none of the dimensions included in them except *warmth* and *severity of toilet training* was significantly correlated with the child's *emotional upset.*

COMMENT

Viewed even from a cross-cultural standpoint, the range of ages at which the mothers began toilet training was wide. An anthropologist might have difficulty in defining just what *the* American custom is. The modal age was between 9 and 11 months, but there were quite a number of mothers who started within the child's first half-year and a good many more who waited until well after the first birthday.

Did these variations make any difference? From the mother's stand-point, yes. By and large, the later the training was started, the more quickly it was accomplished. Likewise, from the child's standpoint, train-ing begun after 20 months produced emotional upset in relatively few of the children. These facts sound like arguments for a late beginning, especially when one notes the high proportion of upsets in those cases in which training began in the 15- to 19-month range.

There are other aspects of the situation to be kept in mind, however. First there is the fact that mothers who began bowel training at the moderately early age of 5 to 9 months found this procedure as successful as a very late start, in the sense that their children accepted the training with few signs of disturbance. Furthermore, we found that the mothers who chose to begin training early were relatively high in sex anxiety. This suggests a problem similar to the one in connection with breast feeding. If toilet-training activity is an emotionally hazardous part of child care, there is something to be said for the mother's getting the process over speedily, instead of trying to overcome her discomfort and delay her training efforts for the sake of a quicker training period later on. Most normal mothers with relatively high sex anxiety do not recognize this quality in themselves. There seems little point in making a categorical assertion that they *should* overcome their reluctance to delay. Sex anxiety cannot be overcome either by exhortation or by a display of factual arguments.

We have said little about the mechanical details of bowel training. Our interviews, coming as they did 3 or 4 years after completion of the process, were not an appropriate method for investigating what might be called "habit training." There are a number of unresolved problems on which we have not sought data. For example, there is a question as to whether children who are "completely trained" during the early months of life have actually attained voluntary control of their sphincters. Some observers have concluded that it is the *mothers* who get trained in these cases. Other observers, basing their reasoning on conditioned re-flex principles, have assumed that such early control is bona fide. An-other question is whether sphincter inhibition or voluntary sphincter release is learned first. Most writers have assumed that a child learns to hold in before he learns to let go. Both these questions are important in relation to a decision about the optimum age for beginning the training process. Since we have no findings that are relevant to them, however, we are disinclined to add further unverified speculations to a literature already burdened with opinion.

Within the limits of our two measures—duration and upset—we

conclude that either of two periods may be chosen for training with an expectation of reasonable comfort. These are the second 6 months of the child's life and the time after 20 months. The training evidently goes more quickly at the later time and produces little upset. The earlier period is also not immediately upsetting to the child, though the process takes longer. We do not know, of course, whether there are later consequences, in the child's personality, resulting from the choice between these two age periods.

A word is in order about the 15- to 19-month period. One reason that bowel training in this period may be upsetting to the child is that the *wrong* habits have become deeply ingrained. There has been little or no experience with the *right* responses. In other words, he has been practicing elimination in a diaper, lying down or walking, and in rooms that are not in the future to be appropriate for sphincter release. He has not been practicing in the presence of such correct cues as sitting on the potty, being undressed, hearing his mother talk about toileting, and so on. A further problem is that if training is begun after the child is old enough to run around, he will resist being kept in one place long enough for evacuation to occur and for him to be rewarded. A 9-months-old baby who is not yet walking, and who is still content to be confined to a play pen for reasonable lengths of time, will also sit happily on the potty for 5 or 10 minutes, especially if someone stays with him. If he is at all regular in his bowel movements this is usually enough time for his bowel movement to coincide. His mother can then follow it with rewards and praise. The child of a year-and-a-half, however, finds it confining to be required to sit still, even for 5 minutes. He is likely to struggle or cry—activity which can in itself prevent sphincter release. Even if it does occur, the child's emotional state is such that his mother has difficulty making the experience rewarding to him, no matter how much she praises and smiles.

In contrast with these various doubts and queries about the most appropriate age for beginning toilet training, there is considerable certainty about the effects of the dimension of severity. The introduction of pressure, impatience, irritability and punishment into toilet training produces resentment, recalcitrance and emotional upset in the child. It does not serve to speed his learning in the slightest, and may, if the mother is rather cold in her relations with him, serve to initiate a prolonged period of bedwetting.

Severe training may be an almost inevitable maternal reaction to external conditions, of course. A child gone balky because he has gotten started wrong in his attempts to gain control is difficult to handle gently under the best of circumstances. A siege of illness in either the mother or child at a critical part of the training can prolong the process and be quite frustrating.

Underlying these more or less fortuitous sources of severity, however, is a general quality of the personality that seems to provide a number of correlated measures. These include several indicators of high demand for conformance to adult standards, punitiveness, and an intolerance of counter-aggression from the child. We have no information from which we can hazard a guess as to why these various qualities are associated with one another.

THE CONCEPT
OF IDENTIFICATION[1]

Jerome Kagan
HARVARD UNIVERSITY

SEVERAL YEARS AGO Sanford (20) presented an analysis of the concept of identification. In brief, Sanford suggested that the term be applied to situations in which "an individual may be observed to respond to the behavior of other people or objects by initiating in fantasy or reality the same behavior himself . . . the individual strives to behave in a way that is exactly like that of the object" (20, p. 109). Sanford further suggested that the motive for this imitative behavior was a threat to the person's self-esteem. By limiting the term "identification" to those imitative behavioral sequences in which the motivation for the act was anxiety over self-esteem, Sanford emphasized two points: (a) mere similarity in overt behavior between a subject and a model was not necessarily a measure of identification, and (b) the motive for the imitative behavior was one of the defining characteristics of an identificatory response.

The various behavioral phenomena which have been labeled "identification" differ in their manifest properties and motivations. The following four classes of behavior have been described as related to the process of identification because they all can lead to similarities in behavior between a subject and a model.

[1] This research was supported, in part, by a research grant (M–1260) from the National Institute of Mental Health of the National Institutes of Health, United States Public Health Service. The views of Wesley Allinsmith, Vaughn J. Crandall, Leonard M. Lansky, and Howard A. Moss are especially acknowledged. A major stimulus for the present essay was a workshop in parent-child relations supported by USPHS Grant 1649 and held at the Merrill-Palmer School, Detroit, Michigan, July 14–27, 1957.

Reprinted from *Psychological Review* (September 1958), **65** (5), pp. 296–305, by permission of the author and the American Psychological Association.

Imitation Learning

This term refers to the initiation and practice of certain responses (gestures, attitudes, speech patterns, dress, etc.) which are not subject to prohibition by the social environment and which are assumed to be the result of an attempt to imitate a model. The behavior has been labeled either "matched-dependent behavior" or "copying" by Miller and Dollard (17). Miller and Dollard posit that initially the imitative act occurs by chance and the act can only be reinforced if some drive is reduced following the execution of the response. According to this view only direct reward from the social environment, like praise or affection, can strengthen the person's tendency to imitate a model. Mowrer (18) distinguishes between developmental and defensive identification. In the former process, the person imitates or reproduces the behavior of a model in order to "reproduce bits of the beloved and longed-for parent" (18, p. 615). Mowrer suggests that most imitation of a model is the result of the desire to reproduce responses which have acquired secondary reward value through association with a nurturant and affectionate model. Thus, Mowrer emphasizes the self-rewarding aspect of certain imitative acts as opposed to Miller and Dollard's emphasis on direct reward from the social environment.

Prohibition Learning

This term refers to the adoption and practice of the prohibitions of the parents and parent substitutes. The acquisition of these prohibitions bears some relation to the process of superego development as described by psychoanalytic theory (2, 3, 4, 11). Several investigators have suggested that a major motivation for the acquisition of some prohibition is anxiety over anticipated loss of love (10, 11, 18, 20, 23). Sanford labeled this process "introjection" and suggested that the learning and maintenance of this class of behavior might be explained without use of the concept of identification.

Identification with the Aggressor

This phrase refers to the adoption of behaviors which are similar to those of an aggressive or threatening model. The motivation for this "imitation" is assumed to be anxiety over anticipated aggression or domination by the threatening model. It is difficult to explain this behavior as a product of either prohibition or imitation learning, since the motive and reinforcement do not seem related to anxiety over anticipated loss of love or desire for a direct, social reward like praise or affection. Anna

Freud (2) has labeled this phenomenon "identification with the aggressor," Mowrer has called this process "defensive identification" (as distinct from developmental identification), and Sanford has suggested that the term "identification proper" be restricted to this class of behavior.

Vicarious Affective Experience

This phrase refers to the experience of positive or negative affect on the part of a person as a result of an event which has occurred to a model. Salient examples of this phenomenon are (a) a child's elation or depression at learning that his parent is a success or failure, or (b) a mother's elation following the success of her child in school. This phenomenon of vicarious, affective experience has been attributed to a person's identification with a model, but this affective response has been difficult to explain and often neglected by psychologists investigating the identification process. These four phenomena (imitation learning, prohibition learning, identification with the aggressor, and vicarious, affective experience) appear to be mediated by different motives and rewards, and an analysis of each of them is one purpose of this paper.[2]

In different contexts, social scientists have used the term "identification" to refer to three different sets of variables: (a) the process of identification; (b) individual differences in the content of the behaviors, motives, and attitudes acquired as a result of the identification process; and (c) the differential effect of various models that are used during the identification process (3, 4, 5, 7, 9, 11, 13, 15, 16, 25, 26). This paper recognizes the relevance of the model and content dimensions but is primarily concerned with the process of identification, and will attempt to analyze this process in behavioral terms. It is suggested that the process remains the same regardless of the models used or the specific behavioral content that is acquired as a result of an identification.

Definitions of Identification

The concept of identification originated in psychoanalytic theory, and Freud made a distinction between primary and secondary identification (3, 4, 5). Primary identification referred to the initial, undifferentiated perception of the infant in which an external object was perceived as part of the self, while secondary identification began after the child

---

[2] In an unpublished paper presented at a symposium at Harvard University in 1957, Bronfenbrenner described three types of identification: (a) anaclitic identification, (b) identification with a source of power, and (c) identification through reinforcement of a role model. These three terms are similar in meaning to the present phrases of prohibition learning, identification with the aggressor, and imitation learning, respectively.

had discriminated a world of objects separate from the self. Freud implied in his later writings that the process of secondary identification was motivated primarily by the motives and anxieties created by the Oedipal situation. In order to reduce the anxiety over anticipated aggression or rejection from the same-sex parent and obtain vicariously the affection of the opposite-sex parent, the child identified with the former. Identification was described by Freud as "the endeavor to mould a person's own ego after the fashion of one that has been taken as a model" (5, p. 63).

Mowrer's concept of "defensive identification," Sanford's definition of "identification proper," and Anna Freud's description of "identification with the aggressor" are all related to the earlier psychoanalytic hypothesis that the threat value of the same-sex parent motivated the child to identify with him in order to reduce the anxiety associated with this threat. However, it is suggested that an individual may identify with a model not only to reduce anxiety over anticipated aggression from a model but also to experience or obtain positive goal states which he perceives that the model commands. The thesis of this paper is that the motivation to command or experience desired goal states of a model is salient in the development and maintenance of an identification.[3] It will be suggested later that two major goal states involved in identification behavior are (a) mastery of the environment and (b) love and affection. However, it is not implied that these are the only goals which an individual desires to command.

Definition

Identification is defined as an acquired, cognitive response within a person (S). The content of this response is that some of the attributes, motives, characteristics, and affective states of a model (M) are part of S's psychological organization. The major implication of this definition is that the S may react to events occurring to M as if they occurred to him.

The Acquisition and Maintenance of an Identification

Although identification has been defined as a cognitive response, it is not implied that the content of the response is available to consciousness or easily verbalized. Thus the terms "cognitive response,"

[3] It is assumed that anticipation of a positive goal state is associated with the anticipation of a change in affect, and thus the phrase "experience goal states of the model" will be used synonymously with the phrase "experience affective states of the model." This assumption agrees with McClelland's definition of a motive as an "anticipation of a change in affective state" (14, p. 466).

"belief," "wish," or "assumption" will be used in this text to include cognitive processes not always available through verbal report. Identification is not viewed as an all-or-none process. Identification is a response that can vary in strength and there will be differences in the degree to which an S believes that the characteristics of a model, whether assets or liabilities, belong to him. In addition, the S may become identified, to differing degrees, with a variety of models. The motives and reinforcements that are involved in the acquisition and maintenance of this cognitive response are elaborated in the following assumptions.

Assumption 1. Initially the S perceives that the M possesses or commands goals and satisfactions that the S desires. This perception leads to a wish to possess these desired goal states.

Assumption 2. This wish to command the goal states of the M leads to the desire to possess the characteristics of the M because S believes that if he were similar to the M he would command the desired goals. That is, the S assumes that the more similarity there is between the S and M the more likely S is to possess or command the desired goal states of the M.

To illustrate, let the S be a child and the M a mother, although S and M could be an adolescent boy and the leader of a group, or a girl and her older sister. The child perceives that the mother can feed the child, restrict the child, obtain articles out of the child's reach, punish the child, etc. Thus, to the S, the M appears to command desired skills and goal states. The discrepancy between the child's perception of his inability to obtain these desired goals and his perception of the more adequate adult elicits the wish to possess or control those goals which he perceives that M commands. The perceptions of the child are subject to distortion, and the child may exaggerate the degree to which M commands desired goals. It was assumed (Assumption 2) that the wish to command these goal states led to the expectation that if S possessed M's characteristics he would also command these desired goals. There often is direct reinforcement of the belief that to "be similar to" a model is equivalent to possessing his positive attributes. Often, the social environment tells the child directly that he is similar to a parent in certain characteristics, and this communication may be contiguous in time with statements related to some of the model's desired goal states. For example, parents and relatives may tell the child, "You have your father's eyes," and often add, "You'll grow up to be big and strong just like Daddy." It is suggested that these statements which associate similarities in external attributes with command of desired goal states have an important effect on the child's learning about himself, and lead the child to the expectation that to be similar to the model is equivalent to possessing his positive and desirable attributes.

Assumption 3. The identification response (i.e., "some of the characteristics of the model are mine") is reinforced each time S perceives or is told that he is similar to the M. One type of reinforcement for the identification response occurs when an S is told directly that he and the M are similar in temperament or appearance. It is suggested that a second type of reinforcement for this cognitive response is S's own perception of similarity to the M. Once again, consider the case of the small child and his parent. Although the child may perceive marked differences in size, strength, and skills between himself and the M, he may perceive a similarity in affective states, such as joy, anger, or sadness. The importance of the perception of similarities in affective states between the S and M is stressed because a major motive for identification is a desire to experience positive affective states of the model. Thus, perception of similarity in affect is assumed to have saliency as a reinforcement. If the parent becomes angry, sad, or happy and communicates these affects to the child, the child has the opportunity to perceive that he and the M experience similar feelings. This perception reinforces the belief that there is similarity between the S and M. In addition to similarity in affective states, perception of similarities in external characteristics will reinforce the identification response. With specific reference to the child-parent relation, it is assumed that perception of similarities in sexual anatomy, dress, amount and distribution of hair, and other external attributes are potential reinforcements of the identification. Thus, while the identification response is being learned, the major reinforcements for the response are perceptions of similarity between the S and M.[4] Freud suggested that perceptions of similarity strengthen an identification, for he wrote,

> Identification . . . may arise with every new perception of a common quality shared with some other person who is not an object of the sexual instinct. The more important this common quality is, the more successful may this partial identification become, and it may thus represent the beginning of a new tie (5, p. 65).

[4] It is suggested that the concept of identification has not yielded to a behavioral analysis because the notion of social reinforcement has been viewed as a specific action directed at an individual by a reinforcing agent. There has been a tendency to overlook the possibility that a perception, fantasy, or thought may be a potential reinforcement of a response. A recent experimental finding by Estes and Johns (1) supports the hypothesis that a person's perception of a situation, even though objectively inaccurate, can reinforce his subsequent behavior.

Assumption 4. In order for the identification belief to be maintained, the S must not only perceive similarity between the S and M but he also must experience some of the desired, affective goal states of the M. Thus, if the M were successful or happy and S believed that M was experiencing positive affect, the S would also feel positive affect appropriate to the success, and this experience would reinforce his identification. The S also may experience affect appropriate to events occurring to M as a result of the expectation that the social environment will respond to him the same way it responds to the M. That is, when the S has developed some degree of identification with the M he may anticipate that when the social environment praises or rewards the M, it will behave similarly to him. If, on the other hand, the M were sad or criticized, S might experience negative affect because of the identification belief that he and the M were similar and the expectation that the environment might react to him as it did to M. However, if no vicarious command of desired goals or positive affect were experienced as a result of the identification, then the response should extinguish just as any other habit does in the absence of positive reinforcement.[5] That is, some degree of identification should be maintained as long as S perceives that the M commands desired goals. When the S no longer perceives the M in this fashion, then both the motivation for the identification and the intensity of the positive reinforcement should decrease.

The Acquisition of Behavior Similar to a Model: The Motives for Imitation, Identification, and Prohibition Learning

Since perceptions of similarity between the S and M reinforce the identification response, the S may imitate the M during the acquisition phase of an identification in order to increase the degree of similarity. It is acknowledged that the social environment rewards imitative behaviors with affection and praise, and these direct, social reinforcements may strengthen the tendency to imitate adults independently of any identification motives. However, it is suggested, along with Sears *et al.* (23), that direct, social reinforcement of imitative behavior cannot account for all of the imitative responses that the S initiates. A 4-year-old child may simulate adult behaviors when the child is alone or in situations where the parents discourage or punish the imitative response.

---

[5] This view of identification suggests a measurement operation which differs from the usual practice of assessing similarities in behavior between an S and an M. One measure of degree of identification would be the degree to which an S's affective state or behavior was influenced as a result of events that occurred to an M. That is, praise or criticism of an M in S's presence should lead to corresponding changes in the affective state of an S who was identified with the M.

However, despite the punishment or absence of social reward for some imitative behaviors, the behavior continues to be practiced. Sears *et al.*, call this behavior "role practice" and assume that it is motivated by the "desire to reproduce pleasant experiences" (23, p. 370). Consider the 3-year-old girl who plays the role of mother alone in her room. It is hypothesized that a potential reinforcement for this behavior is the creation, in fantasy, of perceptual similarity between the behaviors of the S and M. This perception strengthens S's identification with the M and allows S to share vicariously some of the positive goal states which M commands.

A somewhat different phenomenon is the behavior called "identification with the aggressor" by Anna Freud or "defensive identification" by Mowrer. Anna Freud describes a girl who was afraid of ghosts and suddenly began to make peculiar gestures as she ran in the dark. She told her brother, "there is no need to be afraid, you just have to pretend that you're the ghost who might meet you" (2, p. 119). The present theory assumes that the child desired the threatening power of the feared object and this motive elicited the imitative behavior. The fantasied perception of similarity to the feared model gave S a vicarious feeling of power and reduced her anxiety over attack. It is suggested that "identification with the aggressor" does not differ from other identification responses with respect to the basic mechanism of acquisition but does involve a specific motive and goal state. Identification with the aggressor involves a specific relationship between the S and M in which S fears the M. Thus, S desires the aggressive power or threat value of the M in order to reduce his own anxiety over anticipated attack. It may be misleading to classify "identification with the aggressor" as qualitatively different from other identificatory behavior merely because the motive and goal differ from those involved in other identifications.

A third motive which can lead to behavioral similarity between an S and M is anxiety over anticipated loss of love or nurturance. It is suggested that many social prohibitions which the M practices are learned by the S in situations in which this anxiety motivates the acquisition and maintenance of the response. The reinforcement for the learned prohibition is continued acceptance and a consequent reduction in anxiety over rejection. The research of Sears *et al.* (23) suggests a relationship between "high conscience" in a child and a pattern in which the mother is nurturant and uses withdrawal of love as a disciplinary technique. In summary, any one response which is imitative of a model may be mediated by three different motive-reinforcement sequences, and in many instances all three may be involved in producing behavioral similarity between S and M.[6] Thus, "eating neatly," "getting good grades," or "being nonaggressive" could be motivated by the desire for praise as in imitation learning, by anxiety over loss of love as in prohibition learning, or by the desire to create perceptual similarity between the S and M as in identification. Thus, mere similarity in overt behavior between an S and M may not be the most sensitive measure of degree of identification.

At a more speculative level, it is suggested that the behaviors which have been called "self actualizing" (6) could be motivated and reinforced by a desire for perceptual similarity to an M and be an indication of early identification tendencies. Even the most orthodox supporters of the importance of simple imitation learning find it difficult to explain the child's initial imitations of a model. Once the child has begun to imitate a model it is likely that praise and recognition from adults could maintain this behavior. However, why does the child suddenly want to dress himself, sit on the toilet alone, or put on Daddy's shoes? It is difficult to account for the initial display of this imitative behavior, and the term "self actualization" implies that the child has some biological drive to use his potentialities. This hypothesis seems no more parsimonious than the suggestion that the initiation of these "self actualizing" behaviors is motivated by S's desire to create perceptual similarity between himself and a model.

Two Goals Motivating Identification: Mastery and Love

It has been assumed that S's desire to command certain goal states motivates his identification with a model. It is suggested, for the child especially, that two important goal states that the S desires to command are (a) a feeling of power or mastery over the environment and (b) love and affection. Attainment of these goals should lead to diminution in anxiety over helplessness or loneliness. The young child perceives that he is not able to gratify all of his needs while the parental model is perceived as more capable of dealing with the environment. This discrepancy between the S's perception of his own relative helplessness and the power that he perceives M to possess motivates the wish to have M's power and the search for perceptions of similarity between himself and the M.

[6] In a manuscript being prepared for publication, H. Kelman suggests that the response of conformity to the attitudes of another person can be mediated by three different motives. His analysis of conformity parallels the present discussion of imitative behavior.

Unfortunately, there are no empirical studies which directly test these hypotheses because most of the research on identification has used similarities in behavior between an S and M as the measure of identification. However, there are some results which are at least consistent with the view that the child identifies with the more powerful parent and the one who is perceived to command important sources of gratification. Payne and Mussen (19) reported that adolescent boys who perceived the father as rewarding on projective tests were more highly identified with the father (based on similar answers to a personality inventory) than boys who pictured their fathers as nonrewarding. In addition, boys with dominant and "masculine" mothers tended to be poorly identified with the father. P. S. Sears (22) reported a finding that is more difficult to explain without use of the concept of identification. She found, in a doll-play situation, that kindergarten girls used the mother doll as agent significantly more often than the father doll, while boys used both mother and father dolls with more nearly equal frequency. Since the mother is initially the major controller of gratifications for both sexes, one might expect an initial identification with her for both boys and girls. P. S. Sears (22) also reports that the kindergarten boys who used the mother doll most often had mothers who were (a) more nurturant than the father, (b) more critical of the father, and (c) more restrictive of the child's mobility outside the home. This result is consistent with the hypothesis that the child is predisposed to identify with the parental model who is perceived as controlling important goal states.

A study of Maccoby and Wilson (15) furnishes more direct support for the present hypotheses. The authors showed movies to seventh grade boys and girls and then determined the protagonist with whom the child identified. The most significant result was that a "boy's choice of screen character (the one with whom he was presumed to identify) is more closely related to the social class level *to which he aspires* than to the level his family currently occupies" (15, p. 79). This result suggests that the child identified with models who commanded desired goals.

A second goal state which may motivate identification is the desire for nurturance and affection. In addition to Freud's classical hypothesis that the child identified with the same-sex parent in order to receive vicariously the affection of the opposite-sex parent, there are situations in which nonparental models command sources of affection. The relation between siblings is such a situation, and the younger child may identify with an older sibling if the former perceives that the latter commands parental affection. The research of Helen Koch (12) indirectly supports this hypothesis. She reported that school-age boys with older sisters tended to develop more feminine attributes than boys with older brothers. On the other hand, girls with older brothers tend to be more masculine than girls with older sisters. In the experiment of Maccoby and Wilson, described earlier, the authors reported that girls were more likely than boys to recall movie content involving boy-girl interaction while boys were superior on recall of aggressive acts by the hero. If one assumes that the need for affection is stronger for girls than for boys, and that the recalled content is influenced by the model chosen for identification, then these results suggest that the specific goal states desired by the S determine the models chosen for identification.

Factors Influencing the Strength of Identification

The strength of the identification habit, following a basic behavioral law, should be a function of the strength of the motive and the quality and frequency of the reinforcement (8). It would be predicted, therefore, that the most intense identification would occur when the S had strong needs for love and power, felt incapable of gratifying these motives through his own skills, and perceived similarity between himself and an M who commanded these goals. Utilizing this hypothesis, two generalized predictions can be made concerning the strength of identification for different ages and models.

1.   The strength of identification tendencies should decrease with age because, in general, the individual's ability to gratify his needs for mastery and love through his own behavior, rather than through a vicarious mechanism, should increase with development. Thus, the identifications of a young child should be more intense than the identifications of older individuals.

2.   An identification with an M with whom S was in direct contact should be stronger than with an M with whom S was not in contact, assuming that the motivation for identification was constant and the models were perceived as equally potent. This statement is based on the assumption that the reinforcements of perceived similarity are stronger when S perceives the affects and attributes of the M directly as opposed to instances in which he is merely told that he is similar to the M. Thus, degree of identification with a father with whom S was in contact should be greater than with an imagined fantasy father whom S had never seen. Only very indirect evidence is available to support this prediction. However, reports by P. S. Sears (21) and Sears et al. (24) suggest that absence of the father from the home tends to decrease the degree of

"masculine" doll play in preschool boys while this experience has little effect on the doll play of girls. The results are open to alternative interpretations but are not inconsistent with the present hypothesis.

SUMMARY

This paper has attempted to analyze the concept of identification and place the concept within a learning-theory framework. Identification was defined as an acquired, cognitive response. The content of this response was that some of the characteristics of a model belonged to the individual and the individual behaved as if some of the characteristics and affective states of the model belonged to him. Identification was not viewed as an all-or-none process. An identification can vary in strength and the individual can identify, to differing degrees, with a variety of models. The motive for the acquisition and maintenance of the identification response was a desire for the positive goal states commanded by the model, and mastery of the environment and love-nurturance were suggested as two important goals. The reinforcement for the acquisition of the identification was perceived similarity in attributes between the person and the model. Thus, the person may strive to imitate aspects of the model's behavior in order to create perceptual similarity between himself and the model. Once the identification was established, the individual behaved as if the goal states of the model belonged to him and the positive affect derived from this vicarious sharing of desired goal states helped to maintain the identification.

It was suggested that the usual emphasis on similarities in overt behavior between an individual and a model is not the best measure of identification, since the motives and reinforcements involved in imitation and prohibition learning could also explain similarities in behavior between two people. A differentiation of imitative behavior based on imitation learning, prohibition learning, and identification was attempted.

REFERENCES

1. Estes, W. K., & Johns, Marcia D. Probability learning with ambiguity in the reinforcing stimulus. *Amer. J. Psychol.*, 1958, **71**, 219–228.
2. Freud, Anna. *The ego and the mechanisms of defense.* London: Hogarth, 1937.
3. Freud, S. *New introductory lectures in psychoanalysis.* New York: Norton, 1933.
4. Freud, S. *The ego and the id.* London: Hogarth, 1935.

 5. Freud, S. *Group psychology and the analysis of the ego*. London: Hogarth, 1949.
 6. Goldstein, K. *The organism*. New York: American Book, 1939.
 7. Gray, Susan W., & Klaus, R. The assessment of parental identification. *Genet. Psychol. Monogr.*, 1956, **54**, 87–114.
 8. Hull, C. L. *Principles of behavior*. New York: Appleton-Century-Crofts, 1943.
 9. Kagan, J. The child's perception of the parent. *J. abnorm. soc. Psychol.*, 1956, **53**, 257–258.
10. Kagan, J. Socialization of aggression and the perception of parents in fantasy. *Child Develpm.*, 1958, **29**, 311–320.
11. Knight, R. P. Introjection, projection and identification. *Psychoanal. Quart.*, 1940, **9**, 334–341.
12. Koch, Helen L. Attitudes of young children toward their peers as related to certain characteristics of their siblings. *Psychol. Monogr.*, 1956, **70**, No. 19 (Whole No. 426).
13. Lazowick, L. M. On the nature of identification. *J. abnorm. soc. Psychol.*, 1955, **51**, 175–183.
14. McClelland, D. C. *Personality*. New York: Sloane, 1951.
15. Maccoby, Eleanor E., & Wilson, W. C. Identification and observational learning from films. *J. abnorm. soc. Psychol.*, 1957, **55**, 76–87.
16. Martin, W. E. Learning theory and identification: III. The development of value in children. *J. genet. Psychol.*, 1954, **84**, 211–217.
17. Miller, N. E., & Dollard, J. *Social learning and imitation*. New Haven: Yale Univer. Press, 1941.
18. Mowrer, O. H. *Learning theory and personality dynamics*. New York: Ronald, 1950.
19. Payne, D. E., & Mussen, P. H. Parent-child relations and father identification among adolescent boys. *J. abnorm. soc. Psychol.*, 1956, **52**, 358–362.
20. Sanford, R. N. The dynamics of identification. *Psychol. Rev.*, 1955, **62**, 106–118.
21. Sears, Pauline S. Doll play aggression in normal young children: influence of sex, age, sibling status, father's absence. *Psychol. Monogr.*, 1951, **65**, No. 6 (Whole No. 323).
22. Sears, Pauline S. Child rearing factors related to playing sex-typed roles. *Amer. Psychologist*, 1953, **8**, 431. (Abstract)
23. Sears, R. R., Maccoby, Eleanor E., & Levin, H. *Patterns of child rearing*. New York: Harper & Row, 1957.
24. Sears, R. R., Pintler, Margaret H., & Sears, Pauline S. Effect of father separation on pre-school children's doll play aggression. *Child Develpm.*, 1946, **17**, 219–243.
25. Seward, J. P. Learning theory and identification: II. The role of punishment. *J. genet. Psychol.*, 1954, **84**, 201–210.
26. Stoke, S. M. An inquiry into the concept of identification. *J. genet. Psychol.*, 1950, **76**, 163–189.

PARENT-CHILD RELATIONS AND PARENTAL PERSONALITY IN RELATION TO YOUNG CHILDREN'S SEX-ROLE PREFERENCES[1]

Paul Mussen and Eldred Rutherford

UNIVERSITY OF CALIFORNIA, BERKELEY

ACCORDING TO CLASSICAL psychoanalytic theory, the identification process originates in the child's hostility toward his like-sexed parent and consequent fear of that parent's retaliation. In contrast, the more recently formulated developmental identification hypothesis considers the process to be motivated by warmth and affection toward that parent whose characteristics and responses are then taken on as a "total pattern" (2, 13, 18, 22, 28, 29).

Most of the available evidence supporting this latter hypothesis has been derived from studies of boys' identification with their fathers. If the hypothesis has general validity, however, it should apply equally well to the girl's identification with her mother. This hypothesis would not predict, as classical psychoanalysis theory does, that the process is more confused, complex, and slower for girls than for boys (18, 22, 28).[2]

Reprinted from *Child Development* (1963), 34, 589–607, by permission of the authors and the Society for Research in Child Development.

[1] This study was supported by the National Institute of Mental Health, United States Public Health Service, under Research Grant M–3217.

The authors wish to express their appreciation to A. B. Campbell, Assistant Superintendent of Schools of Berkeley, Frank Wylde, Principal of the Jefferson School, and Mrs. Sue Callan, Mrs. Georgia Johnson, Mrs. Virginia Allison, Miss Marcia Morgen, and Mrs. Ruth Lockwood, first grade teachers for their cooperation in this study.

[2] In fact, Sears *et al.* have argued that the opposite is true, stating: ". . . We are inclined to believe that the boy's shift (from identification with mother to identification with the father) retards the smooth development of the (identification) process. His gradual adoption of a new model is doubtless somewhat frustrating to him, and

The primary purpose of the present investigation was to test the developmental identification hypothesis further to determine its general validity and its usefulness in understanding the process of the girl's identification with her mother. A major aspect of the basic design paralleled that of two earlier studies of the antecedents of father identification in kindergarten boys (20, 21) in which masculinity was found to be related to perceptions of the father as more rewarding and nurturant and also the more powerful source of punishment.

In addition to testing the developmental identification hypothesis, the study was designed to permit investigation of the association between certain parental variables not directly related to that hypothesis and one criterion of identification with the same-sexed parent, the development of appropriate sex-role preference. For the sake of simplicity of presentation, the hypotheses tested may be categorized in terms of the relation between sex-role preference and (a) parent-child relationships, (b) parental personality characteristics, and (c) parental encouragement of appropriate sex-typing. A series of hypotheses with parallel versions for boys and girls was formulated.

1. *Hypotheses concerning parent-child relationships.* This category includes the most central hypotheses of this study, those derived from the developmental identification hypothesis. More specifically it was hypothesized that femininity (female sex-role preference) in little girls— generally assumed to be a product or manifestation of identification with the mother—is related to rewarding, nurturant, and affectionate relationships with that parent (hypothesis Ia). Mother-daughter relationships were evaluated, first from the child's point of view, by means of projective doll play, and, secondly, from the mother's account of her interactions with her daughter, given in response to interview questions.

Since most of the research was conducted in a coeducational public grammar school, data on boys were also collected. It was therefore possible to achieve something that is rare in research in personality and development: a replication (but with more subjects) of an earlier study and thus additional independent checks on the developmental, defensive, and role-taking hypotheses of identification as applied to boys. All the hypotheses received some support in the earlier study (20). The develop-

---

puts him in a state of conflict as to whom he should act like. Thus we might expect not only that boys in their sixth year would be less fully identified with their fathers than girls with their mothers, but that they would have a less complete identification with the adult role in general than girls would have. Also, this means they would show less indication of high conscience, as well as other signs of identification, than girls" (28, p. 384).

mental hypothesis states that masculinity in young boys is related to positive, affectionate father-son relationships (hypothesis Ib).

2. *Hypotheses concerning consequents of parental personality structure.* Both theory and empirical findings suggest that certain aspects of parental personality structure would have facilitative effects on the child's appropriate sex identification. Thus it was hypothesized that self-acceptance on the part of the like-sexed parent would promote femininity in girls (hypothesis IIa) and masculinity in boys (hypothesis IIb). The prediction is based on the assumption that the parent who accepts himself (or herself) is satisfied with his own sex role and is therefore more likely than the parent who is not self-accepting to reward responses replicating his (her) own. Helper found that children were more likely to emulate the characteristics of a mother who approved of herself (i.e., accepted herself) as model for her children (*12*). McCandless has pointed out that, if the girl's mother is successful and, hence, self-accepting, "she provides the best available model for the appropriate sex role" (*16*, p. 347). The same kind of reasoning probably applies to the boy, i.e., a self-accepting father provides the best model for the son.

In addition, self-acceptance on the part of the opposite-sexed parent may contribute to the development of appropriate sex-typing of his (her) child's behavior. Assuming that self-acceptance is related to approval of —and respect for—others, the self-accepting mother or father is more likely than the parent who lacks this characteristic to approve of his opposite-sexed child's sex-appropriate responses, rewarding and encouraging them. Thus, it is hypothesized that the mother's self-acceptance would be related to the boy's masculinity of interests (hypothesis IIIa), while the father's self-acceptance would be similarly related to the girl's femininity of interests (hypothesis IIIb).

On the basis of learning theory, it was hypothesized that, in general, more masculine fathers and more feminine mothers would foster their daughters' femininity (hypothesis IVa) and their sons' masculinity (hypothesis IVb). The rationale underlying these hypotheses was twofold. First, it was assumed that highly feminine women and masculine men are good models for their like-sexed children and provide more distinctive cues for their children's sex-appropriate responses and attitudes. Secondly, it seems plausible to assume such parents are more cognizant of those interests and responses that are sex-appropriate and those that are inappropriate. They might then be expected to reward sex-appropriate responses, thus increasing their frequency and intensity, and to discourage and punish sex-inappropriate behavior.

3. *Hypotheses concerning parental encouragement of sex-typed behavior.* Parents may directly encourage their child's participation in activities (games, hobbies, etc.) traditionally engaged in by members of the child's own sex and may even participate in such activities with the child. By doing this, they make it clear to the child that they approve and perhaps expect certain kinds of behavior while others are considered inappropriate. They delineate for the child the distinctive cues of sex-typed behavior and, simultaneously, differentially reward such behavior, thus increasing its habit strength. By generalization, other sex-appropriate responses, not specifically rewarded, may also become more intense and frequent. It was therefore hypothesized that strong parental encouragement of participation in sex-appropriate activities would implement the feminization of girls (hypothesis Va) and the masculinization of boys (hypothesis Vb).

METHOD

Psychoanalytic theory holds that identification with the like-sexed parent follows resolution of the Oedipus complex which takes place around the age of 5 or 6 years. Moreover, it is generally agreed that the child becomes increasingly aware of his sex identification at this time, e.g., "at the kindergarten-first grade level, the little girl is faced with the inevitability of her femininity" (*16*, p. 347). For these reasons, first grade children, between 5½ and 6½ years of age, would seem to be ideal subjects for the study of the familial antecedents of sex-typing of behavior and interests.

Femininity and masculinity of interests were assessed by means of the IT Scale, a projective test of sex-role preference (*3*) which was administered to 57 girls and 46 boys in the first grade of a middle class public school. In this test, the child is given a card with a figure drawing unstructured as to sex and referred to as IT. He is then presented with groups of pictures of toys, objects, and activities and asked to choose, from among these, the things that IT would like. The underlying assumption of the test is that "the child will project himself or herself into the IT figure on the basis of his own sex-role preference and will attribute to IT the child's own role preference." (*3*, p. 5). Scores ranged from 0 (exclusively feminine choices) to 84 (exclusively masculine choices).

To designate male and female subjects high and low in sex-typing, the distributions of the IT Scale scores for each sex separately, were dichotomized at the median. The 29 girls with scores ranging from 0 to

70 were considered high in femininity (i.e., low in masculinity), while the other 28 girls, whose scores were over 70, were considered low in femininity (relatively high in masculinity). Among the boys, the highly masculine group, 24 subjects, scored more than 81 on the IT scale, while the 22 considered low in masculinity had scores ranging between 19 and 80.

Doll Play

About a week after the IT test was administered, each subject was tested individually in a structured doll play situation involving a mother doll, a father doll, and a child doll of the subject's own sex. The subject was asked to use the dolls in playing out, and thus completing, nine incomplete stories designed to elicit the child's attitudes toward, and perceptions of, his (her) parents.[4] The following is illustrative:

> The child wants a certain toy. He can't reach it. He goes into the living room to get help. Both Mommy and Daddy are busy reading. What happens?

In telling the stories, which were completely recorded, the child could depict either father or mother as nurturant and/or punitive. The following scores were derived from the children's stories: Mother Nurturance (MN) and Father Nurturance (FN) scores were the total number of stories in which the mother or father, respectively, gave the child in the story help, care, comfort, or attention. Total Nurturance (TotN) score was the sum of the MN and FN scores. Mother Punishment (MP) and Father Punishment (FP) scores were the number of stories in which the mother and father disciplined, spanked, criticized, or in any way punished the child. Mother Power (MPow) and Father Power (FPow) scores were the number of stories involving either nurturant or punitive relationships with the mother or father, i.e., MN plus MP, and FN plus FP.[5]

Mother Interviews

The other, perhaps more objective, source of information on parent-child relationships consisted of interviews with the mothers, but for many reasons, it was possible to interview only 19 mothers of girl subjects—11 mothers of highs and eight mothers of lows. The interviews consisted of 32 open ended questions, some of them with suggested probes, adapted

---

[4] Dittoed copies of the full set of nine stories and the interview questions may be obtained by writing to the authors.

[5] Since the scoring categories were very explicitly defined, interrater agreement was high. Two scorers agreed in over 90 percent of their scores for 10 protocols (90 stories).

and somewhat modified from the interview schedules used by Sears, Maccoby, and Levin (28). These dealt with various aspects of mother-daughter relationships such as restrictions and demands on the child, types of discipline used, warmth and affection, punitiveness, the child's dependence, and conscience development. Interviews lasted between one and two hours and were conducted by trained interviewers who asked the questions in a prescribed order using the exact wording given in the schedule. All interviews were electrically recorded.

Following completion of the interviews, a trained rater listened to the recordings and then rated each of them on 19 scales taken from Appendix B of *Patterns of Child Rearing*, e.g., warmth of mother to child, acceptance-rejection, and child's conscience (28).[6] It should be noted that neither the interviewer nor the rater were informed of the real purpose of the research and knew nothing about the subjects beforehand. Consequently, neither the interviews nor the ratings could be biased by any knowledge of hypotheses or of the method of selecting the interviewees.

Assessment of Parental Personality

In order to test hypotheses IIa, IIb, IIIa, IIIb, IVa, and IVb as simply and directly as possible, two scales of the California Psychological Inventory, the Femininity and Self-Acceptance scales, were mailed to both parents of each of the subjects. The Femininity scale purports to measure femininity of interests and attitudes, while the Self-Acceptance assesses "factors such as sense of personal worth, self-acceptance, and capacity for independent thinking and action" (*11*, p. 12).

The inventories were completed and returned by 32 girls' mothers (14 mothers of highs, 18 mothers of lows) and by 30 girls' fathers (14 fathers of highs, 16 fathers of lows). Among the parents of the boys, 22 mothers (8 of highs, 14 of lows) and 18 fathers (7 of highs, 11 of lows) returned the tests.

Measurement of Parental Encouragement of Appropriate Sex-Typed Activities

All the parents of the subjects were also sent a "play and games list," a list of 50 well known sex-typed children's games, play activities, and hobbies, taken from a list of activities that had been shown to differentiate significantly between the preferences of the two sexes (25).

---

[6] The two interview raters were trained in scoring comparable interviews with other mothers, but based on the same questions, before they scored the interviews involved in this study. On these "practice" ratings, they achieved 91 percent agreement, based on five interview protocols.

Parents were instructed to complete the questionnaires separately and independently, indicating, for each activity, whether they had "actually played the game with their child," "encouraged the child to play the game," or "discouraged the child from playing the game."

The responses to each item (game or activity) were scored in terms of the child's sex. If the parent indicated that he actually played a girls' game with his daughter, or a boys' game with his son, the item was scored +2. Each indication of simple encouragement of the child's playing a sex-appropriate game or participating in a sex-appropriate activity was scored +1, while "discouraging the child" from an activity or game appropriate to his sex was scored −2. The sum of the scores on the 50 items constituted the parent's "encouragement of appropriate sex-typed behavior" score. This score was used in testing hypotheses Va and Vb dealing with parental encouragement of the child's sex-typed activities and behavior.

RESULTS

Verification of the major hypotheses involved comparing the highs and lows in sex-typing of interests in relevant variables derived from doll play, maternal interviews (in the case of the girl subjects only), parental scores on the CPI, and parental responses to the "play and games" questionnaires. In the interests of simplicity of exposition, the results of the comparisons of the two groups of boys, including the replication of the Mussen and Distler study (20), will be presented first. In general, the present findings on boys substantiate those of the earlier study and may therefore serve as a point of reference for the evaluation and interpretation of the data relevant to the process of identification in girls.

Analysis of Boy's Doll Play Responses

The mean scores of the variables evaluated from the doll play responses of the high and low masculinity groups of boys are given in Table 1. In general, these findings clearly substantiate those of the Mussen-Distler study (20).

The present data, like those of the earlier study, demonstrate that boys with highly masculine interests told significantly more stories involving father nurturance, i.e., scored higher on the average in Father Nurturance (FN) than boys low in masculinity. These data, then, provide further evidence supportive of the developmental hypothesis, showing that "young boys are more likely to identify strongly with their

TABLE 1. *Mean Scores of Boys High and Low in Masculinity on Family Perception (Doll Play) Variables*

Variable	High Masculinity Group (N = 24)	Low Masculinity Group (N = 22)	t	p[a]
Father Nurturance (FN)	1.3	.8	1.66	.05
Mother Nurturance (MN)	.9	1.3	1.33	ns
They Nurturance (TN)	.3	.4	.18	ns
Total Punishment (TotP)	2.5	2.5	.24	ns
Father Punishment (FP)	2.3	1.7	1.33	$<.10$
Mother Punishment (MP)	1.4	1.6	.41	ns
They Punishment (TP)	.6	.6	.00	ns
Total Punishment (TotP)	4.3	3.9	.67	ns
Father Power (FPow)	3.6	2.5	2.19	$<.025$
Mother Power (MPow)	2.3	2.9	1.10	ns

[a] In evaluating the significance of differences in this and the following tables, p values were calculated in terms of a one-tail test when there was *specific* prediction (from hypothesis) about the direction of the difference between the groups. Otherwise, two-tail tests were used.

fathers, and thus to acquire masculine interests, if they perceive their fathers as highly nurturant and rewarding" (20, p. 353).

Table 1 also reveals that there was a tendency (reliable only at the 10 percent level) similar to that discovered in the other study (reliable at the 6 percent level, in that instance) for the highly masculine boys to have higher mean Father Punishment (FP) doll play scores than the less masculine boys. This is in accord with what was predicted on the basis of the defensive identification hypothesis which holds that identification with the father is based on perceptions of him as punitive, threatening, and hostile. However, in both studies, the evidence supportive of this hypothesis was much less impressive than that confirming the developmental identification hypothesis.

Since the Father Power (FPow) score was composed of the Father Nurturance (FN) and Father Punishment (FP) scores, the highly masculine boys, of course, received higher scores in this variable, i.e., perceived their fathers as more powerful than the other group. This may be regarded as support for the role-taking hypothesis of identification which maintains that sex-role learning depends upon the amount of the child's interaction with the identificand and the latter's power or control over the child.

In summary, the findings of the present investigation—involving a larger sample of subjects than the Mussen and Distler study (20) and a different definition of high and low masculinity status (above and below the median score for the entire group rather than extreme scores)—in essence replicated those of the earlier study. In both studies, the most salient variables appeared to be the father's nurturant and (to a less marked degree) punitive qualities, the substantially father-identified (i.e., those with strongly sex-typed interests) tending to view their fathers as possessing more of both.

The present results are also consistent with those of other studies in showing that, for boys, sex-typing of interests is more directly related to perceptions of their fathers than to feelings about their mothers. Thus, as Table 1 shows, none of the mother-child interaction variables, derived from the doll play, significantly differentiated the high and low masculinity groups.

Analysis of CPI and Play and Games List Data of Boys' Parents

The data collected from the parents failed to confirm any of the hypotheses concerning the relations between boys' sex-role preferences and parental personality characteristics (hypotheses IIb, IIIb, and IVb) or parental encouragement of sex-appropriate activities (hypothesis Vb). There was no evidence that sex-typing of parental interests and attitudes (high masculinity of fathers and high femininity of mothers) or parental self-acceptance, as measured by the CPI, fostered high degrees of masculinity in the sons. Moreover, neither the fathers or mothers of the highly masculine boys differed significantly from the other parents in their responses to the "play and games" list. Hence these hypotheses were rejected.

It may be concluded that the boy's perception of his father as a nurturant and powerful individual is of paramount importance in his development of masculinity, but there is no evidence that his parents' personality structures, particularly degree of sex-typing and self-confidence, have any significant influence. Moreover, parental encouragement of their son's participation in masculine activities does not seem to have a significant effect on the youngster's sex-role preferences. In other words, it appears that, if a father is warm and nurturant in his relationships with his son, the latter is likely to become highly masculine, even if the father does not have this characteristic or a high degree of self-acceptance and even if he does not encourage his son to participate in traditionally masculine activities. On the other hand, a ruggedly masculine, self-confident father who has poor relationships with his son is not likely to produce a highly masculine son, even if he actively attempts to stimulate his son's participation in typical male activities.

Analysis of Girls' Doll Play Responses

The means of the doll play scores of the girls low and high in femininity, used in testing hypothesis Ia, are presented in Table 2. As indicated in the table, the groups differed significantly in Mother Nurturance

TABLE 2.   *Mean Scores of Girls High and Low in Femininity on Family Perception (Doll Play) Variables*

Variable	High Femininity Group (N = 29)	Low Femininity Group (N = 28)	t	p[a]
Mother Nurturance (MN)	1.5	1.1	1.65	.05
Father Nurturance (FN)	.8	.5	1.34	ns
They Nurturance (TN)	.2	.3	.21	ns
Total Nurturance (TotN)	2.6	1.9	2.12	<.05
Mother Punishment (MP)	2.4	2.0	1.14	ns
Father Punishment (FP)	1.9	1.9	.07	ns
They Punishment (TP)	.6	.7	.11	ns
Total Punishment (TotP)	4.9	4.6	.30	ns
Mother Power (MPow)	3.9	3.0	1.93	<.05
Father Power (FPow)	2.7	2.5	.18	ns

[a] See footnote to Table 1.

(MN) scores, the mean score of the highly feminine girls in this variable being significantly higher than that of the girls low in femininity. The finding is entirely consistent with, and supports, the developmental identification hypothesis which holds that girls will identify strongly with their mothers—and consequently become more feminine—if they perceive their mothers as warm, nurturant, affectionate, and rewarding.

As the data summarized in Table 2 show, highly feminine girls, compared with girls low in femininity, regarded their mothers as significantly more powerful (i.e., obtained higher scores in MPow). This finding seems analogous to the finding that highly masculine boys scored significantly higher in FPow than the other boys. There is a major difference between the findings for the two sexes, however. The highly masculine group's high FPow scores were due to the group's significantly, or nearly significantly, higher scores in *both* components of the FPow, i.e., in Father Nurturance (FN) and Father Punishment (FP). The highly feminine group's significantly higher Mother Power scores, on the other hand, are almost entirely attributable to the higher scores in only one of the components of that score, Mother Nurturance (MN). The two groups of girls did not differ significantly in the Mother Punishment (MP) variable. It may therefore be concluded that the development of a high degree of femininity is importantly influenced by the girl's perceptions of her mother as an important, warm, and gratifying person, but not by the extent to which she is perceived as punitive and threatening.

It may be tenably assumed that strong fear of loss of maternal love would be reflected in perceptions of the mother as harsh and punitive. If this is true, according to the defensive identification hypothesis, highly feminine girls would obtain relatively higher Mother Punishment (MP) scores than the other girls. This was not the case; the defensive identification hypothesis, as applied to girls, received no support from these data.

While the mean score of the highly feminine girls in Father Nurturance (FN) was greater than that of the other group, the difference was not statistically significant. Since the Total Nurturance (TotN) score is essentially a composite of the Mother Nurturance (MN) and Father Nurturance (FN) scores, the mean score of the highly feminine girls in this variable was, of course, also significantly higher, the difference being attributable primarily to the group difference in MN.

Analysis of Maternal Interviews

These interviews were designed to elicit information on mother-daughter relationships from the mother's point of view, similar to the information obtained on father-son relationships in the Mussen-Distler study (21). The interview protocols were rated on 19 variables, taken from the Sears, Maccoby, and Levin study (28). These included: warmth of mother to child; acceptance-rejection; mother's use of withdrawal of love, scolding, physical punishment, deprivation, and reasoning as disciplinary techniques; restrictions imposed upon the child and expectancy of good conduct; child's conscience, tendency to admit guilt.

Only one of the 19 rating variables significantly differentiated the two groups. While it is true that one significant difference might have been expected on the basis of chance alone, it is interesting to note that the differentiating variable, "warmth of mother to child," is of paramount theoretical importance. The mean rating for the highly feminine group in this variable was 4.1, while for the other group, it was 3.4 ($t = 1.75$,

$p < .05$). As predicted on the basis of the developmental identification hypothesis, young girls were more likely to identify with their mothers, and thus to acquire appropriately sex-typed interests and responses, if their mothers were warm, rewarding, and affectionate. Thus this finding from the interview reinforces the doll play Mother Nurturance (MN) finding and further supports the developmental identification hypothesis.

The interview data, like those from doll play, failed to provide any confirmation for the defensive identification hypothesis and, in fact, contained some suggestive evidence contradictory to that hypothesis. While none of the interview punishment variables was significantly differentiating, there was a slight, statistically nonsignificant, tendency for the mothers of the girls low in femininity to be rated higher in "use of withdrawal of love as a disciplinary technique" (mean rating for mothers of the highs was 1.8, for mothers of the lows 2.4; $t = 1.51$, $p < .20$ for two tail test). If the defensive identification hypothesis is valid, and if it assumed that frequent use of this technique[7] is likely to evoke fear of loss of maternal love, it would be expected that extensive use of this technique would produce high mother-identification and, consequently, high femininity in the daughter. According to these results, however, a high degree of use of this technique by the mother, if it has any effect, tends to produce *less* femininity in the daughter.

There were some striking parallels between these interview findings and those derived from a study of child-rearing antecedents of masculine identification in kindergarten boys (*21*). Maternal interviews in that study showed that, compared with the other fathers, the fathers of highly masculine boys were warmer and more affectionate toward their sons, a finding analogous to the group differences in maternal warmth in the present study. Moreover, the mothers of the highly feminine girls did not differ significantly from the other mothers with respect to the punishment variables, and the fathers of the two groups of boys were not found to differ in degree of punitive or threatening treatment of their sons (although it will be recalled that in doll play there was a tendency for the highly masculine boys to portray their fathers as more punitive) (*20, 21*).

Analysis of CPI Results of Girls' Parents

It has been hypothesized that, compared with the other parents, the parents of highly feminine girls would be more self-accepting and self-

[7] It has been suggested that withdrawal of love is regarded as extremely harsh punishment by girls (*4*).

assured individuals (hypotheses IIa and IIIb), with appropriately sex-typed interests, opinions, and orientations (hypothesis IVa). The hypotheses were tested by comparing the self-acceptance and femininity (in reverse, masculinity) scale scores of the CPI inventories completed by the two groups of parents. Parental scores in these scales are summarized in Table 3.

TABLE 3.   *Mean Scores on Personality Measures (CPI) of Parents of Girls High and Low in Femininity*

Variable	High Femininity Group (N = 15)	Low Femininity Group (N = 16)	t	p^a
Self Acceptance				
mother	22.1	18.5	2.82	<.005
father	19.8	21.7	1.35	ns
Femininity				
mother	24.2	24.1	.26	ns
father	16.7	18.7	1.35	<.10

^{a} See footnote to Table 1.

As that table shows, hypothesis IIa was clearly confirmed. As predicted, the mothers of the highly feminine girls scored significantly higher than the other mothers in the CPI self-acceptance scale, indicating that they possess greater self-confidence, self-assurance, and "capacity for independent thinking and action." The relation between the mothers' security and self-confidence and the daughters' level of femininity may be interpreted in several ways. Perhaps mothers with these characteristics are more able than less secure mothers to maintain warm, affectionate relationships with their daughters, thus fostering their daughter's femininity. Or, mere possession of these characteristics—which must be evident to the child—may make her a stable, successful, and consequently, desirable model for the daughter to emulate. These explanations are, of course, not mutually exclusive and both of them may be valid.

The data did not provide any evidence supportive of hypothesis IVa as it applied to mothers. The mothers of highly feminine girls were not found to be more feminine than the mothers of the other girls. It may be inferred that girls are likely to express a high degree of female sex-role preference if their mothers are warm, nurturant, and self-accepting (self-confident), though not necessarily highly feminine. The nature of the mother-child relationships and the mother's personal security are basic determinants of the girl's acquisition of feminine orientations, but the degree of the mother's femininity in itself does not appear to exert an important influence. In other words, so far as we are able to determine, the differences between the two groups of girls in the degree of feminine sex-role preference cannot be attributed to differences in the quantity or intensity of sex-appropriate characteristics or cues presented by their mothers, for the two groups of mothers are approximately equal in this respect. Rather it may be assumed that the more feminine little girls are more strongly motivated than the others to imitate their mothers' behavior as a consequence of their allegiance to that parent. This may have either or both of the following consequents. The feminine cues presented by the mother may have greater vividness or be more distinctive for the girl (i.e., she pays closer attention to them) and hence she is more likely to assimilate more of these characteristics into her own role behavior. Or, being strongly motivated to imitate her mother, she may also emulate the behavior of other women, some of whom present more highly feminine models than the mother does. In terms of this latter explanation, it may be suggested that the daughter who is securely identified as a female does not need to duplicate her mother's behavior in toto but finds other appropriate, sometimes more feminine, models among others in her environment.

While the two groups of fathers did not differ significantly from each other in either the CPI Femininity or Self-Acceptance scales (Table 3), there was a trend consistent with, and supportive of, that part of hypothesis IVa which concerns the girls' fathers. The fathers of the highly feminine group tended to be more masculine in interests and orientations (scored more masculine, or lower, on the Femininity scale) than the fathers of the other group. Perhaps more highly masculine fathers are more aware of the behaviors appropriate for both sexes and, consequently, are better able to discriminate and reward appropriately sex-typed responses in their daughters, thus encouraging and promoting their feminization.

Analysis of Parental Responses to Play and Games List

The parents' direct encouragement of their daughters' participation in sex-appropriate play and activities (hypothesis Va) was measured by the play and games list score. The data are summarized in Table 4.

Contrary to what was predicted on the basis of hypothesis Va, the scores of the mothers of the highly feminine girls on this questionnaire did not differ significantly from those of the other mothers. Hypothesis Va, as it relates to the mothers of the girls, was therefore refuted. In brief, the two groups of mothers appeared to be alike in the extent to which they participated with their daughters—and encouraged participation—in feminine games and activities. Apparently the mothers of highly

TABLE 4. *Mean Scores on Encouragement of Sex-Appropriate Behavior by Parents of Girls High and Low in Femininity*

| Variable: Play and Games List | High Femininity Group | | Low Femininity Group | | | |
	N	Mean	N	Mean	t	p[a]
Mother	14	31.9	17	32.2	.13	ns
Father	11	29.0	15	19.9	1.97	<.05

[a] See footnote to Table 1.

feminine girls provide good models and in subtle ways motivate their daughters to emulate them. According to these data, they accomplish this primarily by interacting warmly and affectionately with their daughters and by revealing their security and self-confidence, rather than by being highly feminine in interests and orientation or by directly stimulating the girl's participation in sex-appropriate female activities.

Hypothesis Va as it related to the fathers of the girls was supported, however. The fathers of the highly feminine group apparently provide much more encouragement and stimulation of their daughters' participation in sex-appropriate activitities, scoring significantly higher, on the average, on the play and games list than the fathers of the other girls (Table 4). Clearly, these fathers play an important and direct role in steering their daughters into feminine role preferences.

DISCUSSION

The results on boys' father identifications—and consequent appropriate sex-typing of their behavior—are essentially in agreement with those of previous studies. An unexpected finding was that, for girls, the process of identification with the like-sexed parent—assessed in terms of degree of appropriate sex-role preference—appears to be much more complexly determined and contingent upon a greater number of antecedent conditions. This was somewhat surprising in view of the fact that much current psychological theorizing emphasizes that the establishment of appropriate sex identification is as difficult—or perhaps more difficult—for boys as for girls (2, 18, 22, 28).

According to the data of this study, the most crucial determinant of the development of masculinity in young boys is the nature of the father-son relationship. Appropriate sex-role preference in boys was found to be directly correlated with nurturant, affectionate relationships with the father, a finding fully consistent with the developmental identification hypothesis and the conclusions of other studies (19, 20, 21, 26). There was also a tendency for highly masculine boys to perceive their fathers as punitive and threatening, a finding supportive of the defensive identification hypothesis. In general, it may be concluded that the boy who sees his father as a highly salient and powerful person in his life—instrumental in both rewarding and punishing him—is likely to develop highly sex-appropriate responses. Except for those pertaining to father-son relationships, none of the hypotheses about the acquisition of masculine sex-role preference was supported in the present study. That is, according to these data, appropriate sex-typing of boys was not influenced by the boys' relationships with their mothers, the personality structures of their parents (self-acceptance and relative degrees of masculinity or femininity), or parental encouragement of specifically sex-typed activities.

The acquisition of femininity by young girls is not so simply determined, however. In a way that is analogous to the boys' development of masculine interests, a positive mother-daughter relationship is of paramount importance in the girl's establishment of appropriate sex-role preference. In addition to this factor, however, aspects of the parents' personality structure—e.g., high degree of maternal self-acceptance and self-confidence—appear to be conducive to the establishment of a high degree of femininity in the daughter. Furthermore, while the mother's personality and interrelationships with her son seem to have little influence on the boy's sex-role preference, the father's personality and behavior appear to be important factors in the daughter's development of femininity. The father's possession of a high degree of masculinity of interests and attitudes and his active encouragement of the girl's participation in appropriate sex-typed activities tend to foster the girl's development of appropriate sex-role preference.

From a synthesis of these data it may be inferred that the boy who loves his father (regards him as nurturant) and perceives him as a powerful person is highly motivated to incorporate some of that parent's behavior and personal qualities, including his sex-typed characteristics and interests. By generalization, he tends to view other men in the same way and emulates their behavior, thus reinforcing his masculine identification. This may occur even though the parents do not strongly encourage, or give direct tuition in, masculine activities and even though the father is not an outstanding model of masculinity or personal security.

It seems that the boy, being strongly motivated to become masculine—initially as a consequence of his positive feelings toward his father—maintains, and probably increases, this motivation. Under these conditions, there is little need for his parents to present clear-cut models of sex-typing or excellent personal adjustment or to exert strong pressure toward masculinizing him. In brief, given positive father-son relationships, no specific family socialization techniques are required for the boy's achievement of a high level of male typing.

The process of female typing in the little girl, while directly related to mother-daughter relationships, is also facilitated by the presence of a highly adequate mother as the feminine model and a father who tends to be aware of the behavior expected of a young girl, encouraging his daughter to act in feminine ways (i.e., to participate in girls' games).

It may be concluded that, in the development of the young child's appropriate sex-typing, the girl's family must play more forceful and direct roles as teachers and socializers than the boy's. The reasons for this are not clear, but we may speculate that the boy receives more assistance and support from the general social environment in the process of establishing appropriate sex-role behavior than the girl does. This may be true for several reasons. For one thing, in American culture—particularly in the middle class group from which most of these subjects come—maleness (being a male and acting like one) is relatively highly valued, while being a female and behaving in feminine ways are relatively less valued and rewarded (15). Evidence for this comes from the finding that, when asked, boys seldom, if ever, state that they wish they were girls, while girls frequently state that they wish they were boys (30). Moreover, masculine characteristics are rated as more desirable by children and adults of both sexes (17). Among nursery school children, boys identify significantly more strongly with their fathers than with their mothers, while girls often identify with both mother and father (5). Boys generally become firmly sex-typed in their behavior earlier than girls do (24). From these facts it may be inferred that society strongly motivates the boy to acquire his own sex-role characteristics and rewards him for acquiring them. The girl is not so strongly motivated in this way to become feminine and is less likely to be highly rewarded for it if she does.

Moreover, as common observation attests, behavior considered ap-

propriate for boys is more clear-cut and well-defined, and boys' violations
of approved behavior are more likely to elicit punishment and hence to
be extinguished. For example, young boys can wear cowboy outfits and
play ball but would be severely ridiculed if they wore dresses or played
with dolls. Little girls, on the other hand, can wear either outfit and
play either game without suffering such harsh social criticism. In short,
boys can acquire masculine behavior and interests relatively more simply
than girls can assimilate femininity partially because the cues for sex-
appropraite masculine behavior are more distinct, easier to discriminate,
and hence easier to learn.

From the point of view of learning theory, the role of the parents
in masculinizing their sons is primarily that of providing initial motivation
to acquire masculine characteristics and behavior. The general social-
cultural milieu further implements the masculinization by presenting
numerous, well articulated, and distinct cues for the male sex role and
rewards the boy for learning these. If the boy is already highly motivated
to learn this kind of behavior as a consequence of his relationships with
his father, he will not have difficulty acquiring these behaviors.

For girls, the social-cultural milieu gives less support in the assimilation of her sex role. Due to the relatively lesser value of the feminine
role in middle-class American culture and the relative paucity and non-
distinctiveness of cues associated with the female sex role among young
children, her parents must assist her in several ways if she is to achieve
a high degree of femininity. More specifically, parents are forced to assume three feminizing functions with their daughters, only one of which
is like the parents' role in masculinizing boys. They must evoke motivation to acquire femininity, and, in addition, they help the feminizing process by presenting some cues for discriminating the sex roles and by
directly encouraging the girls to adopt at least certain kinds of behavior
characteristic of the feminine role.

It is also possible that, for young boys, masculinization is facilitated
by their tendency to have higher activity levels and greater freedom of
movement. These probably permit them to seek out and establish more
numerous and intense social relationships outside the home than girls
do. Some of the boy's peers and friends are likely to be excellent models
of masculine behavior, and, by imitating these people, the boy's own
appropriate sex-typing will be strengthened. Young girls, having more
limited freedom to make contacts outside the home, may find fewer
good models of sex-appropriate behavior to emulate. For this reason,
the establishment of a high degree of sex-typing in girls may be rela-

tively less influenced by factors outside the home than the masculinization of boys and more importantly affected by parental personality structure and direct efforts at sex-typing.

The data of the present study are consistent with at least one aspect of psychoanalytic theory, for they indicate that, as that theory maintains, the achievement of sex-identification is more complicated for girls than for boys. The greater difficulty involved in feminine than in masculine sex-typing may, however, be plausibly—and probably more parsimoniously—attributed to certain features of the social structure that promote the boys' acquisition of appropriate sex-role behavior more than they do the girl's.

It is impossible to know, without empirical tests, the extent to which findings such as these can be generalized. The results might have been different if other criteria of strength of identification were used. For example, it is possible that the achievement of a high degree of same-sex parental modeling, another criterion of identification (as distinguished from sex identity, the criterion used here), is in fact more complex for boys than for girls in our society. It is at least possible that different manifestations of identification are related to different processes. Thus, as Mowrer has suggested (*18*), sex typing may depend on developmental identification while conscience development or parental modeling may depend on defensive identification.

SUMMARY

This study was designed to test several hypotheses dealing with boys' father-identifications and girls' mother-identifications as these are reflected in the degree of appropriate sex-role preference. The sex-role preference of 46 first grade boys and 57 first grade girls was determined by means of the IT scale. Boys above the boys' median masculinity score and girls above the median for femininity (i.e., below the median for masculinity) were considered to have developed high degrees of appropriate sex-role identification while the others were considered low in this dimension.

The major hypotheses concerned the relations between parent-child interactions and identifications with the like-sexed parent. Doll play techniques provided the basis for assessing the subjects' perceptions of their parents. Analysis of these data substantially supported the developmental identification hypothesis for both sexes. That is, compared with members of their own sex low in appropriate sex-role identification, highly masculine boys and highly feminine girls perceived their like-sexed parents as significantly warmer, more nurturant, and more affectionate. Maternal interviews with the girls' mothers buttressed the doll play findings, the mothers of the highly feminine girls being rated significantly higher than the other mothers in "warmth toward the child." Among the boys—but not among the girls—there was also evidence supportive of the defensive identification hypothesis, for the highly masculine group tended to perceive their fathers as more punitive as well as more rewarding.

The other hypotheses investigated were related to parental characteristics—specifically mothers' femininity, fathers' masculinity, and self-acceptance—and parental encouragement of the child's participation in sex-appropriate activities as antecedents of high degrees of sex-typing. These were evaluated from parental questionnaires which included the CPI Femininity and Self-Acceptance scales and a play and games list in which the parent indicated whether he (she) encouraged or discouraged his (her) child's participation in certain typically male and female activities.

There was no evidence that high masculinity of fathers, femininity of mothers, parental self-acceptance, or encouragement of their son's participation in masculine activities had any significant effect on the boy's masculinization. Apparently the boy's perceptions of his father as a nurturant and powerful individual are crucial in his development of masculinity, but his parents' personality structure and their pressures toward sex-typing him are not significantly influential.

The young girl's feminization, on the other hand, appears to be facilitated by several factors in addition to warm mother-daughter relationships. Thus, the mothers of highly feminine girls were found to be significantly more self-accepting, but not more feminine or more encouraging of their daughters' participation in feminine activities, than the mothers of girls low in femininity.

Fathers of the highly feminine girls also appear to play a vastly important role in their daughters' feminization. Compared with the fathers of girls low in femininity, these fathers tended to be more masculine and gave their daughters significantly more encouragement to participate in feminine activities. It may be concluded that the feminization of young girls involves a greater number of, and more complex, determinants than does the masculinization of boys. In the development of the child's appropriate sex-typing, the girl's family appears to play more forceful and direct roles as teachers and socializers than the boy's. It is suggested that this is true because the male role is more highly valued in middle class American culture and because behavior considered appropriate for the boy is more clear-cut and well-defined. In short, it may be that the boy receives more assistance and support from the general social environment in the process of sex-typing than the girl does.

REFERENCES

1. Bronfenbrenner, U. The study of identification through interpersonal perception. In R. Tagiuri & L. Petrullo (Eds.), *Person perception and interpersonal behavior.* Stanford Univer. Press, 1958. Pp. 110–130.
2. Bronfenbrenner, U. Freudian theories of identification and their derivatives. *Child Develpm.*, 1960, **31**, 15–40.
3. Brown, D. G. Sex role preference in young children. *Psychol. Monogr.*, 1956, **70**, No. 14 (Whole No. 421).
4. Burton, R. V., Maccoby, Eleanor E., & Allinsmith, W. Antecedents of resistance to temptation in four-year-old children. *Child Develpm.*, 1961, **32**, 689–710.
5. Emmerich, W. Parental identification in young children. *Genet. Psychol. Monogr.*, 1959, **60**, 257–308.
6. Freud, Anna. *The ego and the mechanisms of defense.* New York: International Universities Press, 1946.
7. Freud, S. The passing of the Oedipus-complex. In *Collected papers,* Vol. II. London: Hogarth, 1925. Pp. 269–282.
8. Freud, S. On narcissism: an introduction. In *Collected papers,* Vol. IV. London: Hogarth, 1925. Pp. 30–59.
9. Freud, S. *Group psychology and the analysis of the ego.* London: Hogarth Press, 1949.
10. Freud, S. Some psychological consequences of the anatomical distinction between the sexes. In *Collected papers,* Vol. V. London: Hogarth, 1950. Pp. 186–197.
11. Gough, H. G. *The California psychological inventory.* Palo Alto: Consulting Psychology Press, 1957.
12. Helper, M. M. Learning theory and the self-concept. *J. abnorm. soc. Psychol.* 1955, **51**, 184–194.
13. Kagan, J. The concept of identification. *Psychol. Rev.*, 1958, **65**, 296–305.
14. Levin, H. & Sears, R. R. Identification with parents as a determinant of doll play aggression. *Child Develpm.*, 1956, **27**, 135–153.
15. Lynn, D. B. A note on sex differences in the development of masculine and feminine identification. *Psychol. Rev.*, 1959, **66**, 126–135.
16. McCandless, B. R. *Children and adolescents.* Holt, Rinehart & Winston, 1961.
17. McKee, J. P., & Sherriffs, A. C. The differential evaluation of males and females. *J. Pers.*, 1957, **25**, 356–371.

18. Mowrer, O. H. Identification: a link between learning theory and psycho-therapy. In *Learning theory and personality dynamics*. Ronald, 1950. Pp. 573–616.
19. Mussen, P. Some antecedents and consequents of masculine sex-typing in adolescent boys. *Psychol. Monogr.*, 1961, **75**, No. 2 (Whole No. 506).
20. Mussen, P., & Distler, L. Masculinity, identification, and father-son relationships. *J. abnorm. soc. Psychol.*, 1959, **59**, 350–356.
21. Mussen, P., & Distler, L. Child rearing antecedents of masculine identification in kindergarten boys. *Child Develpm.*, 1960, **31**, 89–100.
22. Parsons, T. Family structure and the socialization of the child. In T. Parsons & R. F. Bales (Eds.), *Family, socialization, and interaction process*. Free Press, 1955. Pp. 35–131.
23. Payne, D. E., & Mussen, P. H. Parent-child relations and father identification among adolescent boys. *J. abnorm. soc. Psychol.*, 1956, **52**, 358–362.
24. Rabban, M. Sex-role identification in young children in two diverse social groups. *Genet. Psychol. Monogr.*, 1950, **42**, 81–158.
25. Rosenberg, B. G., & Sutton-Smith, B. The measurement of masculinity and femininity in children. *Child Develpm.*, 1959, **30**, 373–380.
26. Sears, P. S. Child-rearing factors related to playing of sex-typed roles. *Amer. Psychologist*, 1953, **8**, 431. (Abstract)
27. Sears, R. R. Identification as a form of behavior development. In D. B. Harris (Ed.), *The concept of development*. Univer. of Minnesota Press, 1957. Pp. 149–161.
28. Sears, R. R., Maccoby, E. E., & Levin, H. *Patterns of child rearing*. Harper & Row, 1957.
29. Stokes, S. M. An inquiry into the concept of identification. In W. E. Martin & C. B. Stendler (Eds.) *Readings in child development*. Harcourt, Brace, 1954. Pp. 227–239.
30. West, J. *Plainville, U.S.A.* Columbia Univer. Press, 1945.

IDENTIFICATION AS A PROCESS OF INCIDENTAL LEARNING [1]

Albert Bandura and Aletha C. Huston

STANFORD UNIVERSITY

ALTHOUGH PART OF a child's socialization takes place through direct training, much of a child's behavior repertoire is believed to be acquired through identification with the important adults in his life. This process, variously described in behavior as "vicarious" learning (9), observational learning (11, 24), and role taking (10, 23) appears to be more a result of active imitation by the child of attitudes and patterns of behavior that the parents have never directly attempted to teach than of direct reward and punishment of instrumental responses.

While elaborate developmental theories have been proposed to explain this phenomenon, the process subsumed under the term "identification" may be accounted for in terms of incidental learning, that is, learning that apparently takes place in the absence of an induced set or intent to learn the specific behaviors or activities in question (13).

During the parents' social training of a child, the range of cues employed by a child is likely to include both those that the parents consider immediately relevant and other cues of parental behavior which the child has had ample opportunity to observe and to learn even though he has not been instructed to do so. Thus, for example, when a parent punishes a child physically for having aggressed toward peers, the intended outcome of the training is that the child should refrain from hitting others. Concurrent with the intentional learning, however, a certain amount of incidental learning may be expected to occur through imitation, since the child is provided, in the form of the parent's behavior, with

[1] This investigation was supported in part by Research Grant M–1734 from the National Institute of Health Service, and the Lewis S. Haas Child Development Research Fund, Stanford University.

Reprinted from the *Journal of Abnormal and Social Psychology* (1961), **63** (2), 311–318, by permission of the authors and the American Psychological Association.

an example of how to aggress toward others, and this incidental learning may guide the child's behavior in later social interactions.

The use of incidental cues by both human and animal subjects while performing nonimitative learning tasks is well documented by research (4). In addition, studies of imitation and learning of incidental cues by Church (3) and Wilson (26) have demonstrated that subjects learn certain incidental environmental cues while imitating the discrimination behavior of a model and that the incidental learning guides the subjects' discrimination responses in the absence of the model. The purpose of the experiment reported in this paper is to demonstrate that subjects imitate not only discrimination responses but also other behaviors performed by the model.

The incidental learning paradigm was employed in the present study with an important change in procedure in order to create a situation similar to that encountered in learning through identification. Subjects performed an orienting task, but, unlike most incidental learning studies, the experimenter performed the diverting task as well, and the extent to which the subjects patterned their behavior after that of the experimenter-model was measured.

The main hypothesis tested is that nursery school children, while learning a two-choice discrimination problem, also learn to imitate certain of the experimenter's behaviors which are totally irrelevant to the successful performance of the orienting task.

One may expect, on the basis of theories of identification (1), that the presence of affection and nurturance in the adult-child interaction promotes incidental imitative learning, a view to which empirical studies of the correlates of strong and weak identification lend some indirect support. Boys whose fathers are highly rewarding and affectionate have been found to adopt the father-role in doll play activities (21), to show father-son similarity in response to items on a personality questionnaire (20), and to display masculine behaviors (18, 19) to a greater extent than boys whose fathers are relatively cold and unrewarding.

One interpretation of the relationship between nurturance and identification is that affectional reward increase the secondary reinforcing properties of the model and, thus, predispose the imitator to reproduce the behavior of the model for the satisfaction these cues provide (17). Once the parental characteristics have acquired such reward value for the child, conditional withdrawal of positive reinforcers is believed to create additional instigation for the child to perform behaviors resembling that of the parent model, i.e., if the child can reproduce the parent's rewarding behavior, he can, thus, reward himself (22, 25). In line with this theory of identification in terms of secondary reward, it is predicted that children who experience a warm, rewarding interaction with the experimenter-model should reproduce significantly more of the behaviors performed by the model than do children who experience a relatively distant and cold relationship.

METHOD

Subjects

The subjects were 24 boys and 24 girls enrolled in the Stanford University Nursery School. They ranged in age from 45 to 61 months with a mean age of 53 months. The junior author played the role of the model for all 48 children, and two other female experimenters shared in the task of conducting the study.[2]

General Procedure

Forty subjects were matched individually on the basis of sex and ratings of dependency behavior, and subdivided randomly in terms of a nurturant-nonnurturant condition yielding two experimental groups of 20 subjects each. A small control group comprising 8 subjects was also studied.

In the first phase of the experiment half the experimental and control subjects experienced two nurturant rewarding play sessions with the model while the remaining subjects experienced a cold nonnurturant relationship. For the second phase of the experiment subjects performed a diverting two-choice discrimination problem with the model who exhibited fairly explicit, although functionless, behavior during the discrimination trials, and the extent to which the subjects reproduced the model's behavior was measured. The experimental and control procedures differed only in the patterns of behavior displayed by the model.

Matching Variable

Dependency was selected as a matching variable since, on the basis of the theories of identification, dependency would be expected to facilitate imitative learning. There is some evidence, for example, that dependent subjects are strongly oriented toward gaining social rewards in the form of attention and approval (2, 5), and one means of obtaining

[2] The authors wish to express their appreciation to Alice Beach and Mary Lou Funkhouser for their assistance in collecting the data, and to Ruth Barclay and Claire Korn for their help with the behavior observations.

these rewards is to imitate the behavior of others (23). Moreover, such children do not have the habit of responding independently; consequently they are apt to be more dependent on, and therefore more attentive to, the cues produced by the behavior of others (7, 8).

Measures of subjects' dependency behavior were obtained through observations of their social interactions in the nursery school. The observers recorded subjects' behavior using a combined time-sampling and behavior-unit observation method. Each child was observed for twelve 10-minute observation sessions distributed over a period of approximately 10 weeks; each observation session was divided into 30-second intervals, thus, yielding a total of 240 behavioral units.

The children were observed in a predetermined order that was varied randomly to insure that each child would be seen under approximately comparable conditions. In order to provide an estimate of reliability of the ratings, 234 observation sessions (4,680 behavior units) were recorded simultaneously but independently by both observers.

The subjects' emotional dependency was assessed in terms of the frequency of behaviors that were aimed at securing a nurturant response from others. The following four specific categories of dependency behavior were scored: seeking help and assistance, seeking praise and approval, seeking physical contact, and seeking proximity and company of others.

The dependency scores were obtained by summing the observations made of these five different types of behaviors and on the basis of these scores, the subjects were paired and assigned at random to the two experimental conditions.

Experimental Conditions

In the *nonnurturant* condition, the model brought the subject to the experimental room and after instructing the child to play with the toys that were spread on the floor, busied herself with paper work at a desk in the far corner of the room. During this period the model avoided any interaction with the child.

In contrast, during the nurturant sessions, the model sat on the floor close to the subject. She responded readily to the child's bids for help and attention, and in other ways fostered a consistently warm and rewarding interaction.

These experimental social interactions, which preceded the imitation learning, consisted of two 15-minute sessions separated by an interval of approximately 5 days.

Diverting Task

A two-choice discrimination problem similar to the one employed by Miller and Dollard (15) in experiments of matching behavior was used as the diverting task which occupied the subjects' attention while at the same time permitting opportunities for the subjects to observe behavior performed by the model in the absence of any instructions to observe or to reproduce the responses resembling that of the model.

The apparatus consisted of two small boxes, identical in color (red sides, yellow lid) and size (6" x 8" x 10"). The hinged lid of each box was lined with rubber stripping so as to eliminate any auditory cues during the placement of the rewards which consisted of small multi-color pictures of animals and flowers. The boxes were placed on small chairs approximately 5 feet apart and 8 feet from the starting point.

At the end of the second social interaction session the experimenter entered the room with the test apparatus and instructed the model and the subject that they were going to play a game in which the experimenter would hide a picture sticker in one of the boxes and that the object of the game was to guess which box contained the sticker.

The model and the subject then left the room and after the experimenter placed two stickers in the designated box, they were recalled to the starting point in the experimental room and the model was asked to take the first turn. During the model's trial, the subject remained at the starting point where he could observe the model's behavior.

Although initially it was planned to follow the procedure used by Miller and Dollard (15) in which one of two boxes was loaded with two rewards and the child made his choice immediately following the leader's trial, this procedure had to be modified when it became evident during pretesting that approximately 40 percent of the subjects invariably chose the opposite box from the model even though the nonimitative response was consistently unrewarded. McDavid (12) in a recent study of imitative behavior in preschool children, encountered similar difficulties in that 44 percent of his subjects did not learn to imitate the leader even though the subjects were not informed as to whether the leader was or was not rewarded.

In order to overcome this stereotyped nonimitation, the experimenter placed two rewards in a single box, but following the model's trial the model and the subject left the room and were recalled almost immediately (the intratrial interval was approximately 5 seconds), thus, creating the impression that the boxes were reloaded. After the subject completed his trial, the model and the subject left the room. The experimenter recorded the subject's behavior and reloaded the boxes for the second trial. The noncorrection method was used throughout. This procedure was continued until the subject met the learning criterion of four successive imitative discrimination responses, or until 30 acquisition trials had been completed. The slight modification in procedure proved to be effective as evidenced by the fact that only 9 of the 48 children failed to meet the criterion.

In order to eliminate any position habit, the right-left placements of the reward were varied from trial to trial in a fixed irregular order. This sequence was randomly determined except for the limitation that no more than two successive rewards could occur in the same position.

The number of trials to criterion was the measure of the subjects' imitation behavior on the discrimination task.

Although initially it was planned to follow the procedure used by itself, of some theoretical interest, the discrimination problem was intended primarily as an orienting or distraction task. Thus, on each discrimination trial, the model exhibited certain verbal, motor, and aggressive behaviors which were totally irrelevant to the performance of the task to which the subject's attention was directed. At the starting point, for example, the model remarked, "Here I go," and then marched slowly toward the box containing the stickers repeating, "March, march, march." On the lid of each box was a small rubber doll which the model knocked off aggressively when she reached the designated box. She then paused briefly, remarked, "Open the box," removed one sticker and pasted it on a pastoral scene that hung on the wall immediately behind the boxes. The model terminated the trial by replacing the doll on the lid of the container. The model and the subject then left the room briefly. After being recalled to the experimental room the subject took his turn, and the number of the model's behaviors reproduced by the subject was recorded.

Control Group

In addition to the two experimental groups, a control group, consisting of eight subjects, comparable to the experimental groups in terms of sex distribution, dependency ratings, and nurturant-nonnurturant experiences was studied. Since the model performed highly novel patterns of responses unlikely to occur independently of the observation of the behavior of the model, it was decided to assign most of the available subjects to the experimental groups and only a small number of subjects to the control group.

The reasons for the inclusion of a control group were twofold. On

the one hand, it provided a check on whether the subjects' behavior reflected genuine imitative learning or merely the chance occurrence of
behaviors high in the subjects' response hierarchies. Second, it was of
interest to determine whether the subjects would adopt certain aspects
of the model's behavior that involved considerable delay in reward. With
the controls, therefore, the model walked to the box, choosing a highly
circuitous route along the sides of the experimental room; instead of
aggressing toward the doll, the model lifted it gently off the container
and she left the doll on the floor at the completion of a trial. While
walking to the boxes the model repeated, "Walk, walk, walk."

Imitation Scores

On each trial the subjects' performances were scored in terms of the
following imitation response categories: selects box chosen by the model;
marches; repeats the phrases, "Here I go," "March, march," "Open box,"
or "Walk, walk"; aggresses toward the doll; replaces doll on box; imitates
the circuitous route to the box.

Some subjects made a verbal response in the appropriate context
(for example, at the starting point, on the way to the box, before raising
the lid of the container) but did not repeat the model's exact words.
These verbal responses were also scored and interpreted as partially
imitative behavior.

In order to provide an estimate of the reliability of the experimenter's
scoring the performances of 19 subjects were scored independently by
two judges who alternated in observing the experimental sessions through
a one-way mirror from an adjoining observation room.

RESULTS

Reliability of Observations of Dependency Behavior

The reliability of the observers' behavior ratings was estimated by
means of an index of agreement based on the ratio of twice the number of
agreements over the combined ratings of the two observers multiplied
by 100. Since small time discrepancies, due to inevitable slight asynchro-
nism of the observers' timing devices, were expected, a time discrepancy
in rating a given behavior category greater than two 30-second intervals
was interpreted as a disagreement.

The interobserver reliabilities for the dependency categories considered separately were as follows: Positive attention seeking, 84 percent;
help seeking, 72 percent; seeking physical contact, 84 percent; and seeking
proximity, 75 percent.

Reliability of Imitation Scores

The percentage of agreement in scoring imitative behavior in the experimental sessions is presented in Table 1. Except for *other imitative responses*, the subjects' behavior was scored with high reliability and, even in the latter response category, the scoring discrepancies arose primarily from the experimenter's lack of opportunity to observe some of the behaviors in question rather than from differences of interpretation,

TABLE 1.   *Scorer Reliability of Imitative Responses*

Response Category	Percentage Agreement
Aggression	98
Marching	73
Imitative verbal behavior	80
Partially imitative verbal behavior	83
Other imitative responses	50
Replaces doll	99
Circuitous route	96

for example, when the subject made appropriate mouth movements but emitted no sound while marching toward the containers, this partial imitation of the model's verbalizations could not be readily observed by the experimenter (who was at the starting point) but was clearly evident to the rater in the observation room.

Incidental Imitation of Model's Behavior

Since the data disclosed no significant sex differences, the imitation scores for the male and female subgroups were combined in the statistical analyses.

Ninety percent of the subjects in the experimental groups adopted the model's aggressive behavior, 45 percent imitated the marching, and 28 percent reproduced the model's verbalizations. In contrast, none of the control subjects behaved aggressively,[3] marched or verbalized, while 75 percent of the controls and none of the experimental subjects imitated the circuitous route to the containers. Except for replacing the doll on the box, which was performed by most of the experimental and control subjects, there was no overlap in the imitative behavior displayed by the two groups (see Table 2).

While the control subjects replaced the doll on the box slightly more

[3] One subject in the control group hit the doll off the box on one trial only.

often than the subjects in the experimental group, this difference tested by means of the median test was not statistically significant ($X^2 = 1.49$; $df = 1$). Evidently the response of replacing things, undoubtedly overtrained by parents, is so well established that it occurs independently of the behavior of the model. Since this was clearly a nonimitative response, it was not included in the subsequent analyses.

To the extent that behavior of the sort evoked in this study may be considered an elementary prototype of identification, the results presented in Table 2 add support to the interpretation of identification as a process of incidental learning.

TABLE 2. *Amount of Imitative Behavior Displayed by Subjects in the Experimental and Control Groups*

Response Category	Experimental Subjects N = 40		Control Subjects N = 8	
	Percentage Imitating	Mean per Trial	Percentage Imitating	Mean per Trial
Behaviors of experimental model				
marching	45	.23	0	0
verbal responses	28	.10	0	0
aggression	90	.64	13	.01
other imitative responses	18	.03	0	0
partially imitative verbal behavior	43	.11	0	0
replacing doll	90	.60	75	.77
Behaviors of control model				
circuitous route	0	0	75	.58
verbal responses	0	0	13	.10

Note. The mean number of trials for subjects in the experimental group (13.52) and in the control group (15.25) did not differ significantly.

Effects of Nurturance on Imitation

In order to make comparable the imitation scores for the subjects who varied somewhat in the number of trials to criterion, the total imitative responses in a given response category were divided by the number of trials. Since only a small number of subjects in the nonnurturant condition displayed imitative nonaggressive behavior and the distributions of scores were markedly skewed, the sign test was used to

TABLE 3. *Significance of Differences in Imitative Behavior Exhibited by Subjects in the Nurturant and Nonnurturant Experimental Conditions*

Response Category	Number of Subjects Imitating		p
	Nurturant (N = 20)	Nonnurturant (N = 20)	
Nonaggressive behaviors	15	7	.04
marching	13	5	.05
verbal behavior	9	2	.05
other imitative responses	6	1	.06
Aggressive behavior	20	16	ns
Partially imitative verbal responses	12	5	.04

Note. The two groups of subjects did not differ in the mean number of trials to criterion. The means for subjects in the nurturant and nonnurturant conditions were 13.75 and 13.30, respectively.

estimate the significance of differences between the two experimental groups.

The predicted facilitating effect of social rewards on imitation was essentially confirmed (see Table 3). Subjects who experienced the rewarding interaction with the model marched and verbalized imitatively, and reproduced other responses resembling that of the model to a greater extent than did the subjects who experienced the relatively cold and distant relationship. Aggression, interestingly, was readily imitated by subjects regardless of the quality of the model-child relationship.

Imitation of Discrimination Responses

A three-way analysis of variance (*14*, Case XVII) of the trials scores failed to show any significant effects of nurturance or sex of imitator on the imitation of discrimination responses (see Table 4), nor did the two groups or experimental subjects differ significantly in the number of trials in which they imitated the model's choice or in the number of trials to the first imitative discrimination response.

While nurturance did not seem to influence the actual choices the subjects made, it nevertheless affected their predecision behavior. A number of the children displayed considerable conflictful vacillation, often running back and forth between the boxes, prior to making their choice. In the analysis of these data, the vacillation scores were divided by the total number of trials, and the significance of the differences was estimated by means of the sign test since the distribution of scores was markedly skewed. The results of this test revealed that the subjects in the nurturant condition exhibited more conflictful behavior than subjects in the nonnurturant group ($p = .03$). This finding is particularly noteworthy considering that one has to counteract a strong nonimitation bias in getting preschool children to follow a leader in a two-choice discrimination problem as evidenced by McDavid's (*12*) findings as well as those of the present study (i.e., 75 percent of the subjects made nonimitative choices on the first trial).

TABLE 4. *Analysis of Variance of Subjects Trials Scores on the Discrimination Learning Task*

Source of Variance	DF	Variance Estimate	F	P
Sex	1	294	4.20	$.10 > p > .05$
Nurturance	1	4	<1	ns
Sex X Nurturance	1	158	1.45	ns
Matched pairs	14	70		
Remainder	14	109		

Note. One subject who refused to continue the task before he reached the learning criterion and three subjects who could be run for only 20 trials had to be excluded from this analysis. The results, therefore, are based on 32 matched pairs.

Dependency and Imitation

Correlations between the ratings of dependency behavior and the measures of imitation were calculated separately for the nurturant and nonnurturant experimental subgroups, and where the correlation coefficients did not differ significantly the data were combined. The expected positive relationship between dependency and imitation was only partially supported. High dependent subjects expressed more partially imitative verbal behavior ($r_t = .60$; $p < .05$) and exhibited more predecision conflict on the discrimination task ($r = .26$; $p = .05$) than did subjects who were rated low on dependency.

Dependency and total imitation of nonaggressive responses was positively related for boys ($r_t = .31$) but negatively correlated for girls ($r_t = -.46$). These correlations, however, are not statistically significant.

Nor was there any significant relationship between dependency and imitation of aggression ($r = .20$) or discrimination responses ($r = -.03$).

DISCUSSION

The results of this study generally substantiate the hypotheses that children display a good deal of social learning of an incidental imitative sort, and that nurturance is one condition facilitating such imitative learning.

The extent to which the model's behavior had come to influence and control the behavior of subjects is well illustrated by their marching, and by their choice of the circuitous route to the containers. Evidence from the pretesting and from the subjects' behavior during the early discrimination trials revealed that dashing toward the boxes was the dominant response, and that the delay produced by marching or by taking an indirect route that more than doubled the distance to the boxes was clearly incompatible with the subjects' eagerness to get to the containers. Nevertheless, many subjects dutifully followed the example set by the model.

Even more striking was the subjects' imitation of responses performed unwittingly by the model. On one trial with a control subject, for example, the model began to replace the doll on the box at the completion of the trial when suddenly, startled by the realization of the mistake, she quickly replaced the doll on the floor. Sure enough, on the next trial, the subject took the circuitous route, removed the doll gently off the box and, after disposing of the sticker, raised the doll, and then quickly replaced it on the floor reproducing the model's startled reaction as well!

The results for the influence of nurturance on imitation of verbal behavior are in accord with Mowrer's (17) autism theory of word learning. Moreover, the obtained significant effect of nurturance on the production of partially imitative verbal responses indicates that nurturance not only facilitates imitation of the specific behaviors displayed by a model but also increases the probability of responses of a whole response class (for example, verbal behavior). These data are essentially in agreement with those of Milner (16), who found that mothers of children receiving high reading readiness scores were more verbal and affectionately demonstrative in the interactions with their children than were the mothers of subjects in the low reading ability group.

That the incidental cues of the model's behavior may have taken on positive valence and were consequently reproduced by subjects for the mere satisfaction of performing them, is suggested by the fact that children in the nurturant condition not only marched to the containers but also marched in and out of the experimental room and marched about in the anteroom repeating, "March, march, march," etc. while waiting for the next trial. While certain personality patterns may be, thus, incidentally acquired, the stability and persistence of these behaviors in the absence of direct rewards by external agents remains to be studied.

A response cannot be readily imitated unless its components are within the subjects behavior repertoire. The fact that gross motor responses are usually more highly developed than verbal skills in young children, may explain why subjects reproduced the model's marching ($p = .05$) and aggresion ($p < .001$) to a significantly greater extent than they did her verbal behavior. Indeed several subjects imitated the motor component of speech by performing the appropriate mouth movements but emitted no sound. The greater saliency of the model's motor responses might also be a possible explanation of the obtained differences.

"Identification with the aggressor" (6) or "defensive identification" (17), whereby a child presumably transforms himself from object to agent of aggression by adopting the attributes of an aggressive, punitive model so as to allay anxiety, is widely accepted as an explanation of the imitative learning of aggression. The results of the present study, and those of a second experiment now in progress, suggest that the mere observation of aggressive models, regardless of the quality of the model-child relationship, is a sufficient condition for producing imitative aggression in children. A comparative study of subjects' imitation of aggressive models who are feared, liked and esteemed, or who are more or less neutral figures would throw some light on whether or not a more parsimonious theory than the one involved in "identification with the aggressor" can explain the modeling process.

Although the results from the present study provide evidence that nurturance promotes incidental learning, the combination of nurturance followed by its withdrawal would be expected, according to the secondary reinforcement theory of imitation, to furnish stronger incentive than nurturance alone for subjects to reproduce a model's behavior. It is also possible that dependency may be essentially unrelated to imitation under conditions of consistent nurturance, but may emerge as a variable facilitating imitation under conditions where social reinforcers are temporarily withdrawn.

The experiment reported in this paper focused on immediate imitation in the presence of the model. A more crucial test of the transmission of behavior through the process of social imitation involves the generalization of imitative responses to new situations in which the model is absent. A study of this type, involving the delayed imitation of both male and female aggressive models, is currently under way.

SUMMARY

The present study was primarily designed to test the hypotheses that children would learn to imitate behavior exhibited by an experimenter-model, and that a nurturant interaction between the model and the child would enhance the secondary reward properties of the model and thus facilitate such imitative learning.

Forty-eight preschool children performed a diverting two-choice discrimination problem with a model who displayed fairly explicit, although functionless, behaviors during the trials. With the experimental subjects the model marched, emitted specific verbal responses, and aggressed toward dolls located on the discrimination boxes; with the controls the model walked to the boxes choosing a highly circuitous route and behaved in a nonaggressive fashion. Half the subjects in the experimental and control groups experienced a rewarding interaction with the model prior to the imitative learning while the remaining subjects experienced a cold and nonnurturant relationship. The following results were obtained:

1. The experimental and the control subjects not only reproduced behaviors resembling that of their model but also, except for one response category, did not overlap in the types of imitative responses they displayed.
2. The predicted facilitating effect of social rewards on imitation was also confirmed, the only exception being for aggression, which was readily imitated by the subjects regardless of the quality of the model-child relationship.
3. Although nurturance was not found to influence the rate of imitative discrimination learning, subjects in the nurturant condition exhibited significantly more predecision conflict behavior than did subjects in the nonnurturant group.

REFERENCES

1. Bronfenbrenner, U. Freudian theories of identification and their derivatives. *Child Develpm.*, 1960, **31,** 15–40.

2. Cairns, R. B. The influence of dependency-anxiety on the effectiveness of social reinforcers. Unpublished doctoral dissertation, Stanford University, 1959.

3. Church, R. M. Transmission of learned behavior between rats. *J. abnorm. soc. Psychol.*, 1957, 54, 163–165.

4. Easterbrook, J. A. The effect of emotion on cue utilization and the organization of behavior. *Psychol. Rev.*, 1959, 66, 183–201.

5. Endsley, R. C., & Hartup, W. W. Dependency and performance by preschool children on a socially reinforced task. *Amer. Psychologist*, 1960, 15, 399. (Abstract)

6. Freud, Anna. *The ego and the mechanisms of defence.* London: Hogarth, 1937.

7. Jackubczak, L. F., & Walters, R. H. Suggestibility as dependency behavior. *J. abnorm. soc. Psychol.*, 1959, 59, 102–107.

8. Kagan, J., & Mussen, P. H. Dependency themes on the TAT and group conformity. *J. consult. Psychol.*, 1956, 20, 29–32.

9. Logan, F., Olmstead, D. L., Rosner, B. S., Schwartz, R. D., & Stevens, C. M. *Behavior theory and social science.* New Haven: Yale Univer. Press, 1955.

10. Maccoby, Eleanor E. Role-taking in childhood and its consequences for social learning. *Child Develpm.*, 1959, 30, 239–252.

11. Maccoby, Eleanor E., & Wilson, W. C. Identification and observational learning from films. *J. abnorm. soc. Psychol.*, 1957, 55, 76–87.

12. McDavid, J. W. Imitative behavior in preschool children. *Psychol. Monogr.*, 1959, 73 No. 16 (Whole No. 486).

13. McGeoch, J. A., & Irion, A. L. *The psychology of human learning.* New York: Longmans, Green, 1952.

14. McNemar, Q. *Psychological statistics.* New York: Wiley, 1955.

15. Miller, N. E., & Dollard, J. *Social learning and imitation.* Yale Univer. Press, 1941.

16. Milner, Esther. A study of the relationship between reading readiness and patterns of parent-child interaction. *Child Develpm.*, 1951, 22, 95–112.

17. Mowrer, O. H. Identification: a link between learning theory and psychotherapy. In *Learning theory and personality dynamics.* New York: Ronald, 1950. Pp. 573–616.

18. Mussen, P., & Distler, L. M. Masculinity, identification and father-son relationships. *J. abnorm. soc. Psychol.*, 1959, 59, 350–356.

19. Mussen, P., & Distler, L. M. Child-rearing antecedents of masculine identification in kindergarten boys. *Child Develpm.*, 1960, 31, 89–100.

20. Payne, D. E., & Mussen, P. H. Parent-child relationships and father identification among adolescent boys. *J. abnorm. soc. Psychol.*, 1956, 52, 358–362.

21. Sears, Pauline C. Child-rearing factors related to playing of sex-typed roles. *Amer. Psychologist*, 1953, 8, 431. (Abstract)

22. Sears, R. R. Identification as a form of behavioral development. In D. B. Harris (Ed.), *The concept of development.* Minneapolis: Univ. of Minnesota Press, 1957. Pp. 149–161.

23. Sears, R. R., Maccoby, Eleanor E., & Levin, H. *Patterns of child rearing*. Evanston: Row, Peterson, 1957.
24. Warden, C. J., Fjeld, J. A., & Koch, A. M. Imitative behavior in cebus and rhesus monkeys. *J. Genet. Psychol.*, 1940, 56, 311–322.
25. Whiting, J. W. M., & Child, I. L. *Child training and personality*. New Haven: Yale Univer. Press, 1953.
26. Wilson, W. C. Imitation and learning of incidental cues by preschool children. *Child Develpm.*, 1958, 29, 393–397.

SECTION IV   EARLY COGNITIVE DEVELOPMENT

The phrase "cognitive development" refers to the growth and change in such phenomena as thinking, perceiving, imagining, problem-solving, and concept formation. Five major response classes are included: (1) perceptual differentiation of environmental stimuli; (2) development of a vocabulary that allows the child to label external events and internal feelings; (3) acquisition of rules about natural events and the ability to apply rules of reasoning to problem situations; (4) increased capacity for immediate memory resulting, in part, from more efficient use of abstract words to group or "chunk" disparate bits of information; and (5) increased ability to communicate thoughts verbally or graphically.

During the period from birth to 13 years the child perceives the world with ever-increasing accuracy, and with greater differentiation; he acquires more words to facilitate memory and to aid comprehension and communication, and he learns basic relationships and cause-effect sequences. All of these processes are changing simultaneously, and the superior quality of the 7-year-old's intellectual product, in contrast to the 5-year-old's, can rarely be attributed to change in only one of these response systems.

It is generally believed that the increased language resources of the child are of primary relevance, for each time the child learns a new word for an object or an event he becomes better able to differentiate it from other similar objects or events, and to see its relationship to other words that belong in the same conceptual category. Psychologists have traditionally believed that it is profitable to regard words as falling on a continuum from concrete to abstract, implying that the more abstract words the child posseses, the more efficient and mature his thinking. To know the word *animal*, in addition to the specific words *dog, cat, horse*, or *cow*, allows the child to cluster the more specific or concrete words in a more general category. This point of view has led some people to assume that the brighter child has more abstract words and uses them more frequently than words referring to specific objects. Professor Brown's paper, "How Shall a Thing Be Called?" notes the fallacy in this assumption. Some parents teach their children a general term such as silverware before they teach him the specific members of that class (e.g., fork, knife, spoon). To say that a child has acquired an abstract term, therefore, requires proof that he has learned not only the general form, but that he also knows the specific instances of the concept.

The meaning of intelligence.   Civilized man has placed great value on the ability to think and to communicate symbolically, and it is generally assumed that people possess differing amounts of a general ability to think symbolically. During the opening decades of the twentieth century there were many attempts to measure this general mental attribute, and the IQ, as reflected by the score on an intelligence test, came to be regarded as a basic human characteristic. The child's IQ was thought to be stable over long periods of time and not easily modified by experience or changes in personality. Analysis of the questions asked in typical intelligence tests reveals that this assumption is oversimplified and not completely accurate. Most of these questions evaluate the child's vocabulary, immediate memory, and knowledge of basic rules about the environment. It is reasonable to assume, therefore, that the child's desire to learn more about his world should influence his IQ score. Since profound changes in the strength of the child's motivation to learn can occur during the opening years of school, some children should increase in IQ score while others should decrease. Researchers at the Fels Research Institute have analyzed changes in IQ scores, over the age span 3 to 10, of 140 normal children who were studied intensively from birth to adolescence.

The second and third articles in this section, "Mental Growth and Personality Development" and "Personality and IQ change" summarize the major findings of this research and reveal that some children, especially boys, show large increases in IQ score, while others decrease. Moreover, the children who manifest IQ increases, in contrast to those who decrease, are, according to observation of their behavior, more independent, more highly motivated to master new skills, and more likely to be preoccupied with thoughts related to achievement.

Piaget's view of intellectual development. Piaget is one of the outstanding psychologists of this century, and his contribution to our understanding of cognitive development is inestimable. Piaget also believes in a generalized trait of mental ability, but he places a major emphasis on the child's acquisition of rules about the environment. Piaget calls these rules "operations." An operation is an invariant rule about environmental events or the relations among symbols. In most instances an operation is synonymous with a rule of reasoning. The rule: A>B and B>C, then A>C is an operation; the rule that wood floats in water or that quantities do not alter their weight despite changes in shape are also operations. One of the most dramatic demonstrations of the fact that children pass through different stages in acquiring various operations can be seen in experiments with young children in which their notions of mass and weight are investigated. Most 4 or 5-year-olds do not believe that the mass or quantity of a substance (for example, amount of clay) remains the same when the shape of that substance is changed. If a 4-year-old is shown two identical balls of clay he will acknowledge that they are equal in amount. However, if the adult breaks one of the clay balls into a dozen small pieces, the child will insist that the twelve small pieces have more clay than the solid ball. The 7-year-old has learned the operation that masses stay constant (in Piaget's term, remain invariant) despite changes in form, and is apt to laugh if an adult suggests that the ball contains less clay than the twelve small pieces.

Professor Lovell has performed some of these experiments with school age children and the fourth and fifth papers summarize the dramatic age differences in the belief regarding conservation of mass and weight.

The sixth paper, by Professor Piaget, presents a concise summary of some of the major changes in thinking about number, quantity, and geometrical measurement that occur between 4 and 12 years of age.

Changes in stimulus processing. The three studies discussed above deal primarily with growth in the child's vocabulary and reasoning. There are, in addition, important changes in the ways in which new information is processed by the child. Specifically, it appears that young children are prone to react impulsively to new events or problems, whereas older children tend to reflect before labeling a new event or selecting a hypothesis to solve a problem. The 6-year-old is tempted to act on the first hunch that occurs to him when he is faced with a problem situation with several possible answers. The 10-year-old is more likely to consider the differential validity of several possible solutions before acting on one of them. Reflection upon the differential validity of various hypotheses has adaptive consequences, for the child who reacts quickly is more likely to make an error than the one who considers the probable accuracy of his hypothesis.

The seventh paper, by Professor Kagan, reveals that development is accompanied by an increased disposition for reflection, and discusses some of the implications and personality correlates of a reflective approach to problems.

How SHALL A THING BE CALLED?

Roger Brown
HARVARD UNIVERSITY

THE MOST DELIBERATE part of first-language teaching is the business of telling a child what each thing is called. We ordinarily speak of *the* name of a thing as if there were just one, but in fact, of course, every referent has many names. The dime in my pocket is not only a *dime*. It is also *money*, a *metal object*, a *thing*, and, moving to subordinates, it is a *1952 dime*, in fact, a *particular 1952 dime* with a unique pattern of scratches, discolorations, and smooth places. When such an object is named for a very young child how is it called? It may be named *money* or *dime* but probably not *metal object, thing, 1952 dime,* or *particular 1952 dime*. The dog out on the lawn is not only a *dog* but is also a *boxer*, a *quadruped*, an *animate being*; it is the *landlord's dog*, named *Prince*. How will it be identified for a child? Sometimes it will be called a *dog*, sometimes *Prince*, less often a *boxer*, and almost never a *quadruped*, or *animate being*. Listening to many adults name things for many children, I find that their choices are quite uniform and that I can anticipate them from my own inclinations. How are these choices determined and what are their consequences for the cognitive development of the child?

Adults have notions about the kind of language appropriate for use with children. Especially strong and universal is the belief that children have trouble pronouncing long names and so should always be given the shortest possible names. A word is preferable to a phrase and, among words, a monosyllable is better than a polysyllable. This predicts the preference for *dog* and *Prince* over *boxer, quadruped,* and *animate being*. It predicts the choice of *dime* over *metal object* and *particular 1952 dime*.

Zipf (*10*) has shown that the length of a word (in phonemes or

Reprinted from *Psychological Review* (1958), **65** (1), by permission of the author and the American Psychological Association.

syllables) is inversely related to its frequency in the printed language. Consequently the shorter names for any thing will usually also be the most frequently used names for that thing, and so it would seem that the choice of a name is usually predictable from either frequency or brevity. The monosyllables *dog* and *Prince* have much higher frequencies according to the Thorndike-Lorge list (8) than do the polysyllables *boxer, quadruped,* and *animate being.*

It sometimes happens, however, that the frequency-brevity principle makes the wrong prediction. The thing called a *pineapple* is also *fruit. Fruit* is the shorter and more frequent term, but adults will name the thing *pineapple.* Similarly they will say *apple, banana, orange,* and even *pomegranate;* all of them longer and less frequent words than the perfectly appropriate *fruit.* Brevity seems not to be the powerful determinant we had imagined. The frequency principle can survive this kind of example, but only if it is separated from counts like the Thorndike-Lorge of overall frequency in the printed language. On the whole the word *fruit* appears more often than the word *pineapple* (and also is shorter), but we may confidently assume that, when pineapples are being named, the word *pineapple* is more frequent than the word *fruit.* This, of course, is a kind of frequency more directly relevant to our problem. Word counts of general usage are only very roughly applicable to the prediction of what will be said when something is named. What we need is referent-name counts. We don't have them, of course, but if we had them it is easy to see that they would improve our predictions. Bananas are called *banana,* apples, *apple,* and oranges, *orange* more often than any of them is called *fruit.* The broad frequency-brevity principle predicts that *money* and *dime* will be preferred to *metal object, 1952 dime,* and *particular 1952 dime,* but it does not predict the neglect of the common monosyllable *thing.* For this purpose we must again appeal to imagined referent-name counts, according to which dimes would surely be called *dime* or *money* more often than *thing.*

While the conscious preference for a short name can be overcome by frequency, the preference nevertheless affects the naming act. I have heard parents designate the appropriate objects *pineapple, television, vinegar,* and *policeman;* all these to children who cannot reproduce polysyllabic words. Presumably they use the names because that is what the referents are usually called, but the adult's sense of absurdity of giving such words to a child is often evident. He may smile as he says it or remark, "That's too hard for you to say, isn't it?"

Some things are named in the same way by all adults for all children.

This is true of the apple and the orange. Other things have several common names, each of them used by a specifiable group of adults to specifiable children. The same dog is *dog* to most of the world and *Prince* in his own home and perhaps on his own block. The same man is a *man* to most children, *policeman* to some at times, *Mr. Jones* to the neighborhood kids, and *papa* to his own. Referent-name counts from people in general will not predict these several usages. A still more particular name count must be imagined. The name given a thing by an adult for a child is determined by the frequency with which various names have been applied to such things in the experience of the particular adult. General referent-name counts taken from many people will predict much that the individual does, but, for a close prediction, counts specific to the individual would be needed.

The frequencies to which we are now appealing have not, of course, been recorded. We are explaining imagined preferences in names by imagined frequencies of names. It is conceivable, certainly, that some of these specific word counts might be made and a future naming performance independently predicted from a past frequency. Probably, however, such frequencies will never be known, and if we choose to explain particular naming performances by past frequencies we shall usually have to infer the frequency from the performance.

BEYOND THE FREQUENCY PRINCIPLE

A frequency explanation is not very satisfying even when the appeal is to known frequencies. The question will come to mind: Why is one name more common than another? Why is a dog called *dog* more often than *quadruped* and, by some people, called *Prince* more often than *dog?* Perhaps it just happened that way, like driving on the right side of the road in America and on the left in England. The convention is preserved but has no justification outside itself. As things have worked out, coins are usually named by species as *dime, nickel,* or *penny* while the people we know have individual names like *John, Mary,* and *Jim.* Could it just as easily be the other way around? Might we equally well give coins proper names and introduce people as types?

The referent for the word *dime* is a large class of coins. The name is equally appropriate to all members of this class. To name a coin *dime* is to establish its equivalence, for naming purposes, with all other coins of the same denomination. This equivalence for naming purposes corresponds to a more general equivalence for all purposes of economic exchange. In the grocery one dime is as good as another but quite different from any nickel or penny. For a child the name given an object anticipates the equivalences and differences that will need to be observed in most of his dealings with such an object. To make proper denotative use of the word *dime* he must be able to distinguish members of the referent category from everything else. When he learns that, he has solved more than a language problem. He has an essential bit of equipment for doing business. The most common names for coins could not move from the species level to the level of proper names without great alteration in our nonlinguistic culture. We should all be numismatists preparing our children to recognize a particular priceless 1910 dime.

Many things are reliably given the same name by the whole community. The spoon is seldom called anything but *spoon,* although it is also a piece of *silverware,* an *artifact,* and a *particular ill-washed restaurant spoon.* The community-wide preference for the word *spoon* corresponds to the community-wide practice of treating spoons as equivalent but different from knives and forks. There are no proper names for individual spoons because their individuality seldom signifies. It is the same way with pineapples, dimes, doors, and taxicabs. The most common name for each of these categorizes them as they need to be categorized for the community's nonlinguistic purposes. The most common name is at the level of usual utility.

People and pets have individual names as well as several kinds of generic name. The individual name is routinely coined by those who are disposed to treat the referent as unique, and is available afterwards to any others who will see the uniqueness. A man at home has his own name to go with the peculiar privileges and responsibilities binding him to wife and child. But the same man who is a one-of-a-kind *papa* to his own children is simply a *man* to children at large. He is, like the other members of this large category, someone with no time to play and little tolerance for noise. In some circumstances, this same man will be given the name of his occupation. He is a *policeman* equivalent to other policemen but different from *bus drivers* and *Good Humor men.* A policeman is someone to "behave in front of" and to go to when lost. To the kids in the neighborhood the man is Mr. Jones, unique in his way—a crank, bad tempered, likely to shout at you if you play out in front of his house. It is the same way with dogs as with people. He may be a unique *Prince* to his owners, who feed and house him, but he is just a *dog* to the rest of the world. A homeless dog reverts to namelessness, since there is none to single him out from his species. Dimes and nickels have much the same significance for an entire society and their usual names are fixed at this level of significance. People and pets function uniquely for some and in various generic ways for others. They have a corresponding variety of designations, but each name is at the utility level for the group that uses it. Our naming practices for coins and people correspond to our nonlinguistic practices, and it is difficult to imagine changing the one without changing the other.

The names provided by parents for children anticipate the functional structure of the child's world.[1] This is not, of course, something parents are aware of doing. When we name a thing there does not seem to be any process of choice. Each thing has its name, just one, and that is what we give to a child. The one name is, of course, simply the usual name for us. Naming each thing in accordance with local frequencies, parents unwittingly transmit their own cognitive structures. It is a world in which *Prince* is unique among dogs and *papa* among men, *spoons* are all alike but different from *forks*. It may be a world of *bugs* (to be stepped on), of *flowers* (not to be picked), and *birds* (not to be stoned). It may be a world in which *Niggers*, like spoons, are all of a kind. A division of caste creates a vast categorical equivalence and a correspondingly generic name. *Mr. Jones* and *Mr. Smith* do not come out of racial anonymity until their uniqueness is appreciated.

Adults do not invariably provide a child with the name that is at the level of usual utility in the adult world. An effort is sometimes made to imagine the utilities of a child's life. Some parents will, at first, call every sort of coin *money*. This does not prepare a child to buy and sell, but then he may be too young for that. All coins are equivalent for the very young child in that they are objects not to be put into the mouth and not to be dropped down the register, and *money* anticipates that equivalence. A more differentiated terminology can wait upon the age of storegoing. Sometimes an adult is aware of a child's need for a distinction that is not coded in the English lexicon. A new chair comes into

---

[1] The equivalence of dimes and their distinctiveness as a class from nickels and pennies is strongly suggested by the appearance of individual coins as well as by their names. Variations in size, weight, and hue are far greater between classes than within a class. This, of course, is because coins are manufactured in accordance with a categorical scheme which is also represented in our names for coins. It is possible, then, that a child might structure coins in the culturally approved manner if he never heard them named at all. However, we cannot be sure that an untutored child would not put all shiny new coins into one class and all the dingy specimens into another. When the referents are not manufactured articles but are such things as dogs, people, flowers, and insects, it is clear that autochthonous factors in perception do not force any single scheme of categorization. The names applied must be the child's principal clue to the locally functioning scheme.

the house and is not going to be equivalent to the shabby chairs already there. A child is permitted to sit on the old chairs but will not be permitted on the new one. A distinctive name is created from the combinational resources of the language. *The new chair* or *the good chair* is not to be assimilated to *chairs* in general.

Eventually, of course, children learn many more names for each thing than the one that is most frequent and useful. Sometimes a name is supplied in order to bring forward an immediately important property of the referent. A child who starts bouncing the coffee pot needs to be told that it is *glass*. Sometimes a name is supplied to satisfy the child's curiosity as to the place of a referent in a hierarchy of categories. Chairs are *furniture* and so are tables; carrots are a *vegetable* but apples are not. Probably, however, both children and adults make some distinction among these various names. *The* name of a thing, the one that tells what it "really" is, is the name that constitutes the referent as it needs to be constituted for most purposes. The other names represent possible recategorizations useful for one or another purpose. We are even likely to feel that these recategorizations are acts of imagination, whereas the major categorization is a kind of passive recognition of the true character of the referent.

THE CHILD'S CONCRETE VOCABULARY

It is a commonplace saying that the mind of a child is relatively "concrete" and the mind of an adult "abstract." The words "concrete" and "abstract" are sometimes used in the sense of subordinate and superordinate. In this sense a relatively concrete mind would operate with subordinate categories and an abstract mind with superordinate categories. It is recorded in many studies of vocabulary acquisition (e.g., 2, 6) that children ordinarily use the words *milk* and *water* before the word *liquid;* the words *apple* and *orange* before *fruit; table* and *chair* before *furniture; mama* and *daddy* before *parent* or *person;* etc. Very high-level superordinate terms like *article, action, quality,* and *relation,* though they are common in adult speech (8), are very seldom heard from preschool children (2). Presumably this kind of vocabulary comparison is one of the sources of the notion that the child's mind is more concrete than the mind of the adult.[2] However, the vocabulary of a child is not a

[2] From the facts of vocabulary acquisition alone it is not possible to draw safe conclusions about cognitive development. Such conclusions rely on something like the following set of assumptions. A subject, whether animal or human, is ordinarily credited with a cognitive category when he extends some distinctive response to new instances of the category and withholds it from noninstances. Words, when used to

very direct index of his cognitive preferences. The child's vocabulary is more immediately determined by the naming practices of adults.

The occasion for a name is ordinarily some particular thing. In the naming it is categorized. The preference among possible names seems to go to the one that is most commonly applied to the referent in question. That name will ordinarily categorize the referent so as to observe the equivalences and differences that figure in its usual utilization. There are not many purposes for which all liquids are equivalent or all fruits, furniture, or parents; and so the names of these categories are less commonly used for denotation than are the names of categories subordinate to them. It is true that words like *article, action, quality,* and *relation* are rather common in adult written English, but we can be sure that these frequencies in running discourse are not equaled in naming situations. Whatever the purposes for which all articles are equivalent, or all actions, or qualities, they are not among the pressing needs of children.

It is not invariably true that vocabulary builds from concrete to abstract. *Fish* is likely to be learned before *perch* and *bass; house* before *bungalow* and *mansion; car* before *Chevrolet* and *Plymouth* (6). The more concrete vocabulary waits for the child to reach an age where his purposes differentiate kinds of fish and makes of cars. There is much elaborately concrete vocabulary that is not introduced until one takes courses in biology, chemistry, and botany. No one has ever proved that vocabulary builds from the concrete to the abstract more often than it builds from the abstract to the concrete. The best generalization seems to be that each thing is first given its most common name. This name seems to categorize on the level of usual utility. That level sometimes falls on the most concrete categories in a hierarchy (proper names for significant people), and vocabulary then builds toward the more abstract categories (names for ethnic groups, personality types, social classes).

---

denote new referents, are such a distinctive response. If children speak words they probably can make correct denotative use of them, and so the presence of the word in a child's vocabulary may be taken as evidence that he possesses the category to which the word makes reference. The instances of the category are presumed not to be differentiated by the child unless he uses words for such differentiations. If all of these assumptions are made it would seem to follow that the direction of vocabulary growth (from subordinate to superordinate or vice versa) reveals the direction of cognitive development. When the assumptions of such an argument are explicitly stated, it is clear that they are too many and too doubtful. Obviously words may be spoken but not understood; objects may be differentiated by nonlinguistic response even though they are not differentiated linguistically. However, it is not my purpose here to quarrel with these assumptions but rather to show that, even when they are accepted, the facts of vocabulary growth do not compel the conclusion that cognitive development is from the concrete to the abstract.

Utility sometimes centers on a relatively abstract level of categorization (fish) and vocabulary then builds in both directions (perch and vertebrate). Probably utility never centers on the most abstract levels (thing, substance, etc.), and so probably there is no hierarchy within which vocabulary builds in an exclusively concrete direction.

In the literature describing first-language acquisition (5) there is much to indicate that children easily form large abstract categories. There are, to begin with, the numerous cases in which the child overgeneralizes the use of a conventional word. The word *dog* may, at first, be applied to every kind of four-legged animal. It sometimes happens that every man who comes into the house is called *daddy*. When children invent their own words, these often have an enormous semantic range. Wilhelm Stern's (7) son Gunther used *psee* for leaves, trees, and flowers. He used *bebau* for all animals. Lombroso (9) tells of a child who used *qua qua* for both duck and water and *afta* for drinking glass, the contents of a glass, and a pane of glass. Reports of this kind do not suggest that children are deficient in abstracting ability. It even looks as if they may favor large categories.

There are two extreme opinions about the direction of cognitive development. There are those who suppose that we begin by discriminating to the limits of our sensory acuity, seizing each thing in its uniqueness, noting every hair and flea of the particular dog. Cognitive development involves neglect of detail, abstracting from particulars so as to group similars into categories. By this view abstraction is a mature rather than a primitive process. The contrary opinion is that the primitive stage in cognition is one of a comparative lack of differentiation. Probably certain distinctions are inescapable; the difference between a loud noise and near silence, between a bright contour and a dark ground, etc. These inevitable discriminations divide the perceived world into a small number of very large (abstract) categories. Cognitive development is increasing differentiation. The more distinctions we make, the more categories we have and the smaller (more concrete) these are. I think the latter view is favored in psychology today. While there is good empirical and theoretical support (1, 3, 4) for the view that development is differentiation, there is embarrassment for it in the fact that much vocabulary growth is from the concrete to the abstract. This embarrassment can be eliminated.

Suppose a very young child applies the word *dog* to every four-legged creature he sees. He may have abstracted a limited set of attributes and created a large category, but his abstraction will not show up in his vocabulary. Parents will not provide him with a conventional name for his category, e.g., *quadruped,* but instead will require him to narrow his use of *dog* to its proper range. Suppose a child calls all elderly ladies *aunt.* He will not be told that the usual name for his category is *elderly ladies* but, instead, will be taught to cut back *aunt* to accord with standard usage. In short, the sequence in which words are acquired is set by adults rather than children, and may ultimately be determined by the utility of the various categorizations. This will sometimes result in a movement of vocabulary toward higher abstraction and sometimes a movement toward greater concreteness. The cognitive development of the child may nevertheless always take the direction of increasing differentiation or concreteness.

The child who spontaneously hits on the category four-legged animals will be required to give it up in favor of dogs, cats, horses, cows, and the like. When the names of numerous subordinates have been mastered, he may be given the name *quadruped* for the superordinate. This abstraction is not the same as its primitive forerunner. The schoolboy who learns the word *quadruped* has abstracted from differentiated and named subordinates. The child has abstracted through a failure to differentiate. Abstraction after differentiation may be the mature process, and abstraction from a failure to differentiate the primitive. Needless to say, the abstractions occurring on the two levels need not be coincident, as they are in our quadruped example.

SUMMARY

Though we often think of each thing as having a name—a single name—in fact, each thing has many equally correct names. When some thing is named for a child, adults show considerable regularity in their preference for one of the many possible names. This paper is addressed to the question: "What determines the name given to a child for a thing?" The first answer is that adults prefer the shorter to the longer expression. This gives way to the frequency principle. Adults give a thing the name it is most commonly given. We have now come full circle and are left with the question, "Why is one name for a thing more common than another?"

It seems likely that things are first named so as to categorize them in a maximally useful way. For most purposes Referent A is a spoon rather than a piece of silverware, and Referent B is a dime rather than a metal object. The same referent may have its most useful categorization on one level (*Prince*) for one group (the family) and on another level (*dog*) for another group (strangers). The categorization that is most useful for very young children (*money*) may change as they grow older (*dime* and *nickel*).

With some hierarchies of vocabulary the more concrete terms are learned before the abstract; probably the most abstract terms are never learned first, but it often happens that a hierarchy develops in both directions from a middle level of abstraction. Psychologists who believe that mental development is from the abstract to the concrete, from a lack of differentiation to increased differentiation, have been embarrassed by the fact that vocabulary often builds in the opposite direction. This fact need not trouble them, since the sequence in which words are acquired is not determined by the cognitive preferences of children so much as by the naming practices of adults.

REFERENCES

1. Gibson, J. J., & Gibson, Eleanor, J. Perceptual learning: differentiation or enrichment? *Psychol. Rev.*, 1955, **62**, 32–41.
2. International Kindergarten Union. *A study of the vocabulary of children before entering the first grade.* Baltimore: Williams & Wilkins, 1928.
3. Lashley, K. S., & Wade, Marjorie. The Pavlovian theory of generalization. *Psychol. Rev.*, 1946, **53**, 72–87.
4. Lewin, K. *A dynamic theory of personality.* New York: McGraw-Hill, 1935.
5. McCarthy, Dorothea. Language development in children. In L. Carmichael (Ed.), *Manual of child psychology.* New York: Wiley, 1946. Pp. 477–581.
6. Smith, M. E. An investigation of the development of the sentence and the extent of vocabulary in young children. *Univer. Iowa Stud. Child Welfare*, 1926, **3** (5).
7. Stern, Clara, & Stern, W. *Die Kindersprache.* Leipzig: Barth, 1920.
8. Thorndike, E. L., & Lorge, I. *The teacher's word book of 30,000 words.* New York: Bureau of Publications, Teachers Coll., Columbia Univer., 1944.
9. Werner, H. *Comparative psychology of mental development.* Chicago: Follett, 1948.
10. Zipf, G. K. *The psycho-biology of language.* Boston: Houghton-Mifflin, 1935.

MENTAL GROWTH AND

PERSONALITY DEVELOPMENT:

A LONGITUDINAL STUDY

Lester W. Sontag, Charles T. Baker, and
Virginia L. Nelson

FELS RESEARCH INSTITUTE FOR STUDY OF
HUMAN DEVELOPMENT

THE PRESENT RESEARCH is based on a study of 140 Fels children. These children were selected from the total group of Fels children for only one reason. They alone had a relatively complete series of Stanford-Binet Intelligence Tests and other longitudinal records from infancy through at least 10 years of age. There are 89 different families in this group. In some cases all of the children of a family were members of the Fels program; in other cases only one or few of the children participated in the program, although incidental information may have been recorded about the non-Fels siblings. The children used as subjects are, at the time of this writing, all over 12 years of age. The longitudinal records of their complete childhood are the extensive data which will be used in this study.

Two major criteria of IQ change were used in the study: the amount of increase or decrease in IQ between ages 4½ and 6 years and between 6 and 10 years of age. When the former criterion was used the boys tended more frequently to show patterns of gain in IQ. A chi-square between the number of boys and girls falling into the four quartiles was 3.66, which is significant between the .10 and .05 levels. Analysis of the age 6 to 10 distribution also resulted in more boys showing acceleratory

From The Fels Research Institute for the Study of Human Development, Antioch College, Fels Monograph Series, Child Development Publications. Reprinted from Monographs of the Society for Research in Child Development, Inc. (1958), **23** (2), Whole No. 68.

patterns. In this case a chi-square analysis yielded a value of 11.20, significant at less than the .01 level. In all of our analyses by the various criteria, and regardless of which form was used, there was a tendency for boys to gain more at all ages, but this tendency was most pronounced in the years after age 6.

PERSONALITY RATING SCALES

A set of rating scales was developed to aid in making judgments of a number of personality factors. The ratings of personality were based on all the accumulated longitudinal information on each child with the exception of mental measurement data. The central file on each subject consisted of several hundred pages of narrative and objective information.

The central files were read chronologically, individual by individual. Two age periods appeared to fit both the IQ criteria data and the material that was to be rated. It was decided that an individual central file would be read until age 6, at which time ratings would be made on the various personality dimensions. The reader would then continue reading until age 10 at which time a new set of personality ratings would be made (7 point scale).

1. *Emotional Independence from Parents.* The first scale was a rating of the child's attempts to gain satisfaction by getting warmth and approval from one or both parents, or parent surrogates, as opposed to gaining satisfaction from either identification with his peer group, or interest in solitary pursuits.

2. *Aggressiveness in Peer Relationships.* The lowest ratings on this scale were reserved for those children who characteristically were quiet and passive in most play or other group situations involving other children.

3. *Self-Initiated Behavior.* This scale ranged from a low score for conformity with external demands to a high score given to self-initiated behavior. The child given a low rating at age 6 or at age 10 was judged by the observer to be overly well behaved at home. The child was seldom or never a disciplinary problem to his parents.

4. *Socialization.* Children given a low rating on this scale were characteristically withdrawing children in the variety of group situations in which they were observed.

5. *Friendliness.* This scale ranged from a low score for repeated hostile behavior to a high rating for warmth and friendliness toward peers and adults.

6. *Problem-Solving Behavior.* In this scale an attempt was made to judge the child's behavior when he was confronted with an obstacle in various types of situations. These situations included learning situations, group activities, and the use of materials. Behavior which would tend to give the child a low score on this scale included such things as attempts to shift responsibility in problem-solving situations to another person, soliciting the help of an adult, or directly asking other children to complete his project. A child was given a high rating on this scale if he made repeated efforts to find ways to overcome various obstacle situations.

7. *Anticipation of Reward.* The dimension present in this scale involved the relationship between the occurrence of patterns of behavior and the length of time until these behaviors brought reward, approval, or some type of gratification. A child received a low rating at age 6 if many of his characteristic behaviors were ones that would appear to bring immediate gratification rather than bringing rewards later in time.

8. *General Competitiveness.* A child was given a low rating on this scale at age 6 if he typically tended to withdraw from competitive situations in nursery school and in play activity at home. In some cases the child would verbalize his distrust of his own ability to the nursery school teachers. The child who was rated high on this scale, on the other hand, was apt to verbalize realistic self-confidence in a number of areas.

9. *Femininity.* This scale was used in rating only the girls in our sample. This scale was an attempt to separate the girls who appeared to derive great satisfactions from being thought of as pretty, dainty, or charming by adults, or who appeared to seek a considerable amount of approval or admiration for physical attractiveness, in contrast to the girls who tended to compete in more masculine or duo-sexual areas such as sports, scholastic attainment, or class leadership.

10. *Sibling Rivalry.* This scale was an attempt to rate the amount of friction present between siblings as a result of behavior initiated by the subject being rated.

11. *Anxiety.* This scale was an attempt to rate the general level of emotional comfort or freedom of movement in a variety of life situations. A child was given a low rating on this scale at age 6 if there was little evidence in the central file of anxious behaviors. Observers may have commented that he generally appeared poised or self-assured in group situations. He may have been described as "even tempered," "not easily upset," or "he takes physical accidents, difficulties or disappointments in his stride." He tended to gain satisfactions from positive family and peer relationships. A child was given a high rating at this age if

there was a pattern of some particular behavior reflecting upsetting situations or specific fears.

12. *Scholastic Competition.* This was designed to rate competition in academic aspects of school work and was therefore used for rating only at age 10.

13. *Independence in Scholastic Achievement.* In this scale, behaviors were rated which would indicate whether the child sought scholastic achievement out of self-motivation, or whether he conformed to the wishes of parents or teachers in order to gain their approval.

14. *Parental Emphasis on School Achievement.* A rating was made of the amount of affective emphasis on school achievement applicable to the subject at age 10. A high rating was given on this scale if one or both parents appeared to place a high emphasis on school achievement, and if this emphasis was paralled with high scholastic achievement on the part of the subject.

PERSONALITY FACTORS AND IQ CHANGE

Accelerative and decelerative IQ groups were selected on the basis of the criterion described earlier. There was a total of 35 cases with accelerative trends for each of the two age periods studied, and personality ratings were made for these children.

RESULTS

Analysis of Age 6 Ratings

The results of a chi-square analysis of personality ratings made at age 6 of the children who had the greatest amount of change in IQ during the preschool years revealed that only the rating on independence clearly discriminated between the two IQ change groups, with the IQ ascenders being more independent than the IQ descenders. The latter appear to be more emotionally dependent on their parents during this period.

Analysis of Age 10 Ratings

The relationship between personality factors rated at age 10 and the groups with accelerative or decelerative IQ patterns between age 6 and 10 revealed that a definite cluster of personality variables appeared to be associated with IQ change during the elementary school years. Independence, Aggressiveness, Self-Initiation, Problem-Solving, Anticipation, Competitiveness, and the two scales having to do with scholastic competition all appear to be clearly related to an accelerative IQ pattern.

Conclusions and Remarks

From the various analyses made in this chapter it would appear that our major hypotheses regarding personality factors and individual differences in mental growth rate were essentially substantiated in their broader aspects. A study of the various modes of personality by which children attempt to gain satisfaction in their experiences appeared to be of value in predicting IQ change and in understanding the nature of accelerated or decelerated mental growth rate as related to personality factors. During the preschool years, emotional dependence on parents appears to be clearly associated with the subsequent loss in IQ. During the elementary school years, a cluster of personality traits, with the need for achievement as a common dimension, appears to be closely associated with accelerated or decelerated mental growth patterns. It would also appear that during the preschool years the child who develops modes of behavior characterized by aggressiveness, self-initiation, and competitiveness is laying a basic groundwork for future acceleration in performance on mental tasks. As the child develops these pathways of behavior for satisfactorily handling his interactions with peers and adults, it is not surprising to find a generalization of these behaviors to most new learning situations. The child's motivation to learn new things appears to be enhanced by these general personality characteristics.

Our findings regarding the development of personality as related to the development of intellectual ability would appear to be consistent with an increasingly prevalent attitude toward problems in child development. We may regard intelligence as but one aspect of the total personality. The general motives for behavior which characterize the child's adjustment to many life situations may appropriately serve as a conceptual framework for viewing intelligence and other aspects of personality.

REFERENCES

1. Baldwin, A. L., Kalhorn, Joan, & Breese, Faye H. Patterns of parent behavior. *Psychol. Monogr.*, 1945, **58**, No. 3 (Whole No. 268).
2. Baldwin, A. L., Kalhorn, Joan, & Breese, Faye H. The appraisal of parent behavior. *Psychol. Monogr.*, 1949, **63**, No. 4 (Whole No. 299).
3. Bayley, Nancy. Some increasing parent-child similarities during the growth of children. *J. educ. Psychol.*, 1954, **45**, 1–21.

4. Champney, H. Parent behavior as related to child development: I. Mental gain. Paper read to Amer. Assoc. Advancement Sci., December, 1939.
5. Champney, H. The variables of parent behavior. *J. abnorm. soc. Psychol.*, 1941, **36**, 525–542.
6. Crandall, V. J., & Preston, Anne. Patterns and levels of maternal behavior. *Child Develpm.*, 1955, **26**, 267–277.
7. Ebert, Elizabeth, & Simmons, Katherine. The Brush Foundation study of child growth and development: I. Psychometric tests. *Monogr. Soc. Res. Child Develpm.*, 1943, **8**, No. 2 (Whole No. 35).
8. Edwards, A. L. *Experimental design in psychological research.* New York: Rinehart, 1950.
9. Fromm, Erika, & Hartman, Lenore D. *Intelligence—a dynamic approach.* Garden City, N.Y.: Doubleday, 1955.
10. Garn, S. M. Applications of pattern analysis to anthropometric data. *Ann. N.Y. Acad. Sci.*, 1955, **63**, 537–552.
11. Gesell, A. *The mental growth of the preschool child: A psychological outline of normal development from the birth to the sixth year, including a system of developmental diagnosis.* New York: Macmillan, 1925.
12. Honzik, Marjorie P. Developmental study of the relations of family variables to children's intelligence. *Amer. Psychologist*, 1952, **7**, 527–528. (Abstract)
13. Husen, T. The influence of schooling upon IQ. *Theoria*, 1951, **12**, 61–88.
14. Inhelder, Barbel. Patterns of inductive thinking. *Acta Psychologica*, 1955, **11**, 217–218.
15. Lasko, Joan Kalhorn. Parent behavior toward first and second children. *Genet. Psychol. Monogr.*, 1954, **49**, 97–137.
16. McClelland, D. C., Atkinson, J. W., Clark, R. A., & Lowell, E. L. *The achievement motive.* New York: Appleton-Century-Crofts, 1953.
17. MacFarlane, Jean W. The uses and predictive limitations of intelligence tests in infants and young children. *Bull. World Health Organization*, 1953, **9**, 409–415.
18. McNemar, Q. A critical examination of the University of Iowa studies of environmental influences upon the IQ. *Psychol. Bull.*, 1940, **37**, 63–92.
19. Patterson, C. H. A note on concomitant changes in IQ in a pair of siblings. *J. genet. Psychol.*, 1943, **63**, 307–309.
20. Piaget, J. *The origins of intelligence in children.* New York: International Universities Press, 1952.
21. Piaget, J. *La perception.* (Symposium) Paris: Presses Universitaires de France, 1955.
22. Rafferty, Janet E. Use of two interpretive projective techniques for prediction within the social learning theory of personality. Unpublished doctor's dissertation, Ohio State University, 1952.
23. Richards, Esther L. Relationship of declining intelligence quotients to maladjustment of school children. *Arch. neurol. Psychiat.*, 1937, **30**, 817–838.
24. Roberts, Katherine E., & Ball, Rachel S. A study of personality in young children by means of a series of rating scales. *J. genet. Psychol.*, 1938, **52**, 79–149.

25. Sontag, L. W. Dynamics of personality formation. *Personality*, 1951, 1, 119–130.
26. Sontag, L. W., Baker, C. T., & Nelson, Virginia L. Personality as a determinant of performance. *Amer. J. Orthopsychiat.*, 1955, 25, 555–562.
27. Sontag, L. W., Crandall, V. J., & Lacey, J. I. Dynamics of personality: resolution of infantile dependent need. *Amer. J. Orthopsychiat.*, 1952, 22, 534–541.
28. Sontag, L. W., & Reynolds, E. L. The Fels composite sheet: I. A practical method for analyzing growth progress. *J. Pediat.*, 1945, 26, 327–335.
29. Wagenheim, Lillian. The effect of childhood diseases on IQ variability. *J. consult. Psychol.*, 1954, 18, 354.
30. Wallen, J. E. W. The results of multiple Binet retesting of the same subjects. *J. genet. Psychol.*, 1940, 57, 345–391.
31. Wellman, Beth L., & McCandless, B. R. Factors associated with Binet IQ changes of preschool children. *Psychol. Monogr.*, 1946, 60, No. 2 (Whole No. 278).
32. White, C. The use of ranks in a test of significance for comparing two treatments. *Biometrics*, 1952, 8, 33–41.
33. Wilcoxen, F. *Some rapid approximate statistical procedures.* Stamford: Amer. Cyanamid Co., 1949.
34. Winterbottom, Marian R. The relation of childhood training in independence to achievement motivation. Univer. Microfilms, Publ. No. 5113, Univer. of Michigan. (Abstract)

PERSONALITY AND IQ CHANGE[1]

Jerome Kagan, Lester W. Sontag, Charles T. Baker,
and Virginia L. Nelson

HARVARD UNIVERSITY AND FELS RESEARCH INSTITUTE

RESEARCH ON MENTAL DEVELOPMENT during the last twenty years has indicated that a child's IQ score does not necessarily remain constant with age (2, 3, 4, 10). Several reports (9, 10, 12) suggest that changes in environmental conditions can depress or raise IQ level and it is sometimes implied that these changes may be explained by recourse to personality variables. The purpose of this paper is to demonstrate that changes in IQ during childhood are correlated with certain personality predispositions as inferred from projective test data. The personality variable under study is need for achievement.

Performance on an IQ test is assumed to be a function of at least two major variables; the variety of skills and abilities the person brings to the test situation and his motivation to perform well on the test (2, 6). Since the IQ scores of some children change markedly during the school years, it seems plausible to assume that those children who show marked increases in IQ have a very strong motivation to acquire or develop the various intellectual skills tapped by an IQ test and to perform well in a testing situation. It is suggested that need for achievement, competitive strivings, and curiosity about nature motivate the acquisition and improvement of cognitive abilities and by so doing facilitate increases in tested IQ.

The social environment often awards praise and recognition for intellectual accomplishment, and school age children with a high need for achievement might seek to gratify this need through intellectual activity.

[1] This investigation was supported in part by a research grant (PHS M 1260) from the National Institute of Mental Health of the National Institutes of Health, United States Public Health Service. The writers wish to thank Dr. Seymour B. Sarason for his critical reading of the manuscript, and Mary Schnurer for her assistance in assessing the reliability of the scoring.

Thus it was predicted that children showing marked increases in IQ would produce more achievement imagery on the TAT than those with minimal gains in IQ.

METHOD

A sample of 140 Fels subjects (Ss), 70 of each sex, were chosen for study because a fairly complete record of test information was available on them. From ages 2½ to 6, the Stanford-Binet intelligence test (1916 or 1937 revision) was administered to most Ss twice yearly, on their birthdays and six months after their birthdays. From ages 6 to 12, most Ss received alternately Form L or Form M of the 1937 revision annually, on or near each S's birthday. All of the tests were administered by one of the authors (VLN). The mean IQ of the Fels population is near 120, with standard deviation varying from 14 to 20 IQ points.

In order to obtain groups of Ss who showed the most change in IQ score from ages 6 to 10, a smoothed longitudinal plot of each S's IQ was prepared by averaging the mean of three consecutive test scores around each age. This procedure is explained in detail in other reports (1, 10, 11). This technique tends to eliminate erratic variations in IQ and hopefully furnishes a more valid measure of IQ changes. Then each S's smoothed IQ at age 6 was subtracted from his smoothed IQ at age 10, and this distribution of differences, positive if S gained in IQ and negative if S lost in IQ, was divided into quartiles. This report deals with the projective test information on those Ss in the two extreme groups; those who increased and those who decreased the most in IQ score. These will be called Group A, the IQ ascenders, and Group D, the IQ descenders, respectively. There was no significant difference between the mean IQ of the two extreme quartiles at age six, the means being 119 and 116 for Groups A and D respectively. The average amount of increase in IQ for Group A was larger (plus 17 points) than the corresponding decrease for the members of Group D (minus 5 points) and while 46 percent of Group D lost 5 or more points, every child in Group A gained 10 or more points during the years 6 through 10. The mean IQ of the entire sample of 140 tends to increase slightly from ages 6 to 10, probably as a result of practice effects with the same test. Since every S in Group D showed a decrease in IQ, it might be inferred that the members of Group D did not benefit from practice and familiarity with the test, and it is probably more accurate to view Group D Ss in this light rather than as Ss who showed marked decreases in IQ score.

The projective test stimuli used in the analysis were selected TAT pictures. Two factors governed the choice of the TAT cards which were analyzed. Because the protocols were gathered over a period of years, there was not complete comparability for all Ss for the number of cards administered. Secondly, the specific hypotheses of the study dictated the cards chosen for analysis and Cards 1, 3 BM, 3 GF, 5, 6 BM, 12F, 14, and 17 BM were selected for analysis. The age at which the TAT protocols were administered ranged from 8–9 to 14–6 with median at 11–6 and 80 percent of the protocols obtained between the ages of 11 and 12.

Achievement imagery on the TAT was scored according to the definition of McClelland *et al.* (*8*); and themes involving a reference to competition with a standard of excellence were scored achievement imagery.

RESULTS

Although there was a total of 70 Ss in the two extreme quartiles, not all of the Ss had TAT data for the age range under study. Because there were approximately twice as many boys as there were girls in Group A, all comparisons were first made separately by sex and results were only combined if the direction of the result for both boys and girls in the same IQ group was in the predicted direction.

Need achievement. All achievement themes, save one, occurred to Cards 1 and 17 BM. The typical achievement story to Card I concerned a boy who wanted to master the violin and/or become a famous violinist, while the typical achievement theme to 17 BM involved competitive activity with regard to rope climbing. Table 1 shows the percentage of Ss in each group reporting achievement imagery plots to Cards 1, 17 BM, and to both pictures.

TABLE 1. *Percentage of Ss Reporting Achievement Imagery to Cards 1 and 17 BM*

| | Group A | | | Group D | | |
TAT Card	Boys	Girls	Boys and Girls	Boys	Girls	Boys and Girls
Card 1	36.4	50.0	40.6	27.3	15.0	19.4
Card 17 BM	36.4	30.0	34.4	0.0	15.0	9.7
Cards 1 and 17 BM	22.7	10.0	18.8	0.0	0.0	0.0

For both Cards 1 and 17 BM, more male and female Ss in Group A reported achievement imagery than the boys or girls of Group D. For Card 1, the difference between Group A and Group D girls is reliable at the .03 level; the difference for boys is in the predicted direction but not significant. For Cards 17 BM, the difference between Group A and Group D boys is significant ($P = .03$) and in the predicted direction for girls. All P values are for one tail and were evaluated using the exact method suggested by Fisher (5). When the sexes were pooled, comparisons between Groups A and D were significant not only for Cards 1 and 17 BM separately, but also for the number of Ss telling achievement imagery to both Cards 1 and 17 BM ($P < .10$, .03, and .01 respectively). Thus, the Ss who showed increases in IQ were more prone to structure Cards 1 and 17 BM in terms of achievement oriented behavior than the Ss in Group D.

DISCUSSION

In the main, the hypotheses about the differences between Groups A and D have been verified. Boy and girl ascenders produced more TAT achievement imagery than Group D children.

The results are interpreted as indicating that high motivation to achieve may motivate the acquisition of intellectual skills and knowledge which, in turn, facilitates increases in tested IQ. If one accepts the generally assumed notion that boys are more achievement oriented than girls, the fact that there were twice as many boys in Group A as there were girls supports the present interpretation. A recent study using the Edwards Personal Preference Schedule found that high school boys obtained higher need achievement scores than high school girls (7).

These results are not interpreted as indicating that a strong achievement motive is the only variable involved in producing gains in IQ. The Ss in this study are all average or above in IQ and there is not adequate sampling of children with lower IQ levels. One would not expect Ss with low IQs or language handicaps to suddenly show an interest in reading despite achievement needs. The child who spends increased time reading because of a heightened interest in natural processes must have already learned the basic reading skills so that this behavior is not a difficult or unlikely choice for him.

Similarly, needs for achievement should only motivate attempts at improvement of intellectual abilities in a social milieu where praise, recognition, and superior status are awarded for such accomplishment.

That is, achievement-oriented children from homes in which intellectual activity was praised would probably be more likely to master intellectual skills than achievement-oriented children from homes in which such accomplishment was not rewarded. In a cultural environment where athletic ability, fighting prowess, or success with the opposite sex was highly valued, one might expect the child to choose these behavioral channels to gratify his achievement and competitive needs. The parents in the Fels population are predominantly middle class and tend to place importance on intellectual accomplishment. A large majority of the parents have attended college, and since enrollment in the Fels program is voluntary it might be inferred that only parents who valued knowledge and scientific pursuits would be predisposed to become part of the research population. Thus, the children under study tend to come from homes which value intellectual ability.

Study of the educational attainment of the parents of the Ss in Groups A and D revealed no significant difference between the groups with respect to the percentage of families in which both parents attended college (57.1 percent for Group A versus 42.9 percent for Group D; $P >$ .30). Although there is a slight difference favoring the educational level of Group A families, the difference was not dramatic. There may be important differences between Groups A and D with respect to the differential encouragement of intellectual achievement, but measurement of these differences would probably require variables more refined than educational level of the parents. However, even though parental emphasis on intellectual activity may increase the child's desire to improve his cognitive skills, the child's predisposition to adopt or rebel against parental values should selectively influence his motivation to strive for intellectual accomplishment. Thus, the type of relation between parent and child may be an important factor in this process.

Finally, there is the possibility that genetic and/or constitutional variables may play a role in facilitating marked IQ changes. There is considerable data indicating that genetic factors influence general IQ level but less evidence relevant to the role of these variables in producing childhood increases in IQ score. For most of the children in our population, IQs tend to level off during the ages 6–10 and most of the marked changes in level occur during the preschool years. However, the exact relationship between genetic variables and IQ change has yet to be determined. The phenomenon of IQ increase during the school years is admittedly complex and it is not implied that the child's motives are the major factor. However, it is suggested that personality needs may influence this process. Perhaps the most accurate generalization is that for middle-class children with average or above IQ levels, strong achievement needs may facilitate IQ gains by motivating the child to master intellectual skills.

REFERENCES

1. Baker, C. T., Sontag, L. W., & Nelson, Virginia L. Specific ability in IQ change. *J. consult. Psychol.*, 1955, 19, 307–310.
2. Bayley, Nancy. Mental growth in young children. *Yearb. nat. Soc. Stud. Educ.*, 1940, 39, Part II, 11–47.
3. Bayley, Nancy. Consistency and variability in the growth in IQ from birth to eighteen years. *J. genet. Psychol.*, 1949, 75, 165–196.
4. Bradway, Katherine. IQ constancy on the Revised Stanford-Binet from the preschool to the junior high school level. *J. genet Psychol.*, 1944, **65**, 197–217.
5. Fisher, R. A. *Statistical methods for research workers.* (5th ed.) Edinburgh: Oliver & Boyd, 1934.
6. Haggard, E. A., Davis, A., & Havighurst, R. J. Some factors which influence performance of children on intelligence tests. *Amer. Psychol.*, 1948, **3**, 265–266.
7. Klett, C. J. Performance of high school students on the Edwards Personal Preference Schedule. *J. consult. Psychol.*, 1957, **21**, 68–72.
8. McClelland, D. C., Atkinson, J. W., Clark, R. A., & Lowell, E. L. *The achievement motive.* New York: Appleton-Century-Crofts, 1953.
9. Richards, T. W. Mental test performance as a reflection of the child's current life situation: a methodological study. *Child Develpm.*, 1951, **22**, 221–233.
10. Sontag, L. W., Baker, C. T., & Nelson, Virginia L. Personality as a determinant of performance. *Amer. J. Orthopsychiat.*, 1955, **25**, 555–562.
11. Sontag, L. W., Baker, C. T., & Nelson, Virginia L. Mental growth and personality development. *Monogr. Soc. Res. Child Develpm.*, 1958, **23**, No. 2.
12. Wellmann Beth L. & McCandless, B. R. Factors associated with Binet IQ changes of preschool children. *Psychol. Monogr.*, 1946, **60**, No. 2 (Whole No. 278).

THE CONCEPT OF SUBSTANCE

K. Lovell

UNIVERSITY OF LEEDS

BY THE WORD "substance" is meant "amount of matter,"[1] "amount of material," or to use the term of the physicist, "mass." It is intended here to discuss how the child's ideas of "amount of material" develop with age and experience.

Piaget (4, 5, 7) has shown how, in his view, the child slowly builds up the idea of the "object" during the first two years of life. During this period he gradually comes to distinguish between his own body and the other objects of the environment, and builds up a picture of the world as consisting of a number of objects that continue to exist even when they disappear from his sight; and he learns that, as a rule, they maintain their shape and size. He also comes to regard himself as one person among the others around him.

It is not, however, intended to consider further the development of the child's concept of the object at this early age. It is sufficient to say that by the second birthday the ordinary child apprehends a cup of milk, a piece of plasticine, a brick, a doll, etc., as independent entities, and that they remain the same as he looks at them; and that, if they pass from his gaze momentarily, he will find them as he left them, provided they have not been disturbed in the interval. For the adult such a statement is trite, but for the child it indicates real discoveries.

The child's play with sand, water, and the like, whether in the home environment, or nursery and infant school, is of the greatest value to him in helping him to understand that he has a certain quantity of stuff in, say, his hands, or in a tin. Of course maturation as well as experience determines the child's ability to understand. He slowly builds up a vocabulary, and, after a period during which he may use words without

[1] Equally well "quantity of matter."

Reprinted by permission from *The Growth of Mathematical and Scientific Concepts in Children* (1961), Univer. of London Press.

having much idea of their significance, he comes to understand that he has "much," "little," "a lot of," "the same," and so forth, although he cannot, of course, at this stage use terms such as "amount of matter." Furthermore, if he adds sand to the heap he already has, he comes to understand that he has "more," and if he throws away some of his water he comes to know that he has "less." As far as we can judge, the child comes to realize, as a result of age and experience, that the amount of milk in a cup, the quantity of sand in the pit, the lump of plasticine that he sees on the table, remains the same, at least for very short periods, if nothing is added or taken away, and if the substance is not disturbed in any way.

PIAGET'S VIEWS ON THE CHILD'S CONSERVATION OF SUBSTANCE

Only in recent years, however, have we found out that up to 7–8 years of age or so, the average child does not appear to understand that the amount or quantity of matters stays the same regardless of any changes in shape or position. That is an illuminating piece of insight into child thinking for which we have to thank Piaget in the first instance. This concept of conservation of substance (or invariance of substance) is an important one, for the mind can only deal effectively with a lump of plasticine, a glass of water, or a collection of shells, if they remain permanent in amount and independent of the rearrangement of their individual parts.

As was stated when dealing with number, Piaget's work suggests that a child's thinking is largely influenced by his perceptions between 4 and 7 years of age. During this period it seems to be so determined because he centers his attention on one aspect, dimension, or element of the situation and ignores other aspects. But from 7 to 8 years of age onwards he is increasingly able to break away from the influence of his perceptions and, in Piaget's view, gains in power to apply logical thought to practical problems and concrete situations. As we saw earlier, he is supposed to come to appreciate the significance of his own actions, so that they acquire the form of reversible operations in the mind and thus render him less dependent upon perception.

From his many experiments involving the conservation of continuous substances (e.g., plasticine, water) and discontinuous substances (e.g., beads, shells), Piaget concluded that children pass through three stages; namely nonconservation, transition, and conservation. In a typical experiment a child was given two equal balls of modelling clay, which he (the child) agreed were of the same size. One of the balls was then rolled out to look like a sausage. At the first stage the child denied that the amounts of clay in the ball and sausage were the same. He may have made a response such as, "It's more because the sausage is longer." At the transition stage, he arrives at the concept of conservation under some conditions, or at one moment, but will lose the idea under slightly changed conditions. But according to Piaget, from 7 to 8 years of age he increasingly feels the logical necessity for conservation and will support it by argument. For example, Piaget (4, p. 140; 6, p. 16) maintains that the child says the sausage can be returned to the shape of a ball, or what has been lost in one direction has been gained in another, or that nothing has been added or taken away.

In another typical experiment two identical vessels A and B are filled to the same height with a colored liquid. Young children of 4–6 years of age will admit that the amounts of liquid in the two vessels are the same. Next the liquid in vessel A is left undisturbed, but the

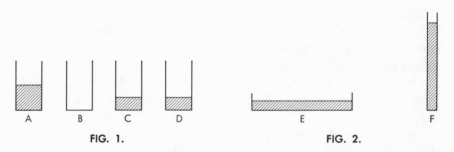

A   B   C   D   E   F

FIG. 1.   FIG. 2.

liquid in B is poured into the vessels C and D, which are identical in size and shape to A and B, so that the amounts of liquid in C and D are the same (Figure 1). The child is then asked, in suitable language, if the amount of liquid in C and in D together is the same as the amount of liquid in A. Children of 4–6 years of age deny that the amounts are still the same. They notice that the levels are lower, and so, for them, there must be less liquid. Or, they notice that there are two vessels, and so consider that there must be more liquid.

Even at 6–7 years of age some children do not affirm that the amounts of liquid are the same. If the liquid in B is poured into the two vessels C and D they may agree; but if it is poured into a wide vessel (E) so that the depth of liquid is very small, or into a thin vessel (F) so that the column of liquid is tall (see Figure 2), they will deny conservation. It seems that it is not a lack of verbal understanding that causes the child's confusion since he admits to conservation when perceptual differences are small, but denies conservation when perceptual differences are great.

By 7–8 years of age, the child admits to conservation and stands firm in his conviction; and, as already stated, Piaget maintains that the child can only arrive at the concept because logical concepts are already at his disposal. He claims that the child can reverse the process in his mind, thus employing the logical concept of an inverse operation; or he can grasp that what has been lost in one dimension has been gained in another, so employing the logical concept of compensation or displacement of parts ("Taking from here and putting there.").

FURTHER EXPERIMENTAL EVIDENCE ON THE CHILD'S CONSERVATION OF SUBSTANCE

Lovell and Ogilvie (3) report work in which 322 children in a north of England junior school were examined individually in order to study the growth of the concept of conservation of substance. Balls of plasticine about two inches in diameter were used. Providing the child agreed that the amounts of plasticine in the two balls were equal to begin with, he was deemed to be a suitable subject for the experiment. One ball was rolled out to form a "sausage," and the subjects were questioned at some length regarding the amounts of material in the "sausage" and ball. The accompanying Table 1 shows the percentage number of children found at each of the three stages mentioned above, for each of the four years of the junior school (7+ to 11+ years); the number of children in the year groups being respectively 83, 65, 99, 75, from youngest to oldest.

TABLE 1.

	Number of Children		Stage 3 Conservation (percent)	Stage 2 Transition (percent)	Stage 1 nonconservation (percent)
1st year	83		36	33	31
2nd year	65		68	12	20
3rd year	99		74	15	11
4th year	75		86	9	5

Hyde (2) also repeated this experiment using plasticine balls and obtained similar results. Thus the stages proposed by Piaget have been confirmed, and the answers given by the children often agree closely with those reported by him. On the other hand the work shows that the development of the concept is much more complex than Piaget reckons. There is no doubt then that if a substance changes its shape it is likely to change in amount.

In a further experiment Lovell and Ogilvie used a rubber band. The children were asked if there was the same amount of rubber in the band when it was stretched, as there had been a moment earlier, when it was unstretched. It was found that about one-third of those who were non-conservers in the experiment involving plasticine were conservers in the experiment employing the rubber band. Hyde also found that some children who were nonconservers in the test using plasticine balls were conservers when a liquid was poured from one vessel into another of different shape. Again, Hyde found that when liquids in vessels A and B, which certain children had agreed were equal in amount, were poured into glasses C and D respectively, they agreed that the amounts in the latter vessels were equal, in spite of the great perceptual differences (Figure 3).

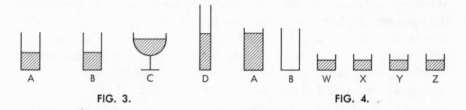

FIG. 3.   FIG. 4.

Yet, when the liquids in A and B were matched again for equality, and the liquid in B was poured into a number of smaller vessels (Figure 4) which were similar to one another, some of those who had previously agreed to conservation, now denied that the total amount of liquid in W, X, Y, and Z was equal to the amount in A. Beard (1) also found, among the sixty 6 to 7-year-olds she tested, that some who were nonconservers when comparing balls of plasticine could conserve when water was poured from one vessel to a number of smaller ones.

The evidence from these experiments strongly suggests that as far as continuous quantities are concerned, children who are conservers of substance in one situation are not inevitably conservers in another. On this point the more recent findings seem to lead to conclusions at variance with those of Piaget. The interpretation usually given to his view is that once the concept of conservation of substance has been attained, it holds in all situations involving conservation of substance, whether continuous or discontinuous quantities are used. If Piaget is understood correctly, the evidence supplied by Lovell and Ogilvie, as well as that of Hyde and Beard, does not support his view, which in our opinion, hides the distinctive traits of child thinking. It seems, rather, that the concept is applicable only in highly specific situations at first, and that it increases in depth and complexity with experience and maturation. Piaget's view that the child arrives at the concept because he is able to argue logically may or may not be correct. It is believed that he underestimates the part played by the experience of the child in experimenting with water, sand, plasticine, etc., in many and varied situations. Sheer experience of the physical world seems to be affecting conservation more than Piaget reckons, and this theme will be developed further, later in the book. It is equally likely that the concept of conservation of substance—indeed, any concept—grows out of the interlocking of several organizations of past impressions that normally remain outside consciousness (schemata), which in turn grow out of many and varied experiences. The child may then invoke logical argument to justify the attainment of a concept which was, in fact, attained on grounds other than logical. Or, it is equally likely that experience and the development of logical thought abet one another and together give certainty.

It is not possible to say how far the inability to conserve substance affects the lives of children and the less intelligent adolescents and adults. Most people, except for those suffering from moderate or severe mental subnormality, probably become aware that the amount of water in a bucket or of cement in a bag remains the same if nothing is added or taken from it or if it is not disturbed in any way. But some of the least able, or least wary, may continue to be uncertain of the concept of invariance of substance even in very simple situations and the uncertainty may influence their lives in ways we know not. For example, Lovell and Ogilvie report that some children will pay more for a piece of toffee when it is in one shape than when it is in another. Such persons may be more often deceived by their perceptions than the majority are, and they are probably more susceptible to deception practiced by the unscrupulous.

REFERENCES

1. Beard, R. An investigation of concept formation among infant school children. Unpublished Ph.D. thesis, University of London Library, 1957.
2. Hyde, D. M. An investigation of Piaget's theories of the development of the concept of number. Unpublished Ph.D. thesis, University of London Library, 1959.

3. Lovell, K., & Ogilvie, E. A study of the conservation of substance in the junior school child. *Brit. J. Educ. Psychol.*, 1960, **30**, 109–118.
4. Piaget, J. *The psychology of intelligence.* London: Routledge and Kegan Paul, 1950.
5. Piaget, J. *The origins of intelligence in the child.* London: Routledge and Kegan Paul, 1953.
6. Piaget, J. *Logic and psychology.* University of Manchester Press, 1953.
7. Piaget, J. *The child's construction of reality.* London: Routledge and Kegan Paul, 1955.

THE CONCEPT OF WEIGHT

K. Lovell

UNIVERSITY OF LEEDS

IT IS USEFUL to begin the study of the concept of weight by defining the term "weight" itself. The shorter Oxford Dictionary defines it as "The quantity of a portion of matter as measured by the amount of its downward force due to gravity." In other words "weight" is a result of the gravitational pull. It is not the same as the amount of matter; the amount of matter in a body remains the same whether at 10,000 feet above mean sea level or 10,000 feet below; but its weight changes. The body will weigh heavier at the bottom of a coal mine than on the mountain top, if weighed on a spring balance, although the quantity of matter will naturally be the same. This distinction between amount or quantity of substance, and weight, will be made again later on; for, according to Piaget, the concept of conservation of weight develops a couple of years later than the concept of conservation of substance.

How then does the child acquire this concept of weight? In his preschool days he will hear words like "heavy" and "light" being used, but it is not until he has picked up objects and by means of his muscle sense felt this gravitational pull—he does not of course know it as such—that he can have any idea of the meanings of words associated with weight. Let it be repeated, the concept of weight commences to develop through muscle sense, and the "picking up" of objects or "carrying loads on the back" comes before the use of scales. The child, then, needs much experience of comparing weights, using his own muscles. These then are some of the activities that will help:

1. Children pick up objects and learn to distinguish by muscle sense which is the heavier. This game can be played with the eyes closed.
2. Children examine groups of objects, each group consisting of two objects. They say, or write down, which of the objects in each group is the heavier, and check their answer by lifting the objects.

Reprinted by permission from *The Growth of Mathematical and Scientific Concepts in Children* (1961), Univer. of London Press.

3. Miming. Children can mime a scene in which one of them carries a heavy sack on his back and another a light one. Another can blow a feather into the air; and another struggle with a heavy bucket of sand.

When adequate experience has been obtained of weight through muscle sense we may proceed to the use of scales; indeed we must do so. With scales the child can find which is the heavier of two objects without having to handle them. At first children do not use standard weights, they balance a stone in one pan against, say, sand in the other. This experiment should be repeated with sand replaced by shells, lead shot, nuts, etc. From such activities the children learn that a small amount of one substance weighs as much as a far larger amount of the other, and from this point one can lead on to the need for standard weights.

The 1-pound weight is the best one to begin with, since it is very widely used in our society. If it is not possible to have a number of these weights for the children to handle, make such weights from a bag of suitable material filled with sand, or dried peas or beans, etc. and clearly marked 1 pound. The pupils should then get plenty of practice in using the scales to weigh out 1 pound of sand, shells, nuts, dried peas, etc. This activity can be linked with the work of the shop, since the materials which are suitable can be weighed, put into bags, and sold.

Soon the need will arise for a unit smaller than the pound. This is the moment to introduce the ounce. Once again there should be a number of 1-ounce weights available, with which children weigh out ounces of various objects. Thus they learn to weigh materials in pounds and ounces. At this point a record of the weighings should be made in their work books; e.g. weight of parcel 1 lb. 7 oz. At a later stage the ½-pound and ¼-pound weights must be introduced. If children have the concepts of weight and of "½" and "¼," they should appreciate that these weights are respectively the equivalent of 8 and 4 ounces. It is also possible to make up bags containing 14 and 28 pounds of sand to give children experience of lifting a stone; the older ones can lift a quarter. Hundredweights and tons, however, can only be discussed in terms of what adults and lorries respectively can carry.

Children should also be introduced to the spring balance. By attaching various weights at the bottom of a thin piece of rubber, a suitable piece of elastic, or a spiral spring, and noting the elongation produced, one can demonstrate the principle of the spring balance. Furthermore, these experiments neatly illustrate weight as being the property of a body due to the pull of the earth.

PIAGET'S VIEWS ON THE GROWTH OF THE CONCEPT OF CONSERVATION OF WEIGHT

We now turn to discuss what is known about the development of the concept of weight in children in greater detail. In a typical experiment carried out by Piaget and his students a ball of clay was taken and either elongated to a "sausage" or cut up into sections. The child was then asked whether the "sausage," or the sections taken together, weighed as much as the original ball. Once again Piaget claims that children go through three stages in which (1) they deny conservation of weight; (2) admit to it sometimes (transition stage); and (3) readily agree to it and stand firm in their conviction (conservation stage). In the first stage, the child may reply, "It is lighter, because it is thin now," or, "It is heavier, because there are more pieces." It seems as if the child centers on only one aspect of the transformation and that his thinking is still too influenced by perception; there has been no intellectualization of the problem and because of this failure there can be no real thought about it. He has not grasped, in Piaget's view, that because the "sausage" can be returned to a ball and the pieces of the ball can be put together again, there must be conservation of weight.

In another experiment, there were four equal rectangular bars of tin A, B, C, D, colored differently, and a piece of lead L. All five objects were of the same weight, but the amount of substance in L was very different from that in A, B, C, D. After an actual experiment using a balance the child was asked (in suitable language):

1. If A balances B, and B balances C, how do A and C compare for weight?
2. If A balances B, and B balances L, how do A and L compare for weight?
3. If A balances B, and C balances D, what is the relation between the weight of A + C, and B + D?
4. If A balances B, and C balances L, what is the relationship between the weight of A + C, and B + L?

At the first stage, which corresponds to the stage of nonconservation of weight, no correct conclusions were arrived at by any of the children. At stage two, corresponding to the stage of transition, problems were solved involving the similar bars A, B, C, D, although the children failed all problems that brought in the lump of lead L. This happened although the age of children suggested that the concept of quantity had been formed. Perhaps, at this stage, children may solve the problem of similar bars by simply considering the amount of matter. If so they executed the logical operations correctly in the case of substance (where conservation or invariance was understood), and obtained the right answer by inadequate reasoning. Hence for Piaget, the intellectualization of the problem in relation to weight had not gone far enough at this stage. They had no concept of invariant weight, and therefore could not solve problems involving L. The child still remained too much dependent on subjective experience. He could be shown in all apparent clarity that the lead bar balanced the blue tin bar, and that the blue tin bar balanced the red tin bar, but he could not derive that the lead balanced the red tin bar. At stage three, where the child was able to execute logical operations in relation to weight, because of added experience and maturation, he could arrive at the concept of invariance of weight. At this stage, too, he could perform the operation of transitivity, viz., he could derive that if $A = B$ in weight, and $B = L$ in weight, then $A = L$ in weight. Stage three does not, in Piaget's view, come until about 9–10 years of age (4).

FURTHER EXPERIMENTAL EVIDENCE ON THE DEVELOPMENT OF THE CHILD'S CONCEPT OF CONSERVATION OF WEIGHT

In experiments carried out by one of the writer's students, (3), a large number of junior school children were shown two balls of plasticine of diameter 1½ and 2 inches respectively, and they had to judge which was the heavier using their hands or scales as they wished. Actually the smaller ball, which had some lead at its center, was clearly heavier than the larger. These balls will later be referred to as R1 (the heavier but smaller ball) and R2 respectively. The latter ball was then rolled out to form a "sausage" and the children were questioned at length, and individually, about the weight of the "sausage" and the ball. Table 1 shows the percentage of children at each year of the junior school who were found at the conservation, transition, and nonconservation stages.

The stages proposed by Piaget are again confirmed, and the answers sometimes agree with those reported by him. Moreover, a comparison of Table 1 below and Table 1 [p. 293] shows that the concept of conservation of weight usually develops later than conservation of substance, although this may not be so in individual cases. . . . See also Hyde (1).

But the experimentation went far beyond this point, and a number of

TABLE 1.

Year	Stage 3 Conservation (percent)	Stage 2 Transition (percent)	Stage 1 Nonconservation (percent)	Number of Children Tested
1st year	4	5	91	57
2nd year	36	36	29	73
3rd year	48	20	32	66
4th year	74	13	13	168
Total				364

findings were clearly established that apparently have been overlooked by the Geneva school. These may be briefly summarized as follows:

1. Some 48 percent of the children at the transition stage, and some 46 percent at the nonconservation stage, could show reversibility of thought, for they gave evidence of being aware of the weight relationship between R1 and R2 at the beginning of the experiment. It follows that reversibility of thought itself is not a sufficient condition for conservation, although it may be a necessary condition. This clearly parallels the results of Lovell and Ogilvie (3, Table 5), who found that 75 percent of those at the transition stage, and 50 percent of those at the nonconservation stage of substance, showed evidence of reversibility.

2. The children were then shown a third ball G which was heavier than R1. They were asked individually, and in suitable language, what the relationship was between the weights of G and R2, if G was heavier than R1 and R1 was heavier than R2. Contrary to what one might expect from Piaget, 67 percent of those at the transition stage and 53 percent of those at the nonconservation stage could perform the operation of transitivity.

3. A number of questions of the type given below were put to 114 of the conservers—so designated on Piaget's criterion.

"What happens to the weight of this ball (R2) if I squeeze it down to the size of this one (R1)?"

"What will happen to the weight of this ball (R2) if I leave it in my cupboard for a time?"

"If the plasticine gets harder does it get heavier? Or does it get lighter?"

The following numbers of conservers said, in effect, that *harder* indicated *heavier*, although this was not believed to be true by all subjects in relation to all substances: first year 2; second year 16, third year 18; fourth year 42; making 78 in all.

4. Children who were conservers when rolling plasticine were asked: (a) What would happen to the weight of a piece of butter if it hardened? (b) If some water was cooled and it changed into ice, would the ice weigh more, the same, or less than the water from which it was formed? (c) What would happen to a lump of clay if it got harder? From answers to these questions, and from the varying percentage of conservers obtained in each case (much the highest in [a]), it is perfectly clear that there is no automatic transfer of reasoning from one substance to another. In the case of butter there is much practical experience of it, through shopping, in which weight is involved; the child also notices it getting harder and softer in the house with changes in temperature. Whereas the child may manipulate plasticine more than butter, the weight as such is rarely considered.

The conclusion to be drawn is that few children in the junior school have generalized their ideas about weight; that is, few of them have conceived of it as a factor abstracted from subjective feelings and linked with quantity and only quantity—so that they will retain conservation of weight provided the quantity of substance does not change. Until the child has learnt from experience that warming, cooling, squeezing, hardening, ageing, lengthening and so on do not alter the weight, he will not conserve weight in the widest sense. In spite of the fact that the child can give evidence of reversibility in relation to weight, that is, he can state the relationships between the weight of balls R1 and R2 at the beginning; and in spite of the fact that he can perform the operation of transitivity, he will not necessarily conserve in the general sense, since he may *believe* that some process one of the balls undergoes actually changes its weight. Piaget's tests of rolling a ball into a "sausage" or of cutting a ball into slices by no means told the whole story. The tests simply showed up those who conserved in a particular kind of experiment using a particular medium. With change of medium and circumstance the percentage of children at the various stages who conserve weight may well change. The kind of experiments described here might be undertaken in the junior school to help the child to learn that weight depends solely upon the amount of material, at least for all practical purposes.

Summing up then, we may say:

1. The concept of the invariance of weight develops in part through prolonged and varied experience of the physical world.

2. Piaget's are only one kind of experiment that could be used to test the development of the concept.

3. The type of experiment used by Piaget, and other types of experiments described here, can be in themselves learning situations.

The concept of conservation of substance arises earlier than that of weight since quantity is under immediate visual perception, whereas weight is not.

It will be appreciated that a child may work exercises involving pounds, ounces, quarts, etc., without conserving weight. Provided he knows the appropriate tables, can manipulate the four rules of number, and can comprehend the question, he can work the exercise, since conservation used in the widest sense is not involved. But in problems of science which involve changes of state, density, etc., his thinking will be based on his preconceptions and may lead him into gross errors.

In connection with this chapter readers might study an article by King (2). His data were not obtained by individual questioning but by means of a questionnaire.

REFERENCES

1. Hyde, D. M. An investigation of Piaget's theories of the development of the concept of number. Unpublished Ph.D. thesis, University of London Library, 1959.
2. King, W. H. The developments of scientific concepts in children. *Brit. J. educ. Psychol.*, 1961, **31**, 1–20.
3. Lovell, K., & Ogilvie, E. A study of the conservation of weight in the junior school child. *Brit. J. educ. Psychol.*, 1961, **31**, 138–144.
4. Piaget, J., & Inhelder, B. *Le développement des quantités chez l'enfant.* Neuchâtel: Delachaux and Niestle, 1941.

HOW CHILDREN FORM
MATHEMATICAL CONCEPTS

Jean Piaget
UNIVERSITY OF GENEVA

IT IS A GREAT MISTAKE to suppose that a child acquires the notion of number and other mathematical concepts just from teaching. On the contrary, to a remarkable degree he develops them himself, independently and spontaneously. When adults try to impose mathematical concepts on a child prematurely, his learning is merely verbal; true understanding of them comes only with his mental growth.

This can easily be shown by a simple experiment. A child of five or six may readily be taught by his parents to name the numbers from 1 to 10. If 10 stones are laid in a row, he can count them correctly. But if the stones are rearranged in a more complex pattern or piled up, he no longer can count them with consistent accuracy. Although the child knows the names of the numbers, he has not yet grasped the essential idea of number: namely, that the number of objects in a group remains the same, is "conserved," no matter how they are shuffled or arranged.

On the other hand, a child of 6½ or 7 often shows that he has spontaneously formed the concept of number even though he may not yet have been taught to count. Given eight red chips and eight blue chips, he will discover by 1 to 1 matching that the number of red is the same as the number of blue, and he will realize that the two groups remain equal in number regardless of the shape they take.

The experiment with 1 to 1 correspondence is very useful for investigating children's development of the number concept. Let us lay down a row of eight red chips, equally spaced about an inch apart, and ask our small subjects to take from a box of blue chips as many chips as there are on the table. Their reactions will depend on age, and we can distinguish three stages of development. A child of 5 or younger, on the average, will lay out blue chips to make a row exactly as long as the red row, but he will put the blue chips close together instead of spacing them. He believes the number is the same if the length of the row is the same. At the age of 6, on the average, children arrive at the second stage; these children will lay a blue chip opposite each red chip and obtain the correct number. But they have not necessarily acquired the concept of number itself. If we spread the red chips, spacing out the row more loosely, the 6-year-olds will think that the longer row now has more chips, though we have not changed the number. At the age of 6½ to 7, on the average, children achieve the third stage: they know that, though we close up or space out one row of chips, the number is still the same as in the other.

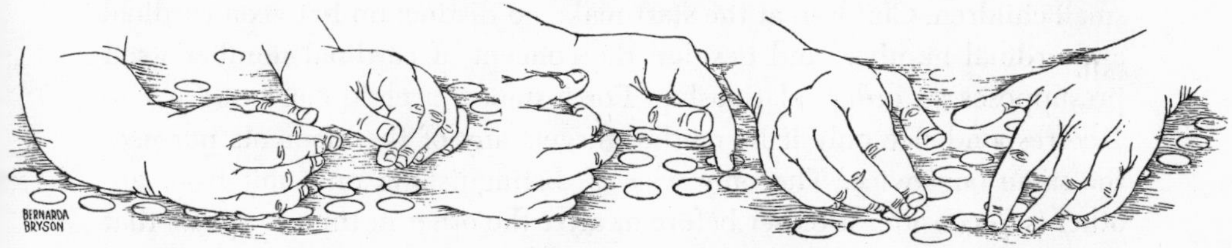

FIG. 1. Experiment with chips demonstrates the development of the concept of number by children from the age of five or younger (*hands at left*), through six (*center*), to six and a half or seven (*right*). The experiment is described in detail in the text. Reprinted with permission. Copyright © 1953, 1961 by Scientific American, Inc. All rights reserved.

In a similar experiment a child is given two receptacles of identical shape and size and is asked to put beads, one at a time, into both receptacles with both hands simultaneously—a blue bead into one box with his right hand and a red bead into the other with his left hand. When he has more or less filled the two receptacles, he is asked how they compare. He is sure that both have the same number of beads. Then he is requested to pour the blue beads into a receptacle of a different size and shape. Here again we see differences in understanding according to age. The smallest children think that the number has changed: if, for instance, the beads fill the new receptacle to a higher level, they think there are more beads in it than in the original one; if to a lower level, they think there are fewer. But children near the age of 7 know that the transfer has not changed the number of beads.

In short, children must grasp the principle of conservation of quantity before they can develop the concept of number. Now conservation of quantity of course is not in itself a numerical notion; rather, it is a logical concept. Thus these experiments in child psychology throw some light on the epistemology of the number concept—a subject which has been examined by many mathematicians and logicians.

The mathematicians Henri Poincaré and L. E. J. Brouwer have held that the number concept is a product of primitive intuition, preceding logical notions. The experiments just described deny this thesis, in our opinion. Bertrand Russell, on the other hand, has supported the view that number is a purely logical concept: that the idea of cardinal number derives from the logical notion of category (a number would be a category made up of equivalent categories) while the notion of ordinal number derives from the logical relationships of order. But Russell's theory does not quite fit the psychological processes as we have observed them in small children. Children at the start make no distinction between cardinal and ordinal number, and besides, the concept of cardinal number itself presupposes an order relationship. For instance, a child can build a 1 to 1 correspondence only if he neither forgets any of the elements nor uses the same one twice. The only way of distinguishing one unit from another is to consider it either before or after the other in time or space, that is, in the order of enumeration.

Study of the child's discovery of spatial relationships—what may be called the child's spontaneous geometry—is no less rewarding than the investigation of his number concepts. A child's order of development in geometry seems to reverse the order of historical discovery. Scientific geometry began with the Euclidean system (concerned with figures, angles and so on), developed in the seventeenth century the so-called projective geometry (dealing with problems of perspective), and finally came in the nineteenth century to topology (describing spatial relationships in a general qualitative way—for instance, the distinction between open and closed structures, interiority and exteriority, proximity and separation). A child begins with the last: his first geometrical discoveries are topological. At the age of 3 he readily distinguishes between open and closed figures: if you ask him to copy a square or a triangle, he draws a closed circle; he draws a cross with two separate lines. If you show him a drawing of a large circle with a small circle inside, he is quite capable of reproducing this relationship, and he can also draw a small circle outside or attached to the edge of the large one. All this he can do before he can draw a rectangle or express the Euclidean characteristics (number of sides, angles, etc.) of a figure. Not until a considerable time after he has mastered topological relationships does he begin to

FIG. 2. Child of three draws this, but not rectangle. Reprinted with permission. Copyright © 1953, 1961 by Scientific American, Inc. All rights reserved.

develop his notions of Euclidean and projective geometry. Then he builds those simultaneously.

Curiously enough, this psychological order is much closer to modern geometry's order of deductive or axiomatic construction than the historical order of discovery was. It offers another example of the kinship between psychological construction and the logical construction of science itself.

Let us test our young subjects on projective constructions. First we set up two "fence posts" (little sticks stuck in bases of modeling clay) some 15 inches apart and ask the child to place other posts in a straight line between them. The youngest children (under the age of 4) proceed to plant one post next to another, forming a more or less wavy line. Their approach is topological: the elements are joined by the simple relationship of proximity rather then by projection of a line as such. At the next stage, beyond the age of 4, the child may form a straight fence if the two end posts parallel the edge of the table, or if there is some other straight line to guide him. If the end posts are diagonally across the table, he may start building the line parallel to the table's edge and then change direction and form a curve to reach the second post. Occasionally a youngster may make a straight line, but he does so only by trial-and-error and not by system.

At the age of 7 years, on the average, a child can build a straight fence consistently in any direction across the table, and he will check the straightness of the line by shutting one eye and sighting along it, as a gardener lines up bean poles. Here we have the essence of the projective concept; the line is still a topological line, but the child has grasped that the projective relationship depends on the angle of vision, or point of view.

One can proceed to study this with other experiments. For instance, you stand a doll on a table and place before it an object oriented in a certain direction: a pencil lying crosswise, diagonally or lengthwise with respect to the doll's line of vision, or a watch lying flat on the table or standing up. Then you ask the child to draw the doll's view of the object, or, better still, ask him to choose from two or three drawings the one that represents the doll's point of view. Not until the age of about 7 or 8 can a child deduce correctly the doll's angle of vision.

FIG. 3. Child of seven straightens a row of "fence posts" by sighting along them. Reprinted with permission. Copyright © 1953, 1961 by Scientific American, Inc. All rights reserved.

A similar experiment testing the same point yields the same conclusions. Objects of different shapes are placed in various positions between a light and a screen, and the child is asked to predict the shape of the shadow the object will cast on the screen.

Ability to coordinate different perspectives does not come until the age of 9 or 10. This is illustrated by an experiment I suggested some time ago to my collaborator, Dr. Edith Meyer. The experimenter sits at a table opposite the child, and between the child and herself she places a cardboard range of mountains. The two see the range from opposite perspectives. The child is then asked to select from several drawings the ones that picture both his own and the opposite person's views of the mountain range. Naturally the youngest children can pick out only the picture that corresponds to their own view; they imagine that all the points of view are like their own. What is more interesting, if the child changes places with the experimenter and sees the mountains from the other side, he now thinks that his new view is the only correct one; he cannot reconstruct the point of view that was his own just a little while before. This is a clear example of the egocentricity so characteristic of children—the primitive reasoning which prevents them from understanding that there may be more than one point of view.

It takes a considerable evolution for children to come, at around the age of 9 or 10, to the ability to distinguish between and coordinate the different possible perspectives. At this stage they can grasp projective space in its concrete or practical form, but naturally not in its theoretical aspects.

At the same time the child forms the concept of projective space, he also constructs Euclidean space; the two kinds of construction are based upon one another. For example, in lining up a straight row of fence posts he may not only use the sighting method but may line up his hands parallel to each other to give him the direction. That is, he is applying the concept of conservation of direction, which is a Euclidean principle. Here is another illustration of the fact that children form mathematical notions on a qualitative or logical basis.

The conservation principle arises in various forms. There is first the conservation of length. If you place a block on another of the same length and then push one block so that its end projects beyond the other, a child under 6 will supopse that the two blocks are no longer of equal length. Not until near the age of 7, on the average, does the child understand that what is gained at one end of the block is lost at the other. He arrives at this concept of the conservation of length, be it noted, by a process of logic.

Experiments on a child's discovery of the conservation of distance are especially illuminating. Between two small toy trees standing apart from each other on a table you place a wall formed of a block or a thick piece of cardboard, and you ask the child (in his own language, of course) whether the trees are still the same distance apart. The smallest children think the distance has changed; they are simply unable to add up two parts of a distance to a total distance. Children of 5 or 6 believe the distance has been reduced, claiming that the width of the wall does not count as distance; in other words, a filled-up space does not have the same value as an empty space. Only near the age of 7 do children come to the realization that intervening objects do not change the distance.

However you test them, you find the same thing true: children do not appreciate the principle of conservation of length or surface until, somewhere around the age of 7, they discover the reversibility that shows the original quantity has remained the same (e.g., the realignment of equal-length blocks, the removal of the wall, and so on). Thus the discovery of logical relationships is a prerequisite to the construction of geometrical concepts, as it is in the formation of the concept of number.

This applies to measurement itself, which is only a derived concept. It is interesting to study how children spontaneously learn to measure. One of my collaborators, Dr. Inhelder, and I have made the following experiment: We show the child a tower of blocks on a table and ask him to build a second tower of the same height on another table (lower or higher than the first) with blocks of a different size. Naturally we provide the child with all the necessary measuring tools. Children's attempts to deal with this problem go through a fascinating evolution. The youngest children build up the second tower to the same visual level as the first, without worrying about the difference in height of the tables. They compare the towers by stepping back and sighting them. At a slightly more advanced stage a child lays a long rod across the tops of the two towers to make sure that they are level. Somewhat later he notices that the base of his tower is not at the same level as the model's. He then wants to place his tower next to the model on the same table to compare them. Reminded that the rules of the game forbid him to move his tower, he begins to look around for a measuring standard. Interestingly enough, the first that comes to his mind is his own body. He puts one hand on top

FIG. 4. Child of six measures the height of a tower of blocks with her body. Reprinted with permission. Copyright © 1953, 1961 by Scientific American, Inc. All rights reserved.

of his tower and the other at its base, and then, trying to keep his hand the same distance apart, he moves over to the other tower to compare it. Children of about the age of 6 often carry out this work in a most assured manner, as if their hands could not change position on the way! Soon they discover that the method is not reliable, and then they resort to reference points on the body. The child will line up his shoulder with the top of his tower, mark the spot opposite the base on his thigh with his hand and walk over to the model to see whether the distance is the same.

Eventually the idea of an independent measuring tool occurs to the child. His first attempt in this direction is likely to be the building of a third tower next to and the same height as the one he has already erected. Having built it, he moves it over to the first table and matches it against the model; this is allowed by the rules. The child's arrival at this stage presupposes a process of logical reasoning. If we call the model tower

A, the second tower C, and the movable tower B, the child has reasoned that $B = C$ and $B = A$, therefore $A = C$.

Later the child replaces the third tower with a rod, but at first the rod must be just the same length as the height of the tower to be measured. He then conceives the idea of using a longer rod and marking the tower height on it with his finger. Finally, and this is the beginning of true measurement, he realizes that he can use a shorter rod and measure the height of the tower by applying the rod a certain number of times up the side.

The last discovery involves two new operations of logic. The first is the process of division which permits the child to conceive that the whole is composed of a number of parts added together. The second is the displacement, or substitution, which enables him to apply one part upon others and thus to build a system of units. One may therefore say that measurement is a synthesis of division into parts and of substitution, just as number is a synthesis of the inclusion of categories and of serial order. But measurement develops later than the number concept, because it is more difficult to divide a continuous whole into interchangeable units than to enumerate elements which are already separate.

To study measurement in two dimensions, we give the child a large sheet of paper with a pencil dot on it and ask him to put a dot in the same position on another sheet of the same size. He may use rods, strips of paper, strings, rulers or any other measuring tools he needs. The youngest subjects are satisfied to make a visual approximation, using no tools. Later a child applies a measuring tool, but he measures only the distance of the point from the side or bottom edge of the paper and is surprised that this single measurement does not give him the correct position. Then he measures the distance of the point from a corner of the paper, trying to keep the same slant (angle) when he applies the ruler to his own sheet. Finally, at about the age of 8 or 9, he discovers that he must break up the measurement into two operations: the horizontal distance from a side edge and the perpendicular distance from the bottom or top edge. Similar experiments with a bead in a box show that a child discovers how to make three-dimensional measurements at about the same age.

Measurement in two or three dimensions brings us to the central idea of Euclidean space, namely the axes of coordinates—a system founded on the horizontality or verticality of physical objects. It may seem that even a baby should grasp these concepts, for after all it can distinguish between the upright and lying-down positions. But actually the representation of vertical and horizontal lines brings up quite another problem from this subjective awareness of postural space. Dr. Inhelder and I have studied it with the following experiments: Using a jar half-filled with colored water, we ask our young subjects to predict what level the water will take when the jar is tipped one way or another. Not until the age of 9, on the average, does a child grasp the idea of horizontality and predict correctly. Similar experiments with a plumb line or a toy sailboat with a tall mast demonstrate that comprehension of verticality comes at about the same time. The child's tardiness in acquiring these concepts is not really surprising, for they require not only a grasp of the internal relationships of an object but also reference to external elements (e.g., a table or the floor or walls of the room).

When a child has discovered how to construct these coordinate axes by reference to natural objects, which he does at about the same time that he conceives the coordination of perspectives, he has completed his conception of how to represent space. By that time he has developed his fundamental mathematical concepts, which spring spontaneously from his own logical operations.

The experiments I have described, simple as they are, have been surprisingly fruitful and have brought to light many unexpected facts. These facts are illuminating from the psychological and pedagogical points of view; more than that, they teach us a number of lessons about human knowledge in general.

INFORMATION PROCESSING IN THE CHILD [1]

Jerome Kagan

HARVARD UNIVERSITY

THE VARIED and murky phenomena implied by the word cognition range from the unrestrained racing of images and words to the more orderly, goal directed sequence of mediated steps that are tripped into action by the desire to solve a problem or acquire a new piece of knowledge. This paper restricts itself to the latter domain of cognitive events, and specifically, to the processes of stimulus classification and hypothesis selection. Three sequential operations typically occur when a person is confronted with a problem: an initial categorization of the relevant information, storage of the coded categorization, and, finally, the imposing of rules of reasoning or transformations (e.g., a complex set of verbal associations) upon the encoded data. The nature of the categorization, transformation, or elaborative mediation is goverened, of course, by the nature of the problem. Students of cognitive development have generally assumed that the striking differences between the intellectual products of children of different ages or among children of the same age were attributable primarily to differences in the availability of vocabulary, possession of deductive or inductive rules, and richness of the associational network. In essence, the superior intellectual performance of older, in contrast to younger, children has been ascribed to the greater knowledge repertoire of the older children. This supposition is intuitively attractive and empirically verified. It is not surprising, therefore, that psychologists have not seriously entertained the possibility that other factors may contribute to age and individual differences in the form

[1] This research was supported, in part, by Grant M–4464 from the National Institute of Mental Health, United States Public Health Service. Parts of this paper represent a condensation and abridgement of a longer monograph: Kagan, J. *et al.* Information processing in the child: significance of analytic and reflective attitudes. *Psychological Monograph* (1964), **78** (1), Whole No. 578.

and quality of cognitive products. Specifically, there has been a tendency to ignore the relevance of differences in rate of information processing—individual differences in the degree of reflection attendant upon classification and hypothesis selection. It appears that children and adults have a clear and stable preference with respect to the speed with which they offer hypotheses in problem situations. Some children are fast; others slow.

The reflection-impulsivity dimension describes the degree to which the child reflects upon the differential validity of alternative classifications of a stimulus or solution hypotheses in situations in which many response possibilities are available simultaneously. In these situations some children have a fast conceptual tempo; they impulsively report the first classification that occurs to them or the first solution sequence that appears appropriate. The reflective children, on the other hand, characteristically delay before reporting a classification or solution hypothesis. They actively consider the alternatives available to them and evaluate their differential validity. The reflective child behaves as if he cared that his first response be as close to correct as possible. The operational definition of the reflection variable is response time in problem situations in which the subject is presented with a standard stimulus and an array containing the standard and 5 to 10 highly similar variants. The child is required to select the one stimulus in the array that is identical to the standard. There is typically a negative correlation between response time and number of errors (i.e., incorrect selections) in these problem situations. Children who delay before offering their first answer make fewer errors. The adjective "reflective" is most descriptive of the child who has long response times and few errors.

Reflection-Impulsivity: Measurement and Developmental Changes

This section describes the test situations used most frequently with children to assess the reflection-impulsivity dimension and the relations among the major variable derived from these tests.

Delayed recall of designs (DRT). In this test a simple design was presented for 5 seconds. This standard was then removed, and after 15 seconds an array of 8, 9, or 10 stimuli was presented. The S selected the one design that was identical to the standard. The major variables derived were number of errors (a secondary distinction was made between major and minor errors), and average response time. Figure 1 illustrates two sample items.[2]

---

[2] These stimuli were designed originally by Eleanor J. Gibson and her colleagues at Cornell University and have been used by the Cornell group in a research project on reading.

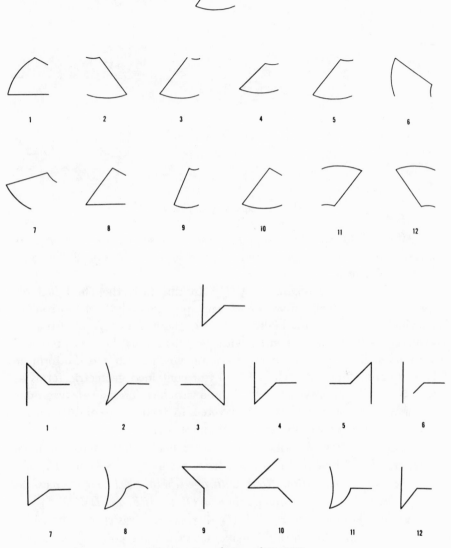

FIG. 1. Sample items from DRT.

Matching familiar figures (MFF). This task was basically similar to the DRT, but illustrated familiar objects rather than geometric designs and, unlike DRT, contained no memory requirement. The S was shown a picture (the standard) and six similar stimuli, only one of which was identical to the standard. The S selected the one stimulus that was identical to the standard. The standard and variations were always

FIG. 2.   Sample items from MFF.

available to the subject. The major variables scored were number of errors, and average response time to first selection. Figure 2 illustrates two sample items.

Haptic visual matching (HVM). In this task, the child first explored with his fingers a wooden form (approximately 3 inches square) to which he had no visual access. He was allowed an unlimited time to explore the form, and when he withdrew his hands, he was presented with a visual array of five stimuli, one of which illustrated the form he had explored haptically. The 20 item test contained geometric forms as well as familiar objects and yielded three variables: errors, response time, and palpation time (i.e., time S devoted to tactual exploration of the wooden form). Figure 3 illustrates two sample items.

The three tests described above have been administered to large numbers of children in Grades 1–4 from a variety of schools. *The developmental trends indicate that, with age, there is a linear decrease in errors and an increase in response time on DRT, MFF, and HVM.*

Since the DRT, MFF, and HVM tasks are easier for the older children, and the older children make less errors, the positive correlation between response time and age suggests that a disposition favoring reflection over alternative solution hypotheses grows stronger as the child matures. Supplementary data from other studies support this conclusion.

Relationships Among Response Time, Recognition Errors, and Verbal Ability

The three perceptual recognition tasks (DRT, MFF and HVM) were similar in their psychological requirements, and all yielded the two

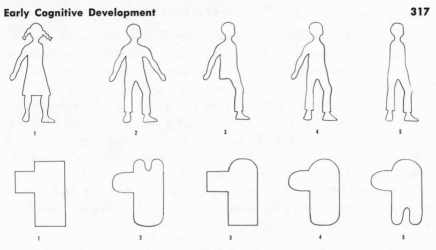

FIG. 3.   Sample items from HVM.

variables of recognition errors and response time. In almost every sample studied there has been a negative relationship between frequency of recognition errors and average response time (i.e., the latency between presentation of the array of alternatives and the child's first selection), the coefficients typically ranging between —.30 and —.60. That is, the children who offered hypotheses quickly made the most errors. There was also a negative, but reduced, relation between recognition errors and verbal ability (mean score on three verbal subtests of the WISC; vocabulary, information, and similarities). The relation between errors and verbal ability was typically lower for boys than for girls. Response time to these recognition tasks, however, was independent of verbal ability; the correlations typically falling below .20. Thus, the reflection-impulsivity dimension appeared to be relatively orthogonal to the traditional construct of verbal ability. The moderate relation between recognition errors and verbal skills, for girls especially, suggests that the basic cognitive processes implied by the phrase "high verbal intelligence" (e.g., richer verbal resources, greater self confidence, problem solving skills, stronger motivation to perform with competence) have some relevance for accuracy in perceptual recognition tasks among school age children. Multiple correlation coefficients with recognition errors as the criterion and verbal ability and response time as the two predictors have yielded coefficients in the 70's. That is, one can predict the number of errors a child will make with greater accuracy if one takes into account both his verbal skills and his speed of decision.

There was remarkable consistency of recognition error scores across the three tasks (coefficients typically ranged from .30 to .60 for different groups), and even higher inter-tasks consistency for response times across the three tasks. Moreover, average response time on one task (DRT, for example) predicted not only response time but also errors on a second recognition task (MFF or HVM). Finally, both recognition errors and response time on DRT were highly stable over short (9 weeks) and long (17 months) periods. In sum, response time appears to be a critical conceptual variable; it shows generality over tasks, stability over time, and is relatively independent of verbal skills. The occurrence of recognition errors is a more complex variable, for it is related both to response time and to the many psychological processes implied by high verbal skills.

Generality of the Reflection-Impulsivity Dimension

The child's tendency to manifest long or short response times to problems with high response uncertainty showed remarkable generality across tasks that were somewhat different than DRT, MFF, or HVM. For example, the average response time to tachistoscopic exposures of six different pictures was positively related to response time on MFF (average $r = .40$). The phrase "conceptual tempo" communicates the connotative meaning assigned to the reflection variable. Some children consistently spew out the first reasonable hypothesis that occurs to them without pausing to reflect on its probable validity. Their strategy of problem solving has a shotgun character; the child firing a fusillade of answers in the hope that one will be correct. The impulsive child seems to need quick success and appears minimally anxious over making mistakes. The reflective child characteristically pauses to consider the differential validity of several hypotheses. He behaves as if he had a strong desire to be as correct as possible on his first attempt. He is unwilling to make a mistake and able to tolerate the ambiguity and tension inherent in the period of silence that is an inevitable concomitant of response selection.

In one study, where recognition errors or response time on DRT or MFF were the indexes of reflection-impulsivity, impulsive children (i.e., those with high errors and fast response times) showed a marked increase in errors of commission on a second serial learning task after threat. That is, the impulsive children reported words not originally present on the list after being told that their performance on a first serial learning task was inadequate. The more impulsive the child (on DRT or MFF), the greater his increase in errors of commission following this threat to his self-esteem. Moreover, even prior to threat, impulsive children produced more errors of commission than reflective children.

There is much similarity between recognition errors on DRT, HVM, or MFF, on the one hand, and orthographic errors in reading. One might expect these two classes of errors to be related in young children learning to read. In one study of 130 first grade children there was a strong positive relationship between errors in recognizing three-letter words (i.e., big, dog, cat, nap) and errors and fast response times on MFF or HVM. However, there was a minimal relationship between the accuracy of recognition of single letters and errors or response time. For example, the correlations between *errors* or *response time* on MFF and word recognition errors were .31 and —.36 for boys and .50 and —.41 for girls. The corresponding correlations for single letter errors were .12 and —.25 for boys; .23 and —.13 for girls.

The significance of reflection-impulsivity. The tendency to have long response times shows impressive inter-task consistency and stability over time (e.g., the reliability of response times over a 9-week period was in the high 70s). It is to be noted that the generality of response time is limited to those problems that have many response alternatives available simultaneously—problems with high response uncertainty. This consistency should not necessarily occur on tasks with only one alternative, or on tasks for which the alternatives are not quickly and simultaneously available. Response times to simple rote questions (e.g., What is your name? What is the month?); to difficult arithmetic questions; or on simple motor reaction time tasks should not necessarily correlate highly with each other or with response times on tasks like MFF or HVM.

Reflection is defined as the consideration of alternative solution hypotheses (either classifications or problem solving sequences) when many alternatives are available simultaneously. Reflection does not refer to delay that is the result of fear of failure, timidity, or inability to generate any solution. The tasks used in this work minimize fear of failure, but further efforts to guarantee this control are necessary.

Significance of Recognition Errors. Recognition errors on MFF or HVM are multiply determined with reflection as the major variable, and verbal skills as a secondary factor. Error scores on DRT or MFF were consistently related to verbal ability; whereas, response times were usually independent of verbal skills. The potpourri of processes implied by the phrase "verbal intelligence" influence quality of performance on problems that do not require complex reasoning operations or rich verbal expression. A "verbal intelligence" index encompasses a variety of more fundamental factors such as expectancy of task success, availability of verbal labels for unique classification of stimuli, special problem solving skills and strategies, and motivation to perform well. When a child believes that a problem has a definite answer and requires concentration for success, it is usually the case that a global index of intelligence relates positively to performance score when the sample tested contains an adequate range of IQ scores (e.g., 90–120). The tendency to reflect on alternative solution possibilities is only one problem solving strategy that has indirect implications for performance.

Antecedents of Reflection-Impulsivity. A tendency toward reflection versus impulsivity displayed a stability over time and a generality across tasks that is unusual for psychological attributes, and tempts one to conclude that this disposition is a basic component of a child's behavioral organization. It is critical, therefore, to understand the antecedents of this predisposition. Why are some children more reflective than others? Three possibilities deserve exploration: constitutional predispositions, degree of involvement in tasks, and differential utility attached to quick success versus possible failure.

There is growing evidence suggesting that one of the possible consequences of minimal brain damage during the perinatal and early postnatal periods is increased restlessness and distractibility and inability to inhibit inappropriate responses during the pre- and early school years. It is possible that extreme impulsivity at age 6 is a partial consequent of subtle cerebral insult early in life. Biological processes, unrelated to CNS insult, could also account for large individual differences in activity level and, as an epiphenomenon, conceptual impulsivity. Schaefer and Bayley (4) found that very active 10-month-old boys were rated as low on attentiveness during the period 27–96 months of age. Preliminary results from an intensive longitudinal study of infant activity and attention at the Fels Institute suggest that vigor of motor activity and degree of sustained attenion to visual stimuli are inversely correlated during the first year of life. The evidence is still thin, but strong enough to support the conjecture that some of the basic determinants of conceptual reflection versus impulsivity can be previewed in the activity and attentional behavior of the infant.

A second set of psychological factors that might influence the reflection dimension is degree of involvement in the task. The child who has high standards of performance should be more likely to reflect on alternative hypotheses. The child who cared less about the quality of his product should be more likely to accept his first hypothesis and adopt an impulsive trial-and-error strategy to the DRT or MFF.

A final hypothesis concerning the basic psychological determinants of reflection-impulsivity involves the differential value the child places on two exhortations that the school and social environment typically promote. The two standards are: *"get the answer quickly"* and *"do not make a mistake."*

In most problems with high response uncertainty, these two standards are incompatible for, as we have seen, errors and response time on HVM or MFF are always negatively related. Difficult problems require reflection in order to avoid offering an incorrect answer. It is possible that children differ in the value they attach to each of these standards. The child who values quick success and is minimally anxious about mistakes should behave impulsively. The child who has high anxiety over making an error and places less value on quick success should be reflective.

Methodological Implications of Reflection and Analysis. A response to a psychological test, be it an ink blot interpretation, a story to a picture, or the selection of an answer in a multiple choice inventory, usually involves processing of information and the selection of one best response from a set of alternatives. *Motives, conflicts, and defenses are not the only factors that affect the final cognitive product in these test situations.* The dimension of reflection-impulsivity may influence the manner in which information is classified and, consequently, the content of the final response. The acknowledgement of individual differences in mode of information processing leads one to look at personality test mode of information processing leads one to look at personality test data, for example, through lenses that differ from the conventional kind (1).

A second methodological implication of this work touches the validity of the assumption that factor analysis of group administered tests can yield the basic components of intellective activity. It is difficult to obtain sensitive indexes of response time from group administered test procedures. The data summarized suggest that the reflection-impulsivity dimension may be a basic variable, but it is not likely that a factor analysis of the data derived from most group-administered test batteries would yield a "reflection" factor.

Problem Solving. A final implication of the reflection-impulsivity dimension concerns the gradual establishment of permanent attitudes toward problem solving and strategies of solution with novel problem tasks. In complex problems with alternate routes to solution, reflection upon the probable validity of varied solution sequences is critical for the ease with which success is achieved. The child who does not reflect upon the differential validity of several solution possibilities is apt to implement mentally the first idea that occurs to him. This strategy is more likely to end up in failure than one that is characterized by reflection. For the impulsive child who reaches a cul-de-sac in a problem solving sequence and recognizes he has not solved the problem is likely to become more anxious than he was initially. As a result of the increased anxiety his selection and evaluation of a second solution path is apt to be impaired, and the probability of success attenuated. This maladaptive cycle may become entrenched with time, and after five years of experiencing the sequence: problem . . . → impulsive selection of invalid solution sequence . . . → failure . . . → anxiety . . . → selection of second sequence . . . → failure . . . → etc., the child may gradually withdraw involvement from problem situations, and become apathetic or hostile toward intellectual situations.

Relation to basic research and theory. The points of contact between the reflection-impulsivity constructs and the main stream of psychological theory in cognition are still unclear. Witkin and his colleagues (5) have used solution time on the Embedded Figures Test as an index of the construct of field independence. The data gathered to date indicate no strong relation between field independence and reflection-impulsivity. Experimental psychologists have noted, recently that discrimination response time is not only a function of information transmitted (i.e., stimulus uncertainty), but is also determined by response uncertainty (3).

It is believed that further investigations of response uncertainty will provide an important bridge between the traditionally isolated domains of cognition and personality. For available data suggest that individual difference variables like motivation, expectation of failure, and hyperkinesis are responsible, in part, for the dramatic variability associated with laboratory studies of response time, perceptual dynamics, and human learning. The data generated by studies in these three substantive areas are influenced, in varying degrees, by the S's characteristic strategy in situations with high response uncertainty.

Theoretical conceptualizations of intellective development have been mainly concerned with the growth and dynamics of mediational systems and cognitive operations (e.g., associational transformations, algorithms, rules of reasoning). Piaget's theorizing, for example, has centered on the characteristics of cognitive structures at different stages of development, and Piaget assumes that differences in these structures explain age differences in cognitive productions. Both European and American psychologists have typically been indifferent to the cognitive phenomena that describe the beginning and end of a problem solving sequence: the initial coding of information, the selection of a "best" solution hypothesis, and the psychological characteristics of the response the child uses to communicate his answer to a social agent. The reflection dimension is an essential aspect of these processes.

The final paragraph is an attempt to dilute any tendency the reader may have to conclude that the reflective child is necessarily the better or brighter child. It seems reasonable to assume that efficient learning and performance on varied intellective tasks will sometimes be facilitated by a reflective approach; sometimes by a more impulsive orientation. Some of the academic contents children must master require reflection, especially the disciplines with deductive structures such as mathematics and physical science. But mastery and productivity in the humanities, arts, and social sciences can be hampered by an excessively strong reflective orientation. New pedagogical procedures should acknowledge the interactions between the dispositions of the learner and the material, and tailor presentations to the preferred strategy of the child.

REFERENCES

1. Kagan, J., Moss, H. A., & Sigel, I. E. Psychological significance of styles of conceptualization. In J. C. Wright and J. Kagan (Eds.), Basic cognitive processes in children. *Monogr. Soc. Res. Child Develpm.*, 1963, **28**, No. 2 (Whole No. 86). Pp. 73–112.
2. Kagan, J., with Rosman, Bernice L., Day, Deborah, Albert, J., & Phillips, W. Information processing in the child. *Psychol. Monogr.*, 1964, **78** (Whole No. 578).
3. Morin, R. E., & Forrin, B. Response equivocation and reaction time. *J. exp. Psychol.*, 1963, **66**, 30–36.
4. Schaefer, E. S., & Bayley, Nancy. Maternal behavior, child behavior, and their intercorrelations from infancy through adolescence. *Monogr. Soc. Res. Child Develpm.*, 1963, **28**, No. 87 (Whole No. 3).
5. Witkin, H. A., Dyk, R. B., Faterson, H. F., Goodenough, D. R., & Karp, S. A. *Psychological differentiation.* New York: John Wiley, 1962.

SECTION V BEHAVIORAL DIFFERENTIATION: FAMILY AND SOCIAL INFLUENCES

The years from school entrance to pubescence are characterized by marked and dramatic differentiation in the child's behavior. The changes are the result of many developments, such as the establishment of relatively stable ways of coping with anxiety; the hierarchical arrangement of various motives; and the learning of inhibition of those responses prohibited by the child's reference groups. The behavior and characteristics of the typical 11-year-old provide a fairly accurate preview of his personality during adolescence and early adulthood. The strength of dependent or aggressive behaviors, the zeal for mastery of intellectual skills, or the degree of anxiety accompanying social interaction in an 11-year-old are not easily altered. The first selection in this section, by Kagan and Moss, illustrates the long term stability of passive and dependent behavior from preadolescence through early adulthood in a group of normal girls, but not for boys. The results demonstrate that society's differential permissiveness toward passivity and dependency in boys and girls influences the continuity of these behaviors.

During the first five years, the child's parents are clearly the primary influences on him, but, in the second half-decade of life, parental impacts may become diluted as peers, teachers, and the public media become more influential. Acceptance or rejection by peers contributes to the child's self image and self-esteem, and the values of the majority culture are transmitted, in large measure, by the peer group. The teacher is viewed by most children as a parent surrogate; hence, his or her nurturance and competence affect the child's tendency to model his own values upon those of the teacher's. The mass media also confront the child with models to emulate and, in so doing, may directly mold his motives and standards. All of these influences—parents, peers, teacher, and public media—are acting simultaneously in a specific social class context. But the values and motives of parents, peers, and teachers from different social class groups differ dramatically. Dr. Kohn's paper, the second in this section, suggests some salient differences in values of middle and working class parents. It emphasizes the fact that middle class parents reward and encourage the development of internal standards of responsibility and self-control in their children, while lower class parents tend to place greater value on obedience and a fear of authority.

Marshall and McCandless, in the third paper of this section, report a study of the relation between the child's behavior and peer acceptance. Their data show that the overly dependent preschool child is less likely to be accepted by his peers or teachers than the more independent youngster.

The effect of specific parental practices on the child's behavior is a thorny problem and one in which progress is being made slowly. It is generally believed that the parent's role as a model for the child, in combination with his specific practices, are the critical variables to study and both factors must be taken into account.

Rosen and D'Andrade have studied achievement motivation in school age boys and they suggest that maternal affection and encouragement of intellectual mastery, together with a laissez-faire paternal attitude, are maximally predictive of a desire for intellectual mastery in the young boy.

The selection by Crandall and his colleagues, the fifth article of this section, suggests that parents' behavior affects boys' and girls' acquisition of intellectual skills differentially, and, moreover, the influence of mother and father may be felt in different ways. A girl is most likely to be precocious in reading skills if her mother is a model for intellectual mastery and sets high standards for her daughter, while her father rewards her efforts with nurturance and affection. There were minimal relations between parental reactions and the boys' reading achievement, supporting other results indicating that it is more difficult to predict the level of school achievement from familial milieu for boys than for girls.

THE STABILITY OF PASSIVE AND DEPENDENT BEHAVIOR FROM CHILDHOOD THROUGH ADULTHOOD[1]

Jerome Kagan and Howard A. Moss

HARVARD UNIVERSITY AND NATIONAL INSTITUTES
OF HEALTH

A BASIC ASSUMPTION of developmental theory is that adult behaviors are often established in early childhood. Although retrospective reports obtained from the verbal protocols of adults support this assumption, it has been difficult to produce a more objective demonstration of the long term stability of childhood behavior patterns. This unhappy state of affairs is a consequence of the expense and difficulty associated with collecting long term longitudinal information on a large sample of children. Only extensive, longitudinal research programs, as exemplified by the Berkeley Growth Study or the Fels Research Institute, can furnish the answers to this developmental problem.

This paper presents one set of results which have emerged from a recent study of a group of "normal" adults from the Fels longitudinal research population for whom extensive information was available from birth through adolescence. The findings deal specifically with the long term stability of passive and dependent behavior in the face of situations which are frustrating and/or demand problem solving activity. This particular behavioral variable was chosen for initial analysis because theoretical essays on personality development emphasize that the early dependence of the child on the parent is of the utmost importance in

[1] This research was supported, in part, by research grant M-1260 from the National Institute of Mental Health, United States Public Health Service. Parts of this paper were presented at the annual meeting of the Midwestern Psychological Association in Chicago, May 1959.

shaping his future personality. That is, the development of a variety of adult motives and behaviors are based on the quality and intensity of the dependent relationship with the mother and mother-substitute figures. Further, psychological symptoms are theoretically attributed to inconsistency in the gratification of the child's dependent overtures and/or to denial or inhibition of dependent motives or behavior.

In addition to the longitudinal material, each subject was recently assessed during early adulthood by means of both interview and test procedures. The adult assessment was focused on the behavioral variables of dependency, aggression, achievement, and sexuality and on the degree of conflict and type of defensive responses associated with behavioral strivings in these areas. It was anticipated that there might be important sex differences with respect to occurrence of these behaviors, and the assessment procedures were designed to detect these potential sex differences.

METHOD

The Sample

The subjects (Ss) in this analysis were 27 male and 27 female Caucasian adults born between 1930 and 1939 who had recently been through a comprehensive assessment program which included an average of five hours of tape recorded interview and a variety of test procedures. The Ss were between 20 and 29 years of age at the time of the assessment. In addition, these Ss had fairly complete longitudinal records from 3 to 10 years of age. The Ss were predominantly middle class but came from a variety of vocational backgrounds including agricultural, skilled labor, tradesmen, and professional groups. The religious affiliations of the group included 43 Protestants, 10 Catholics and 1 Jewish subject. The mean Wechsler-Bellevue IQ of the group was 120 with an IQ range of 97 to 142.

Interview Variables: Adult Assessment

Each S was interviewed by the senior author for approximately five hours over two to three sessions. *The interviewer had absolutely no knowledge of any of the longitudinal information on the Ss.* Since these Ss had been studied by psychologists for over 20 years, rapport was usually excellent, and defensive and evasive answers were infrequent. Following the interviews, each S was rated (7-point scale) on 59 variables. Six of these adult interview variables dealt specifically with passive and dependent behavior; abridged definitions of these variables follow:

Degree to which dependent gratifications were sought in choice of vocation. This variable assessed the degree to which security was an important aspect of job choice, the degree to which the subject looked to his employer for gratification of his dependent needs, reluctance to shift jobs because of temporary loss of security. For nonworking women, emphasis was placed on her attitudes about the importance of security in her husband's job.

Degree of dependent behavior toward a love object. This variable assessed the degree to which the subject sought advice and emotional support from a love object (sweetheart, husband, wife), degree to which the subject looked for stability and wisdom in a love object, degree to which responsibility for decision making was given to love object.

Degree of dependent behavior with parents. This variable assessed the degree to which the subject looked for advice, support, emotional encouragement, and nurturance from one or both parents.

Degree of dependent behavior toward nonparental figures. This variable assessed the degree to which the subject sought advice, emotional support, and nurturance from nonparental figures who were not love objects, e.g., friends, relatives, and teachers.

Tendency to display behavioral withdrawal in the face of anticipated failure. This variable assessed the frequency and consistency with which S tended to withdraw from tasks and situations which he thought were difficult to master and in which failure was anticipated.

Degree of conflict over dependent behavior. This variable assessed the degree to which the subject avoided placing himself in dependent positions, his derogation of dependent behavior in self and others and his emphasis on the value and importance of independent behavior.

A random sampling of 32 taped interviews were independently studied and rated. The interrater reliabilities for the six dependency variables ranged from .63 to .82 with an average coefficient of .74.

Procedure for Evaluation of Childhood Behavior

The junior author, who had no knowledge of the adult psychological status of the Ss, evaluated narrative reports based on direct observation of the child in a variety of situations. Summaries of interviews with the child and the mothers were also available. The observation reports were based on (a) semiannual visits to the home in which a staff member observed the child interact with mother and siblings for a 2 to 4 hour period, (b) semiannual or annual observations of the child in the Fels experimental nursery school and day camp settings, (c) interviews with

the child, and (d) observations of the child in the classroom. After studying this material, the psychologist rated each child for a comprehensive
set of variables (7-point scale). The rater studied the material for each
S for ages 3 to 6 and made his ratings. Following a period of interpolated
work, he then studied all the material for each S for ages 6 to 10 and
again made the ratings. A period of approximately six months intervened
between the evaluation of the material for any one child for ages 3 to
6 and 6 to 10. The rater felt that retroactive inhibition was sufficiently
intense to mask any halo effect of the preschool ratings upon the later
ratings made for 6 to 10 years of age. That is, the amount of material
studied and the large number of variables rated militated against the
recall of specific ratings over such a long period of time. In addition, the
high degree of interrater reliability for these ratings supports the above
statement. Independent ratings of the four childhood dependency variables by a second psychologist produced satisfactory interrater reliabilities. The product-moment correlations for each variable were all in
the .80s with an average reliability of .86. The four childhood variables
which involved passive and dependent behavior were defined as follows:

*Tendency to behave in a passive manner when faced with environ-
mental obstacles or stress* (rated for ages 3 to 6 and 6 to 10). This variable
assessed the degree to which the child was behaviorally passive in the
face of external frustrations and failed to make any active mastery
attempts to obtain desired goal objects following frustration. The rating
of a passive behavioral reaction emphasized withdrawal from the frustration but included whining, crying, and soliciting help.

*Tendency to seek support, nurturance, and assistance from female
adults when under stress: general dependence* (rated for age 3 to 6).
This variable assessed the S's behavioral tendency to obtain assistance,
nurturance, or affection from mother and other female adults when
confronted with a threat to his well-being, a problem, or loss of a desired
goal object. Dependent behavior included seeking out adults when faced
with a problem or personal injury, reluctance to start a task without help
or encouragement, seeking assistance of others, seeking affection from and
close contact with female adults.

Tendency to seek affection and emotional support from female adults
(rated for ages 6 to 10).   This variable assessed the degree to which the
child sought affection or emotional encouragement from mother or mother
substitute figures. Evidence included kissing, holding hands, clinging,
seeking encouragement or proximity to female adults.

Tendency to seek instrumental assistance from female adults (rated for ages 6 to 10). This variable assessed the degree to which the child sought instrumental help with specific problems from mother, teachers, or other female authority figures. Instrumental dependent acts included seeking help with tasks, and seeking help when physically threatened.

As mentioned above the average interrater reliability for these four variables was +.86.

The distributions for both the childhood and interview variables were normal. Product-moment correlations were computed between each of the childhood variables and the six interview-based dependency variables obtained in adulthood with separate analyses for males and females.

Tachistoscopic Perception

After the interviews and interview ratings were completed, each adult S was seen for a variety of test procedures, one of which was a tachistoscopic perception task. A series of 14 scenes were drawn to suggest action in the areas of dependency, aggression, sexuality, and physical danger. Three motivationally neutral, control pictures were also included.[2] For nine of the 14 pictures, separate pairs of illustrations were made for males and females so that the sex of the central figure was the same as the sex of the subject. The pictures were black and white line drawings with minimal background details. A brief description of the three dependency pictures follows:

1. A young adult in the foreground (male for male Ss and female for female Ss) is on his knees clutching the waist of a figure of the same age but of opposite sex who is standing and looking forward. The figure on the floor is looking up at the face of the standing figure.
2. A young adult in the foreground (male for male Ss and female for female Ss) has his arms extended in an imploring gesture toward an adult of the same sex who is standing in the background with his back to the figure in the foreground.
3. A young adult (male for male Ss and female for female Ss) is seated on a chair with head buried in the abdomen of an adult of the opposite sex who is standing and comforting the seated figure.

The 14 pictures were presented seven times at seven different exposure speeds and in six different orders. The seven speeds ranged from .01 to 1.0 seconds. The pictures were shown initially at the fastest exposure (.01 seconds), and each succeeding series was presented at a

---

[2] Photostats of the 14 stimuli are available upon request.

TABLE 1.　*Correlations Between Passive-Dependent Behavior in Childhood and Adulthood*

	Adult Dependency Variables			
	Dependency in vocation		Dependency on love object	
Childhood Variables	M	F	M	F
Passivity (ages 3 to 6)	−.07	.24	.10	.23
Passivity (ages 6 to 10)	.11	.73[a]	.25	.36[b]
General dependence (ages 3 to 6)	−.06	.21	.13	.20
Emotional dependence (ages 6 to 10)	.21	.08	.18	.37[b]
Instrumental dependence (ages 6 to 10)	.19	.39[b]	.06	.58[a]

[a] $p < .01$, one tail.　　[b] $p < .05$, one tail.

slower exposure speed. All exposures were above threshold and all Ss reported seeing something at each exposure. The S sat in a light proof room, 22 inches from a flash-opal milk glass screen. The image was projected from the back of the screen, and the field was constantly illuminated by a 35 mm. projector (30 footcandles at the screen). The subject was told to state for each picture (a) the sex of each figure, (b) the approximate ages of each figure, and (c) what each figure in the picture was doing. The S was given three practice pictures to adapt him to the task and its requirements, and the entire protocol was electrically recorded and transcribed verbatim.

The protocols were scored for recognition threshold for each picture. Recognition threshold was defined as the first series at which the picture was described accurately and all succeeding trials were accurately described. The distributions of recognition thresholds differed among the 14 pictures and were markedly skewed either to the low or high end of the scale. Thus, the distribution of recognition thresholds for each picture was divided at the median into early and late recognition groups for statistical operations.

RESULTS

Stability of Dependent Behavior

Table 1 presents the product-moment correlations between the childhood and adult ratings of passive and dependent behavior.

The major result is that passive and dependent behaviors were fairly

Adult Dependency Variables (cont.)							
Dependency on parents		Dependency on others		Withdrawal to failure		Dependency conflict	
M	F	M	F	M	F	M	F
—.28	.25	.04	.19	.06	.26	.03	.01
—.20	.54[a]	.04	.06	.21	.52[a]	—.26	—.63[a]
—.07	.07	.11	—.06	.12	.00	.05	.26
.02	.51[a]	—.02	.06	.35[b]	.37[b]	—.12	—.31
.14	.32	.37[b]	.01	.09	.39[b]	—.04	—.17

stable for females but not for males. For girls the ratings of passivity during ages 6 to 10 correlated significantly with the adult ratings of a dependent orientation in vocational choice, dependency on love object, dependency on parents, and withdrawal to failure. Childhood passivity was inversely correlated with adult conflict over dependent behavior. That is, females who were passive as children were apt to accept their dependent behavior in adulthood and show minimal anxiety over their dependent motives. Only dependent behavior toward nonparental figures failed to show a significant positive correlation with the childhood ratings of passivity. Similarly, the childhood ratings of both instrumental and emotional dependency on female adults, for girls aged 6 to 10, predicted adult ratings of dependency on love object, dependency on parents, and withdrawal to anticipated failure situations.

For the men there were only two significant correlations between the childhood dependency ratings and those based on the adult interview. Boys who were high on instrumental dependency for ages 6 to 10 were high on dependent behavior towards nonparental figures in adulthood. Second, emotional dependence during ages 6 to 10 was positively correlated with adult withdrawal to failure.

Of the 18 correlations between each of the three childhood variables for ages 6 to 10 and the six adult variables, 60 percent were significant in the expected direction for females, while only 9 percent were significant for the men.

Tables 2 and 3 present the intercorrelations among the childhood and adult interview variables respectively.

The correlations among the passive and dependency variables be-

TABLE 2. *Intercorrelations Among Childhood Dependency Variables*

	Passivity (6 to 10)		General Dependence (3 to 6)		Emotional Dependence (6 to 10)		Instrumental Dependence (6 to 10)	
	M	F	M	F	M	F	M	F
Passivity (3 to 6)	.82[a]	.76[a]	.74[a]	.83[a]	.26	.80[a]	.38	.79[a]
Passivity (6 to 10)	—	—	.40[b]	.63[a]	.43[b]	.65[a]	.53[a]	.61[a]
General dependence (3 to 6)	—	—	—	—	.37	.61[a]	.38[b]	.63[a]
Emotional dependence (6 to 10)	—	—	—	—	—	—	.60[a]	.79[a]
Instrumental dependence (6 to 10)	—	—	—	—	—	—	—	—

[a] $p < .01$, two tails. [b] $p < .05$, two tails.

TABLE 3. *Intercorrelations Among Adult Dependency Variables*

	Dependence Love Object		Parents Dependence		Others Dependence		Withdrawal		Conflict Dependence	
	M	F	M	F	M	F	M	F	M	F
Dependence vocation	.61[a]	.42[b]	.53[a]	.49[a]	.12	−.10	.41[b]	.50[a]	−.61[a]	−.56[a]
Dependence love object	—	—	.24	.54[a]	.48[a]	.16	.49[a]	.54[a]	−.66[a]	−.50[a]
Dependence parents	—	—	—	—	.39[b]	.03	.44[a]	.57[a]	−.59[a]	−.71[a]
Dependence others	—	—	—	—	—	—	.38[b]	−.15	−.46[a]	.15
Withdrawal	—	—	—	—	—	—	—	—	−.57[a]	−.70[a]
Dependence conflict	—	—	—	—	—	—	—	—	—	—

[a] $p < .01$, two tails. [b] $p < .05$, two tails.

tween ages 3 to 6 and 6 to 10 were generally more consistent for girls than for boys. That is, for girls the correlations among passivity and general dependence for ages 3 to 6 and the three variables for ages 6 to 10 were all consistently high. For boys the stability of the passivity rating for ages 3 to 6 and 6 to 10 was quite high. However, the relationships between passivity for 3 to 6 and the two dependency behaviors for 6 to 10 were not as high as they were for girls. This finding suggests that overt seeking of affection and/or instrumental aid in school age boys begins to be dissociated from a passive withdrawal reaction to problem situations.

The intercorrelations among the adult dependency variables were generally positive for both sexes. Dependency on parents and dependency on love objects were each associated with withdrawal to failure and negatively related to conflict over dependency. It is interesting to note that women who are dependent on their parents tended to be dependent on their love object but not on friends or authority figures. Men, on the other hand, who were dependent on their parents tended to be dependent on friends and authority figures rather than on a love object. Dependency on parents and friends usually involves instrumental aid with problems, while dependency on a love object more often included the soliciting of emotional support and affection. It will be recalled that one of the two significant correlations for males between childhood and adult dependency involved instrumental dependency for ages 6 to 10 with adult dependency on nonparental authority figures. Emotional dependency for boys age 6 to 10 showed no correlations with the adult dependency variables. Thus, male dependent behavior is apt to emphasize the seeking of instrumental assistance with problems, while females are likely to seek affection and emotional support in addition to instrumental aid.

It is important to note that passive and dependent behavior for ages 6 to 10 showed a better relation to adult dependent behavior than the ratings for 3 to 6 years of age. This finding indicates that important age changes occur between ages 3 and 10 and that behavior displayed during the first few years of school is a better index of adult functioning than the earlier preschool behavior patterns.

Tachistoscopic Perception of Dependent Pictures

There were significant sex differences in recognition thresholds for the three dependency pictures with the females recognizing all three pictures earlier than the males. The scene that depicted a person imploring a same sexed adult (picture 2) yielded the most significant sex difference ($p < .001$, two tails). The picture of the adult on his knees clutching on to an opposite sexed adult (picture 1) and that of the seated adult holding on to an opposite sexed adult (picture 3) yielded sex differences significant at the .005 and .08 levels, respectively, for two tails. The aggressive pictures, on the other hand, produced opposite results, for the females recognized two of the four aggression pictures significantly later than the men ($p < .01$, two tails). There were no significant sex differences for the sex, physical danger, or three neutral scenes.

There was not a highly consistent relationship between recognition threshold for the dependent scenes and the interview ratings of dependency conflict. Only recognition of the scene that illustrated a man on his knees in front of a woman (picture 1) showed a relation to dependency conflict, and this held only for males. The males who were above the median in recognition threshold for this scene (late recognition) were rated as more conflicted over dependent behavior than males who recognized this picture early ($p = .07$, two tails). For the females, recognition threshold for the dependency pictures showed no significant relation to ratings of dependency conflict.

DISCUSSION

The results support a basic hypothesis of developmental theory which states that the acquisition of certain adult response patterns begins in early childhood. The differential stability of passive-dependent behavior for men and women is probably the result of several factors. However, one set of processes which may contribute to this phenomenon is derived from the commonly accepted hypothesis that passive and dependent behavior is less punished in females than in males. Further, females are often encouraged to be passive while men are expected to be independent and autonomous in the face of frustration. Parental and peer group punishment for passive and dependent behavior should result in some inhibition of this behavior in males. Thus, we would not expect this class of behavior to be as stable for men as for women. Studies of both overt behavior and fantasy (2, 3, 4, 6, 7) all indicate that dependent responses are more frequent for girls than for boys. Further, the sex stereotypes presented by communication media fit this description. The analysis of children's books by Child, Potter, and Levine (1) indicated that girls are portrayed as passive while boys are presented as independent and heroic. Finally, a study of the likes and dislikes of

10-year old children (5) confirms the belief that girls accept passive behavior as more appropriate for their sex role than do boys.

The present tachistoscopic threshold data support the notion that men
are more conflicted over dependent behavior than women. It will be
recalled that the women recognized all three scenes depicting dependent
behavior much earlier than the men. This finding suggests that the
tendency to perceive dependent behavior in adults is much weaker in
men than it is in women. One possible cause of this "weaker perceptual
hypothesis" is that dependent action is less acceptable to men, i.e., that
men are more conflicted over dependent behavior. This conclusion finds
support in the correlation, for men, between late recognition of dependency and the interview rating of dependency conflict.

Detailed analysis of the 54 cases indicates that there was a greater
proportion of men, than women, who shifted from high dependency
during childhood to independent behavior as adults. The women tended
to be either dependent or independent for both childhood and adulthood.
For example, in comparing emotional dependence for ages 6 to 10 with
adult dependency on parents, not one female showed a major shift from
high dependency in childhood to low dependency in adulthood. For the
men, however, 20 percent were rated very dependent during the ages 6
to 10 and very independent in adulthood.

The authors do not suggest that passive and dependent behavior in
girls is rigidly fixed at school age and that change is a rare or unusual
phenomenon. It must be kept in mind that the social milieu of these
particular subjects remained rather constant throughout their lives. Their
familial and extrafamilial environments were not disrupted to any marked
degree. The parents and peers of these Ss retained their same values,
their reference groups remained constant, and, in most cases, their geo-
graphical travel was limited. Thus, the degree of behavioral stability
obtained for these females might not hold for populations that are more
mobile or transient, for different ethnic or class samples, or for people
subjected to major traumata during adolescence and early adulthood.

Implicit in these results is a strategy for certain research problems
in developmental psychology. It would appear that a select group of
theoretically relevant behaviors become clearly established as preferential response tendencies as early as 6 to 10 years of age. This means that
one can study the child longitudinally without having to wait 15 to 20
years before asking important questions of the data. Since the current
philosophy of financial support for research allows an investigator to
chart a 5 to 10 year program, it is now feasible for one investigator to

see the products of a longitudinally orientated project in a reasonable length of time.

Although case history material can never prove an hypothesis, it often facilitates scientific communication by placing some flesh on the skeleton of a correlation matrix. The following case material is presented to give the reader a clearer picture of the material upon which our childhood evaluations were based and to illustrate dramatically the degree of constancy of behavioral passivity for two specific individuals.

Case A. Miss A is a 21-year-old, unmarried woman, who was in her senior year in an Eastern college. She was one of the most independent women in our sample and one who showed a strong reaction against dependent behavior in a wide variety of situations. As an adult she was described as a woman with a very strong need for recognition by others combined with a striving for achievement related goals. She had a strong desire to nurture others and often sought out situations in which she could give advice, support, and encouragement to peers. Miss A stated during the interview that she liked to keep her personal problems to herself. She did not like to discuss her personal problems because she felt that this behavior made her appear "helpless and weak." Statements like this indicate very strong conflict and anxiety over being in a passive-dependent position with other people. She was trying to sever any semblance of a dependent relation with her mother and derogated the latter because the mother seemed to be dependent upon her for companionship. Miss A sometimes felt lonely but said that she fights these feelings and tries to be able to live with them, for she does not like to admit that she needs friends or companionship. Her relationship with men seems to be consistent with the above pattern, for she tends to withdraw from heterosexual relationships that become too intense. Miss A said that she does not like men that make demands upon her, and she avoids men who attempt to place her in a passive role or position.

The following material represents selected verbatim excerpts from the longitudinal material on this subject.

Age 3 years, 4 months: Summary of Fels Nursery School Observations. S seems to be able to control and channel her behavior so that she got done just what she wanted to get done. In this activity she was very independent and capable. She was very social but also had a streak of aloof self-sufficiency, and she always made her individuality felt. She was what might be called a strong personality, often very intense, quite stubborn.

. . . Her most outstanding characteristic was her consistent independence and integrity. In spite of the fact that she imitated and followed certain boys, she seemed to do this very much from her own choice, and she never lost the flavor of her individuality. She was capable of being social and seemed to enjoy contacts but at all times she was her own master. She would often withdraw from play and go on in her own direction at any time that she wished. . . . She was independent with adults and at times negativistic just to be devilish. She seemed somewhat self-conscious and had some cute little tricks.

. . . In all, she could be characterized best by being called "tough minded." She shows determination and will, originality and spark, curiosity and interest in factual detail. She likes to quibble and argue, to verbalize, to construct, to accomplish. She is an individualist, independent and stubborn.

Age 5 years, 4 months: Fels Nursery School Observation. S seems to be a vigorous, ruthless, competitive, highly sensual young woman, but one felt quite often that antagonism toward others was simply a direct response to their behavior. . . . She has grown far more social and also popular with an increasingly large crowd of special friends in a gang. She could be, when she chose, quite a successful leader, forging ahead and organizing a group on a hike, directing them and arranging things, and particularly keeping order in a fair sharing of the tools in the carpentry shop. . . . Many of S's conflicts with the adult world seemed a direct imitation of a certain boy. She needed a chance to grumble, would scornfully refuse any adult suggestions or orders, would usually go officially ahead to carry them out. She was quite demanding, often shouting an order to an assistant. . . . With her other work the same drive for strong achievement was also evident, sticking to anything until it was finished, whatever the group stimuli. S still had real trouble in fine motor coordination, would growl as she worked, "I'm doing this as well as I can steer my pencil." For all her teeth gritted effort, the final results would still be relatively crude. She was very skilled in the use of puzzles and interested in the problems of designs and the way things fit together. She scorned any of the ready-made designs for the Christmas tree decorations.

Age 7 years: Observation in Fels Day Camp. S came accompanied by one friend. S did not seem overwhelmed by the large proportion of adults around, but in her sturdy, self-sufficient manner went ahead with her own activities. Her friend was at first rather shy and withdrawn and S, with her usual confident bullying and bossing of the adults, tended to take the girls under her wing and make sure she had a good time. S remains an exceptionally eager, imperturbable young woman. On a number of small issues she did insist on her own way, on just how long she would stay in the gym and play before lunch, but was quite reasonable about making compromises. She chose a rather difficult necklace to make and got quite mad when it didn't work out well. She kept doggedly with it, very self-sufficient, and continuing all on her own after getting some initial advice. . . . Her major effort was put on self-appointed tasks, to be able to master jumping over the horse at the gym where she took numerous tumbles until she succeeded. In spite of her distractability and preference for the apparatus she did set herself to learning the new skills required there.

Age 9 years: Report from Teacher. S is one of the most responsible children in the group. . . . She is self-reliant, independent, and knows how to plan her time well. She enters all games with enthusiasm, is very well coordinated, is full of personality and joie de vivre.

Case B.   Miss B is a 23-year-old, unmarried woman, who is working and living with her parents. She was one of the most overtly dependent women in the sample. During the interview she was very dependent on the interviewer for structure and was rather mild and meek. Her most typical reaction to failure or stressful situations is to deny or withdraw and she says quite blithely, "I'm not a worrier." She is very sensitive to the opinions of other people and usually conforms with their expectations for her. She accepts her passive-dependent role with authority people and with love objects. S tends to be very dependent on peers for advice, likes being close to the family, and tends to see herself as inadequate in the face of problem situations.

Following are selected excerpts from her longitudinal records:

Age 2 years, 6 months: Fels Nursery School Observation.   At the first day of nursery school, S seemed rather frightened and very reluctant to leave her mother this morning. The mother had to carry her and hold her in the car until the door was shut. For the first few miles she cried and then suddenly stopped and began to take an interest in the various animals and objects. She cried when she reached the nursery school but stopped as soon as she left the other children. On the second day of nursery school she cried again but seemed much less frightened and more angry. During the nursery school she stood watching the other children and at one point ran to another girl and stood beside her. The other little girl paid no attention, and S trailed after her. S wandered around and, when the teacher went to the house, S rushed to follow her and stood around the teacher. S tagged after another little girl all morning. During the nursery school 2-week period she was timid and tense.

Age 3 years: Fels Nursery School Summary. At first, S was timid and tense and was gathered under the wing of another peer and her cohorts. From then on she was "at home" with the group. She followed another girl's lead and joined in the activities the other girl organized. On days when this girl was absent she was at loose-ends and tended to return to her original dependence on an adult. Several weeks after her nursery school stay she visited the school one morning for several hours. She was a little apprehensive at first but made no real protest. She stood around not joining in the play until an adult suggested an activity.

Age 4 years: Fels Nursery School Summary. S cried the first day of nursery school after she saw another girl cry. She stayed close to the teacher the first few days and watched the other children with a worried expression on her face. Indoors she chose small blocks or color cubes to play with. In the yard S was very cautious about trying out the apparatus, particularly when there was any balancing involved. She has a high, whining, nasal voice, and several letter substitutions made her speech rather difficult to understand. She was quite compliant with adult requests. Frequently, she appealed to adults for help in conflicts, such as getting a turn to slide, which is a situation she could have handled for herself.

Age 6 years: Visit to the School. S is retiring, quiet, and shy. She doesn't show the enthusiasm that most of the children in the class do. She seems content. . . . She goes to the teacher for suggestions and skips to her seat jubilantly with a word of approval from the teacher. S recites a bit timidly in front of the whole class but accepts the teacher's support and gets through successfully. Her voice is a little soft and her enunciation is not clear. S volunteers information a bit tentatively and without enthusiasm. The teacher reports that S is about the brightest of the average group. S is not a leader but she is very sweet and cooperative and is never any trouble.

Age 6 years, 6 months: Summary of Fels Day Camp Observations. S was outclassed in almost every respect in this group but fluttered happily about after the others doing the best she could. She occasionally withdrew or grew silent but, when encouraged by an adult, she soon recovered. She was not insensitive and did not seem to have her security disturbed more than momentarily. She seems to feel a great confidence and trust in adults and could always be bought off or led along. She lacked initiative in almost every way. She could not go ahead on any craft project nor could she assert herself socially. She needed help and encouragement, hung about the adults, not exposing herself to the center of the group. She is essentially a conformist and wanted only to do what was right. She got into no mischief and had little sense of fun. She was happiest when settled into a situation that was approved and guided by an adult, and at these times she would proddle along very happily. Her main interests lay in conforming to any plans laid by adults and working on simple handcrafts. She was rather unsure in her accomplishments. She was often physically apprehensive.

Age 7 years, 6 months: Summary of Fels Day Camp Observations. The most characteristic aspect of S's day camp behavior was her ability, high conformity, and social reticence. She did not participate in social activities to any extent and was generally ignored by the other children. She clung to adults, wanted to assist them when possible, and wanted their approval and comforting in all her activities. She seemed to be somewhat apprehensive about physical contacts, especially if they became at all rough. She was apprehensive about almost any physical danger. Her actual physical ability was not particularly poor, and, when she was put into athletic situations, she did surprisingly well. Her general lack of physical participation seems not to be due to poor ability as much as to lack of motivation and apprehension.

Age 8 years: Visit to the School. S is always anxious to do what is right all of the time. She is not a discipline problem. S shows no interest in physical activities. Initially, she is lost at school work and takes some time to adjust to new work. S was pretty tentative in her first attempt to get the teacher's attention and held up her paper hesitantly. She was very pleased when the teacher came to her. She was uncertain about the problems although they had similar ones before.

Age 8 years: 8 months: Fels Day Camp Summary. S is a small, dark looking girl, bent over, with thick dark hair and a tired face. Her voice is high but with no force; her hands hanging limp at the wrists. Much of this lack of force seemed related to her personality, and at the races she surprised us by doing remarkably well. S obeyed adults implicitly and wanted to have their sanction for even small acts which the group had already been given permission for. She has a rather cringing, servile manner. This clinging around adults was particularly marked the first day when she ate her lunch with them.

Age 9 years, 8 months: Fels Day Camp Summary. S is a rather pathetic looking little girl. Rather thin, droopy eyed, clammy handed, somehow reminiscent of an orphan in an old melodrama. She seems nearer to seven or eight than her actual age and with a kind of naivete and unsureness about all she did. She was an exceedingly compliant child in taking the tests, even the reading tests which she obviously disliked, without a murmur.

SUMMARY

This paper summarized some results from a larger investigation of the stability of behavior in a group of subjects who were part of the Fels Research Institute's longitudinal population. This report dealt specifically with the long term stability of passive and dependent behavior from childhood through adulthood.

The Ss were 27 males and 27 females for whom extensive longitudinal information was available from birth through adolescence. One psychologist studied narrative reports based on observations of the child in various settings and rated each child on four variables describing types of passive and dependent behavior for ages 3 to 6 and 6 to 10. A second psychologist, who had no knowledge of the childhood data, interviewed each S in adulthood and rated each S on six variables related to aspects of adult passive and dependent behavior. In addition, each adult S was administered a tachistoscopic perception task in which scenes illustrating dependent activity were presented at seven different exposure speeds.

The results revealed that passive and dependent behaviors were quite stable for women, but minimally stable for men. Over 60 percent of the correlations between the childhood (ages 6 to 10) and adult ratings of dependency were statistically significant for females, while only 9 percent were significant for men. For example, the correlation between passive withdrawal from problem situations for ages 6 to 10 and adulthood was .52 ($p < .01$) for women and .21 for men. Similarly, the correlation between emotional dependence for ages 6 to 10 and adult dependency on parents was .51 ($p < .01$) for women and .02 for men. The correlations between the ratings for ages 3 to 6 and adulthood were considerably lower and not statistically significant.

It was suggested that environmental disapproval and punishment of dependent behavior in young males led to inhibition of and conflict over dependency in the growing boy. The social acceptance of passive and dependent behavior in females would be expected to result in greater stability for this class of responses for women than for men. The fact that females recognized the tachistoscopically presented dependency scenes earlier than the men was interpreted as support for this explanation.

Case history material for two female subjects was presented to illustrate the type of information utilized in this study.

REFERENCES

1. Child, I. L., Potter, E. H., & Levine, Estelle M. Children's textbooks and personality development: an exploration in the social psychology of education. *Psychol. Monogr.*, 1946, **60**, No. 279.
2. Hattwick, Bertha. Sex differences in behavior of nursery school children. *Child Develpm.*, 1937, **8**, 323–355.
3. Kagan, J. The stability of TAT fantasy and stimulus ambiguity. *J. consult. Psychol.*, 1959, **23**, 266–271.
4. Sanford, R. N., Adkins, M. M., Miller, R. B., & Cobb, E. N. Physique, Personality, and Scholarship: a comprehensive study of school children. *Monogr. Soc. Res. Child Develpm.*, 1943, **8**, No. 1.
5. Tyler, Leona E. The development of vocational interests: I. The organization of likes and dislikes in ten-year-old children. *J. genet. Psychol.*, 1955, **86**, 33–44.
6. Watson, R. I. *Psychology of the child.* New York: Wiley, 1959.
7. Whitehouse, Elizabeth. Norms for certain aspects of the thematic apperception test on a group of nine and ten-year-old children. *J. Pers.*, 1949, **1**, 12–15.

SOCIAL CLASS AND PARENTAL VALUES[1]

Melvin L. Kohn

NATIONAL INSTITUTES OF HEALTH

WE UNDERTAKE THIS inquiry into the relationship between social class and parental values in the hope that a fuller understanding of the ways in which parents of different social classes differ in their values may help us to understand why they differ in their practices.[2] This hope, of course, rests on two assumptions: that it is reasonable to conceive of social classes as subcultures of the larger society, each with a relatively distinct value-orientation, and that values really affect behavior.

SAMPLE AND METHOD OF DATA COLLECTION

Washington, D.C.—the locus of this study—has a large proportion of people employed by government, relatively little heavy industry, few recent immigrants, a white working class drawn heavily from rural areas, and a large proportion of Negroes, particularly at lower economic levels. Generalizations based on this or any other sample of one city during one limited period of time are, of course, tentative.

[1] Revision of paper presented at the annual meeting of the American Sociological Society, August, 1957. This is the first portion of a more general inquiry into the relationship of class and family directed by the author and John A. Clausen, with collaboration and aid of Eleanor Carroll, Mary Freeman, Paul Hanlon, Alexander Shakow, and Eleanor Wolff.

[2] There now exists a rather substantial, if somewhat inconsistent body of literature on the relationship of social class to the ways that parents raise their children. For a fine analytic summary see Urie Bronfenbrenner (2). Bronfenbrenner gives references to the major studies of class and child-rearing practices that have been done.

For the most relevant studies on class and *values* see Evelyn M. Duvall (3); David F. Aberle and Kaspar D. Naegele (1); Herbert H. Hyman (5).

Reprinted by permission from *The American Journal of Sociology* (January, 1959), **64** (4).

Our intent in selecting the families to be studied was to secure approximately two hundred representative white working-class families and
another two hundred representative white middle-class families, each
family having a child within a narrowly delimited age range. We decided
on fifth-grade children because we wanted to direct the interviews to
relationships involving a child old enough to have a developed capacity
for verbal communication.

The sampling procedure[3] involved two steps: the first, selection of
census tracts. Tracts with 20 percent or more Negro population were
excluded, as were those in the highest quartile with respect to median
income. From among the remaining tracts we then selected a small
number representative of each of the three distinct types of residential
area in which the population to be studied live: four tracts with a predominantly working-class population, four predominantly middle-class,
and three having large proportions of each. The final selection of tracts
was based on their occupational distribution and their median income,
education, rent (of rented homes), and value (of owner-occupied homes).
The second step in the sampling procedure involved selection of families.
From records made available by the public and parochial school systems
we compiled lists of all families with fifth-grade children who lived in
the selected tracts. Two hundred families were then randomly selected
from among those in which the father had a "white-collar" occupation
and another two hundred from among those in which the father had a
manual occupation.

In all four hundred families the mothers were to be interviewed. In
every fourth family we scheduled interviews with the father and the
fifth-grade child as well.[4] (When a broken family fell into this subsample, a substitute was chosen from our overall sample, and the broken
family was retained in the overall sample of four hundred families.)

When interviews with both parents were scheduled, two members of

[3] I owe a considerable debt of gratitude to Samuel W. Greenhouse, chief of the
Section on Statistics and Mathematics, Biometrics Branch NIMH, for his expert help
in sample design, as well as for his advice on general statistical problems of the
research.

[4] The interviewing staff was composed of Eleanor Carroll, Mary Freeman, Paul
Hanlon, and Melvin Kohn. We were aided from time to time by three volunteers from
the NIMH staff: Leila Deasy, Erwin Linn, and Harriet Murphy. Field work was
conducted between March, 1956, and March, 1957.

We secured the cooperation of 86 percent of the families where the mother
alone was to be interviewed, and 82 percent of the families where mother, father,
and child were to be interviewed. Rates of nonresponse do not vary by social class,
type of neighborhood, or type of school. This, of course, does not rule out other
possible selective biases introduced by the nonrespondents.

the staff visited the home together—a male to interview the father, a female to interview the mother. The interviews were conducted independently, in separate rooms, but with essentially identical schedules. The first person to complete his interview with the parent interviewed the child.

INDEXES OF SOCIAL CLASS AND VALUES

Social class. Each family's social position has been determined by the Hollingshead Index of Social Position, assigning the father's occupational status a relative weight of 7 and his educational status a weight of 4. We are considering Hollingshead's Classes I, II, and III to be "middle class," and Classes IV and V to be "working class." The middle-class sample is composed of two relatively distinct groups: Classes I and II are almost entirely professionals, proprietors, and managers with at least some college training. Class III is made up of small shopkeepers, clerks, and salespersons but includes a small number of foremen and skilled workers of unusually high educational status. The working-class sample is composed entirely of manual workers but preponderantly those of higher skill levels. These families are of the "stable working class" rather than "lower class" in the sense that the men have steady jobs, and their education, income, and skill levels are above those of the lowest socioeconomic strata.

Values. We shall use Kluckhohn's (6) definition: "A value is a conception, explicit or implicit, distinctive of an individual or characteristic of a group, of the desirable which influences the selection from available modes, means, and ends of action."

Our inquiry was limited to the values that parents would most like to see embodied in their children's behavior. We asked the parents to choose, from among several alternative characteristics that might be seen as desirable, those few which they considered *most* important for a child of the appropriate age. Specifically, we offered each parent a card listing 17 characteristics that had been suggested by other parents, in the pretest interviews, as being highly desirable. (These appear down the left margin of Table 1. The order in which they were listed was varied from interview to interview.) Then we asked: "Which three of the things listed on this card would you say are the *most* important in a boy (or girl) of (fifth-grade child's) age?" The selection of a particular characteristic was taken as our index of value.

Later in this report we shall subject this index to intensive scrutiny.

TABLE 1. *Proportion of Mothers Who Select Each Characteristic as One of Three "Most Desirable" in a 10- or 11-Year-Old Child*

Characteristics	For Boys		For Girls		Combined	
	Middle Class	Working Class	Middle Class	Working Class	Middle Class	Working Class
1. That he is honest	0.44	0.57	0.44	0.48	0.44	0.53
2. That he is happy	.44[a]	.27	.48	.45	.46[a]	.36
3. That he is considerate of others	.40	.30	.38[a]	.24	.39[a]	.27
4. That he obeys his parents well	.18[a]	.37	.23	.30	.20[a]	.33
5. That he is dependable	.27	.27	.20	.14	.24	.21
6. That he has good manners	.16	.17	.23	.32	.19	.24
7. That he has self-control	.24	.14	.20	.13	.22[a]	.13
8. That he is popular with other children	.13	.15	.17	.20	.15	.18
9. That he is a good student	.17	.23	.13	.11	.15	.17
10. That he is neat and clean	.07	.13	.15[a]	.28	.11[a]	.20
11. That he is curious about things	.20[a]	.06	.15	.07	.18[a]	.06
12. That he is ambitious	.09	.18	.06	.08	.07	.13
13. That he is able to defend himself	.13	.05	.06	.08	.10	.06
14. That he is affectionate	.03	.05	.07	.04	.05	.04
15. That he is liked by adults	.03	.05	.07	.04	.05	.04
16. That he is able to play by himself	.01	.02	.00	.03	.01	.02
17. That he acts in a serious way	0.00	0.01	0.00	0.00	0.00	0.01
N	90	85	84	80	174	165

[a] Social-class differences statistically significant, 0.05 level or better, using chi-squared test.

CLASS AND VALUES

Middle- and working-class mothers share a broadly common set of values—but not an identical set of values by any means (see Table 1). There is considerable agreement among mothers of both social classes that happiness and such standards of conduct as honesty, consideration, obedience, dependability, manners, and self-control are highly desirable for both boys and girls of this age.

Popularity, being a good student (especially for boys), neatness and cleanliness (especially for girls), and curiosity are next most likely to be regarded as desirable. Relatively few mothers choose ambition, ability to defend one's self, affectionate responsiveness, being liked by adults, ability to play by one's self, or seriousness as highly desirable for either boys or girls of this age. All of these, of course, might be highly valued for children of other ages.

Although agreement obtains on this broad level, working-class mothers differ significantly[5] from middle-class mothers in the relative emphasis they place on particular characteristics. Significantly fewer working-class mothers regard happiness as highly desirable for *boys*. Although characteristics that define standards of conduct are valued by many mothers of both social classes, there are revealing differences of emphasis here too. Working-class mothers are more likely to value obedience; they would have their children be responsive to parental authority. Middle-class mothers are more likely to value both consideration and self-control; they would have their children develop inner control and sympathetic concern for other people. Furthermore, middle-class mothers are more likely to regard curiosity as a prime virtue. By contrast, working-class mothers put the emphasis on neatness and cleanliness, valuing the imaginative and exploring child relatively less than the presentable child.[6]

Middle-class mothers' conceptions of what is desirable for boys are much the same as their conceptions of what is desirable for girls. But

[5] The criterion of statistical significance used throughout this paper is the 5 percent level of probability, based, except where noted, on the chi-squared test.

[6] Compare these results with Bronfenbrenner's (2) conclusion, based on an analysis of reports of studies of social class and child-rearing methods over the last 25 years: "In this modern working-class world there may be greater freedom of emotional expression, but there is no laxity or vagueness with respect to goals of child training. Consistently over the past 25 years, the parent in this group has emphasized what are usually regarded as the traditional middle-class virtues of cleanliness, conformity, and (parental) control, and although his methods are not so effective as those of his middle-class neighbors, they are perhaps more desperate."

working-class mothers make a clear distinction between the sexes: they are more likely to regard dependability, being a good student, and ambition as desirable for boys and to regard happiness, good manners, neatness, and cleanliness as desirable for girls.

What of the *fathers'* values? Judging from our subsample of 82 fathers, their values are similar to those of the mothers (see Table 2). Essentially the same rank-order of choices holds for fathers as for mothers, with one major exception: fathers are not so likely to value happiness for their daughters. Among fathers as well as mothers, consideration and self-control are more likely to be regarded as desirable by the middle class; middle-class fathers are also more likely to value another standard of conduct—dependability. Working-class fathers, like their wives, are more likely to value obedience; they are also more likely to regard it as desirable that their children be able to defend themselves.[7]

We take this to indicate that middle-class parents (fathers as well as mothers) are more likely to ascribe predominant importance to the child's acting on the basis of internal standards of conduct, working-class parents to the child's compliance with parental authority.

There are important differences between middle- and working-class parents, too, in the way in which their choice of any one characteristic is related to their choice of each of the others.[8]

[7] A comparison of the values of the fathers in this subsample with those of the mothers in this same subsample yields essentially the same conclusions.

We do not find that fathers of either social class are significantly more likely to choose any characteristic for boys than they are to choose it for girls, or the reverse. But this may well be an artifact of the small number of fathers in our sample; Aberle and Naegele (1) have found that middle-class fathers are more likely to value such characteristics as responsibility, initiative, good school performance, ability to stand up for one's self, and athletic ability for boys and being "nice," "sweet," pretty, affectionate, and well-liked for girls.

[8] A logical procedure for examining these patterns of choice is to compare the proportions of parents who choose any given characteristic, B, among those who do and who do not choose another characteristic, A. But since a parent who selects characteristic A has exhausted one of his three choices, the a priori probability of his selecting any other characteristic is only two-thirds as great as the probability that a parent who has not chosen A will do so. (A straightforward application of probability considerations to the problem of selecting three things from seventeen when one is interested only in the joint occurrence of two, say, A and B, shows that we can expect B to occur $\frac{2}{16}$ of the time among selections containing A and $\frac{3}{16}$ of the time among those not containing A.) This, however, can be taken into account by computing the ratio of the two proportions: p_1, the proportion of parents who choose B among those who choose A, and p_2, the proportion who choose B among those who do *not* choose A. If the ratio of these proportions (p_1/p_2) is significantly larger than two-thirds, the two are positively related; if significantly smaller, they are negatively related.

The test of statistical significance is based on the confidence interval on a ratio, originally given by Fieller (4), with the modification that we deal here with the ratio of two independent proportions whose variances under the null hypothesis (chance)

TABLE 2. *Proportion of Fathers Who Select Each Characteristic as One of Three "Most Desirable" in a 10- or 11-Year-Old Child*

Characteristics	For Boys		For Girls		Combined	
	Middle Class	Working Class	Middle Class	Working Class	Middle Class	Working Class
1. That he is honest	0.60	0.60	0.43	0.55	0.52	0.58
2. That he is happy	.48	.24	.24	.18	.37	.22
3. That he is considerate of others	.32	.16	.38	.09	.35[a]	.14
4. That he obeys his parents well	.12[a]	.40	.14[a]	.36	.13[a]	.39
5. That he is dependable	.36[a]	.12	.29	.00	.33[a]	.08
6. That he has good manners	.24	.28	.24	.18	.24	.25
7. That he has self-control	.20	.08	.19	.00	.20[a]	.06
8. That he is popular with other children	.08	.16	.24	.45	.15	.25
9. That he is a good student	.04	.12	.10	.36	.07	.19
10. That he is neat and clean	.16	.20	.14	.09	.15	.17
11. That he is curious about things	.16	.12	.10	.00	.13	.08
12. That he is ambitious	.20	.12	.14	.00	.17	.08
13. That he is able to defend himself	.04	.16	.00[a]	.18	.02[a]	.17
14. That he is affectionate	.00	.04	.05	.18	.02	.08
15. That he is liked by adults	.00	.08	.00	.09	.00	.08
16. That he is able to play by himself	.00	.08	.05	.00	.02	.06
17. That he acts in a serious way	0.00	0.04	0.00	0.00	0.00	0.03
N	25	25	21	11	46	36

[a] Social-class differences statistically significant, 0.05 level or better, using chi-squared test.

We have already seen that parents of both social classes are very likely to accord honesty first-rank importance. But the choice of honesty is quite differently related to the choices of other characteristics in the two classes (see Table 3). Middle-class mothers[9] who choose honesty are more likely than are other middle-class mothers to regard consideration, manners, and (for boys) dependability as highly desirable; and those mothers who regard any of these as desirable are more likely to value honesty highly. Consideration, in turn, is positively related to self-control, and manners to neatness. Honesty, then, is the core of a set of standards of conduct, a set consisting primarily of honesty, consideration, manners, and dependability, together with self-control and neatness. As such, it is to be seen as one among several (albeit the central) standards of conduct that middle-class mothers want their children to adopt.

This is not the case for working-class mothers. Those who regard honesty as predominantly important are not especially likely to think of consideration, manners, or dependability as comparable in importance; nor are those who value any of these especially likely to value honesty. Instead the mothers who are most likely to attribute importance to honesty are those who are concerned that the child be happy, popular, and able to defend himself. It is not that the child should conduct himself in a considerate, mannerly, or dependable fashion but that he should *be* happy, *be* esteemed by his peers, and, if the necessity arise, *be* able to protect himself. It suggests that honesty is treated less as a standard of

---

are known and whose distribution we assume to be normal. The 95 percent confidence interval on the true ratio, R, of the two proportions, p_1 and p_2, that hold for any given A and B is given by:

$$R = r \pm \frac{(1/8p_2)\sqrt{(28/n_1) + (39r^2/n_2) - [(28 \times 39)/64n_1n_2p_2^2]}}{[1 - (39/64n_2p_2^2)]}$$

where p_1 and p_2 are the observed sample proportions, $r = p_1/p_2$, $n_1 =$ the number of persons selecting A, and $n_2 =$ the number of persons who do not select A.

The logic of the testing procedure is as follows: if the interval contains the null hypothesis value of $R = \frac{2}{3}$ implied by chance selection, then we assume no association between B and A. If the interval excludes $\frac{2}{3}$ such that the lower limit is larger than $\frac{2}{3}$, we conclude that the true R is greater than we expect on the basis of randomness and hence that B is positively associated with A. On the other hand, if the upper limit of the interval is smaller than $\frac{2}{3}$, then we conclude that the true R is smaller than $\frac{2}{3}$ and hence B and A are negatively related.

This procedure was suggested by Samuel W. Greenhouse. For the derivation of the test see E. C. Fieller (4) and Pandurang V. Sukhatme (7).

[9] This analysis and those to follow will be limited to the mothers, since the sample of fathers is small. For simplicity, we shall present data separately for boys and for girls only where the relationship under discussion appears to differ for the two sexes considered separately.

TABLE 3. *All Cases[1] Where Mothers' Choice of One Characteristic as "Desirable" Is Significantly Related to Their Choice of Any Other Characteristic as "Desirable"*

Characteristic A	B	Proportion Who Choose B Among Those Who: Choose A (p_1)	Do Not Choose A (p_2)	p_1/p_2
Middle-Class Mothers				
Positive relationships:				
1. Honesty	Consideration	0.42	0.37	1.14
2. Honesty	Manners	.22	.16	1.38
3. Honesty	Dependability (boys)	.33	.22	1.50
4. Consideration	Honesty	.47	.42	1.12
5. Manners	Honesty	.52	.43	1.21
6. Dependability	Honesty (boys)	.54	.41	1.32
7. Consideration	Self-control	.24	.22	1.09
8. Self-control	Consideration	.41	.39	1.05
9. Manners	Neatness	.24	.08	3.00
10. Neatness	Manners	.42	.16	2.63
11. Curiosity	Happiness	.58	.43	1.35
12. Happiness	Curiosity	.23	.14	1.64
13. Happiness	Ambition (boys)	.13	.06	2.17
Negative relationships:				
1. Honesty	Popularity	.04	.24	0.17
2. Popularity	Honesty	.12	.50	0.24
3. Curiosity	Obedience	.03	.24	0.38
4. Obedience	Consideration	0.17	0.45	0.13
Working-Class Mothers				
Positive relationships:				
1. Happiness	Honesty	0.51	0.55	0.93
2. Popularity	Honesty	.62	.51	1.22
3. Honesty	Popularity	.20	.14	1.43
4. Honesty	Defend self	.07	.05	1.40
5. Consideration	Manners (girls)	.42	.30	1.40
6. Manners	Consideration (girls)	.31	.20	1.55
7. Consideration	Curiosity	.11	.04	2.75
8. Ambition	Dependability	.29	.19	1.53
9. Happiness	Consideration (boys)	.35	.27	1.30
10. Consideration	Happiness (boys)	.32	.25	1.28
11. Happiness	Popularity (girls)	.25	.16	1.56
Negative relationships:				
1. Obedience	Popularity	.05	.24	0.21
2. Manners	Popularity	.00	.23	0.00
3. Consideration	Popularity	.02	.23	0.09
4. Popularity	Obedience	.10	.38	0.26
5. Popularity	Manners	.00	.29	0.00
6. Popularity	Consideration	.03	.32	0.09
7. Manners	Dependability (girls)	0.00	0.20	0.00

[1] Where it is not specified whether relationship holds for boys or girls, it holds for both sexes. In all the relationships, p_1 and p_2 are each based on a minimum of 20 cases.

conduct and more as a quality of the person; the emphasis is on being a person of inherent honesty rather than on acting in an honest way.

Note especially the relationship of popularity to honesty. For middle-class mothers these are *negatively* related. To value honesty is to forego valuing popularity; to value popularity is to forego valuing honesty. One must choose between honesty "at the risk of offending" and popularity at the sacrifice of absolute honesty. The exact opposite obtains for working-class mothers: those who accord high valuation to either are *more* likely to value the other. The very mothers who deem it most important that their children enjoy popularity are those who attribute great importance to honesty. Honesty does not interfere with popularity; on the contrary, it enhances the probability that one will enjoy the respect of one's peers.

However, working-class mothers who value obedience, manners, or consideration are distinctly unlikely to value popularity, and vice versa. They do see each of these standards of conduct as inconsistent with popularity.[10] This further substantiates the view that working-class mothers are more likely to view honesty as a quality of the person, a desideratum of moral worth, rather than as one among several highly valued standards of conduct.

Happiness, in distinction to honesty, implies neither constraints upon action nor a moral quality; rather, it indicates a desired goal, achievable in several different ways. One way of specifying what is implied when happiness is regarded as a major value is to ascertain the other values most likely to be related to the choice of happiness.

The two choices positively related to the choice of happiness by middle-class mothers are curiosity and (for boys) ambition. Those middle-class mothers who deem it exceedingly important that their children aspire for knowledge or success are even more likely than are middle-class mothers in general to value their children's happiness highly.

Working-class mothers who value these, however, are no more likely to value happiness. Instead, curiosity is related to consideration, to the child's concern for others' well-being, and ambition to dependability, to his being the type of person who can be counted on. The values that are positively related to happiness by working-class mothers are honesty,

10 It may be said that these three characteristics have more in common than that they are all standards of conduct. The fact that working-class mothers who value consideration for their *daughters* are especially likely to value manners, and the converse, suggests the possibility that consideration may be seen as a near-equivalent to manners by at least a sizable portion of working-class mothers. If so, all three values negatively related to popularity can be viewed as reflecting close conformance to directives from parents—as contrasted with directives from within. (Note in this connection, that working-class mothers who would have their daughters be mannerly are distinctly unlikely to deem it important that they be dependable.)

consideration (for boys), and popularity (for girls). Not aspirations for knowledge or for success, but being an honest—a worthy person; not the desire to outdistance others, but, for boys, concern for others' well-being and, for girls, enjoyment of the respect and confidence of peers: these are the conceptions of the desirable that accompany working-class mothers' wishes that their children be happy.

Still the, perhaps, equally important fact is that no choice, by mothers of either social class, is negatively related to the choice of happiness.

The final bit of information that these data provide concerns the conception of *obedience* entertained in the two classes. Middle-class mothers who value curiosity are unlikely to value obedience; those who value obedience are unlikely to value consideration. For middle-class mothers, but not for working-class mothers, obedience would appear to have a rather narrow connotation; it seems to approximate blind obedience.

CLASS, SUBCULTURE, AND VALUES

In discussing the relationship of social class to values we have talked as if American society were composed of two relatively homogeneous groups, manual and white-collar workers, together with their families. Yet it is likely that there is considerable variation in values, associated with other bases of social differentiation, *within* each class. If so, it should be possible to divide the classes into subgroups in such a way as to specify more precisely the relationship of social class to values.

Consider, first, the use we have made of the concept "social class." Are the differences we have found between the values of middle- and working-class mothers a product of this dichotomy alone, or do values parallel status gradations more generally? It is possible to arrive at an approximate answer by dividing the mothers into the five socioeconomic strata delineated by the Hollingshead Index (see Table 4). An examination of the choices made by mothers in each stratum indicates that variation in values parallels socioeconomic status rather closely.

1. The higher a mother's status, the higher the probability that she will choose consideration, curiosity, self-control, and (for boys)[11] happiness as highly desirable; curiosity is particularly likely to be chosen by mothers in the highest stratum.
2. The lower her status, the higher the probability that she will select

[11] The choice of happiness is, as we have seen, related to social class for boys only. Consequently, in each comparison we shall make in this section the choice of happiness for *girls* will prove to be an exception to the general order.

TABLE 4.   *Mothers' Socioeconomic Status and Their Choice of Characteristics as "Most Desirable" in a 10- or 11-Year-Old Child*

	Proportion Who Select Each Characteristic Socioeconomic Stratum (on Hollingshead Index)				
Characteristic	I	II	III	IV	V
Obedience	0.14	0.19	0.25	0.35	0.27
Neatness, cleanliness	.06	.07	.16	.18	.27
Consideration	.41	.37	.39	.25	.32
Curiosity	.37	.12	.09	.07	.03
Self-control	.24	.30	.18	.13	.14
Happiness	.61	.40	.40	.38	.30
boys		.48	.40		.27
girls		.54	.40		.45
Honesty	0.37	0.49	0.46	0.50	0.65
N	51	43	80	128	37

obedience, neatness, and cleanliness; it appears, too, that mothers in the lowest stratum are more likely than are those in the highest to value *honesty*.

Mothers' values also are directly related to their own occupational positions and educational attainments, independently of their families' class status. (The family's class status has been indexed on the basis of the husband's occupation and education.) It happens that a considerable proportion of the mothers we have classified as working class hold white-collar jobs.[12] Those who do are, by and large, closer to middle-class mothers in their values than are other working-class mothers (see Table 5). But those who hold manual jobs are even further from middle-class mothers in their values than are working-class mothers who do not have jobs outside the home.

So, too, for mothers' educational attainments: a middle-class mother of *relatively* low educational attainment (one who has gone no further than graduation from high school) is less likely to value curiosity and more likely to value (for girls) neatness and cleanliness (see Table 6). A working-class mother of *relatively* high educational attainment (one who has at least graduated from high school) is more likely to value self-control for boys and both consideration and curiosity for girls. The

[12] No middle-class mothers have manual jobs, so the comparable situation does not exist. Those middle-class women who do work (at white-collar jobs) are less likely to value neatness and cleanliness and more likely to value obedience and curiosity.

TABLE 5. *Working-Class Mothers' Own Occupations and Their Choice of Characteristics as "Most Desirable" in a 10- or 11-Year-Old Child*

| Characteristic | Proportion Who Select Each Characteristic | | |
	White-Collar Job	No Job	Manual Job
Obedience	.26	.35	.53
Neatness, cleanliness	.16	.18	.42
Consideration	.39	.21	.05
Curiosity	.10	.04	.00
Self-control	.13	.14	.11
Happiness	.33	.40	.26
boys	.32	.21	—
girls	.36	.59	—
N	69	77	19

TABLE 6. *Mothers' Education and Their Choice of Characteristics as "Most Desirable" in a 10- or 11-Year-Old Child*

| Characteristic | Proportion Who Select Each Characteristic | | | |
| | Male Child | | Female Child | |
	At Least Some College	High School Graduate or Less	At Least Some College	High School Graduate or Less
Middle-Class Mothers				
Obedience	0.11	0.22	0.13	0.29
Neatness, cleanliness	.03	.09	.03[a]	.23
Consideration	.47	.35	.41	.37
Curiosity	.31[a]	.13	.31[a]	.06
Self-control	.33	.19	.19	.21
Happiness	0.50	0.41	0.59	0.40
N	36	54	32	52
Working-Class Mothers				
Obedience	0.29	0.43	0.28	0.32
Neatness, cleanliness	.12	.14	.21	.35
Consideration	.32	.27	.33[a]	.14
Curiosity	.07	.05	.12[a]	.00
Self-control	.22[a]	.07	.16	.08
Happiness	0.27	0.27	0.47	0.43
N	41	44	43	37

[a] Difference between mothers of differing educational status statistically significant, 0.05 level or better, using chi-squared test.

largest differences obtain between those middle-class mothers of highest educational attainments and those working-class mothers of lowest educational attainments.

Even when we restrict ourselves to considerations of social status and its various ramifications, we find that values vary appreciably within each of the two broad classes. And, as sociologists would expect, variation in values proceeds along other major lines of social demarcation as well. Religious background is particularly useful as a criterion for distinguishing subcultures within the social classes. It does *not* exert so powerful an effect that Protestant mothers differ significantly from Catholic mothers of the same social class in their values.[13] But the combination of class and religious background does enable us to isolate groups that are more homogeneous in their values than are the social classes in toto. We find

TABLE 7. *Mothers' Religious Background and Their Choice of Characteristics as "Most Desirable" in a 10- or 11-Year-Old Child*

| | Proportion Who Select Each Characteristic | | | |
Characteristic	Middle-Class Protestant	Middle-Class Catholic	Working-Class Protestant	Working-Class Catholic
Obedience	0.17	0.25	0.33	0.36
Neatness, cleanliness	.08	.15	.17	.27
Consideration	.36	.38	.26	.29
Curiosity	.24	.12	.07	.05
Self-control	.28	.15	.15	.09
Happiness	.47	.42	.38	.30
boys	.48	.32	.35	.13
girls	0.45	0.52	0.42	0.54
N	88	52	107	56

that there is an ordering, consistent for all class-related values, proceeding from middle-class Protestant mothers, to middle-class Catholic, to working-class Protestant, to working-class Catholic (see Table 7). Middle-class Protestants and working-class Catholics constitute the two extremes whose values are most dissimilar.

[13] The index here is based on the question "May I ask what is your religious background?"
Even when the comparison is restricted to Catholic mothers who send their children to Catholic school versus Protestant mothers of the same social class, there are no significant differences in values.
Jewish mothers (almost all of them in this sample are middle class) are very similar to middle-class Protestant mothers in their values, with two notable exceptions. More Jewish than Protestant mothers select popularity and ability to defend one's self—two values that are not related to social class.

Another relevant line of social demarcation is the distinction between urban and rural background.[14] As we did for religious background, we can arrange the mothers into four groups delineated on the basis of class and rural-urban background in an order that is reasonably consistent for all class-related values. The order is: middle-class urban, middle-class rural, working-class urban, working-class rural (see Table 8). The extremes are middle-class mothers raised in the city and working-class mothers raised on farms.

Several other variables fail to differentiate mothers of the same social class into groups having appreciably different values. These include the mother's age, the size of the family, the ordinal position of the child in the family, the length of time the family has lived in the neighborhood, whether or not the mother has been socially mobile (from the

TABLE 8. *Rural Versus Urban Background of Mothers and Their Choices of Characteristics as "Most Desirable" in a 10- or 11-Year-Old Child*

| | Proportion Who Select Each Characteristic | | | |
Characteristic	Middle-Class Urban	Middle-Class Rural	Working-Class Urban	Working-Class Rural
Obedience	0.19	0.24	0.29	0.42
Neatness, cleanliness	.11	.12	.17	.25
Consideration	.42	.27	.31	.18
Curiosity	.19	.12	.07	.04
Self-control	.20	.33	.15	.11
Happiness	.47	.42	.41	.25
boys	.44	.47	.28	.25
girls	0.50	0.37	0.57	0.26
N	141	33	110	55

status of her childhood family), and her class identification. Nor are these results a function of the large proportion of families of government workers included in the sample: wives of government employees do not differ from other mothers of the same social class in their values.

In sum, we find that it is possible to specify the relationship between social class and values more precisely by dividing the social classes into

14 We asked, "Have you ever lived on a farm?" and then classified all mothers who had lived on a farm for some time other than simply summer vacations, prior to age 15, as having had a rural background.

Ordinarily, one further line of cultural demarcation would be considered at this point—nationality background. The present sample, however, is composed predominantly of parents who are at least second-generation, United States-born, so this is not possible.

subgroups on the basis of other lines of social demarcation—but that social class seems to provide the single most relevant line of demarcation.

ADEQUACY OF INDEX VALUES

The form in which our major question was asked enabled us to set the same ground rules for all parents. No premium was put on imaginativeness or articulateness. But the fact that we limited their choice to these particular characteristics means that we denied them the opportunity to select others that they might have regarded as even more desirable. However, we had *previously* asked each parent: "When you think of a boy (or girl) of (child's) age, are there *any* things you look for as most important or most desirable?" Only three additional characteristics were suggested by any appreciable number of parents. The first, suggested by a significantly larger proportion of middle- than of working-class parents, was "self-reliance" or "independence"—a result entirely consistent with the rest of this study. The second, variously labeled "friendliness," "cooperativeness," or "ability to get along well with others" was also predominantly a middle-class concern. It indicates that we may have underrepresented the proportion of middle-class parents who value their children's ability to relate to others. Finally, several parents (of both social classes) said that they considered it desirable that the child not "act too old," "too young," or be effeminate (in a boy) or masculine (in a girl). There seems to be a certain concern, not adequately indexed by our major question, that the child conform to his parent's conception of what constitutes the proper age and sex role.

Of course, parents might have selected other characteristics as well, had we suggested them. These possible limitations notwithstanding, it appears that the index is reasonably comprehensive.

More important than the question of comprehensiveness is whether or not it is really possible for parents to select characteristics as desirable independently of the way that they rate their own children's behavior. Since each parent was later asked to rate his child's performance with respect to each characteristic, we can compare the ratings given by parents who chose a characteristic with those given by parents of the same social class who did not. Parents who chose each characteristic were no more and no less likely to describe their children as excelling in that characteristic; nor were they any more or less likely than other parents to feel that their children were deficient. The parents have not imputed desirability to the characteristics that they feel represent their children's virtues or their children's deficiencies.

The final and most important question: Is it wise to accept some-one's assertion that something is a value to him? After all, assertions are subject to distortion.[15] To the degree that we can ascertain that parents act in reasonable conformity to the values they assert, however, we gain confidence in an index based on assertions.

This study does not provide disinterested observations of the parents' behavior. Our closest approximation derives from interviews with the parents themselves—interviews in which we questioned them in con-siderable detail about their relevant actions. Perhaps the most crucial of these data are those bearing on their actions in situations where their children behave in *disvalued* ways. We have, for example, questioned parents in some detail about what they do when their children lose their tempers. We began by asking whether or not the child in question "ever really loses his temper." From those parents who said that the child does lose his temper, we then proceeded to find out precisely what behavior they considered to be "loss of temper"; what they "generally do when he acts this way"; whether they "ever find it necessary to do anything else"; if so, what else they do, and "under what circumstances." Our concern here is with what the parent reports he does as a matter of last resort.[16]

Mothers who regard *self-control* as an important value are more likely to report that they punish the child—be it physically, by isolation, or by restriction of activities; they are unlikely merely to scold or to ignore his loss of temper altogether (see Table 9).

To punish a child who has lost his temper may not be a particularly effective way of inducing self-control. One might even have predicted that mothers who value self-control would be less likely to punish breaches of control, more likely to explain, even ignore. They do not, however, and we must put the issue more simply: mothers who assert the value are more likely to report that they apply negative sanctions in situations where the child violates that value. This response would certainly seem to conform to their value assertion.

A parallel series of questions deals with the mother's reactions when

[15] But inferring values from observed behavior may not be satisfactory either, for we cannot be certain that we are correctly distinguishing the normative from other components of action. As Robin Williams (8) states: "No student of human conduct can accept uncritically, as final evidence, people's testimony as to their own values. Yet actions may deceive as well as words, and there seems no reason for always giving one precedence over the other."

[16] This comparison and those to follow are limited to parents who say that the child does in fact behave in the disvalued way, at least on occasion. (Approximately equal proportions of middle- and working-class mothers report that their children do behave in each of these ways.)

TABLE 9. *Choice of "Self-Control" as "Most Desirable" Characteristic and Most Extreme Actions That Mothers Report They Take When Their Children Lose Their Tempers*

	Middle-Class		Proportion Working-Class		Both	
	Choose Self-Control	Don't Choose Self-Control	Choose Self-Control	Don't Choose Self-Control	Choose Self-Control	Don't Choose Self-Control
Punish physically	0.26	0.20	0.44	0.26	0.32	0.23
Isolate	.20	.11	.11	.12	.17	.11
Restrict activities, other punishments	.06	.05	.17	.14	.10	.10
Threaten punishment	.06	.03	.00	.02	.04	.02
Scold, admonish, etc.	.31	.40	.17	.31	.26	.36
Ignore	0.11	0.21	0.11	0.15	0.11	0.18
	1.00	1.00	1.00	1.00	1.00	1.00
N	35	113	18	113	53	226

her child "refuses to do what she tells him to do." Mothers who assert that they regard *obedience* as important are more likely to report that they punish in one way or another when their children refuse.[17] There is also evidence that mothers who value *consideration* are more likely to respond to their children's "fighting with other children," an action that need not necessarily be seen as inconsistent with consideration by punishing them, or at least by separating them from the others.[18]

In all three instances, then, the reports on parental reactions to behavior that seem to violate the value in question indicate that mothers who profess high regard for the value are more likely to apply negative sanctions.

[17] The figures are 47 versus 29 percent for middle-class mothers; 36 versus 18 percent for working-class mothers.

[18] The figures are 42 and 29 percent for middle-class mothers; 61 versus 37 percent for working-class mothers.

There is also some indication that *working-class* mothers who value *honesty* have been more prone to insist that their children make restitution when they have "swiped" something, but the number of mothers who say that their children have ever swiped something is too small for this evidence to be conclusive. (The figures for working-class mothers are 63 versus 35 percent; for middle-class mothers, 38 versus 33 percent.)

The interviews with the children provide further evidence that parents have acted consistently with their values—for example, children whose mothers assert high valuation of dependability are more likely to tell us that the reason their parents want them to do their chores is to train them in responsibility (not to relieve the parents of work).

INTERPRETATION

Our first conclusion is that parents, whatever their social class, deem it very important indeed that their children be honest, happy, considerate, obedient, and dependable.

The second conclusion is that, whatever the reasons may be, parents' values are related to their social position, particularly their class position.

There still remains, however, the task of interpreting the relationship between parents' social position and their values. In particular: What underlie the differences between the values of middle- and of working-class parents?

One relevant consideration is that some parents may "take for granted" values that others hold dear. For example, middle-class parents may take "neatness and cleanliness" for granted, while working-class parents regard it as highly desirable. But what does it mean to say that middle-class parents take neatness and cleanliness for granted? In essence, the argument is that middle-class parents value neatness and cleanliness as greatly as do working-class parents but not so greatly as they value such things as happiness and self-control. If this be the case, it can only mean that in the circumstances of middle-class life neatness and cleanliness are easily enough attained to be of less immediate concern than are these other values.

A second consideration lies in the probability that these value-concepts have differing meanings for parents of different cultural backgrounds. For example, one might argue that honesty is a central standard of conduct for middle-class parents because they see honesty as meaning truthfulness; and that it is more a quality of the person for working-class parents because they see it as meaning trustworthiness. Perhaps so; but to suggest that a difference in meaning underlies a difference in values raises the further problem of explaining this difference in meaning.

It would be reasonable for working-class parents to be more likely to see honesty as trustworthiness. The working-class situation is one of less material security and less assured protection from the dishonesty of others. For these reasons, trustworthiness is more at issue for working-class than for middle-class parents.

Both considerations lead us to view differences in the values of middle- and working-class parents in terms of their differing circumstances of life and, by implication, their conceptions of the effects that these circumstances may have on their children's future lives. We believe that parents are most likely to accord high priority to those values that seem both *problematic,* in the sense that they are difficult of achievement, and *important,* in the sense that failure to achieve them would affect the child's future adversely. From this perspective it is reasonable that working-class parents cannot afford to take neatness and cleanliness as much for granted as can middle-class parents. It is reasonable, too, that working-class parents are more likely to see honesty as implying trustworthiness and this connotation of honesty is seen as problematic.

These characteristics—honesty and neatness—are important to the child's future precisely because they assure him a respectable social position. Just as "poor but honest" has traditionally been an important line of social demarcation, their high valuation of these qualities may express working-class parents' concern that their children occupy a position unequivocally above that of persons who are not neat or who are not scrupulously honest. These are the qualities of respectable, worthwhile people.

So, too, is obedience. The obedient child follows his parents' dictates rather than his own standards. He acts, in his subordinate role as a child, in conformity with the prescriptions of established authority.

Even in the way they differentiate what is desirable for boys from what is desirable for girls, working-class mothers show a keen appreciation of the qualities making for respectable social position.

The characteristics that middle-class parents are more likely to value for their children are internal standards for governing one's relationships with other people and, in the final analysis, with one's self. It is not that middle-class parents are less concerned than are working-class parents about social position. The qualities of person that assure respectability may be taken for granted, but in a world where social relationships are determinative of position, these standards of conduct are both more problematic and more important.

The middle-class emphasis on internal standards is evident in their choice of the cluster of characteristics centering around honesty; in their being less likely than are working-class parents to value obedience and more likely to value self-control and consideration; and in their seeing obedience as inconsistent with both consideration and curiosity. The child is to act appropriately, not because his parents tell him to, but because he wants to. Not conformity to authority, but inner control; not because you're told to but because you take the other person into consideration—these are the middle-class ideals.

These values place responsibility directly upon the individual. He cannot rely upon authority, nor can he simply conform to what is presented to him as proper. He should be impelled to come to his own understanding of the situation.[19] He is to govern himself in such a way as to be able to act consistently with his principles. The basic importance of relationship to self is explicit in the concept of self-control. It is implicit, too, in consideration—a standard that demands of the individual that he respond sympathetically to others' needs even if they be in conflict with his own; and in the high valuation of honesty as central to other standards of conduct: "to thine own self be true."

Perhaps, considering this, it should not be surprising that so many middle-class mothers attribute first-rank importance to happiness, even for boys. We cannot assume that their children's happiness is any less important to working-class mothers than it is to middle-class mothers; in fact, working-class mothers are equally likely to value happiness for *girls*. For their sons, however, happiness is second choice to honesty and obedience. Apparently, middle-class mothers can afford instead to be concerned about their son's happiness. And perhaps they are right in being concerned. We have noted that those middle-class mothers who deem it most important that their sons outdistance others are especially likely to be concerned about their sons' happiness; and even those mothers who do not are asking their children to accept considerable responsibility.

REFERENCES

1. Aberle, D. F., & Naegele, K. D. Middle-class fathers' occupational role and attitudes toward children. *Amer. J. Orthopsychiat.*, 1952, **22**, 366–378.
2. Bronfenbrenner, U. Socialization and social class through time and space. In Eleanor E. Maccoby *et al.*, *Readings in social psychology*. New York: Henry Holt & Co., new edition in press.
3. Duvall, Evelyn M. Conceptions of parenthood. *Amer. J. Sociol.*, 1946, **52**, 193–203.
4. Fieller, E. C. A fundamental formula in the statistics of biological assay, and some applications. *Quart. J. Pharmacy & Pharmac.*, 1944, **17**, 117–123.
5. Hyman, H. H. The value systems of different classes. In R. Bendix & S. M. Lipset (Eds.), *Class, status and power*. Glencoe, Ill.: Free Press, 1953. Pp. 426–442.

[19] Curiosity provides a particularly interesting example of how closely parents' values are related to their circumstances of life and expectations: the proportion of mothers who value curiosity rises very slowly from status level to status level until we reach the wives of professionals and the more highly educated businessmen; then it jumps suddenly (see Table 4). The value is given priority in precisely that portion of the middle class where it is most appropriate and where its importance for the child's future is most apparent.

6. Kluckhohn, C. Values and value orientations. In T. Parsons & E. A. Shils (Eds.), *Toward a general theory of action.* Cambridge, Mass.: Harvard University Press, 1951. P. 395.

7. Sukhatme, P. V. *Sampling theory of surveys with applications.* Ames, I.: Iowa State College Press, 1954. Pp. 158–160.

8. Williams, R. *American society: a sociological interpretation.* New York: Alfred A. Knopf, 1951. P. 378.

RELATIONSHIPS BETWEEN DEPENDENCE ON ADULTS AND SOCIAL ACCEPTANCE BY PEERS

Helen R. Marshall and Boyd R. McCandless

UNIVERSITY OF KENTUCKY AND INDIANA UNIVERSITY

THE BELIEF is widely held by those responsible for guidance of children that extreme dependence upon adults in a nursery school situation indicates that the child has not had his needs met for satisfaction in contacts with adults, particularly his parents. It is also commonly assumed that a warm and satisfactory dependent relationship with adults (particularly parents) must exist before a child can be secure enough to gain emotional satisfaction from social competence with and acceptance by peers. Sears' (7) position provides some support for these points of view. He has thought of extreme preschool-aged dependency as being possibly due to weaning and feeding frustration in infancy, these having aroused anxiety associated with adults so that adult controlling and manipulating behavior is essential to the child's emotional economy. Dependency is the expression of this controlling behavior.

The opinion is seldom advanced that adult dependency in preschool situations may be due to lack of techniques for relating with peers, without other dynamic determinants. Rarely expressed also is the opinion that extremely gratifying parents may develop habits of dependency in their children (probably reinforced by the same kind of teachers), thus perhaps reducing or precluding the possibility that the children can find equivalent satisfaction with their peers.

To the authors' knowledge, it has not been established empirically that any relationship, positive or negative, exists between dependence on adults and competence with peers, including acceptance by them. While

Reprinted from *Child Development* (December, 1957), **28** (4), by permission of the authors and the Society for Research in Child Development.

Heathers (1) has studied relations between preschool children's dependence on teachers and their types of play with peers, he has not dealt with social acceptance as such, and its relationship with dependency. One investigation deals with this subject indirectly: McCollum (4) reported that a teacher's rating of "mature dependency" and sociometric status were related positively to a test of creativity for 4- and 5-year-old children.

The authors have reported a technique for eliciting sociometric choices from preschool-aged children, using pictures (3), that is both reliable and useful. They have also revised the Hyde and York (2) "moving sociometric technique" of observation so as to be able relatively quickly to gain reliable quantitative data on adult-child and peer social interactions in a nursery school free play situation (5).

Using the observed number of adult-child interactions as the measure of dependency, this paper asks two questions: (1) Is the degree of preschool children's dependency on adults in free play situations related to their participation with and acceptance by peers? (2) If such a relationship is found, is it affected by the progress of acquaintance in a preschool group from its inception through time?

SUBJECTS AND PROCEDURE

Ss constituted two groups in the Laboratory Preschools of the University of Iowa's Child Welfare Research Station. Children were selected for these groups and teachers assigned by regular Station procedures, independently of the present authors. Fathers of all children were engaged in professional or business-managerial occupations. It was the first Station preschool experience for the majority of the children in each group, although three children were members of both groups. One boy of these three was absent from school too often in Group I to be used as an S, leaving 10 girls and 9 boys in Group I (I). School absence also eliminated a girl in Group II (II), leaving as Ss 9 girls and 10 boys. Mean CA at the time of beginning observations for I was 4–4 years; II averaged 4–11 years at the time of beginning of the first of two play observation series (IIA). The two groups were combined into a single sample of 36 Ss for the correlations listed in Table I of this paper, and for these, Group II records and tests were used for the three children belonging to both groups. There was no teacher overlap between groups, and each group was staffed with an experienced head teacher and two graduate teaching assistants. Interactions with other adults (e.g., the present investigators, student observers, graduate assistants, parents) are included in the dependency measures.

Peers and child-adult interactions were recorded in similar fashion by a modification of the Hyde-York (2) observation technique, as described more fully in another paper (1). The interactions were recorded for 2-minute periods in the following categories for both peer and child-adult interactions: (a) Association: apparent mutual awareness of a common activity or interest, and as further defined by Parten (6). (b) Friendly approach or response that is neutral, pleasant, friendly, or helpful. It may be limited to one word or include many words. (c) Conversation: Ss converse in a friendly fashion for one-half minute or more of the 2-minute observation time (used for II only). (d) Hostile: verbal or physical approach or response that interferes with the ongoing activity of the S, is a direct attack, or is judged deliberate "snubbing" withdrawal from some approach of the child or adult.

An adult dependency score was obtained for each child by adding the observed incidence of adult-child interactions, by category or combinations of categories (as indicated in Tables 1 and 2), and dividing this sum by the total number of minutes of observation for the child.

For Ss in I, a minimum of 100 minutes of observation per child was obtained over one calendar month. At least 200 minutes of observation—two 100-minute series designated as IIA (earlier) and IIB (later)—were recorded for each S of II over 6 calendar weeks. In all observations, Ss were in indoor and outdoor free play situations offering a wide variety of companions and activities. All preschool hours and activities were included in the observations except situations where spontaneous social interactions between children were not encouraged or could not develop, such as listening to stories, resting, juice service, or dressing.

Odd-even sampling reliability of dependency scores was computed only for the friendly approach category and its combinations, since zero scores were obtained in the split halves of other categories for many Ss. Odd-even split-half dependency scores for this category and its combinations in IIA had Guttman coefficients of .69 to .72. Sampling reliability over time was computed for two different split-halves. The two 100-minute series of II had the following Guttman coefficients for dependency scores; friendly approach, .65; conversation (for the 14 Ss with scores), .84; association plus friendly approach, .74; association plus friendly approach plus conversation, .77. However, in the split of the first and second 50-minute scores of IIA, friendly approach dependency scores had a Guttman coefficient of only .16. Sampling reliability of de-

TABLE 1. *Correlation Coefficients for Adult Dependency Scores and Peer Acceptance or Participation Scores for Sample of 36 Ss*

Peer Acceptance or Participation Scores	Adult Dependency Scores[a]				
	A		FA	A+FA	H
	r_{bis}	r^b	r	r	$r_{bis}{}^c$
Sociometric scores	−.59[d]	−.27	−.26	−.32	−.51[d]
Teacher judgment scores	−.50[d]	−.21	−.39[d]	−.40[d]	−.23
Observed social acceptance scores	−.13	−.25	−.49[e]	−.45[e]	−.09
Peer interaction scores:[a]					
A	−.40	−.23	−.42[d]	−.45[e]	−.15
FA	−.54[d]	−.37	−.64[e]	−.67[e]	−.24
H	−.09	.16	−.11	−.07	.19
A+FA	−.50[d]	−.32	−.56[e]	−.59[e]	−.21[d]

[a] Observation category letters are abbreviations for names of the categories, as follows: A = Association; FA = Friendly Approach; H = Hostile.
[b] N = 30.
[c] 11 Ss had zero scores in the hostile "dependency" category.
[d] r or r_{bis} is significant at <.05 level.
[e] r is significant at <.01 level.

TABLE 2. *Correlation Coefficients of Dependency Scores with Other Measures Obtained During Observation Series IIA, N = 19*

Peer Acceptance or Participation Scores	Adult Dependency Scores[a]			
	FA	C^b	A+FA	A+FA+C
Sociometric scores:				
first sociometric	−.02	.11	−.03	−.02
second sociometric	−.03	−.04	−.09	−.10
Teacher judgment scores:				
first judgment	−.32	−.15	.22	.15
second judgment	.08	.01	.04	.01
Observed social acceptance scores	.01	.16	.01	.02
Peer Interaction Scores:[a]				
A	−.07	.16	−.10	−.08
FA	.15	.10	.08	.08
C	.00	.24	−.01	.02
H	.33	.31	.35	.39
A+FA	.07	.13	.01	.01
A+FA+C	−.07	.10	−.11	−.10

[a] Observation category letters are abbreviations for names of the categories, as follows: A = Association; FA = Friendly Approach; H = Hostile.
[b] There were two zero conversation dependency categories, hence N = 17.

pendency scores, then, is low to moderate, where high sampling reliability was obtained for peer interaction scores. These latter ranged from
.80 to .95 in all splits of observation records (5).

Four measures of peer social acceptance and participation were used
in this investigation: (a) Sociometric score, obtained from verbal choices
of Ss (3). The scores in Table 1 were obtained from choices during the
fourth of a series of four test periods for I and the third of three for II.
(b) Teacher judgment (of social status) score (3). The score used in Table
1 was obtained from judgments of teachers made at the same time that
the sociometric choices were obtained. (c) Observed social acceptance
score (5), or, roughly, the sum of the number of children for whom the
S was observed to be one of the three peers played with most frequently
in I and IIB records. (d) Peer interaction score for single and combined
categories of observed interaction. Limited to social interactions with
other children, this score was obtained in the same way (5) as the dependency score and is a measure of degree and kind of social participation with peers. For Table 1 analyses, scores from observation records
of I and IIB were used.

RESULTS

1. Is the degree of preschool children's dependency on adults in free
play situations related to measures of social acceptance by and interaction with peers?

Table 1 gives product-moment and biserial correlation coefficients
obtained between dependency scores and measures of social acceptance
and participation for the sample of 36 Ss. All but two of the 35 coefficients
are negative, 15 of them being significant at the $p = .05$ or less level.
When the same correlations were computed for each group separately, a
similar consistency in negative direction and size of coefficients was obtained for both I and IIB. The consistency of direction and frequency of
significance of these relationships indicates that dependence on adults in
the preschool situation accompanies relatively low social status and group
participation.

The practical importance of the significant negative correlations between dependency and the categories of association (A) and friendly
approach (FA) is pointed up when it is noted that A + FA make up 86
percent of all the observed peer social interactions of these children, A
composing 36 percent, FA 50 percent.

The negative relation between children's sociometric scores and dependency scores differed significantly from zero for the biserial coefficients of association and hostile dependency scores, as shown in Table 1. All dependency scores except those for the hostile category correlated negatively and significantly with teacher judgments of social status. Observed social acceptance scores correlated significantly with dependency scores in the friendly approach category and the additive combination of categories. In general, then, negative relations were found to exist between dependency scores and each of these three measures of social acceptance obtained after several weeks of acquaintance.

The negative relationship between dependency scores and degree of social participation with peers was most marked for the correlations of the friendly approach category peer interaction scores. This category of peer interaction scores was related negatively and significantly to all dependency scores except those of the hostile category. The product-moment r's were the largest in size of any obtained for the total sample. For the friendly approach dependency scores, the r obtained with the same category of peer interaction scores differed significantly from the r's obtained with association (.02 level) and hostile (.01 level) peer interaction scores. Hostile peer interaction scores appear to be unrelated to either friendly or hostile dependence on adults.

The conversation category of interactions with adults was recorded only in observations for II. In IIB, conversation dependency scores correlated negatively and significantly with friendly approach ($r = .50$) and $A + FA$ ($r = -.49$) peer interaction scores. However, the correlations with the three measures of social acceptance were not significant (r's = $-.39$ to $-.45$). Conversation peer interaction scores correlated significantly with association dependency scores ($r_{bis} = -.52$) and with the combination dependency scores ($r = -.52$).

2. Is there any indication that the degree of a child's dependence on adults and its relation to other scores change as acquaintance progresses in a newly formed preschool group?

The 100 minutes of observation records of series IIA were collected for the 19 Ss in the initial 3 to 4 weeks of the group's existence. The product-moment correlation coefficients between friendly dependency scores and other measures taken during this series, presented in Table 2, are neither significant nor consistent in direction. The only correlations approaching significance are positive relations between dependency scores and hostile peer interaction scores; these correlations hovered around zero in observation series IIB. These data, considered in conjunction with the data presented in the previous section, suggest that negative relations between dependence on adults and measures of social status and participation with children may come to exist only after a period of several weeks' acquaintance in a preschool group.

Additional evidence of a change in dependence on adults is furnished by tests of differences in dependency scores obtained in the IIA and IIB observation series. The mean differences in scores were significant beyond the .001 level by two-tailed t tests for all categories, although the direction of the difference was not the same for all categories. Friendly approach and the additive combination dependency scores were larger in IIA than in IIB, while conversation dependency scores were higher in IIB.

Zero scores in the dependency categories of association and hostile prohibited treatment as continuous variables. Twelve Ss had no association interaction with adults in IIA but only four Ss had zero association dependency scores in IIB. Hostile "dependency" interactions were recorded for 7 children in IIA and for 11 children in IIB.

SUMMARY AND CONCLUSIONS

Relations between dependence on adults and social acceptance by peers were studied, using as Ss 38 children attending two newly formed preschool groups. Dependency was measured as the observed number of social interactions with adults in nursery school free play situations.

A negative relation was obtained consistently between dependency scores and measures of peer social acceptance obtained after several weeks of acquaintance. Significance of r's varied for categories of dependency scores but, in general, significant negative relations were found to exist between dependency and sociometric scores, teacher judgments of popularity, observed social acceptance in play, and number of observed friendly interactions with playmates (but not with hostile interactions). These data indicate that dependence on adults in the preschool situation accompanies relatively low social status and participation.

One of the groups of 19 Ss was observed and tested at the beginning of acquaintance. The relations between dependency scores and peer social acceptance measures were neither significant nor consistent in direction. Changes in dependence on adults as acquaintances progressed suggest that further investigations of social interactions of both adults and children in newly formed preschool groups may contribute knowledge of how dependence waxes and wanes in children as they function in groups.

REFERENCES

1. Heathers, G. Emotional dependence and independence in nursery school play. *J. genet. Psychol.*, 1955, 87, 37–57.
2. Hyde, R. W., & York, R. H. A technique for investigating interpersonal relationships in a mental hospital. *J. abnorm. soc. Psychol.*, 1948, 43, 287–299.
3. McCandless, B. R., & Marshall, Helen R. A picture-sociometric technique for preschool children and its relation to teacher judgments of friendship. *Child Develpm.*, 1957, 28, 139–147.
4. McCollum, Margaret E. An experimental study of creativity in the preschool child. Unpublished master's thesis, University of Toronto, 1954.
5. Marshall, Helen R., & McCandless, B. R. A study in prediction of social behavior of preschool children. *Child Develpm.*, 1957, 28, 149–159.
6. Parten, Mildred B. Social participation among preschool children by a time sample technique. *J. abnorm. soc. Psychol.*, 1932, 27, 243–269.
7. Sears, R. R. Ordinal position in the family as a psychological variable. *Amer. sociol. Rev.*, 1950, 15, 397–401.

THE PSYCHOSOCIAL ORIGINS
OF ACHIEVEMENT MOTIVATION [1]

Bernard C. Rosen and Roy D'Andrade

UNIVERSITY OF NEBRASKA AND STANFORD UNIVERSITY

THE PURPOSE of this study is to examine the origins of achievement motivation (*n* Achievement) within the context of the individual's membership in two important groups: family and social class. Specifically, this paper explores, through the observation of family interaction, the relationship between achievement motivation and certain child-training practices, and the relationship between these practices and the parent's social class membership.

Since many socialization practices are known to be dissimilar between social groups (*3, 4*), it might be expected that independence training practices would also differ. A study by McClelland *et al.* (*8*), later replicated by Rosen (*10*), demonstrated this to be the case: middle-class parents place greater stress upon independence training than lower-class parents. The deduction from this finding that classes differ in their level of *n* Achievement was shown to be correct by Rosen (*9*) who found that,

[1] This paper is a condensed report of an investigation supported by a research grant (M–1495) to the senior writer from the National Institute of Mental Health, Public Health Service. The generous support, advice, and encouragement of David C. McClelland is gratefully acknowledged. The contributions of James Sakoda for his help on statistical procedures, Shirley Rosen for her work in administering the Thematic Apperception Test and in the preparation of the manuscript, and Marion Winterbottom for her work in scoring the TAT protocols are deeply appreciated. Roland Bonato, Diane D'Andrade, and June Schmelzer assisted in the collection of the data. David Bakum and Thomas Shipley made many helpful suggestions.

A special expression of thanks is due Superintendent Richard C. Briggs, Mansfield School system; Arthur H. Illing, Manchester School system; and Charles Northrup, Windham School system; Principals Stephen J. Ardel, Buchanan School; Harriet Atwood, Highland Park School; David J. DiSessa, Annie Vinton School; Esther Granstrom, Bowers School; Robert L. Perry, Natchaug School; Catherine Shea, Verplanck School; Lawrence Smith, Windham Center School.

Abridged and reprinted from *Sociometry* (1959), **22**, 185–218, by permission of the authors and the American Sociological Association.

on the average, n Achievement scores for middle-class adolescents were significantly higher than those for their lower-class counterparts.

Significantly, although these studies flow logically from one another, in none of them were all three variables—group membership, child training practices, and n Achievement—studied simultaneously. Furthermore, there were certain gaps in these studies which called for theoretical and methodological modifications and additions. The nature of these gaps, and the contributions which it was the research objective of this study to make, are as follows:

Theoretical. The keystone around which studies of the origins of achievement motivation have been built is the notion that training in independent mastery is an antecedent condition of n Achievement (6, 15). This approach grew out of McClelland's and his associates' theory of the nature and origins of motivation. They argue that all motives are learned, that "they develop out of repeated affective experiences connected with certain types of situations and types of behavior. In the case of achievement motivation, the situation should involve 'standards of excellence,' presumably imposed on the child by the culture, or more particularly by the parents as representatives of the culture, and the behavior should involve either 'competition' with those standards of excellence or attempts to meet them which, if successful, produce positive effects or, if unsuccessful, negative effect. It follows that those cultures or families which stress competition with standards of excellence or which insist *that the child be able to perform certain tasks well by himself* . . . should produce children with high achievement motivation" (7).

Two distinctly different kinds of child-training practices are implicit in this theory. The first is the idea that the child is trained to do things "well"; the second, the notion that he is trained to perform tasks "by himself." The former has been called *achievement training* (2) in that it stresses competition in situations involving standards of excellence; the latter has been called *independence training* in that it involves putting the child on his own. The failure to disentangle these two concepts has resulted in a focus of attention upon independence training largely to the exclusion of achievement training, although the former is primarily concerned with developing self-reliance, often in areas involving self-care-taking (e.g., cleaning, dressing, amusing, or defending oneself). Although both kinds of training practices frequently occur together, they are different in content and consequences and needed to be examined separately.

Methodological. This study departed from two practices common in studies of the origins of n Achievement. The first practice is to derive data exclusively from ethnographic materials; the second to obtain information through questionnaire-type interviews with mothers. Interviews and ethnographies can be valuable sources of information, but they are often contaminated by interviewer and respondent biases, particularly those of perceptual distortion, inadequate recall, and deliberate inaccuracies. There was a need for data derived from systematic observation of parent-child relations. It is not enough to know what parents *say* their child-rearing practices are; these statements should be checked against more objective data, preferably acquired under controlled experimental conditions, that would permit us to *see* that they do. In this study, experiments were employed which enabled a team of investigators to observe parent-child interaction in problem-solving situations that were standardized for all groups and required no special competence associated with age or sex.

EXPERIMENTAL PROCEDURE

The subjects selected to provide data needed for the testing of these hypotheses about the origins of achievement motivation were 120 persons who made up 40 family groups composed of a father, mother, and their son, aged 9, 10, or 11. The selection of the family groups began with testing the boy. Seven schools in three northeastern Connecticut towns were visited by the same field worker who administered a Thematic Apperception Test individually and privately to 140 boys aged 9, 10, or 11. As is customary in the TAT procedure, the subject was presented with a set of four ambiguous pictures and asked to tell a story about each. His imaginative responses were then scored according to a method developed by McClelland and his associates which involves identifying and counting the frequency with which imagery about evaluated performance in competition with a standard of excellence appears in the thoughts of a person when he tells a brief story under time pressure. Experience has shown that this imagery can be identified objectively and reliably. It is the assumption of this test that the more the individual shows indications of evaluated performance connected with affect in his fantasy, the greater the degree to which achievement motivation is part of his personality (7). The stories were scored by two judges; the Pearsonian coefficient of correlation between scorers was .87, a level of reliability similar to those reported in earlier studies with this measure.

Subjects with scores of plus 2 to minus 4 (approximately the bottom quartile) were leveled as having low n Achievement, those with scores of plus 9 to plus 22 (approximately the top quartile) as having high n Achievement. Any boy with an IQ score below 98, with physical defects, whose parents were separated, or who had been raised during part of his life by persons or relatives other than his parents (e.g., grandparents) was eliminated from the sample.

Forty boys, matched by age, race, IQ, and social class were chosen for further study. All were white, native born, and between 9 and 11 years of age; the average was 10 years. Half of the boys had high n Achievement scores, half had low scores. In each achievement motivation category, half of the boys were middle class, half were lower class. Their social class position was determined according to a modified version of the Hollingshead Index of Social Position (5) which uses the occupation and education of the chief wage earner—usually the father—as the principal criteria of status. The middle-class father (class II or III) held either a professional, managerial, white-collar position, or was self-employed as an owner of a small-to-medium size business. Often one or both parents in middle-class families were college graduates; all were high-school graduates. The parents of lower-class (IV or V) boys were quasi-skilled or skilled workers in local factories, or owners of very small farms—often the farmers held factory jobs as well. Relatively few of these parents had completed high school, none had gone beyond high school. A pair of observers visited each family group, usually at night. There were two teams of observers, each composed of a man and a woman. Both teams had been trained together to ensure adequate intra- and inter-team reliability.

Once in the home, the observers explained that they were interested in studying the factors related to success in school and eventually to a career, and that the son was one of many boys selected from a cross-section of the community. When rapport had been established, the parents and their son were placed at a table—usually in the kitchen—and it was explained that the boy was going to perform certain tasks.

Experimental Tasks

The observers wanted to create an experimental situation from which could be derived objective measures of the parents' response to their son as he engaged in achievement behavior. Tasks were devised which the boy could do and which would involve the parents in their son's task performance. The tasks were constructed so that the subjects were often faced with a choice of giving or refusing help. At times they were permitted to structure the situation according to their own norms; at other times the experimenters set the norms. In some situations they were faced with decision conflicts over various alternatives in the problem-solving process. The observation of the parents' behavior as their son engaged in these experimental tasks provided information about the demands and the amount of independence the child had developed in relations with his parents.

In creating the experimental tasks an effort was made to simulate two conditions normally present when boys are solving problems in the presence of their parents: (1) tasks were constructed to make the boys relatively dependent upon their parents for aid, and (2) the situation was arranged so that the parents either knew the solution to the problem or were in a position to do the task better than their son. In addition, tasks were created which tapped manual skills as well as intellectual capacities, although intelligence is a factor in any problem-solving situation. It was for this reason that the experimenters controlled for IQ.

Pretesting had shown that no single task would provide sufficient data to test all hypotheses. Hence, five tasks were constructed, each designed to attack the problem from a somewhat different angle and yet provide certain classes of data that could be scored across tasks. The five tasks in this study are as follows:

1. *Block Stacking*. The boys were asked to build towers out of very irregularly shaped blocks. They were blindfolded and told to use only one hand in order to create a situation in which the boy was relatively dependent upon his parents for help. His parents were told that this was a test of their son's ability to build things, and that they could *say* anything to their son but could not touch the blocks. A performance norm was set for the experiment by telling the parents that the average boy could build a tower of eight blocks; they were asked to write down privately their estimate of how high they thought their son could build his tower. The purposes of this experiment were (a) to see how high were the parents' aspirations for and evaluations of their son, e.g., if they set their estimates at above or below the norm; (b) to see how self-reliant they expected or permitted their son to be, e.g., how much help they would give him.

There were three trials for this task. The first provided measures of parental evaluations and aspirations not affected by the boy's performance; the second and third estimates provided measures affected by the boy's performance. The procedure for the third trial differed from the first two in that the boy was told that he would be given a nickel for each block he stacked. Each member of the family was asked to estimate privately how high the boy should build his tower. No money would be given for blocks stacked higher than the estimate nor would the subject receive anything if the stack tumbled before he reached the estimate. Conservative estimates, hence, provided security but little opportunity for gain; high estimates involved more opporunity for gain but greater risk. The private estimates were then revealed to all and the family was asked to reach a group decision. In addition to securing objective measures of parental aspiration-evaluation levels, the observers scored the interaction between subjects, thus obtaining data as to the kind and amount of instructions the parents gave their son, the amount of help the son asked for or rejected, and the amount and kind of affect generated during the experiment.

2. *Anagrams.* In this task the boys were asked to make words of three letters or more out of six prescribed letters: G, H, K, N, O, R. The letters, which could be reused after each word was made, were printed on wooden blocks so that they could be manipulated. The parents were given three additional lettered blocks, T, U, and B, and a list of words that could be built with each new letter. They were informed that they could give the boy a new letter (in the sequence T, U, B) whenever they wished and could say anything to him, short of telling him what word to build. There was a 10-minute time limit for this experiment. Since this is a familiar game, no efforts were made to explain the functions of the task.

3. *Patterns.* In this experiment the parents were shown eight patterns, graduated in difficulty, that could be made with Kohs blocks. The subjects were informed that pattern 1 was easier to make than pattern 2, pattern 3 was more difficult than 2, but easier than 4, and so forth. The subjects were told that this was a test of the boy's ability to remember and reproduce patterns quickly and accurately. Each parent and boy was asked to select privately three patterns which the boy would be asked to make from memory after having seen the pattern for 5 seconds. All three patterns were chosen *before* the boy began the problem solving so that his performance in this task would not affect the choice of the patterns. Where there were differences of choice, as inevitably there were, the subjects were asked to discuss their differences and make a group decision. Insofar as possible the observers took a verbatim account of the decision-making process, scoring for three kinds of variables: (a) the number of acts each subject contributed to the decision-making process, (b) the number of times each individual initiated a decision,

and (c) the number of times each subject was successful in having the group accept his decision or in seeing to it that a decision was made.

4. *Ring Toss.* In this experiment each member of the group was asked to choose privately ten positions, from each of which the boy was to throw three rings at a peg. The distance from the peg was delineated by a tape with 1-foot graduations laid on the floor. The subjects were told that this was a test of discrimination and judgment and that after each set of three tosses they would be asked to make a judgment as to the best distance from which to make the next set of tosses. Group decisions were made as to where the boy should stand.

5. *Hatrack.* The Maier Hatrack Problem was used in this experiment. The boy was given two sticks and a C-clamp and instructed to build a rack strong enough to hold a coat and hat. His parents were told that this was a test of the boy's ability to build things. In this task no one was given the solution at the beginning of the experiment. For the first time the parents had no advantage over the boy—a most uncomfortable position for many parents, particularly the fathers. This stress situation was created deliberately to maximize the possibility of the problem generating effect, as was often the case, with some hostility being directed at the observers. After seven minutes the parents were given the solution to the problem.

Category System

References have been made to the use of a category system for scoring interaction between subjects. A brief description of this system, shown in Diagram 1, is in order. Most of the subjects' verbal and some of their motor behavior (e.g., laughing, hand-clapping, scowling) was scored in one of twelve categories. In eight of these categories were placed acts involving relatively strong affect. Four additional categories were used to distinguish between various kinds of statements—either giving, requesting, or rejecting directions—which contained very little affect. A distinction was made between negative and positive affective acts. Affective acts associated with explicit or implicit evaluations of the boy's performance which aimed at motivating or changing his behavior were scored differently from affective acts which involved reactions to the boy and only indirectly to his performance.

Directional acts by the parents were remarks designed to help the boy perform his task. A distinction was made between *specific* directions (S) which were acts instructing the subject to do particular things which would facilitate task completion, and nonspecific (N) which were acts aimed at giving the subject some information but not specific enough to enable him to rely entirely upon it. It was believed that nonspecific statements were more likely than specific statements to create self-reliance in the child.

The affective acts were schematized in two sets—one positive, the other negative. The first set was comprised of acts involving direct expressions of emotions toward another person, not necessarily in the context of task performance, either of a positive character (+X), such as expressions of love or approval, or of a negative character (−X), such as indications of hostility and rejection. Another set was of acts involving release of tension, either associated with positive affect (+T) such as grins, laughter, jokes, or negative affect (−T) such as scowls, coughs, or irritated gestures. Tension-release acts differ from acts of direct emotion (X) in that the former were not focused toward any person but were diffused, undirected reactions to the general situation. The next set of acts involved parental evaluation of the boy's performance. Those acts in which the parents stated that the boy was doing the task well were scored as positive evaluations (+E). The last two categories involved acts aimed at urging or pushing the boy to perform more effectively. These "pushing up the performance level acts" were scored in one of two categories. Those acts in which the parents "cheered" the boy on while at the same time indicating that they expected him to do better were scored as positive pushing acts (+P); negative pushing acts (−P) were statements in which the parents sought to improve the boy's performance by indicating in a threatening way that they thought he could do better.

Only four kinds of acts were scored for the boy: whether he asked for aid (aa), rejected aid (ra), showed positive tension (+T) or negative tension (−T). An act was defined as the smallest segment of verbal or motor behavior which could be recognized as belonging to one of the twelve categories in the system. The actor rather than the target of the acts was used as the observer's frame of reference.

EXPERIMENTAL FINDINGS

Achievement Training and Achievement Motivation

Measures of achievement training were obtained from the estimates and choices made by the parents in three tasks: Block Stacking, Patterns, and Ring Toss. Each task provided measures of achievement training which, though positively related to one another, were sufficiently independent to require their being treated as separate scores. This situation

+X	Expresses approval, gives love, comfort, affection.
+T	Shows positive tension release, jokes, laughs.
+E	Gives explicit positive evaluation of performance, indicates job well done.
+P	Attempts to push up performance through expression of enthusiasm, urges, cheers on.
N	Gives nonspecific directions, gives hints, clues, general suggestions.
S	Gives specific directions, gives detailed information about how to do a task.
aa	Asks for aid, information, or advice.
ra	Rejects aid, information, or advice.
—P	Attempts to push up performance through expressions of displeasure; urges on, indicating disappointment at speed and level of performance.
—E	Gives explicit negative evaluation of performance, indicates a job poorly done.
—T	Shows negative tension release, shows irritation, coughs.
—X	Expresses hostility, denigrates, makes sarcastic remarks.

DIAGRAM 1.   The system of categories used in scoring parent-child interaction.

was a result of intended fundamental differences between the tasks. Thus, in one task (Block Stacking) the parents were asked how well their son would do, in a second situation (Patterns) they were asked to choose a task for him to perform, while on the last problem (Ring Toss) they were given an open-end situation which they could structure in a number of ways.

Parental Aspirations and Evaluations

The parents' estimates of how well their son would do in the Block Stacking task are considered measures of their aspirations for and evaluations of him. In this case the estimates were made against a stated norm. The parents' first estimate, unaffected by any previous performance in this task, is conceived to be primarily a measure of parental aspirations for the boy. Undoubtedly, this estimate is somewhat affected by the parents' evaluation of the boy's competence, for aspiration and evaluation levels are often intricately mixed. Nonetheless, since presumably the parents had never seen their son perform a block-stacking test with one hand while blindfolded, we believe the element of aspiration level to be dominant in this measure.

We began by comparing the fathers of boys with high n Achievement with the fathers of boys with low n Achievement, and the mothers of high n Achievement boys with low n Achievement. It had been predicted that the parents of the boys with high n Achievement scores would give higher estimates than parents of boys with low scores. And in fact the data are in the predicted direction; the fathers and mothers of boys with high n Achievement scores on the average give higher estimates, but the differences are not statistically significant. However, when father's and mother's scores are summed together the differences between parental group is significant ($F = 4.09, p < .05$).

Parental estimates for the second and third trials of this task were combined to form a single score. Since the means and standard deviations of both estimates were about the same, no transformation into standard scores was necessary. Both estimates had been influenced considerably by the boy's performance. The combined score was considered as a measure of the parents' aspiration-evaluation of the boy as affected by his performance against a given standard of excellence. The data show that the mothers of boys with high n Achievement scores give considerably higher estimates for the second and third trials of this task than do the mothers of boys with low scores ($F = 10.28, p < .005$). The differences between the fathers, although in the predicted direction in that the fathers of boys with high n Achievement scores tend to give higher estimates, are not statistically significant.

The Patterns task was designed to provide additional and supplemental measures of parental aspiration-evaluation levels. In this situation the parents were not asked to estimate how well their son would do, but actually to select three tasks, graded in difficulty, for their son to perform. Since all three choices were made before their son began the problem, these scores could be considered as performance-free measures of the parents' evaluation of the boy's capacity to do the task, plus their aspiration for him to do the more difficult task in a situation structured by degree of difficulty with no stated norm or group average.

Each subject's three choices were combined simply by addition (no transformation of scores was necessary) to provide a single score for each person. We had expected that the parents of boys with high achievement motivation scores—in keeping with their tendency to have higher aspirations for and evaluations of their boys—would choose the more difficult patterns for their sons. The data indicate a difference in this direction, but the differences are small and not significant for either fathers or mothers.

Parental Standards of Excellence

In the two experiments just described some parents would very likely have imposed standards of excellence upon the tasks even if the experimenters had not done so. However, since they had been asked to make their estimates or choices in situations where standards were explicit (as in the Block Stacking task where a group performance norm had been given, or in the Patterns task where the complexity of the patterns had been clearly graded by the experimenters) it could not be clearly seen from these experiments whether parents differed in their tendencies to impose standards upon the problems their children were expected to solve. The Ring Toss experiment was devised for this purpose. In this experiment no norm or group standard of excellence was set by the investigators. Each parent was asked to make ten choices of "the best place for your son to stand." After each choice the boy threw three rings at the peg. A measure of the height of the standard of excellence each parent sets for the boy was derived by summing the choices (number of feet the boy is asked to stand from the peg) of each parent.

We hypothesized that parents who imposed standards of excellence upon this normless task would be most likely to structure tasks generally in these terms. Our expectation was that the parents of boys with high motivation scores would be more likely to impose standards of excellence upon this task in that they would place their sons farther from the peg than would parents of boys with low scores. The data tend to support this expectation: the fathers and mothers of high n Achievement boys, on the average, chose positions further from the peg than the parents of children with low achievement motivation. The differences, however, are significant only in the case of the mothers ($F = 5.47$, $p < .25$). Combining the scores for fathers and mothers increases the differences between parental groups ($F = 6.99$, $p < .01$).

The Anagrams experiment involved another task for which the investigators had set no explicit standard of excellence, the parents and boy merely being provided with lettered blocks out of which words could be made. This experiment had been designed primarily to provide measures of independence training. The sum of the times at which new letters (the parents shared three letters) were given by both (or either) parents was treated originally as a measure of self-reliance training, i.e., the longer the parents delayed in giving the boy new letters the more indication that they expected him to work longer and harder at a problem on his own. This experiment revealed a clear difference between parental groups but not in the direction we predicted: the parents of high n Achievement boys gave new letters *sooner* than the parents of boys with low n Achievement ($F = 6.28$, $p < .025$).

This finding, so different from what had been expected, prompted a reevaluation of the task and a further (albeit ex post facto) interpretation of the data. We believe, now, that we were mistaken in assuming that this task would only measure self-reliance training. Rather, our observations indicate that this experiment elicited from some parents a type of achievement training in which the element of competition with a standard of excellence was very strong. The parents (especially the mothers) of boys with strong achievement motivation, it appeared, tended to perceive the task not so much as one which their son should do on his own, *but as a challenge to do well.* They reacted to this experiment with more emotion and competitiveness than displayed toward any other problem. The mother, in particular, was eager for her son to do well and often became anxious when he stopped making words. Both parents typically showed keener pleasure and disappointment at the boy's success or failure than was ordinarily displayed by the parents of boys with weak achievement motivation. The boy with strong motivation tended to receive letters sooner, we believe, because his parents were eager to see him make more words and because of their reluctance to frustrate him to a point where his motive to excel in this important area would be destroyed.

In choosing to structure this task in terms of achievement training rather than self-reliance training—a decision congruent with our theoretical position that the former is the more important in the development of achievement motivation, the parents of high n Achievement boys are nonetheless exhibiting less self-reliance training than the parents of low n Achievement boys. This is contrary to our theoretical expectations, but is similar, as we shall see below, to other empirical data which indicate that the mothers of high n Achievement boys score low on self-reliance training—and typically the mother played her most prominent role in the Anagrams experiment.

Achievement Training and Performance Levels

The behavior of people with high achievement motivation is characterized by persistent striving and general competitiveness. It would follow from this, other things being equal, that boys with high achievement motivation would perform better than those with low motivation—and in fact this proved to be the case. Boys with high n Achievement tend to build higher towers of blocks, construct patterns faster, and make more words in the Anagrams task. The differences are significant in the case of the Block Stacking task ($F = 8.16$, $p < .005$), but not for the Patterns and Anagrams experiments. In the latter two tasks the individual's performance is very greatly affected by his intelligence. Since IQ score was one of the variables controlled in this study (there were no differences between the mean IQ scores of boys with high n Achievement and their peers with low achievement motivation), even these small differences are surprising. The superior performance of high n Achievement boys appears to be more a function of greater self-reliance and zest in competitive activity than of intelligence. Thus, boys with high achievement motivation tend to ask for less aid (aa), are more likely to reject offers of help from their parents (ra), and appear to get more pleasure out of participating in the experiments—they show less evidence of negative affect ($-T$) and more of positive feelings ($+T$). Although for only one of these variables—asks aid ($F = 5.76$, $p < .05$)—is there a significant difference between groups, the direction of the differences in all four cases consistently points to greater self-reliance and self-assurance on the part of boys with high need for achievement.

The question arises, then, whether the higher estimates of the parents of boys with high n Achievement are not a natural response to his superior performance, rather than a measure of their aspirations for and evaluations of him. In two tasks, Block Stacking and Anagrams, where there were significant differences between parental groups, the analysis of covariance technique was used to control the effect of the boy's performance upon parental estimates. This technique enabled us to compute what the parents' estimates of the boy's performance, or their willingness to give him a new letter, would be if the performance of high and low n Achievement boys were made comparable. An analysis of covariance of the mother's estimates for the second and third trials in the Block Stacking tasks—there had been no significant difference between fathers—provided an adjusted F ratio for the mother's estimates which, although reduced, is still statistically significant ($F = 6.17, p < .05$).

In order to see whether the speed with which the parents give their sons new letters in the Anagrams task is merely a function of the rate at which the boy builds words—it will be remembered that high n Achievement boys made more words during the ten-minute time limit for this task than boys with low achievement motivation—an analysis of covariance was computed with the number of words controlled. The adjusted F ratio not only remained significant but increased very slightly from 6.28 to 6.45, both ratios being significant at the .05 level.

In the Ring Toss experiment there was no question of whether superior performance by high n Achievement boys had influenced their
parents to make significantly higher choices, because in this task high n
Achievement boys were less successful in placing rings around the peg
than their low n Achievement peers. The reason for this is simple: the
parents of high n Achievement boys tended to place their sons farther
away from the peg and consequently the number of their successes were
smaller; the tetrachoric correlation between the number of successes and
the distance away from the peg is —.31.

These data clearly indicate that the parents were not responding
merely to the boy's performance, but this is not to say his ability had no
influence on their estimates and choices. In the Block Stacking experiment, for example, the parents' aspirations and evaluations tend to go
up as the boy's performance improves. This is particularly true for the
mothers of high n Achievement boys, who are more affected by the boy's
performance than the fathers. Thus, for the first trial of the Block Stacking task the F ratio for fathers of high n Achievement boys is larger than
the mothers', but for the second and third trials the mothers' F ratio jumps
from 1.24 to 10.12, while the fathers' F increases only slightly, from 2.78
to 3.45. This is particularly interesting in view of the fact that fathers
were more active in this task than mothers, who seemed to feel that this
was the sort of task about which males were more informed. Nonetheless,
even though the mothers of high n Achievement boys did not generally
perceive this task as falling under their area of parental training, they
responded quite strongly to their son's performance in their aspirations
and evaluations. From a longer developmental point of view, of course,
these data do not permit us to state with certainty as to which came first,
the higher aspiration-evaluation levels of the parents, or the boy's superior performance; the data strongly suggest that they very probably
interact.

INDEPENDENCE TRAINING, SANCTIONS, AND
ACHIEVEMENT MOTIVATION

Earlier we distinguished between achievement training and independence training; the latter was broken down into two components:
self-reliance training and the granting of relative autonomy in decision
making. Associated with *both* independence and achievement training
are sanctions—rewards and punishments—administered by the parents to
reinforce appropriate behavior in the child. The data to index these

variables were obtained by examining the interaction between parents and child as they engaged in the experimental tasks, and by observing the decision-making process in those instances where the subjects were asked to make a group estimate or choice of what the boy should do.

Sanctions

Typically, positive and negative reinforcements are associated with any learning situation—rewards for success and punishment for failure. We had predicted that the parents of boys with high achievement motivation would score higher on Warmth (positive affect) and lower on Rejection (negative affect) than the parents of low n Achievement boys. The data show that the mothers of high n Achievement boys score significantly higher on Warmth than the mothers of low n Achievement boys ($F = 8.87$, $p < .01$). The differences between fathers, although in the predicted direction, are not significant ($F = 4.13$, $p < 1.0$).

Parental Profiles and Motivation

In the analysis of data so far the relationship of each variable to achievement motivation was examined separately. The Split Plot type of analysis of variance was next employed to permit the examination of all variables simultaneously for each parent. All scores were transformed into standard scores, and in the case of four variables (S, Pushing, Rejection, and Autonomy) where low parental scores for parents had been hypothesized as producing high n Achievement the direction of the scores was reversed. Hence, we have labeled these as "Fewer Specific Statements," "Less Pushing," "Less Rejection"; a high score for Autonomy means that the parents have given their son a relatively high amount of autonomy. This was done in order to make it possible to sum across all variables and arrive at a meaningful figure for each parent. A mean score for each variable for fathers and mothers was computed and the distance from the mean in standard deviations was plotted; the profiles for fathers are shown in Chart 1, for mothers in Chart 2.

A Split Plot analysis of variance reveals that there are significant differences *in levels* between the profiles of the parents of boys with high achievement motivation and the parents of boys with low n Achievement. The difference in levels for fathers is greater ($F = 10.09$, $p < .005$) than for mothers ($F = 4.77$, $p < .05$). By difference in level we mean that when the scores for each variable are summed for each parent, the parents of high n Achievement boys have a significantly higher *total* score than the parents of low n Achievement boys. Thus, although some variables are not significant when tested separately, and others only barely

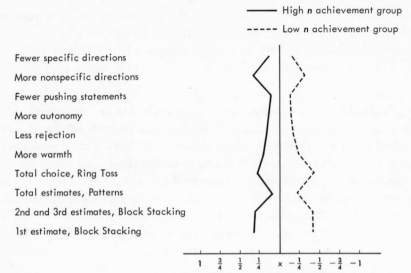

Fewer specific directions

More nonspecific directions

Fewer pushing statements

More autonomy

Less rejection

More warmth

Total choice, Ring Toss

Total estimates, Patterns

2nd and 3rd estimates, Block Stacking

1st estimate, Block Stacking

$1 \quad \frac{3}{4} \quad \frac{1}{2} \quad \frac{1}{4} \quad x \quad -\frac{1}{4} \quad -\frac{1}{2} \quad -\frac{3}{4} \quad -1$

Mean differences in standard deviations

CHART 1. Profiles for fathers: High *n* Achievement group and low *n* Achievement group.

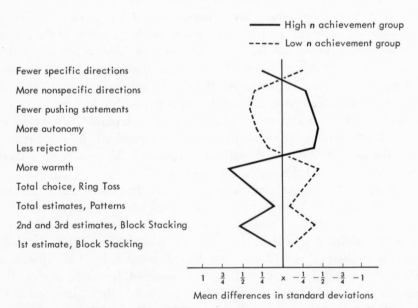

Fewer specific directions

More nonspecific directions

Fewer pushing statements

More autonomy

Less rejection

More warmth

Total choice, Ring Toss

Total estimates, Patterns

2nd and 3rd estimates, Block Stacking

1st estimate, Block Stacking

$1 \quad \frac{3}{4} \quad \frac{1}{2} \quad \frac{1}{4} \quad x \quad -\frac{1}{4} \quad -\frac{1}{2} \quad -\frac{3}{4} \quad -1$

Mean differences in standard deviations

CHART 2. Profiles for mothers: High *n* Achievement group and low *n* Achievement group.

significant, when the scores of all the variables are pooled together each contributes something to the total variance and the result is a significant difference between groups. This is most apparent in Chart 1 where the fathers profiles are compared. It can be seen that the mean scores for the fathers of boys with high achievement motivation are higher for every variable, where "highness" was predicted as being positively related to high n Achievement. It should be remembered that the scores for S, P, Rejection, and Autonomy were reversed so that what appears as a "high" score in the chart is in fact, a low score. In the case of these four variables, low parental scores were predicted as tending to produce high n Achievement. The difference between the two groups of fathers is not great, it is the *consistency* of the direction of these differences which when summed together make for a significant difference between the two groups. Another way of saying this is to point out that since the profiles of the two groups are almost parallel, there is no significant interaction between n Achievement groups and test variables when the level differences are taken out of the profiles.

The profiles for mothers are not parallel so that, even when level differences are taken out, the profiles for the mothers of high n Achievement boys remains significantly different from that of the mothers of low n Achievement boys ($F = 2.30$, $p < .025$). The fact that there are interaction differences for mothers is not surprising when we remember that some of the variables which discriminate between groups for fathers do not do so for mothers, while other variables which are not significant for fathers are highly significant for mothers (e.g., Warmth). There are even some reversals in that mothers of high n Achievement boys give fewer nonspecific directions, more pushing statements, and are more dominant than the mothers of low n Achievement boys.

Another way of examining the differences between the parents of high and low n Achievement boys is shown in Chart 3. On this chart there is a profile for fathers and a profile for mothers. Each profile is obtained by computing the mean differences between the scores of the fathers, and then of the mothers, of high and low n Achievement boys. For example, for the first estimate Block Stacking the average standard score of the fathers of low n Achievement boys is subtracted from the average standard score of the fathers of boys with high achievement motivation. The difference is positive, that is, on the average, the father of a high n Achievement boy had a higher score than the average father of a boy with low n Achievement. If the difference had been negative the point would have been plotted below the zero line, indicating that the average father

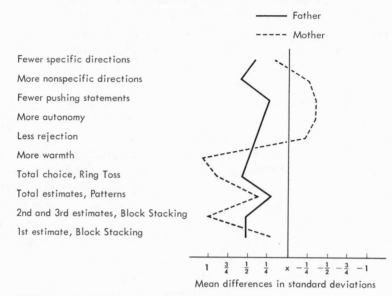

CHART 3.   Profiles for fathers and mothers: Mean difference between fathers of "highs" and fathers of "lows"; mothers of "highs" and mothers of "lows."

of a low *n* Achievement boy had made the higher estimate. If there had been no difference, the point would have been on the zero line; the farther the point is plotted away from the zero line, the greater the difference between groups. Thus, for mothers with respect to the variable Warmth, the difference between *n* Achievement groups is more than plus ¾ indicating that the average score for the mothers of high *n* Achievement boys is more than three quarters of a standard deviation higher than that of the mothers of low *n* Achievement boys.

Chart 3 shows that the fathers of high *n* Achievement boys when compared with the fathers of low *n* Achievement boys tend to give higher estimates and choices for the Block Stacking and Patterns tasks, place their sons farther away from the peg in the Ring Toss experiment, are more warm, less rejecting, give their boy more autonomy, are less pushing, and give more nonspecific directions and fewer specific ones. The two groups of mothers when compared with one another present a somewhat different picture. The mothers of high *n* Achievement boys also tend to give higher estimates and choices for the Block Stacking and Patterns tasks, place their sons farther away from the peg in the Ring Toss experiment, give fewer specific directions, and are more warm. However, they are more rejecting, give the boy less autonomy, are more pushing, and give fewer nonspecific directions.

Parental Role Relationships and Achievement Motivation

The relationships of achievement motivation to certain training practices employed by *fathers and mothers considered separately* have now been described. But we know that the boy is subject to the influence of both parents, and that he belongs to a family unit in which the expectations and role behavior of both parents may have important consequences for his motivation. We know also that the parental pairs in this study did not always have the same expectations of the boy or the same reactions to his performance. The question then arises: Is there a difference between the parents of high and low *n* Achievement boys *when the parents are considered as a family pair?* Specifically, are the scores of the parents of high *n* Achievement boys more likely to be similar or dissimilar to one another than are the scores of the parents of boys with low achievement motivation? And what are the consequences of these similarities or dissimilarities for the development of achievement motivation?

The correlation technique made it possible to determine the relationship between the scores of fathers and mothers *considered as pairs*. Two sets of Pearsonian coefficients of correlation were computed for each variable; one set for the fathers and mothers of boys with high motivation, the other for the parents of the low motivation group. These correlations are taken as measures of the role relationships between parental pairs. A positive correlation is considered as indicating a *similar* role relationship; i.e., the parental scores tend to be high or low together. A negative correlation is considered as indicating a *dissimilar* role relationship, with parental scores moving in opposite directions. It must be stressed that these correlations tell us nothing about how high or low the scores are, merely that they are similar or dissimilar. To discover if there were any significant differences between the parents of high and low *n* Achievement boys the correlation coefficients were transformed into Z scores and the Standard Error of Difference was then computed. The ratio of the difference between Z's and the Standard Error of Difference was then computed and tested for significance and Table 1 presents the correlations for each measure.

For the tasks performed in this study the optimal learning situation would be one in which the parental aspirations and choices are in agreement or, in terms of the correlation analysis of parental pairs, one in which the parents play similar roles. The data show that for several achievement training measures (estimates and choices in Block Stacking and Patterns) the parents of high *n* Achievement boys tend to play more similar roles than do the parents of low *n* Achievement boys. That is, six of the seven correlations are positive and five are higher for the parents of

TABLE 1. *Correlation Analysis of Pairs of Parents
of High* n *Achievement Boys Compared with Pairs of Parents of
Low* n *Achievement Boys*

	F X M (Highs)	F X M (Lows)	p
Achievement training			
1st estimate, Block Stacking	.50	.36	.308
2nd estimate, Block Stacking	.57	.31	.171
3rd estimate, Block Stacking	.36	.35	.480
1st choice, Patterns	.36	−.09	.087
2nd choice, Patterns	.37	−.27	.026
3rd choice, Patterns	−.01	.06	.496
Ring Toss	.83	.86	.500
Independence training			
Self-reliance training:			
number of specific directions	.28	.31	.460
number of nonspecific directions	.01	.33	.159
number of pushing statements	−.02	.12	.348
Autonomy:			
number of times "initiator"	−.248	−.728	.026
number of times "decider"	−.258	−.276	.480
number of acts in decision process	.086	−.149	.245
Sanctions			
number of warmth responses	−.39	.23	.030
number of rejection responses	.23	.70	.032

the "highs" than for the parents of the "lows." The extremely high correlations for Total Choices, Ring Toss, is a result of the fact that each parent was asked to make a series of successive choices with both parents basing each choice on the previous position of the boy. There is one significant difference between the correlations for the parents of high and low n Achievement groups: the second choice in the Patterns task. This is interesting when we remember that the patterns chosen by the parents of the "highs" were not significantly more difficult than those chosen by the parents of the "lows." There is, however, greater agreement between the parents of high n Achievement boys as to how difficult the task should be, and in general this is more likely to be the case among parents of high than of low n Achievement boys.

The situation is reversed for the measures of self-reliance training, i.e., S, N, and P type statements. For these variables, the parents of low n Achievement boys tend to have the more similar roles. Thus, for all three variables the correlations are positive and are higher between parents of the "lows," although the differences between the two groups are not statistically significant. This finding lends additional credence to our hypothesis that self-reliance training, when not associated with high achievement training, is not a sufficient cause of n Achievement. The consistency with which both parents of low n Achievement boys put their sons on their own is especially significant in the light of the greater dissimilarity in their willingness to let the boy assert himself in the decision-making process. The correlations between fathers and mothers of low n Achievement boys for the three measures of autonomy are all negative and higher than the correlations for the parents of the "highs." For one measure, "number of times initiator," the difference between high or low groups is statistically significant at the .026 level. This greater dissimilarity in parental roles indicates a tendency for one person to dominate the decision-making process and suggests a greater loss of autonomy for low n Achievement boys. Where both parents try to affect the decision-making process the boy has some freedom of movement, and can, in the terminology of Simmel, even play the role of the "third who enjoys," but where one parent lays down the law, the boy has fewer alternatives. It should be noted that in two of the measures of autonomy, the parents of high n Achievement boys also play somewhat dissimilar roles, and that for the measure "number of times decider," there is virtually no difference between "high" and "low" groups, which is probably a function of this aspect of the decision-making process where only one person wins.

The affect given out by the parents is considered to be the basic factor determining the child's affective arousal to standards of excellence. We believe that the child's sensitivity to parental affect is increased when he is faced with a situation where there is a difference between parents in the amount and kind of affect they display, or where a single parent is both warm and rejecting. Positive affect (Warmth), in particular, becomes more valued as it is both given and withheld; thus a parent who is both warm and rejecting will have more effect on the child than one who is uniformly warm. Hence, both dissimilarity between parents, or dissimilar affect from one parent, will result in a greater value placed upon warmth by the child. This notion is supported by the finding of Sears, Maccoby, Levin, et al. (12) who note that the child who has "high conscience" has a mother who is relatively warm and uses withdrawal of love fairly often; neither warmth nor withdrawal of love when used alone is effective in producing "high conscience."

This finding has particular relevance for the data on positive sanctions shown in Table 1 where it can be seen that the parents of the "highs" play far more dissimilar roles than the parents of the "lows"; the correlation between the fathers and parents of high n Achievement boys for Warmth is —.39, as compared with .23 for the parents of low n Achievement boys. This difference between groups is significant at the .03 level. It should be remembered that both parents of the "highs" were above average for Warmth, although this difference was not significant for fathers, and that the mothers of high n Achievement boys were more warm and rejecting than the mothers of the "lows." We believe that this dissimilarity between parents and variations in the affect given out by the mother sensitizes the high n Achievement boy to the need for approval and increases his willingness to internalize the standards and expectations of his parents.

The role relationships of parents with respect to Rejection is unlike that found for Warmth. Correlations for this variable are positive for both groups, but the correlation is higher for the parents of the "lows" (.70) than for the parents of the "highs" (.23): the difference is significant at the .032 level. These data indicate that when the low n Achievement boy experiences rejection he is far more likely to receive it from both parents than is the high n Achievement boy. Negative affect, then, when not associated with compensating warmth from one or both of the parents, seems not likely to generate high need achievement.

Social Class and Child-Training Practices

The research design made it improbable that the class differences in training practices would be great, for the sample was selected in such a way as to make both classes equal with respect to the dependent variable. That is, the n Achievement scores of lower-class boys were on the average equal to the scores of middle-class boys—a situation known not to be true for the more general universe of middle- and lower-class boys. Hence, if the independent variables examined in this study are necessary and sufficient causes of n Achievement, and the measures of these variables valid, there should be no significant difference in the training practices of the middle- and lower-class parents *in this sample*. Significant class differences would be found only if these variables were non-causally related to n Achievement but associated with social class—a conclusion which had not been apparent when the original hypotheses were formulated.

The data reveal class differences, but with one exception they are not significant; nor is it always the middle-class group whose scores are in the direction hypothesized as generating high n Achievement.

It would appear then, that when IQ and achievement motivation levels are controlled, social class membership is not a significant variable in determining performance, at least for the tasks included in this study. The one clear difference between middle- and lower-class parents for a measure of achievement training is Total Choices, Ring Toss. In this case it is the lower-class parent who tends to place the boy farthest away from the peg ($F = 6.99$, $p < .01$), quite in variance with what we had anticipated, and for which no satisfactory explanation can be offered.

With respect to the independence training variables (S, N, P, and autonomy), it is the direction rather than the statistical significance of the differences which warrant their being reported. Middle-class mothers give somewhat more independence training than lower-class mothers: they have higher scores for nonspecific directions, make fewer pushing remarks, and give their sons somewhat more autonomy; however, they also give more specific directions. The direction of all these scores is exactly the reverse of what was found to be characteristic of the mothers of high n Achievement boys. The profile for fathers is almost point for point different. In this case it is the lower-class father who gives fewer specific statements, more nonspecific statements, is less pushing, and gives the boy more autonomy. All these data are exactly contrary to what we had expected. It is important to note, however, that none of these differences is statistically significant at the 1-in-10 level.

In the case of our two measures of sanctions, Warmth and Rejection, we found, as was expected, that the middle-class father and mother are warmer and less rejecting than lower-class parents. The greatest difference is among fathers ($F = 4.13$, $p < .06$).

These data, though sometimes in the direction predicted, indicate that the training practices of middle-class parents are not on the whole markedly different from those of lower-class parents. However, it may be that by controlling n Achievement we, in effect, cancelled out for this sample any differences in training practices which might normally differentiate the social classes.

DISCUSSION AND SUMMARY

The question of how achievement training, independence training, and sanctions are related to achievement motivation may be rephrased by asking, How does the behavior of parents of boys with high *n* Achievement differ from the behavior of parents whose sons have low *n* Achievement?

To begin with, the observers' subjective impressions are that the parents of high *n* Achievement boys tend to be more competitive, show more involvement, and seem to take more pleasure in the problem-solving experiments. They appear to be more interested and concerned with their son's performance; they tend to give him more things to manipulate rather than fewer; on the average they put out more affective acts. More objective data show that the parents of a boy with high *n* Achievement tend to have higher aspirations for him to do well at any given task, and they seem to have a higher regard for his competence at problem solving. They set up standards of excellence for the boy even when none is given, or if a standard is given will expect him to do "better than average." As he progresses they tend to react to his performance with warmth and approval, or, in the case of the mothers especially, with disapproval if he performs poorly.

Fathers and mothers both provide achievement training and independence training, but the fathers seem to contribute much more to the latter than do the mothers. Fathers tend to let their sons develop self-reliance by giving hints (N) rather than always telling "how to do it" (S). They are less likely to push (P) and more likely to give the boy a greater degree of autonomy in making his own decisions. Fathers of high *n* Achievement boys often appear to be competent men who are willing to take a back seat while their sons are performing. They tend to beckon from ahead rather than push from behind.

The mothers of boys with high achievement motivation tend to stress achievement training rather than independence training. In fact, they are likely to be more dominant and to expect less self-reliance than the mothers of boys with low *n* Achievement. But their aspirations for their sons are higher and their concern over success greater. Thus, they expect the boys to build higher towers and place them farther away from the peg in the Ring Toss experiment. As a boy works his mother tends to become emotionally involved. Not only is she more likely to reward him with approval (Warmth) but also to punish him with hostility (Rejection). *In a way, it is this factor of involvement that most clearly sets the mothers of high* n *Achievement boys apart from the mothers of low* n *Achievement boys:* the former score higher on every variable, except specific direction. And although these mothers are likely to give them less option about doing something and doing it well, observers report that the mothers of high n Achievement boys tend to be striving, competent persons. Apparently they expect their sons to be the same.

REFERENCES

1. Bales, R. F. *Interaction process analysis*. Cambridge, Mass.: Addison-Wesley, 1951.
2. Child, I. L., Storm, T., & Veroff, J. Achievement themes in folk tales related to socialization practice. In J. W. Atkinson (Ed.), *Motives in fantasy, action and society*. Princeton, N.J.: Van Nostrand, 1958.
3. Erickson, M. C. Social status and child-rearing practices. In T. Newcomb and E. Hartley (Eds.), *Readings in social psychology*, New York: Holt, 1947.
4. Havighurst, R. J., & Davis, A. Social class differences in child-rearing. *Amer. sociol. Rev.*, 1955, **20**, 438–442.
5. Hollingshead, A., & Redlich, F. Social stratification and psychiatric disorders. *Amer. sociol. Rev.*, 1953, **18**, 163–169.
6. McClelland, D. C., & Friedman, G. A. A cross-cultural study of the relationship between child-training practices and achievement motivation, appearing in folk tales. In G. E. Swanson, Newcomb, T. M., & Hartley, E. L. (Eds.), *Readings in social psychology*, New York: Holt, 1952.
7. McClelland, D. C., Atkinson, J. W., Clark, R., & Lowell, E. *The achievement motive*. New York: Appleton-Century-Crofts, 1953.
8. McClelland, D. C., Rindlisbacher, A., & deCharms, R. Religious and other sources of parental attitudes toward independence training. In D. C. McClelland (Ed.), Studies in motivation. New York: Appleton-Century-Crofts, 1955.
9. Rosen, B. C. The achievement syndrome: a psychocultural dimension of social stratification. *Amer. sociol. Rev.*, 1956, **21**, 203–211.
10. Rosen, B. C. Race, ethnicity, and the achievement syndrome. *Amer. sociol. Rev.*, 1959, **24**, 47–60.
11. Sakoda, J. M. Directions for a multiple-group method of factor analysis. Mimeographed paper, University of Connecticut, June, 1955.
12. Sears, R. R., Maccoby, Eleanor E., & Levin, H. *Patterns of child rearing*. Evanston, Ill.: Row, Peterson, 1957.
13. Strodtbeck, F. L. Family interaction, values, and achievement. In D. C. McClelland, A. L. Baldwin, U. Bronfenbrenner, & F. L. Strodtbeck (Eds.), *Talent and society*. Princeton, N.J.: Van Nostrand, 1958.
14. Tryon, R. C. *Cluster analysis*. Ann Arbor, Mich.: Edwards Brothers, 1939.
15. Winterbottom, M. R. The relation of need for achievement to learning experiences in independence and mastery. In J. W. Atkinson. *Motives in fantasy, action, and society*. Princeton, N.J.: Van Nostrand, 1958.

PARENTS' ATTITUDES AND BEHAVIORS AND GRADE SCHOOL CHILDREN'S ACADEMIC ACHIEVEMENTS[1]

Vaughn J. Crandall, Rachel Dewey,
Walter Katkovsky, and Ann Preston

THE FELS RESEARCH INSTITUTE FOR THE STUDY OF HUMAN
DEVELOPMENT

SINCE THE TIME of Binet's pioneering attempts to predict children's academic achievements from their performance on intelligence tests, psychologists and educators have been concerned with factors producing individual differences in young children's scholastic attainments. Early research addressed to this question was primarily devoted to the role which general intellectual abilities played in academic performances. More recently, educational and child development researchers have concerned themselves with factors other than ability which might also contribute to performance differences. Personality variables such as achievement motivation and anxiety have been brought into the picture. The achievement need has been the center of recent concerted research efforts by a number of investigators, e.g., McClelland and his colleagues (7; Atkinson, 1). So, too, has anxiety been used as a predictor variable for intellectual and academic performances, e.g., McCandless and Castaneda (6), and Sarason, Davidson, Lighthall, Waite and Ruebush (8).

Research on determinants of achievement performances has indicated that both ability and motivational variables are useful and necessary predictors. Another broad and basic question still remains: what are the *antecedents* of differences in children's intellectual achievement motivations and performances? In other words, what environmental factors in

[1] This study was a part of the project, "Parents as identification models and reinforcers of children's achievement development," partially supported by USPH Grant M-2238 awarded the first-listed author.

Reprinted from the *Journal of Genetic Psychology*, in press, by permission of the authors and publisher.

children's everyday experiences facilitate or impede the development of intellectual and academic competence? Many persons and situations influence a child's personality development. Parents, teachers, siblings, and peers all interact with a child in the course of his daily experiences, and each of these individuals can be an important social reinforcer of the child's behaviors. This is true whether the area of personality under consideration is the development of aggressive, dependent, affiliative, or achievement behaviors.

Concerning the development of achievement motivations and behaviors, it is apparent to the careful observer that most children have developed, by the time they enter grade school, fairly consistent differences in the values they attach to intellectual and academic achievements, in their expectations of success in these activities, in the standards they use to judge their efforts, and in the methods and strategies they employ in their attempts to attain achievement goals. What factors produce these differences? This is the general question to which this research is directed. The present article describes one study of a larger research project concerned with parents as identification models and reinforcers of young children's achievement behaviors.[1] The investigation explored relationships between parents' attitudes and behaviors and their early-grade-school-age children's academic performances.

METHODS

The sample. The sample was comprised of 120 Ss; 40 early-grade-school-age children, and their fathers and mothers. The child sample contained 20 boys and 20 girls equally distributed in the second, third, and fourth grades at the time they were administered academic achievement tests. The socioeconomic status of the families was assessed by Hollingshead's Two-Factor Index of Social Position (5). The proportions of families in Hollingshead's social classifications I through V were 10, 30, 29, 31 and 0 respectively, indicating that all but the lowest social classification was reasonably represented. Slightly more than one-half of the fathers and one-fourth of the mothers were college graduates. Table 1 presents information regarding the intellectual levels and academic achievement test performances of the children. The children's intellectual abilities were assessed with the Stanford-Binet Intelligence Test; their academic performances, with the California Achievement Test.[2] As indi-

[2] The second author of this report administered the academic achievement tests. Appreciation is expressed to Dr. Virginia Nelson who gave the Stanford-Binet Intelligence Tests to the children.

TABLE 1. *Intelligence and Academic Achievement Test Performances of the Children*

		Number of Children
A.	Stanford-Binet IQ	
	Below 100	2
	100–114	9
	115–129	13
	130–144	14
	145 and over	2
B.	Reading age *vs.* chronological age	
	RA less than CA	2
	RA 1–9 months beyond CA	7
	RA 10–19 months beyond CA	19
	RA 20–29 months beyond CA	5
	RA 30–39 months beyond CA	4
	RA 40–49 months beyond CA	2
C.	Arithmetic age *vs.* chronological age	
	AA less than CA	5
	AA 1–9 months beyond CA	12
	AA 10–19 months beyond CA	13
	AA 20–29 months beyond CA	7
	AA 30–39 months beyond CA	3

cated in Table 1, the children of the study were intellectually superior to national norms; all but two had IQs above one hundred, and approximately three-fourths of the children obtained scores more than one standard deviation above the national average. The mean IQ of the group was 124. Intellectual abilities within the sample, however, varied appreciably. The children's IQs ranged from 79 to 164 with a SD of 16. As might be expected from their intelligence test scores, the children's performances on the standard academic achievement tests were generally above grade level. Only two of the children were reading below grade level, and only five were not performing at or above their grade level in arithmetic.

Assessment of parent attitudes and behaviors. The parents were interviewed individually at Fels Research Institute for the Study of Human Development. To prevent communication between parents, each set of parents was interviewed concurrently but separately.[3] The interview sessions averaged from 2½ to 3 hours and were electronically re-

[3] The fathers were interviewed by the third-listed author; the mothers, by the fourth author.

corded for subsequent interview analyses. Two interviews were given each parent during the interview session. The first was concerned with the parent's attitudes and reported behavior toward his child's everyday achievement efforts. This interview covered four achievement areas, only one of which—the intellectual achievement area—is relevant to the present study. The second interview covered several general (nonspecific to achievement) behaviors of the parents. These included parental affection, rejection, and nurturance.[4] Copies of the parent interview schedules and rating scales may be found elsewhere (4).

Interview I obtained information regarding the following parental attitudinal and behavioral variables: (a) *The parent's attainment value for his child's intellectual performances.* This referred to the degree of importance or value the parent attached to his child's intellectual achievements. This rating assessed the intensity of the parent's desire that his child show interest and participate in intellectual activities, and the value the parent placed on his child's effort, persistence, and competence in these situations. (b) *The parent's evaluation of his child's intellectual competence.* This variable was concerned with the level of competence the parent felt his child characteristically demonstrated in intellectual activities. (c) *The parent's satisfaction-dissatisfaction with his child's intellectual achievement performances.* Ratings of this variable focused on the amount of satisfaction versus dissatisfaction the parent expressed regarding his child's intellectual achievement performances. This rating was exclusively concerned with relevant parental feelings as these were expressed to the interviewer; the parent's reported overt reactions (praise, criticism, etc.) to his child's efforts were *not* a part of the rating. (d) *The parent's minimal standards for his child's intellectual achievement performances.* Here the "personal yardstick" the parent used to judge his child's intellectual performances was considered. The major judgment for this rating entailed the determination of the minimal level of intellectual competence below which the child's performance produced parental dissatisfaction and above which the parent felt more satisfied than dissatisfied with his child's efforts. (e) *Parental instigation of intellectual activities.* This, and the remaining variables of Interview I, was concerned with reported parental behaviors rather than parental attitudes. Parental instigation referred to the frequency and intensity of the parent's attempts to increase his child's participation and competence in intellectual activities. The parent's reactions to his child's efforts *after* he had per-

---

[4] A fourth general parental behavior variable, dominance, was also assessed in Interview II for a study other than the present one, and is not discussed in this report.

formed were not included here. To be a relevant behavioral referent for this variable, the parent's behavior must have preceded some activity on the part of his child. Examples of instigation included such events as the parent arranging for his child to receive special lessons or experiences in some intellectual pursuit, the parent making a special effort to convey to his child the importance of intellectual experiences, and the parent encouraging and/or demanding that his child participate in intellectual achievement activities. (f) *The parent's participation with his child in intellectual achievement activities.* This variable pertained to the extent that the parent actively engaged in intellectual achievement pursuits with his child. Both the frequency of parental participation and the amount of personal involvement while so engaged constituted rating referents for this variable. (g) *Positive parental reactions.* Here the frequency and intensity of the parent's positive reactions to his child's intellectual achievement behaviors were assessed. These included the degree that the parent responded favorably to his child's interest and participation in intellectual achievement activities, as well as the parent's positive reactions to the effort and the competence his child exhibited in these pursuits. Positive parental reactions might take the form of direct verbal approval or other less direct symbols of approbation such as granting special privileges or giving rewards (e.g., money, gifts, etc.) for intellectual achievements. (h) *Negative parental reactions.* This variable was concerned with the frequency and intensity of disapproval and criticism which the parent expressed to his child for any lack of interest, participation, effort, and/or competence in intellectual achievement activities.

Interview II. This interview sampled the parents' reported behaviors with their children which were nonspecific to the children's intellectual achievement performances, but were aspects of parent-child interaction which might possibly influence (either directly or indirectly) children's intellectual achievement efforts. The variables rated were: (a) *Parental affection.* This variable pertained to the amount of overt affection and acceptance which the parent reported expressing toward his child. (b) *Parental rejection.* Here the raters focused on the degree that the parent directly expressed dissatisfaction with, was critical of, or punitive about, his child's general personality attributes or characteristic behaviors. (c) *Parental nurturance.* The behavioral referents for this rating were those relevant to the frequency and quality of emotional support and instrumental help given the child by the parent.

Rating procedures and methods of data analysis. The criterion rater for Parent Interview I rated all interviews of the eighty parents from typescripts of the interviews. Reliability raters rated forty randomly picked father and mother interviews. All identifying information (e.g., parent, child, and sibling names, etc.) was removed before the interview protocols were rated. Interview II was rated after the raters listened to the interview recordings.[5] It was felt that while the data in Interview I was concerned with specific parental attitudes and behaviors which could be assessed from typescripts, Interview II data included important parental feelings and expressions which were less likely to be accurately represented in typed protocols. For example, in Interview II two factors (or mothers) might say that their children were "little hellions" in certain situations, yet one parent might mean (and convey) that he thoroughly disapproved of this behavior, while a second parent might make the same statement but indicate (through his intonation) that he actually approved of these behaviors on the part of his child.

The children's academic achievement test scores used in the study were achievement ratio scores; the reading achievement score for each child was his reading age divided by his chronological age, and his arithmetic score was obtained by dividing his arithmetic age by his chronological age.

Statistical analyses employed in the study were exclusively nonparametric tests. The rank difference correlation was used for all measures of association, and Wilcoxin's Unpaired Replicates Test was employed for all assessments of differences (Siegel, 9).

RESULTS AND DISCUSSION

Inter-rater reliabilities. The inter-rater reliability coefficients for Parent Interview I are presented in Table 2. The magnitude of rater concordance for these variables, with one noticeable exception (the mothers' reported negative reactions), ranged from moderately-acceptable to highly-acceptable agreement. Inter-rater reliabilities of the mother interviews of Parent Interview II were, for the variables of affection, rejection, and nurturance respectively, .87, .61, and .68. Correlations of inter-rater agreement for the same variables in the father interviews were .76, .85, and .78.

[5] The criterion rater for Parent Interview I was the senior author. The reliability raters for this interview were the third author for the mother interviews, and the fourth author for the father interviews. The criterion rater of Parent Interview II was Virginia Crandall. The reliability ratings, made from 40 randomly selected mother and father interviews, were the third author and the fourth author respectively.

TABLE 2. *Inter-rater Reliabilities for Parent Interview I (Parent Attitudes and Reported Behaviors Toward the Children's Intellectual Achievement Efforts)*

Parent Variable	Reported Mothers	Reported Fathers
Attainment value	.50	.80
Evaluation of competence	.78	.94
Satisfaction-dissatisfaction	.85	.96
Achievement standards	.63	.57
Instigation	.63	.76
Participation	.70	.84
Positive reactions	.86	.80
Negative reactions	.22	.79

The child variables. Relations between the children's IQs and their scholastic achievement test performances were assessed. Intelligence test scores correlated .57 and .59 with reading and arithmetic achievement test scores respectively for the girls, and .66 and .50 for the boys. These correlations are similar in magnitude to associations found in most previous studies of children's intelligence and their performances on standard academic achievement tests. These data indicate, as have the results of previous investigations, that general intelligence is one major factor in children's academic achievements. However, the fact that less than one third of the variance was held in common by these sets of variables (i.e., intelligence and achievement test performance) suggests that other factors may also be influential. Parents' attitudes and behaviors influencing children's intellectual achievement motivations and behaviors may account for some of this variance.

Relations between general parental behaviors and the children's academic achievement test performances. Associations between general parental behaviors (i.e., affection, rejection, and nurturance) and the children's reading and arithmetic test performances were evaluated separately by sex of parent and sex of child. Of the 24 correlations run, only 3 were significant beyond the .05 level of confidence according to Old's Tables (Siegel, 9). This is only slightly better than might be anticipated by chance. That the significant correlations obtained were probably not chance occurrences, however, is suggested by the fact that all significant associations pertained *only* to the mothers and their daughters. Girls who were competent readers had both less affectionate and less nurturant mothers than did the girls who demonstrated less proficiency in that academic area; correlations between the girls' reading achievement test scores and their mothers' affection and nurturance were —.38 and —.43 respectively. In addition, girls who performed better on the arithmetic achievement test had mothers who were also relatively low on nurturance; the Rho obtained was —.45.

Why should low maternal nurturance and affection seem to foster academic competence in the girls? Several possibilities are likely. First, the affectionate and nurturant mothers, by rewarding their daughters' affection-seeking and dependent behaviors may have "taught" these girls to expect such overtures to be more effective means of attaining personal security than behaviors requiring independent initiative and achievement striving. In contrast, girls who did not receive as much maternal affection and support, might have turned to other potential sources of satisfaction and security such as achievement per se. Second, previous research has demonstrated that maternal nurturance fosters children's dependence and impedes the development of independence and achievement behaviors (Crandall, Preston & Rabson, 2; Winterbottom, 10). Restrictions of learning experiences in independence and achievement in the more highly-nurtured girls of the present study may have produced (a) fewer possibilities for developing independent problem-solving techniques to handle achievement situations and (b) less confidence (and more anxiety) regarding abilities to do so. One final explanation for the negative relations obtained between maternal nurturance and affection and the girls' academic achievements pertains to young girls' attempted identification with, and emulation of, their mothers. All parents act as learning models for, as well as direct reinforcers of, their children's behaviors. The mother who readily proffers love and help to her child may derive personal satisfaction from such maternal behaviors, and may serve as a model to her daughter to this effect. On the other hand, the mother who withholds affection or rejects her child's help-seeking and emotional support-seeking may be less involved with the maternal role and be more achievement-oriented. Consequently, her daughter is, to the degree she uses her mother as an identification model, more likely to emulate her mother's achievement behaviors, values, and motivations, and to attempt to become competent in academic achievement situations.

Relations between the parents' specific attitudes and behaviors toward their children's intellectual achievement efforts and the children's performances on standard achievement tests. Data relevant to this portion of the study are summarized in Tables 3 and 4. The first four parent variables listed in these tables are attitudinal variables; the last four

TABLE 3.   *Parents' Attitudes and Actions and Children's
Reading Achievement*[a]

Parent Variable	Mothers Reported		Fathers Reported	
	Girls	Boys	Girls	Boys
Attainment value	—.14	.35	—.38	.03
Evaluations	.44	.48	.28	.21
Satisfaction-dissatisfaction	.51	.48	.38	.23
Standards	.48	.18	.15	.26
Instigation	—.52	.18	—.43	—.07
Participation	—.10	.06	—.28	—.25
Positive reactions	—.11	.09	.42	—.17
Negative reactions	—.27	—.18	—.45	.06

[a] Italicized correlations are significant at or beyond the .05 level of confidence (one-tailed test).

TABLE 4.   *Parents' Attitudes and Actions and Children's
Arithmetic Achievement*[a]

Parent Variable	Mothers Reported		Fathers Reported	
	Girls	Boys	Girls	Boys
Attainment value	.17	.23	—.26	—.05
Evaluations	.23	.35	.20	.04
Satisfaction-dissatisfaction	.76	.28	.19	.07
Standards	.50	.00	—.12	.34
Instigation	—.42	.05	—.38	—.31
Participation	.13	.05	—.09	—.55
Positive reactions	.14	.01	.41	—.19
Negative reactions	—.33	—.24	—.44	—.14

[a] Italicized correlations are significant at or beyond the .05 level of confidence (one-tailed test).

are behavioral variables. Each will be discussed in turn. The *attainment
values* the parents placed on their children's intellectual competence
were essentially unrelated to their children's academic achievement test
performances. In fact, the only significant correlation of the eight pertaining to this variable was an unanticipated negative one; fathers who
expressed strong desires that their daughters be intellectually competent
had daughters who performed less adequately on the reading achievement test than did daughters of fathers who were less concerned with
their daughters' intellectual activities and abilities.

The mothers' *evaluations* of their children's general intellectual
competence were associated with their children's academic performances,

but the evaluations of the fathers were not. Both the boys' and girls' reading test performances were positively and significantly related to their mothers' assessments of their general intellectual competence. The children's arithmetic test performances were positively correlated with the mothers' evaluations, though falling just short of statistical significance. In contrast, none of the fathers' evaluations of their children was related to these children's scholastic achievement test-taking behaviors. This finding, that the mothers' evaluations of their children's general intellectual performances were similar to their children's academic performances while the fathers' evaluations were not, may have been due to the fact that mothers are usually home to receive the after-school reports from their children regarding their academic successes and failures, while most fathers are not. In addition, it is a common observation that mothers far outnumber fathers in school situations where concrete information is provided regarding their children's academic performances, (e.g., PTA meetings and parent-teacher conferences). Finally, it may be that fathers more frequently based their judgments of their children's general intellectual competence on their intellectual performances observed in the home (e.g., efforts on puzzles, quiz games, etc.) than did the mothers.

Consistent with the findings on evaluations was the fact that the mothers' *satisfactions and dissatisfactions* with their children's general intellectual achievement efforts were also more often positively associated with the children's achievement test performances than were those of the fathers; three of the four significant correlations obtained pertained to the mothers' expressed satisfaction with the adequacy of their children's intellectual achievement performances.

Parental *standards* for the children's general intellectual performances were unrelated to the children's demonstrated competence on the academic achievement tests with two exceptions. Both of these pertained to the standards the mothers held for their daughters. Mothers who set high standards for their daughters' intellectual achievement efforts, in contrast with mothers whose standards were less demanding, had daughters who were more proficient on both the reading and arithmetic achievement tests. These correlations, as well as a number of those found in the tables which follow, illustrate an inevitable problem inherent in most parent-child research. When significant correlations are obtained between parent and child behaviors, when might it be legitimate to assume the former caused the latter and when might the opposite be true? The positive association of the mothers' achievement standards for their daughters and these girls' academic test performances may have been a function of the following: (a) high maternal achievement standards induced the girls to strive for, and become proficient in, the academic areas under consideration, while low maternal standards produced the opposite effect; or (b) the mothers adjusted their intellectual achievement standards for their daughters according to the girls' demonstrated academic proficiencies; or (c) the correlations obtained may be a function of both (a) and (b).

The remaining correlations listed in Tables 3 and 4 focus on reported parental behaviors rather than parental attitudes. The degree of the parents' *instigation* of their children toward intellectual achievement pursuits was predictive of the children's achievement test performances only for the girls. Girls who performed especially well on the tests had mothers and fathers who were less prone to encourage and push them toward intellectual acitivities than did parents of the less academically proficient girls. Regarding the parents' *participation* with the children in intellectual activities, these parental behaviors bore little relation to the competence the children demonstrated on the academic achievement tests. In only one instance, i.e., the fathers' participation and their sons' performances on the arithmetic achievement test, was the correlation significant; fathers of boys were especially competent in this area spent less time with their sons in intellectual activities than did the fathers of the less competent boys. There was, thus, no evidence in the present study that the amount of parental participation with children in intellectual activities per se had any positive impact on the children's academic achievements. The negative correlations obtained between parental instigation and participation and the children's achievement test performances suggest, though cannot prove, that these parental behaviors might be reactions to the children's efforts rather than antecedent and causal factors in these perfomances. It is possible, for example, that many parents of grade-school-age children—when their child's academic efforts are competent ones—feel little need to encourage such endeavors or spend additional time with them in these pursuits. Conversely, parents of a child who performs relatively poorly in academic situations may become concerned wih his ineptitude, and increase their instigational efforts and participation with him in intellectual achievement activities.

The two final antecedent variables of this study pertained to *parental reactions* to the children's intellectual achievement behaviors as these predicted the children's academic achievement test performances. These variables, historically, have been the major focus of attention of researchers concerned with parent behaviors as determinants of children's personality development. In the current investigation, an attempt was made to assess the reactions of the parents to their children's intellectual achievement efforts and to relate these reactions to the levels of performance which the children evidenced on standard academic achievement tests. The only finding indicating an influence of these parental behaviors on the children's performance—if a causal relationship is assumed—was a cross-sex one; both positive and negative reactions of the fathers to their daughters' intellectual efforts predicted their daughters' academic proficiency. The mothers' reactions, in contrast, were essentially unrelated to their daughter's performances, while neither the fathers' nor the mothers' reported praise or criticism was predictive of their sons' achievement test scores. In short, the only evidence that the parents' direct rewards and punishments may have influenced their children's academic performances occurred exclusively between fathers and their daughters. Girls who performed especially well on the reading achievement test had fathers who more often praised and rewarded, and less often criticized and punished, their general intellectual achievement behaviors. A similar relation obtained for the girls' arithmetic performances.

When the total pattern of significant correlations found in the current study is evaluated, the most striking finding is that the parents' attitudes and behaviors (both general and specific) were associated with their daughters' performances on the scholastic achievement tests much more frequently than with those of their sons. Of the twenty-one significant correlations obtained between the Parent Interview I and II data and the children's demonstrated academic competence, only three pertained to the boys. Why should these differences obtain? One possibility for this finding is that grade-school-age boys may differ from girls in their susceptibility to adult influence. Two unpublished sets of data by the authors of this report support this idea. First, ratings of free-play behavior of another sample of children in the same age-range as the current child sample revealed that the amount of the children's achievement efforts and the amount of their approval-seeking from adults were positively and significantly related for the girls (Rho $= .46$), but unrelated (Rho $= .03$) for the boys. In other words, the girls' achievement strivings were directly related to their apparent desire for approval from adults, while the boys' achievement behaviors were more autonomously determined. It appeared that the boys had less need to use adults' reactions to define the competence of their efforts than did the girls, possibly because the boys may have developed more internalized achievement standards. Additional evidence suggesting that young boys' achievement performances may be less contingent on the reactions of others than are those of girls' was obtained on the sample of Ss employed in the current study. As a part of a different (as yet unpublished) investigation, the children were administered a specially constructed Children's Intellectual Achievement Responsibility Questionnaire. This questionnaire was designed to measure the extent a child attributes his intellectual achievement successes and failures to his own instrumental behaviors rather than as a product of the behaviors and reactions of other persons. The boys' belief in self-responsibility correlated positively with their performances on the academic achievement tests used in the current study, while these variables were not significantly related for the girls. The specific correlations between the boys' belief in self-responsibility and their reading and arithmetic achievement test performances were .49 and .36 respectively. For the girls, these correlations were —.16 and —.23. In summary, to the degree that boys' achievement striving has been found to be unrelated to their approval-seeking from adults, and, to the degree that their academic proficiencies were associated with their belief in self-responsibility, their achievement behaviors appeared to be more independent and autonomous of adult reactions than those of the girls. Because of this, parental attitudes and behaviors may have less impact on, and therefore be less predictive of, the academic performances of boys of this age than of girls. The findings of the current study are congruent with this possibility. It should be strongly emphasized, however, that this reasoning rests on several assumptions, as well as limited research data, and must await more definitive tests in future investigations.

SUMMARY

This study investigated relations between parents' attitudes and behaviors toward their children's general intellectual achievement efforts, and their children's performances on standard academic achievement tests. The sample was comprised of 40 early-grade-school-age children and their fathers and mothers. The children were administered standard intelligence and scholastic achievement tests. The parents were individually interviewed regarding their general parental behaviors (affection, rejection, nurturance) as well as their specific attitudes and reactions to their children's everyday intellectual achievement efforts.

The following results were obtained: (a) Correlations between the children's IQ scores and their performances on the scholastic achievement tests were of the same general magnitude found in most past research on children's intelligence and academic performances. (b) General parental behaviors which significantly predicted the children's academic test performances pertained solely to mothers and their daughters; mothers of academically competent girls were less affectionate and less nurturant toward their daughters than were the mothers of the girls who were less proficient. (c) Certain specific attitudes and behaviors of the parents toward their children's intellectual achievement behaviors were predictive of the children's academic test performances; others were not. First, neither the mothers' nor fathers' expressed values for the children's intellectual experiences were positively associated with the children's observed performances. Second, both the mothers' evaluations of, and satisfaction with their children's general intellectual competence were positively related to these children's actual academic performances while those of the fathers were not. Third, parental instigation and participation, when correlations were significant, were negatively associated with the children's academic performances. Fourth, the positive and negative reactions of the parents to the children's intellectual achievement efforts were predictive of the children's academic achievement test performances for father-daughter combinations only; the more proficient girls had fathers who more often praised and less often criticized their everyday intellectual achievement attempts than did the less academically competent girls. (d) Many more significant relations obtained between the parents' attitudes and behaviors and their daughters' academic proficiency than occurred between these parental attitudes and behaviors and the boys' performances.

REFERENCES

1. Atkinson, J. (Ed.) *Motives in fantasy, action and society.* New York: Van Nostrand, 1958.
2. Crandall, V., Preston, Anne, Rabson, Alice. Maternal reactions and the development of independence and achievement behavior in young children. *Child Develpm.*, 1960, 31, 243–251.
3. Crandall, V., Katkovsky, W., & Preston, Anne. Motivational and ability determinants of children's intellectual achievement behaviors. *Child Develpm.*, in press.
4. Crandall, V., Katkovsky, W., & Preston, Anne. Parent behavior and children's achievement development. *Genet. psychol. Monogr.*, in press.
5. Hollingshead, A., & Redlich, F. Social stratification and psychiatric disorders. *Amer. soc. Rev.*, 1953, 18, 163–169.

6. McCandless, B., & Castaneda, A. Anxiety in children, school achievement and intelligence. *Child Develpm.*, 1956, **27**, 379–382.

7. McClelland, D., Atkinson, J., Clark, R., & Lowell, E. *The achievement motive.* New York: Appleton-Century-Crofts, 1953.

8. Sarason, S., Davidson, K., Lighthall, F., Waite, R., & Ruebush, B. *Anxiety in elementary school children.* New York: Wiley, 1960.

9. Siegel, S. *Nonparametric statistics for the behavioral sciences.* New York: McGraw-Hill, 1956.

10. Winterbottom, Marion. The relation of need for achievement in learning experiences in independence and mastery. In J. W. Atkinson (Ed.), *Motives in fantasy, action and society.* New York: Van Nostrand, 1958. Pp. 453–478.

SECTION VI ADOLESCENCE

In most societies, adolescence is viewed as a period of special difficulty in adjustment—a "critical period" in the individual's development. This is true of the more technologically advanced societies, such as our own, as well as a substantial number of nonliterate ones.

This should not appear too surprising if we stop to consider the special stresses to which the adolescent is typically subjected, in comparison to children at many other age levels. Problems of adjustment are minimized during periods when a fairly well-stabilized individual is confronted with environmental demands with which he is for the most part familiar, and for which he has already developed appropriate and need-satisfying responses. Neither condition characterizes adolescence in our culture.

In the first place, the onset of puberty brings with it a host of physiological changes, including increases in sex hormone and changes in body structure and function, which not only present special adjustment problems in themselves, but which also challenge the individual's basic sense of self, or what Erikson has called his "ego identity." As he says, "in puberty and adolescence,

415

all sameness and continuities relied on earlier are questioned again because of a rapidity of body growth which equals that of early childhood and because of the entirely new addition of physical genital maturity."

At the same time that the adolescent in our culture is confronted with the uncertainties brought on by rapid physical and physiological changes, and the flood of unfamiliar subjective feelings which accompany them, he is also confronted with a whole set of societal demands from which he has heretofore been protected. In the few short years between puberty and nominal adulthood, he is suddenly expected to prepare himself for a job; for changed political and social status as a citizen; for marriage; for relatively complete separation from his parents and the setting up of an independent household; and for a mature philosophy of life.

Small wonder, then, that adolescence constitutes a "critical period." Small wonder, too, that a significant number of adolescents, unable to achieve a satisfying resolution of the various conflicting forces to which they are subjected, are forced into inadequate, and ultimately self-defeating, compromises in their search for a psychological modus vivendi—some into neurosis or even psychosis, others into delinquency and other forms of asocial or antisocial behavior. The really remarkable fact is that so many of today's adolescents survive their parents' and society's most extreme fears, and grow into reasonably happy, effective, and responsible adults—no worse, and quite possibly better fitted for life, than their parents.

The three articles included in this section illustrate the principle issues discussed above. In the first, Paul Mussen and Mary Cover Jones make clear, not only that the very fact of rapid physical change creates problems for adolescents generally, but that deviations from the average timetables for these changes pose special problems for the young people involved, often with profound psychological consequences. In their study of early and late maturing boys, they found that boys who mature late are likely to feel anxious and inadequate, and to have stronger needs for social acceptance than early maturing boys, while at the same time having a greater fear of rejection by others. The fact that adolescents of both sexes are intensely aware of idealized group norms in appearance, ability, and interests, and are seriously affected by deviations from them, should not seem too surprising when we realize the special importance that identification with a peer group assumes at a time when the individual is still struggling with, and is not too sure of, his own identity.

In the second selection in this section, Erik Erikson, a gifted psychoanalyst and writer, with a background in social anthropology and comparative education, discusses the adolescent search for a *sense of identity*—for an answer to the fundamental question, "Who am I?" which he calls the "central problem of the period." As he points out, unless the adolescent, despite the host of other demands placed upon him, can find a reasonably workable resolution of this issue, he is left adrift on the sea of his own fate, subject at best to the whims of an "other-directed" culture, as David Riesman has called it, and at worst, to complete psychological defeat.

One possible outcome of a failure to achieve a meaningful sense of personal identity is juvenile delinquency. Delinquency is by no means a new problem, but there seems little doubt that it is an increasingly serious social concern in our ever more complex, fragmented society. And just as a *sense of identity* has its earliest roots in what Erikson calls the "basic trust" of infancy, so too does adolescent delinquency often find its antecedents in the early years of childhood. In the final selection of this section, John Conger, Wilbur Miller, and Charles Walsmith show that the personality characteristics of future delinquents differ from those of nondelinquents even in the early school years, and even after the possible effects of such factors as socioeconomic status, sex, intelligence, residence area, school background, and ethnic group membership have been controlled through a matching technique. Perhaps most importantly, they demonstrate that it is relatively meaningless to speak of overall personality differences between delinquents and nondelinquents, without first taking into account the social class background and intelligence of the individuals studied.

SELF-CONCEPTIONS, MOTIVATIONS, AND INTERPERSONAL ATTITUDES OF LATE- AND EARLY-MATURING BOYS

Paul Henry Mussen and Mary Cover Jones
UNIVERSITY OF CALIFORNIA, BERKELEY

WHILE INTENSIVE CASE STUDIES show that personal and social adjustment during adolescence may be profoundly influenced by rate of physical maturation, there is a scarcity of systematic data on the relationship between the adolescent's physical status and his underlying motivations, self-conceptions, and interpersonal attitudes. There is, however, a small body of evidence which demonstrates that greater physical maturity is associated with greater maturity of interest among girls (10) and that early-maturing boys differ from their late-maturing peers in both overt behavior and reputational status. In one study (8) in which a staff of trained observers assessed a large group of adolescents on a number of personality variables, boys who were consistently retarded in physical development were rated lower than those who were consistently accelerated in physical attractiveness, grooming, and matter-of-factness; and higher in sociability, social initiative (often of a childish, attention-getting sort), and eagerness. Reputation Test (11) data indicated that classmates regarded the late-maturing boys as more attention-getting, more restless, more bossy, less grown-up and less good-looking than those who were physically accelerated.

On the basis of these findings, it may be inferred that adult and peer attitudes toward the adolescent, as well as their treatment and acceptance of him, are related to his physical status. This means that the socio-

Reprinted from *Child Development* (1957), **28**, 243–256, by permission of the authors and the Society for Research in Child Development.

psychological environment to which late-maturers are subjected—and consequently the social learning situations they encounter—may be significantly different from that of their early-maturing peers. As a consequence, according to the ratings summarized above, they acquire different patterns of overt social behavior. It seems reasonable to hypothesize that groups differing in physical status will also differ in more covert aspects of behavior and personality.

Indirect evidence relevant to this hypothesis comes from an investigation of the long-term consequences of physical acceleration or retardation during adolescence. Jones (6) found that group differences in physique had practically disappeared by the time her early- and late-maturing subjects reached their early thirties. Nevertheless, young adults who had been physically retarded adolescents differed from those who had been accelerated in several important psychological characteristics. In general, it appeared that the adult subjects could be described much as they had been during adolescence. Thus, those who had been early-maturers scored higher on the good impression, socialization, dominance, self-control (low score on impulsivity), and responsibility scales of the California Psychological Inventory, while those who had been slow in maturing scored higher on the flexibility scale. On the Edwards Personal Preference Schedule, early-maturers scored significantly higher on the dominance scale, while the late-maturing were high in succorance. Jones concludes that the early-maturing "present a consistently favorable personality picture with regard to . . . important social variables" (6). Moreover, there was some evidence that these men had attained more stable vocational adjustments than those who had been late in maturing. These group differences in later adjustment suggest that the sociopsychological atmosphere in which the adolescent lives may have profound immediate and enduring effects on his personality structure as well as on his overt behavior.

The present study was designed to investigate the relationship between maturational status and certain important covert aspects of personality during late adolescence. Personality structure was assessed by means of the Thematic Apperception Test (TAT) which seems to be the most appropriate and sensitive instrument for this purpose. More specifically, on the basis of the literature reviewed above and other general works on the psychology of adolescence (1, 4, 5), we formulated and tested a series of propositions relating to differences between the physically retarded and accelerated in self-conceptions, underlying motivations, and basic interpersonal attitudes. These variables were translated into TAT categories—needs (n), Press (p), and descriptions (defined briefly in

Table 1)—and the scores of early- and late-maturers in each of these categories were compared. The propositions and the rationale underlying
them, together with the TAT variables involved, follow.

1. In view of their obvious physical retardation, relatively unfavorable
    reputations and disadvantageous competitive position in many ac-
    tivities, the late-maturing boys are more likely to have feelings of in-
    adequacy. Hence, more boys in this group than in the early-maturing
    group are likely to have negative self-conceptions (TAT category:
    negative characteristics).

2. The adolescent in our culture generally desires some independence
    and adult status. This may be the source of a major problem for the
    late-maturer, however, since he is often regarded and treated as a
    small boy by adults and peers and is not likely to be granted inde-
    pendence as early as physically accelerated boys. Therefore, it may
    be anticipated that more late- than early-maturers regard adults, par-
    ticularly their parents, as dominating, forcing them to do things they
    don't want to or preventing them from doing things they want to do
    (high scores in *p Dominance*). Moreover, the parental treatment these
    boys experience and parental refusal to grant them independent status
    may be interpreted as personal rejection. Hence we predicted that
    more late-maturing boys would score high in *p Rejection*.

3. These feelings of being dominated and rejected may result in attitudes
    of rebellion against the family and in feelings of hostility. We there-
    fore expected that more of the late-maturing group would reveal
    strong aggressive needs (high scores in *n Aggression*) and desires to
    escape from (*n Autonomy*—leaving parents), or to defy, the family
    (*n Autonomy*—defying parents).

4. On the basis of the data indicating that slow-maturers showed a great
    deal of social interest (although often of an immature kind), we hy-
    pothesized that more members of this, than of the early-maturing
    group would reveal strong interests in friendly, intimate interpersonal
    relationships (high scores in *n Affiliation*).

5. Assuming that, as Jones and Bayley (8) suggest, the social initiative
    and attention-getting devices of the late-maturers are of a compen-
    satory nature, we would expect this group to be basically dependent
    and to have strong needs for support from others. These should be
    manifest by higher scores in TAT *n Succorance* and *p Nurturance*.
    The latter may be considered a more indirect measure of dependence,
    a kind of wish-fulfilling view of the world as helpful and friendly.

6. The early-maturer, being regarded and treated as more adult, is more

likely to become self-confident, and to acquire high status goals. For these reasons, we predicted that more of the physically accelerated would give evidence of high achievement goals (high scores in *n Achievement*) and concern with personal recognition (high scores in *n Recognition*).

7. Late-maturing boys in our culture probably face more problems of personal adjustment than do their early-maturing peers. As a result of this, they may become more aware of their problems, and, as the high degree of flexibility of young adults who had been retarded in maturing suggests, more insightful. Hence we predicted that they would be more willing and able than early-maturers to face their own feelings and emotions (low score in the TAT variable *denial of feeling*).

In summary, we attempted to test seven propositions related to difference in the personalities of early- and late-maturing boys. It was hypothesized that more late-maturers would score high in variables relating to negative self-conceptions, dependence, aggression, affiliation, rebelliousness, and feelings of being dominated and rejected. More early-maturers, on the other hand, were expected to reveal strong achievement and recognition needs, feelings of personal success, and tendencies toward denial of feelings.

PROCEDURE

The thirty-three 17-year-old male subjects of this investigation were members of the Adolescent Growth Study which included a normal sample of boys in an urban public school system (3). The subjects of the present investigation represented two contrasting groups, selected on the basis of their physical maturity status: 16 of them had been among the most consistently accelerated throughout the adolescent period; the other 17 had been among the most consistently retarded.[1] All of them took the Thematic Apperception Test, which provides the basic data of this study, at age 17.

The TAT consisted of 18 pictures: nine from the Murray set which is now standard (cards 1, 5, 6, 7BM, 10, 11, 14, 15, 17); five pictures from the set generally used in 1938 when these data were collected (a man and

[1] The present sample includes 27 of Jones and Bayley's (8) 32 subjects (the 16 most consistently retarded and 16 most consistently accelerated boys in the study). The other five boys had not taken the TAT at age 17. The six subjects who were in the present study but not in Jones and Bayley's study are the three "runners-up" from each end of the physical maturity distribution, i.e., the three who were closest to the 16 most accelerated cases and the three cases next to the 16 most retarded.

woman seated on a park bench; a bearded old man writing in an open book; a thin, sullen, young man standing behind a well-dressed older man; a tea table and two chairs; an abstract drawing of two bearded men); and four designed especially for this investigation (the nave of a large church; a madonna and child; a dramatic view of mountains; a boy gazing at a cross which is wreathed in clouds).

The tests were administered individually. Each card was projected on a screen while the subject told a story which was recorded verbatim. Standard instructions were given for the Murray cards, and subjects were asked to describe the feelings elicited by the other four pictures. Most of the stories were brief, consisting of only one or two sentences.

As we noted earlier, each of the personality variables involved in the seven propositions was translated into a TAT scoring category. The scoring scheme involved counting the relevant needs, press, and descriptions of the heroes of the stories, the assumption being that the storyteller has identified with the hero: the hero's needs are the same as the boy's; the press that impinge upon the hero are the ones that affect the boy telling the story. A total of 20 needs, press, and descriptive categories, each defined as specifically as possible, was developed in the analysis of the protocols. A score for each subject for each TAT category was derived by counting the number of stories in which it appeared. A list of the categories used, together with brief descriptions of them, is found in Table 1.

To test the reliability of this analysis, one of the authors (PM) and another psychologist[2] independently scored 15 complete protocols (300 stories). The percentage of interrater agreement was 90, computed by the usual formula (number of agreements divided by number of agreements plus number of disagreements).

In order to eliminate bias, the scoring used in the present study was done "blind," that is, independent of knowledge of the subject's maturational status.

RESULTS

Frequency distributions of the scores of all subjects were made for all the TAT variables. Each distribution was then dichotomized at the point which most nearly enable the placing of half of the 33 subjects above, and half of them below, the dividing point. Subjects having scores above this point were considered high in this particular variable; those with scores below this point were considered low in this variable. Chi-

[2] We are indebted to Dr. Virginia B. Ware for her participation in this aspect of the study.

TABLE 1. *Number of Early- and Late-Maturers Scoring High in TAT Variables*

TAT Variable	Definition of Variable	High Early-Maturers	High Late-Maturers	Chi-Square Value	P
Proposition 1					
Negative characteristics	H is described in negative terms (e.g., imbecile, weakling, fanatic)	5	13	6.80	<.01
Proposition 2		4	8	1.73	
p Dominance 1	H forced by parents to do something he doesn't want to do				.09
p Dominance 2	H prevented by parents from doing something he wants to do	6	8	.31	>.30
p Dominance 3	Total instances of H's being forced by parents to do something and/or prevented from doing something	7	11	1.46	.11
p Rejection	H rejected, scorned, or disapproved of by parents or authorities	5	11	3.69	.03
Proposition 3					
n Aggression 1	H is aggressive in physical, asocial way	8	3	3.88	.02
n Aggression 2	H is mad at someone, argues	7	4	1.52	.10
n Aggression 3	Total of all H's aggressive actions	11	8	1.26	.10
n Autonomy 1	H leaves home	7	10	.75	.20

square tests were used to test the seven propositions, i.e., to ascertain whether or not high scores in certain TAT variables were in fact more characteristic of one group (late- or early-maturers) than of the other.

Table 1 lists the TAT variables, the number of late- and early-maturers with high scores in the variable, the chi-square value obtained and the level of significance. It should be noted that the hypotheses tested were one-sided hypotheses, while the chi-square value is in terms of a two-sided hypothesis. When chi-square has only one degree of freedom, the square root of chi-square has a distribution which is the right hand half of a normal distribution. In order to test a one-sided hypothesis, the chi-

TABLE 1. *(Continued)*

TAT Variable	Definition of Variable	High Early-Maturers	High Late-Maturers	Chi-Square Value	P
n Autonomy 2	H disobeys or defies parents	7	11	1.46	.11
n Autonomy 3	Total of instances in which hero leaves and/or defies his parents	3	9	4.16	.02
Proposition 4					
n Affiliation 1	H establishes good relations with his parents	8	8	.00	>.50
n Affiliation 2	H falls in love, has a romance, marries	9	14	2.66	.05
n Affiliation 3	Total instances in which H establishes and/or maintains friendly relations	8	12	1.46	.11
Proposition 5					
n Succorance	H feels helpless, seeks aid or sympathy	7	12	2.43	.06
p Nurturance 1	H is helped, encouraged, or given something by parents	5	8	.93	.18
p Nurturance 2	H is helped, encouraged, or given something by someone else (not parents)	8	14	3.88	.02
Proposition 6					
n Achievement	H attempts to attain a high goal or to do something creditable	9	10	.02	>.50
n Recognition	H seeks fame and/or high prestige status	9	8	.28	>.30
Proposition 7					
Denial of feeling	S states that picture elicits no thoughts or feelings	9	5	2.43	.06

square test must be converted into the equivalent value in terms of a unit normal deviate (2). The levels of significance reported in Table 1 were evaluated in these terms.

Table 1 shows that, as had been predicted, more late-maturing than early-maturing boys revealed feelings of inadequacy and negative self-concepts, i.e., scored high in the TAT variable *negative characteristics*. Hence proposition 1 was confirmed. This finding is consistent with the frequently made clinical observation that retardation in physical maturation may be an important source of personal maladjustment and attitudes of inferiority.

Proposition 2 stated that more late-maturers regard their parents as highly dominating and rejecting. The evidence summarized in Table 1 substantially supported this proposition. While the difference was not statistically significant, more late- than early-maturers scored high in *p Dominance by parents* (total). There was a marked difference between the groups in the variable which involves parental domination by forcing the child to do something he does not want to do (*p Dominance by parents, forcing*). However, examination of the data with respect to the variable *p Dominance by parents (prevention)* makes it necessary to reject that part of the proposition which maintains that late-maturers are more likely to view their parents as highly restrictive of their activities.

That aspect of proposition 2 which deals with feelings of rejection was confirmed by our data. Compared with the early-maturing group a significantly greater proportion of the late-maturers told stories in which the hero was rejected by parents or authority figures. These feelings of rejection may stem from different sources. In some cases, the parents' behavior may make it clear that they are disappointed in their physically retarded son whom they regard as immature. The boy, perceiving this attitude, may interpret it as rejection. In other cases, parental reluctance to allow the late-maturing boy to establish his independence may lead to considerable tension in the family and the boy's feelings of rejection may simply reflect the ongoing parent-child conflict.

It is possible that earlier in their teens, soon after the physical changes of adolescence became apparent, many of the early-maturing boys also experienced conflicts with their parents, arising from difficulties in establishing their independence or in handling emerging heterosexual interests. At that time they too may have felt dominated or rejected. However, by the age of 17, when these data were collected, these boys were ordinarily treated as adults and granted more freedom. Hence, they were more likely to have resolved many of their conflicts with their parents and to feel accepted and independent.

The hypothesis (part of proposition 3) that more late-maturers would be highly aggressive was rejected on the basis of the evidence given in Table 1. In fact, the differences between the two groups on all the TAT aggression variables were in the opposite direction from the prediction. High scores in the variables relating to aggression of the most overt and violent type were significantly more frequent among the early-maturers, and more members of this group also scored high in measures of milder (verbal) aggression and of total aggression. While late-maturers may experience more problems of adjustment and greater frustrations than their early-maturing peers, they apparently do not manifest greater aggressive motivation. It may be that their own feelings of inadequacy or fears of retaliation and punishment for aggression inhibit their expression of hostile feelings, even in fantasy. On the other hand, the early-maturers who feel more secure personally, and recognize their own relatively advantageous physical and social status, may feel freer to express their aggressive needs. Since aggression is a culturally stereotyped masculine trait, it seems possible that the physically accelerated, being accepted as mature and identifying readily with adult males, are more likely to acquire this characteristic. In any case, the finding that early-maturers express higher aggressive motivation during late adolescence seems consistent with Jones' finding that, as young adults, they score high on the dominance scale of the Edwards Personal Preference test (6). Perhaps the relatively strong aggressive motivation of the early-maturer, or the mature sex-role identification it may imply, serves as a basis for the development of later qualities of leadership and persuasiveness (7).

As Table 1 indicates, the other aspect of proposition 3 was confirmed: a significantly greater proportion of late- than of early-maturers displayed strong motivations to escape from, or defy, their parents. These may be essentially aggressive reactions, stemming from feelings of parental domination and rejection, or they may reflect the late-maturers awareness of their strife with their parents whom they perceive as blocking their drives for independence. These strong needs for escape and defiance may also be considered evidence of a generally immature way of handling parent-child conflicts. Perhaps, by the age of 17, the early-maturers have already resolved many of their conflicts with their families and/or have learned to handle these in less rebellious and in more direct and mature ways.

Proposition 4 stated that, compared with their early-maturing peers, more late-maturers would manifest strong needs for establishing close social contacts with others. While there was some confirmatory evidence, the results were not clear-cut. When all affiliative needs were considered together (score for n Affiliation—total), the group differences were in the predicted direction, but not statistically significant. Examination of the protocols revealed that almost all instances of affiliation concerned either parents or the opposite sex; there were very few stories involving close, friendly associations between like-sexed peers. The two major types of affiliation were scored separately. As Table 1 shows, late-maturers did not differ from early-maturers with respect to need for affiliation with parents, but a significantly greater proportion of the former group displayed strong motivation for heterosexual affiliation.

In view of the late-maturers' strong feelings of inadequacy and dependent needs (see below), it is surprising that a greater proportion of this group did not exhibit strong needs to establish and maintain close bonds with their parents. This may be due to the late-maturers' more intense conflicts with their parents at this age (17 years), their fears of being rejected and dominated by them, and their generally defiant attitudes which prevent them from admitting, even in fantasy, their strong underlying needs to form close contacts with them.

The significant difference between groups in *n Affiliation* (*love, romance, marriage*) is subject to several possible interpretations. For one thing, this category may refer to general needs to establish close relations with others (with peers or adults other than parents) and not merely to desire for contact with the opposite sex. The set of stimulus cards may not have been adequate to elicit responses indicative of more general affiliative needs; hence, these were expressed through responses in the heterosexual affiliation category. If this is true, proposition 4 was confirmed, and the late-maturers' high scores in this variable indicate their greater general interest in establishing and maintaining friendly relationships.

It is also possible that the late-maturers' strong affiliative needs are actually directed only toward members of the opposite sex, i.e., that *n Affiliation* (*love, romance, marriage*) measures specifically heterosexual interests. Assuming that this is true, there is another plausible explanation for the discovered difference. As we saw earlier, the late-maturer may be afraid to admit that he desires close associations with his parents. He may also feel that his immaturity and poor reputational status prevent him from establishing successful social relationships with like-sexed peers. Hence, he may "displace" his affiliative needs to members of the opposite sex, who in his fantasies, may seem more responsive.

A third possible explanation of the difference is based on Jones and Bayley's findings that the late-maturers show less overt interest in girls and are regarded as less good-looking (8). From these data, it may be inferred that the physically retarded probably do not have successful and rewarding experiences with girls. Hence their heightened need for affiliation with the opposite sex, expressed in the TAT, may reflect their attempts to satisfy in fantasy needs which they cannot satisfy adequately in reality.

The data were generally supportive of proposition 5 which stated that late-maturers are likely to have strong underlying dependent needs. A higher proportion of this group than of their early-maturing peers scored high in *n Succorance,* the difference between the two groups approaching statistical significance ($p = .06$). Furthermore, high scores in the category involving receiving help and support from others (not including parents) (*p Nurturance—nonparents*)—an indirect measure of dependent needs—were significantly more characteristic of the physically retarded than of the physically accelerated. In view of the late-maturers' attitudes toward their parents, discussed above, it is not surprising to find that perceptions of parents as kindly and supportive (high scores in *p Nurturance-parents*) were not significantly more common in this group than in the early-maturing group.

On the basis of the data involving the TAT variables *n Achievement* and *n Recognition,* we rejected proposition 6 which stated that more early-maturers would be self-confident and have high needs for achievement and personal recognition. In our culture there is strong pressure to develop needs for achievement and personal recognition, and, according to our results, these needs and feelings may become intense regardless of— or perhaps in spite of—the child's maturational status, feelings of personal adequacy, dependency, and adjustment to parents.

Two interesting incidental findings from the TAT data seem to be consistent with the proposition that more early- than late-maturers are likely to be self-confident. Seven boys in this sample of 33 adolescents told stories in which the hero was helpful or kind to someone else (*n Nurturance*). Of this group, six were early-maturers, while only one was a late-maturer ($X^2 = 2.09$, $p = .07$). Insofar as *n Nurturance* may be a measure of the storyteller's own feelings that he can accept an active, mature role, more of the accelerated group feel self-assured with respect to having attained mature status.

The other incidental finding which seems to support proposition 6 is based on responses only to card 1 of the Murray series which depicts a young boy contemplating a violin which rests on a table in front of him. Eight of the subjects spoke of the boy (the hero) as a prodigy or a genius. Of these, seven were early-maturers; only one was physically retarded ($X^2 = 5.25$, $p = .01$). If the attribution of this prestige status and accomplishment to the hero reflects the subject's own feeling that he has been an achiever, it follows that more of the physically accelerated have positive self-concepts. In view of the small number of cases involved, both of these findings must be considered tentative, but they do offer some evidence in support of proposition 6.

Proposition 7, which stated that relatively few of the physically retarded boys are unwilling or unable to face their own feelings and emotions, received some support from the TAT data summarized in Table 1. A smaller proportion of the members of this group than of the physically accelerated group specifically denied that the pictures evoked any feelings or emotions (e.g., "It doesn't make me think of anything."). While this variable may not adequately measure *denial of feeling* as a major defense mechanism, this result seems to indicate that late-maturers are more sensitive to their own feelings and more ready to admit and face them openly. Since these qualities are basic to the development of psychological insight, it may be inferred that late-maturers, as a group, are more likely to become insightful individuals.

DISCUSSION

The results of the study support the general hypothesis that, in our culture, the boy whose physical development is retarded is exposed to a sociopsychological environment which may have adverse effects on his personality development. Apparently, being in a disadvantageous competitive position in athletic activities, as well as being regarded and treated as immature by others, may lead to negative self-conceptions, heightened feelings of rejection by others, prolonged dependent needs, and rebellious attitudes toward parents. Hence, the physically retarded boy is more likely than his early-maturing peer to be personally and socially maladjusted during late adolescence. Moreover, some of his attitudes are likely to interfere with the process of identification with his parents, which is generally based on perceptions of them as warm and accepting (9). This, in turn, may inhibit or delay the acquisition of mature characteristics and attitudes which are ordinarily established through identification with parents. Fortunately for the late-maturers' subsequent adjustments, they seem more willing and able to face their feelings and emotions. This may be a result of their awareness of others' attitudes toward their immaturity or their feelings of personal inadequacy and dependency.

The physically accelerated boys, on the other hand, are likely to experience environmental circumstances which are much more conducive to good psychological adjustment. Hence, their psychological picture, as reflected in their TAT stories, is much more favorable. By the time they were 17, relatively few early-maturers harbored strong feelings of inadequacy, perceived themselves as rejected or dominated by parents or authorities, or felt rebellious toward their families. As a group, they appeared to have acquired more self-confidence and had probably made stronger identifications with mature adults. Hence, they perceived themselves as more mature individuals, less dependent and in need of help, and more capable of playing an adult male role in interpersonal relationships.

These findings assume additional, probably greater, importance when they are considered in the light of Jones' findings on the early adult (age 33) adjustments of boys who had been retarded or accelerated in physical maturing (6). It should be recalled that by this age physical differences between the two groups had practically disappeared. Certain important psychological differences were noted, however, and these were consistent with the differences at age 17, reported in the present study. For example, the responses of the early-maturing group to two paper-and-pencil tests revealed that, as young adults, they were more dominant, more able to make a good impression, and more likely to be turned to for advice and reassurance; more self-controlled; and more willing and able to carry social responsibility. In short, they present a general picture of psychological maturity. Moreover, more of the early-maturers seemed to have made successful vocational adjustments. In contrast to this, when the late-maturers became adults, they tended to be highly dependent individuals who could be described, on the basis of their test responses, as tending to be rebellious, touchy, impulsive, self-indulgent, and insightful. Most of these characteristics are indicative of poor adjustment and psychological immaturity. Fewer of this group had made good vocational adjustments.

The striking correspondence between the two descriptions of the groups, derived from different kinds of tests and collected at widely separated periods of time, lends further support to Jones' conclusion that "the adolescent handicaps and advantages associated with late- or early-maturing appear to carry over into adulthood to some extent" (6). It seems clear that many attributes of adolescent personality (patterns of motivation, self-conceptions, and attitudes toward others) characteristic of late- and early-maturing boys are relatively stable and durable rather than situational and transitory. This may be attributable to the fact that in our culture adolescence is generally a critical and difficult period of adjustment. Within a relatively brief interval of time, the child must work out numerous complex and vitally important personal problems, e.g., adaptation to his changed biological and social status, establishment of independence, vocational adjustment. In dealing with these problems, he may acquire new behaviors and personality attributes which have broad ramifications, not only on his current adjustment, but also on his subsequent development. If the adolescent can cope with his problems without too much inner stress and turmoil, his self-esteem, feelings of adequacy, and consequently his subsequent adjustment, are likely to be enhanced. On the other hand, if his problems induce great tension and anxiety, he is likely to feel frustrated and inadequate, and, if these feelings are maintained, to adjust less satisfactorily as an adult.

Obviously, the adolescent's success or failure, as well as ease or tension, in handling his problems will be determined to a large degree by the sociopsychological forces to which he is subjected during this time, and these, as we have seen, may be significantly related to his rate of maturation. Thus, physical status during adolescence—mediated through the sociopsychological environment—may exert profound and lasting influences on personality. For this reason, many aspects of the adult's behavior and personality seem consistent with his adolescent adjustments, attitudes and motivations.

Insofar as our results permit generalization, they suggest that some important aspects of motivation, such as needs for achievement and personal recognition, are not significantly affected by maturational status. It may be that among subjects whose achievements are strongly encouraged and rewarded from very early childhood, the need to achieve becomes powerful and resistant to change even in the face of feelings of helplessness and inadequacy. The latter may inhibit the achievement-oriented overt behavior of some late-maturers, but the underlying motivation to achieve seems as strong in this group as it is among the physically accelerated.

In conclusion, it should be noted that, although rate of maturing and associated factors may affect personality development, the relationship between physical status and psychological characteristics is by no means simple. A vast number of complex, interacting factors, including rate of maturation, determine each adolescent's unique personality structure. Hence, in any specific instance, the *group* findings of the present study may not be directly applicable, for other physical, psychological, or social factors may attenuate the effects of late- or early-maturing. For example, an adolescent boy who is fundamentally secure and has warm, accepting parents and generally rewarding social relationships may not develop strong feelings of inadequacy even if he matures slowly. Analogously, the early-maturing boy who has deep feelings of insecurity, for whatever reasons, will probably not gain self-confidence simply because he matures early. In summary, in understanding any individual case, generalizations based on the data of the present study must be particularized in the light of the individual's past history and present circumstances.

SUMMARY

The present investigation was designed to test seven propositions concerning the relationship between rate of physical maturation and important aspects of personality structure, specifically, self-conceptions, underlying motivations, and basic interpersonal attitudes. The TAT protocols of thirty-three 17-year-old boys—16 who had been consistently physically accelerated throughout adolescence and 17 who had been consistently retarded—were analyzed according to a scoring schema involving 20 needs, press, and descriptive categories. The scores of early- and late-maturers in each of the categories were compared.

An earlier study (8) demonstrated that late-maturing boys are more likely than their early-maturing peers to encounter a generally unfavorable sociopsychological environment. Analysis of the data of the present study indicates that this situation may have adverse effects on the personalities of the physically retarded. These boys are more likely to have negative self-conceptions, feelings of inadequacy, strong feelings of being rejected and dominated, prolonged dependency needs, and rebellious attitudes toward parents. In contrast, the early-maturing boys present a much more favorable psychological picture during adolescence. Relatively few of them felt inadequate, rejected, dominated, or rebellious toward their families. More of them appeared to be self-confident, independent, and capable of playing an adult role in interpersonal relationships. Early- and late-maturing groups did not differ significantly from each other in needs for achievement or personal recognition.

These findings make it clear that rate of physical maturing may affect personality development in crucially important ways. However, it is important to note that in any particular case, the effects of early- or late-maturing may be significantly modified by the individual's psychological history and present circumstances.

REFERENCES

1. Farnham, M. L. *The adolescent.* New York: Harper, 1951.
2. Fisher, R. A. *Statistical methods for research workers.* (7th ed.) Oliver & Boyd, 1938.
3. Jones, H. E. Observational methods in the study of individual development. *J. consult. Psychol.,* 1940, **4,** 234–238.
4. Jones, H. E. *Development in adolescence: approaches to the study of the individual.* Appleton-Century-Crofts, 1943.

5. Jones, H. E. Adolescence in our society. In Anniversary Papers of the Community Service Society of New York, *The family in a democratic society*. Columbia Univ. Press, 1949. Pp. 70–82.

6. Jones, M. C. The later careers of boys who were early- or late-maturing. *Child Develpm.*, 1957, **28**, 113–128.

7. Jones, M. C. A study of socialization patterns at the high school level. *J. genet. Psychol.*, 1959, **93**, 87–111.

8. Jones, M. C., & Bayley, N. Physical maturing among boys as related to behavior. *J. educ. Psychol.*, 1950, **41**, 129–148.

9. Payne, D. E., & Mussen, P. H. Parent-child relations and father identification among adolescent boys. *J. abnorm. soc. Psychol.*, 1956, **52**, 358–362.

10. Stone, C. P., & Barker, R. G. The attitudes and interests of premenarcheal and postmenarcheal girls. *J. genet. Psychol.*, 1939, **54**, 27–71.

11. Tryon, C. M. Evaluations of adolescent personality by adolescents. *Monogr. Soc. Res. Child Develpm.*, 1939, **4** (4).

IDENTITY

VERSUS IDENTITY DIFFUSION

Erik H. Erikson
HARVARD UNIVERSITY

I

WITH THE ESTABLISHMENT of a good relationship to the world of skills and
to those who teach and share the new skills, childhood proper comes to
an end. Youth begins. But in puberty and adolescence all sameness and
continuities relied on earlier are questioned again because of a rapidity
of body growth which equals that of early childhood and because of the
entirely new addition of physical genital maturity. The growing and developing young people, faced with this physiological revolution within
them, are now primarily concerned with attempts at consolidating their
social roles. They are sometimes morbidly, often curiously, preoccupied
with what they appear to be in the eyes of others as compared with what
they feel they are and with the question of how to connect the earlier
cultivated roles and skills with the ideal prototypes of the day. In their
search for a new sense of continuity and sameness, some adolescents
have to refight many of the crises of earlier years, and they are never ready
to install lasting idols and ideals as guardians of a final identity.

The integration now taking place in the form of the ego identity is
more than the sum of the childhood identifications. It is the inner capital
accrued from all those experiences of each successive stage, when successful identification led to a successful alignment of the individual's *basic
drives* with his *endowment* and his *opportunities*. In psychoanalysis we
ascribe such successful alignments to "ego synthesis"; I have tried to
demonstrate that the ego values accrued in childhood culminate in what

Reprinted by permission from "Growth and Crises of the Healthy Personality:
VI. Identity versus self-diffusion. In M. J. E. Senn (Ed.), *Symposium on the Healthy
Personality*. II: Problems of Infancy and Childhood. New York: Josiah Macy, Jr.
Foundation, (1950), pp. 134–140.

I have called a *sense of ego identity*. The sense of ego identity, then, is the accrued confidence that one's ability to maintain inner sameness and continuity (one's ego in the psychological sense) is matched by the sameness and continuity of one's meaning for others. To go back into early childhood once more: a child who has just found himself able to walk, more or less coaxed or ignored by those around him, seems driven to repeat the act for the pure enjoyment of functioning and out of the need to master and perfect a newly initiated function. But he also acts under the immediate awareness of the new status and stature of "one who can walk," although different peoples and different people may express this according to a great variety of expectations: "one who will go far," "one who will be able to stand on his own feet," "one who will be upright," "one who must be watched because he might go too far," or sometimes "one who will surely fall." At any rate, to become "one who can walk" is one of the many steps in child development which suddenly give an experience of physical mastery and of cultural meaning, of pleasure in activity and of social prestige; it thus is one building stone of self-esteem. This self-esteem, confirmed at the end of each major crisis, grows to be a conviction that one is learning effective steps toward a tangible future, that one is developing a defined personality within a social reality which one understands. The growing child must, at every step, derive a vitalizing sense of reality from the awareness that his individual way of mastering experience is a successful variant of the way other people around him master experience and recognize such mastery.

In this, children cannot be fooled by empty praise and condescending encouragement. They may have to accept artificial bolstering of their self-esteem in lieu of something better, but what I call their accruing ego identity gains real strength only from wholehearted and consistent recognition of real accomplishment, that is, achievement that has meaning in their culture. A child has quite a number of opportunities to identify himself, more or less experimentally, with habits, traits, occupations, and ideas of real or fictitious people of either sex. Certain crises force him to make radical selections. However, this historical era in which he lives offers only a limited number of socially meaningful models for workable combinations of identification fragments. His usefulness depends on the way in which he simultaneously meets the requirements of his maturational stage and his habits of adjustment. But, should a child feel that the environment tries to deprive him too radically of all the forms of expression which permit him to develop and to integrate the next step in this ego identity, he will resist with the astonishing strength encountered in animals who are suddenly forced to defend their lives. Indeed, in the social jungle of human existence, there is no feeling of being alive without a sense of ego identity. To understand this would be to understand the trouble of adolescents better, especially the trouble of all those who cannot just be "nice" boys and girls, but are desperately seeking for a satisfactory sense of belonging, be it in cliques and gangs here in our country or in inspiring mass movements in others.

Ego identity, then, develops out of a gradual integration of all identifications, but here, if anywhere, the whole has a different quality than the sum of its parts. Under favorable circumstances children have the nucleus of a separate identity in early life; often they must defend it against any pressure which would make them overidentify with one of their parents. This is difficult to learn from patients, because the neurotic ego has, by definition, fallen prey to overidentification and to faulty identifications with disturbed parents, a circumstance which isolated the small individual both from his budding identity and from his milieu. But we can study it profitably in the children of minority-group Americans who, having successfully graduated from a marked and well-guided stage of autonomy, enter the most decisive stage of American childhood: that of initiative and industry.

Minority groups of a lesser degree of Americanization (Negroes, Indians, Mexicans, and certain European groups) often are privileged in the enjoyment of a more sensual early childhood. Their crises come when their parents and teachers, losing trust in themselves and using sudden correctives in order to approach the vague but pervasive Anglo-Saxon ideal, create violent discontinuities; or where, indeed, the children themselves learn to disavow their sensual and overprotective mothers as temptations and a hindrance to the formation of a more American personality.

On the whole, it can be said that American schools successfully meet the challenge of training children of play-school age and of the elementary grades in a spirit of self-reliance and enterprise. Children of these ages seem remarkably free of prejudice and apprehension, preoccupied as they still are with growing and learning and with the new pleasures of association outside their families. This, to forestall the sense of individual inferiority, must lead to a hope for "industrial association," for equality with all those who apply themselves wholeheartedly to the same skills and adventures in learning. Many individual successes, on the other hand, only expose the now overly encouraged children of mixed backgrounds and somewhat deviant endowments to the shock of American adolescence: the standardization of individuality and the intolerance of "differences." The emerging ego identity, then, bridges the early childhood stages, when the body and the parent images were given their specific meanings, and the later stages, when a variety of social roles become available and increasingly coercive. A lasting ego identity cannot begin to exist without the trust of the first oral stage; it cannot be completed without a promise of fulfillment which from the dominant image of adulthood reaches down into the baby's beginnings and which creates at every step an accruing sense of ego strength.

II

The danger of this stage is *self-diffusion;* as Biff puts it in Arthur Miller's *Death of a Salesman,* "I just can't take hold, Mom, I can't take hold of some kind of a life." Where such a dilemma is based on a strong previous doubt of one's ethnic and sexual identity, delinquent and outright psychotic incidents are not uncommon. Youth after youth, bewildered by some assumed role, a role forced on him by the inexorable standardization of American adolescence, runs away in one form or another; leaving schools and jobs, staying out all night, or withdrawing into bizarre and inaccessible moods. Once "delinquent," his greatest need and often his only salvation, is the refusal on the part of older friends, advisers, and judiciary personnel to type him further by pat diagnoses and social judgments which ignore the special dynamic conditions of adolescence. For if diagnosed and treated correctly, seemingly psychotic and criminal incidents do not in adolescence have the same fatal significance which they have at other ages. Yet many a youth, finding that the authorities expect him to be "a bum," or "a queer," or "off the beam," perversely obliges society by becoming just that.

In general it is primarily the inability to settle on an occupational identity which disturbs young people. To keep themselves together they temporarily overidentify, to the point of apparent complete loss of identity, with the heroes of cliques and crowds. On the other hand, they become remarkably clannish, intolerant, and cruel in their exclusion of others who are "different," in skin color or cultural background, in tastes and gifts, and often in entirely petty aspects of dress and gesture arbitrarily selected as *the* signs of an in-grouper or out-grouper. It is important to understand (which does not mean condone or participate in) such intolerance as the necessary *defense against a sense of identity diffusion,* which is unavoidable at a time of life when the body changes its proportions radically, when genital maturity floods body and imagination with all manners of drives, when intimacy with the other sex approaches and is, on occasion, forced on the youngster, and when life lies before one with a variety of conflicting possibilities and choices. Adolescents help one another temporarily through such discomfort by forming cliques and by stereotyping themselves and their ideals.

It is important to understand this because it makes clear the appeal which simple totalitarian doctrines have on the minds of the youth of such countries and classes as have lost or are losing their group identities (feudal, agrarian, national, and so forth) in these times of world-wide industrialization, emancipation, and wider intercommunication. The dynamic quality of the tempestuous adolescences lived through in patri-archal and agrarian countries (countries which face the most radical changes in political structure and in economy) explains the fact that their young people find convincing and satisfactory identities in the simple totalitarian doctrines of race, class, or nation. Even though we may be forced to win wars against their leaders, we still are faced with the job of winning the peace with these grim youths by convincingly demon-strating to them (by living it) a democratic identity which can be strong and yet tolerant, judicious and still determined.

But it is increasingly important to understand this also in order to treat the intolerances of our adolescents at home with understanding and guidance rather than with verbal stereotypes or prohibitions. It is difficult to be tolerant if deep down you are not quite sure that you are a man (or a woman), that you will ever grow together again and be attractive, that you will be able to master your drives, that you really know who you are,[1] that you know what you want to be, that you know what you look like to others, and that you will know how to make the right decisions without, once for all, committing yourself to the wrong friend, girl, or career. Religions help the integration of such identity with "confirma-tions" of a clearly defined way of life. In many countries, nationalism supports a sense of identity. In primitive tribes puberty rites help to standardize the new identity, often with horrifying, impressive rituals.

Democracy in a country like America poses special problems in that it insists on *self-made identities* ready to grasp many chances and ready to adjust to changing necessities of booms and busts, of peace and war, of migration and determined sedentary life. Our democracy, furthermore, must present the adolescent with ideals which can be shared by youths of many backgrounds and which emphasize autonomy in the form of inde-

[1] On the wall of a cowboys' bar in the wide-open West hangs a saying: "I ain't what I ought to be, I ain't what I'm going to be, but I ain't what I was."

pendence and initiative in the form of enterprise. These promises, in turn, are not easy to fulfill in increasingly complex and centralized systems of economic and political organization, systems which, if geared to war, must automatically neglect the "self-made" identities of millions of individuals and put them where they are most needed. This is hard on many young Americans because their whole upbringing, and therefore the development of a healthy personality, depends on a certain degree of *choice*, a certain hope for an individual *chance*, and a certain conviction in freedom of *self-determination*.

We are speaking here not only of high privileges and lofty ideals but also of psychological necessities. Psychologically speaking, a gradually accruing ego identity is the only safeguard against the *anarchy of drives* as well as the *autocracy of conscience*, that is, the cruel overconscientiousness which is the inner residue in the adult of his past inequality in regard to his parent. Any loss of a sense of identity exposes the individual to his own childhood conflicts—as could be observed, for example, in the neuroses of World War II among men and women who could not stand the general dislocation of their careers or a variety of other special pressures of war. Our adversaries, it seems, understand this. Their psychological warfare consists in the determined continuation of general conditions which permit them to indoctrinate mankind within their orbit with the simple and yet for them undoubtedly effective identities of class warfare and nationalism, while they know that the psychology, as well as the economy, of free enterprise and of self-determination is stretched to the breaking point under conditions of long-drawn-out cold and lukewarm war. It is clear, therefore, that we must bend every effort to present our young men and women with the tangible and trustworthy promise of opportunities for a rededication to the life for which the country's history, as well as their own childhood, has prepared them. Among the tasks of national defense, this one must not be forgotten.

I have tentatively referred to the relationship of the problem of trust to matters of adult faith; to that of the problem of autonomy to matters of adult independence in work and citizenship. I have pointed to the connection between a sense of initiative and the kind of enterprise sanctioned in the economic system, and between the sense of industry and a culture's technology. In searching for the social values which guide identity, one confronts the problem of aristocracy, in its widest possible sense, which connotes the conviction that the best people rule and that that rule, as defined in society, develops the best in people. In order not to become cynically or apathetically lost, young people in search of an identity must somewhere be able to convince themselves that those who succeed acquire not only the conviction that they have proven to be better than others, but also the obligation of being the best, that is, of personifying the nation's ideals. In this country, as in any other, we have those success-ful types who become the cynical representatives of the "inside track," the "bosses" of impersonal machinery. . . . In a culture once pervaded with the value of the self-made man, a special danger ensues from the idea of a synthetic personality: as if you are what you can appear to be, or as if you are what you can buy. Here the very special influence of the entertainment industry must be considered. This can be counteracted only by a system of education that transmits values and goals which determinedly aspire beyond mere "functioning" and "making the grade."

ANTECEDENTS OF DELINQUENCY: PERSONALITY, SOCIAL CLASS, AND INTELLIGENCE[1]

John J. Conger, Wilbur C. Miller, and Charles R. Walsmith

UNIVERSITY OF COLORADO SCHOOL OF MEDICINE
AND UNIVERSITY OF DENVER

A CONSIDERABLE NUMBER of studies have examined the relationship between delinquency and such variables as social class, intelligence, and residence area (2, 3, 5, 6, 9, 10, 11, 12, 13, 16). Many others, including such pioneering efforts as those of Healy and Bronner (8) and the Gluecks (6), have investigated the relationship of personality traits to delinquency within various populations (1, 7, 14, 15, 16).

It may well be, however, that the relationship of these variables to delinquency cannot properly be considered independently of their relation to one another. Thus, it is perfectly possible that personality characteristics which are related to delinquency in some intelligence and social-class subgroups may not be related in other subgroups. For example, traits which differentiate delinquents from nondelinquents in a high-IQ, socioeconomically favored subgroup may fail to be differentiating in a deprived subgroup of average intelligence.

If this is the case, it is not enough, in studying the relationship of antecedent personality characteristics to later delinquency, simply to control for the possible effects of other factors, such as socioeconomic status, residence area, intelligence, sex, educational background, and ethnic group membership. This is clearly a necessary step, and one which

[1] This study, and the more extended research project of which it is a part, was made possible by a grant (MH-03040) from the National Institute of Mental Health. We would like to express our indebtedness to the following colleagues and research assistants for their help in the conduct of this study: Joan Happel, Rosamond Putsch, Robert V. Rainey, Ann A. Shenefield, Joan Searles, and Donald Stilson.

442

the more adequate studies in this field have attempted to take, but it is not a sufficient step.

The study reported here in condensed form is a part of a larger, longitudinal study of personality, social class, and delinquency, to be published elsewhere (4). The principle aims of the present study were to determine (1) whether personality traits manifested by boys in the period from kindergarten through the third grade are significantly related to future delinquency after the potential effects of other factors have been controlled through a matching technique, and (2) whether the nature, extent, and direction of such relationships may vary, depending on the intelligence and social class status of the child.

The population from which the subjects of this study were drawn comprised all males in the tenth grade of all high schools in a large Western city ($N = 2,348$). Subjects actually employed met several additional requirements, including presence in the school system of this city in the period from kindergarten through the third grade (K-3) and continued residence in this city, at least through age 18.

Teacher ratings of "personal-social behavior," made on a three-point scale twice yearly during the early school years, were available for use as antecedent variables, as were more informal, unstructured comments made by teachers about their pupils during the same period. The latter were subjected to a content analysis, from which the investigators derived a "Teacher Comment Check List," consisting of 97 discrete behavioral traits and environmental influences (e.g., "good attention, concentration," "distractable, poor attention, daydreams," "independent, self-sufficient," "resents and rejects authority," "parent interest and cooperation"), reflecting the principle kinds of statements which teachers tended to make spontaneously about their pupils at this age. Two trained judges, with experience both in psychology and in elementary education, then applied the check list independently to a sample of 100 sets of teacher comments. For purposes of the present study, a set comprised all of the comments made by teachers about a particular child in the K-3 period. Only those check list items showing interjudge reliabilities of .65 and above at this age level were employed in the study.

Delinquency criterion. All boys in the population who became delinquent prior to age 18 were subsequently identified. The criterion for delinquency employed in this study was formal acceptance of the case by the Juvenile Court. As we have noted elsewhere (4), and as Bandura and Walters (1) also note, delinquency as such is a sociolegal, rather than a psychological phenomenon. In fact, a primary purpose of this investigation was to determine what, if any, were the relationships of psychological variables to this sociolegal phenomenon. As a result, any operationally defined criterion of delinquency had to involve some degree of contact with law enforcement officials—either police or judicial.

Because of the organization of juvenile authorities in this particular city, we were faced with these alternatives: we could have defined as delinquent all youths who had any contact either with the court or juvenile bureau of the police department. This, however, would have meant including as "delinquents" a large number of boys who were involved in very trivial incidents, such as minor pranks, and who were talked to briefly, turned over to their parents or sent home, and never seen again. The local juvenile bureau of the police department has estimated that out of every five cases seen, only two are eventually considered serious enough, either because of the gravity of the offense or because of recidivism, to be turned over to the juvenile court.

In turn, of the youths carried on the records of the juvenile court, only about one in eight is brought to trial, convicted, and sentenced to an institution—either because of failure to respond to assistance by probation workers, or because of the gravity of the offense.

It was our belief that to have used the first of these possible criteria would have diluted the meaning of the term delinquency to the point of absurdity (e.g., calling a child delinquent because he was once involved in a minor bit of mischief which came to the attention of the police). On the other hand, we were convinced that it would be equally inappropriate to designate as delinquent only those youths whose offenses were extremely serious or chronic, and who proved completely refractory to help from juvenile workers. Not only would such a definition exclude many youths in considerable trouble with the law, but it would also render subsequent comparisons between repeaters and nonrepeaters, or treatable and refractory cases, impossible.

It was our conclusion that selecting the middle ground, and defining delinquency as acceptance of the case by the juvenile court, had the greatest promise for this investigation, and was also in closest accord with common usage. The distribution of offenses and ages of offenses for males in our population are shown in Figure 1 and Table 1. As may be seen, the highest incidence of delinquent offenses occurs at age 15.5, with a marked decline in number of offenses below age 14 and above age 16.

Selection of study samples. After identifying the delinquent males in our population for whom relatively complete records were available (N = 271), each was investigated individually to determine the following

Number of offenses

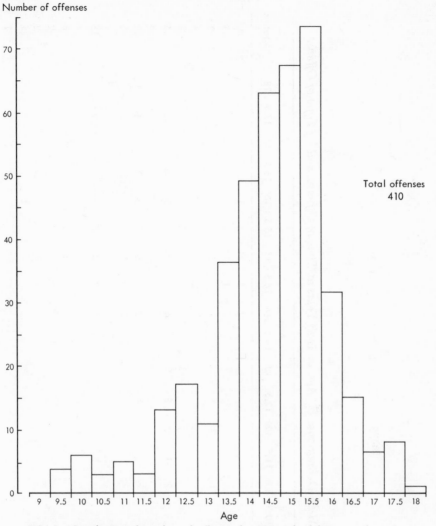

Age

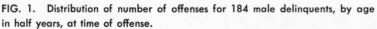

FIG. 1. Distribution of number of offenses for 184 male delinquents, by age in half years, at time of offense.

relevant characteristics: age, socioeconomic status (three levels: high, medium, low), residence area characteristics, IQ (seven levels: very superior, superior, bright normal, average, dull normal, borderline, mentally defective), school background (schools attended) and ethnic group membership. More detailed information regarding the techniques employed in determining such characteristics as socioeconomic status is available elsewhere (4).

TABLE 1. *Distribution of 184 Male Delinquents by Age in Half-Years at Time of Offense, and by Type of Offense*

Type of Offense												Age							
	9.5	10	10.5	11	11.5	12	12.5	13	13.5	14	14.5	15	15.5	16	16.5	17	17.5	18	Totals
Aggravated assault										2	1	1	5	1					10
Aggravated robbery											1	1	1						3
Arson				1		1	1												3
Assault and battery									1	3									4
Attempted car theft													2						2
Burglary	1	2	1	2	1	3	3	5	7	4	2	10	7	3	4		1		56
Car prowl											3	1							4
Car theft							1			2	1	5	5	6	1			1	22
Carrying concealed weapon										1	3	1							5
Cruelty to animals												1							1
Curfew violation					1		1			1	2	2	6				2		15
Destroying city property											1								1
Disturbances												1	3	1		1			6
Escape from Juvenile Hall									1				1						2
False fire alarm											1	1							2
False registration														1					1
Forgery															1	1			2

	1	2	3	4	5	6	7	8	9	10	11	12	13	14	15	16	17	18	Total
Gangs												1							1
Hit and run						2			1	1	2	1							7
Incorrigible	1	2	1			2	3	2	8	4	13	9	7	5	3	1		3	64
Indecent acts				1								1							2
Indecent language									1	1		1							3
Joyriding	1			1		1		1	13	17	18	8	5	5	1				71
Larceny		1	1			2		2	6	7	10	5	7	2	2	1	1		47
Loitering													2						2
Malicious mischief	1	1		1		1		1	5	5	3	3	3	3			1	1	29
Receiving stolen goods						1					1		1		1			1	5
Resisting arrest												1							1
Runaway	1					1			2	2	3	1	2	3					15
Sex offenses						1				1	1	2		3					8
Threats									1										1
Traffic violation											1	3							4
Truancy	1		2			2			2					1					8
Vandalism					1														1
Wearing women's clothing																1			1
Witness to stabbing																	1		1
Totals	4	6	3	5	3	13	17	11	36	49	62	67	73	31	15	6	8	1	N410

Each delinquent was then matched *individually* with a nondelinquent on all the above variables. Because of the obvious impossibility of finding complete matches for all delinquents, this procedure reduced the number of potentially usable delinquents from 271 to 184.

Absence of teacher ratings or teacher comments on some of these boys during the K-3 period further reduced this number to 86. Thus, the final number of subjects employed in this study was 172, divided equally between delinquents and nondelinquents.

Study I: Personal-Social Behavior of Future Delinquents and Nondelinquents During the Early School Years

The first, and statistically much the simpler, of the two analyses presented in this paper involved a comparison of the personality character-istics of future delinquents and their nondelinquent matches in the period from kindergarten through the third grade. As noted above, two kinds of developmental personality measures were available in this period: teacher ratings of personal-social development and the Teacher Comment Check List. Each will be discussed in turn.

TABLE 2. *Number of Pairs in Which Both Delinquent-Nondelinquent Pair Members Received Ratings for Each Item of Personal-Social Behavior at Grade 3*

Teacher Rating	Number of Delinquent-Nondelinquent Pairs
Physical skill	22
Creativeness	25
Clear thinking	20
Openmindedness	25
Leadership ability	50
Regard for persons	48
Sense of responsibility	52
Response to authority	49
Social acceptability	48
Work habits	49
Interests	15
Appreciations	4
Ideals (ambitions, wishes)	7
Physical health resources	12
Physical health problems	9
Home resources	5
Home problems	5
Overall	0

1. *Ratings of personal-social development.* The behaviors rated here are listed in Table 2, and described in more detail elsewhere (4). Each behavior was rated on a three-point scale: low (lower 25 percent), middle (middle 50 percent), and high (upper 25 percent). For purposes of statistical analysis, these ratings were given numerical values of 1, 2, and 3, respectively. Teachers were permitted to omit ratings where they did not feel that they had sufficient evidence to justify a judgment. While these same behaviors were rated at all elementary school grade levels, we selected the children's third grade ratings to represent the early school years. This was done for two reasons: (1) analyzing the ratings at all grade levels would have been prohibitive in terms of time and expense; (2) teachers apparently felt capable of rating more behaviors at this grade level than at earlier ones (though still less capable than at later grade levels). Thus, we had a greater total number of ratings with which to work at grade three.

It was our hypothesis, in view of the operational descriptions of these behaviors which were provided to teachers, that future nondelinquents would obtain higher scores on each of the traits rated. In testing this hypothesis we wanted to preserve the benefits of individual matching of delinquent and nondelinquent subjects and also to be able *later* to analyze for the effects, separately and in interaction, of social class-IQ subgroup membership. Consequently, for reasons to be described in more detail later in this paper, a 2 x 5 analysis of variance design for matched pairs (main effect for delinquency) was employed to test for the significance of delinquent-nondelinquent differences. For present purposes, and for the benefit of nonstatistically oriented readers, it is sufficient to note that this technique permitted us to test for the statistical significance of delinquent-nondelinquent differences on each personality measure.

Table 2 shows the number of times teachers rated *both* members of delinquent-nondelinquent pairs for each of the 18 traits rated at grade three. As may be seen, it appears that teachers felt little confidence at grade three in making ratings for most children on such variables as physical skill, creativeness, clear thinking, and open-mindedness (less than 30 pairs rated on each of these traits); and virtually no confidence in rating interest, appreciations, ideals, physical health resources, physical health problems, home resources, home problems, and overall adjustment (15 or fewer pairs rated).

On the other hand, they seemed to feel relatively confident (more than 45 pairs rated at this grade level) in rating: leadership ability, regard for persons, sense of responsibility, response to authority, social acceptability, and work habits. It is interesting to note that each of these six variables involves readily identifiable, relatively objective behaviors, common to the classroom situation; while many of the other variables involve behaviors or information not necessarily observable or known in the classroom, or they involve clinical inferences or unusually subtle judgments (e.g., "creativeness").

Nondelinquents scored higher than delinquents on 15 of the 18 traits, although, of course, in a fair number of instances the total number of ratings was too small to make statistical analysis possible. (Only on *interests, physical health resources,* and *physical health problems* did the delinquents obtain higher scores, and on none of these traits were more than 15 ratings made).

However, as may be seen in Table 3, which presents means and significance levels for each rating involving over 45 pairs, of the six most commonly (and presumably most confidently) rated traits at the third

TABLE 3. *Mean Scores of Male Delinquents and Nondelinquents on Teacher Ratings (Grade 3)*

Teacher Rating	Delinquent Mean	Nondelinquent Mean	Number of Matched Pairs	F Ratio
Leadership	2.10	2.10	50	.00
Regard for persons	1.95	2.22	48	5.64[a]
Sense of responsibility	1.80	2.11	52	8.40[b]
Response to authority	2.10	2.28	49	2.48
Social acceptability	2.04	2.37	48	6.67[a]
Work habits	1.93	2.04	49	.62

[a] Significant at .05 level
[b] Significant at .01 level

grade level, three (*regard for persons, sense of responsibility,* and *social acceptability*) significantly differentiate nondelinquents from delinquents in the predicted direction at the $.05^2$ level or better, despite relatively small numbers. A fourth trait, *response to authority*, shows a possible trend toward significance (approaching the .10 level). Only two of the six

[2] A word of explanation for the nonstatistically oriented reader may be in order. A significance level of .025 simply means that there are only 25 chances in 1,000 that differences this large or larger would be obtained by chance alone. Similarly, a significance level of .01 indicated that there is only 1 chance in 100 that such results would occur by chance alone.

variables, *work habits* and *leadership,* clearly fail to show any trend toward significance.[3]

2. *Teacher Comment Check List.* It may be recalled that only those items on the Teacher Comment Check List which had an interjudge reliability coefficient of .65 or higher at this age level were employed in the present study. These are listed in Table 4, and are described in more detail elsewhere (4).

The data emerging from the check list were analyzed in two ways. On the basis of a priori hypotheses about the relation to delinquency of specific personality traits, each trait was postulated as more likely to be associated with delinquency or more likely to be associated with nondelinquency. All instances of the former in a record were arbitrarily scored + 1, and all instances of the latter — 1. By summing all instances of the former and subtracting all instances of the latter, a hypothetical "D" (or delinquency) score was obtained for each subject. This procedure has, of course, both advantages and disadvantages. On the positive side, items occurring sufficiently infrequently that their individual validity cannot be assessed have an opportunity, if they are in fact valid, of contributing to the discriminating power of the overall D-score. On the other hand, even though the D-score itself proves capable of discriminating delinquents from nondelinquents, one cannot be sure just which rare items are making a valid (as opposed to a chance) contribution to this discrimination.

One can, however, test the individual significance of D-score items which occur frequently enough to make a statistical test of their discriminating power possible.

Table 4 shows the D-score rating ($+1$, or -1) for each of the reliable teacher comment categories, as well as the distribution of these categories for matched pairs of delinquents and nondelinquents, for the period kindergarten through third grade. The D-scores for all subjects were obtained, means for delinquents and nondelinquents were computed, and the significance of the delinquent-nondelinquent difference was run.[4] A

[3] *Statistical note:* These same data were also analyzed using a nonparametric sign test, based on the number of times the score of the nondelinquent member of a pair exceeded his match for each trait. Similar results were obtained, except that *response to authority,* discriminated in this latter analysis at the .05 level, rather than simply showing a possible trend. *Sense of responsibility* and *social acceptability* showed somewhat higher significance levels (.001 and .004, respectively) and *regard for persons* remained about the same (.035). *Work habits* and *leadership* continued to be nondiscriminating.

[4] Based on the main effect for delinquency in an analysis of variance design for D-score.

TABLE 4. *Distribution of Reliable Teacher Comment Categories for Matched Pairs of Male Delinquents and Nondelinquents, and D-Score Ratings for Each Category*

Teacher Comment Category	D-Score Ratings	Delinquent Only	Nondelinquent Only	Both	Neither	Significance Level (if $p<.10$)
1. Special ability or interest	—	7	15	5	59	.067
2. Below average ability	+	1	2[a]	0	83	
3. Slow learner	+	1	2	0	83	
4. Works up to capacity	—	2	4	0	80	
5. Underachieving	+	12	14	1	59	
6. Good reader	—	7	6[a]	3	70	
7. Poor reader	+	11	17[a]	9	49	
8. Good work habits	—	9	7[a]	1	69	
9. Careful worker	—	7	8	0	71	
10. Careless worker	+	6	4	3	73	
11. Good attention, concentration	—	6	8	0	72	
12. Distractible, poor attention, daydreams	+	21	9	4	52	.003
13. Shows effort to improve	—	16	23	11	36	
14. Lacks persistence, gives up easily	+	9	7	0	70	
15. Conscientious, dependable	—	9	11	2	64	
16. Cooperative	—	11	13	1	61	
17. Poor attitude toward school	+	2	2	1	81	
18. Good attendance	—	1	1	0	84	
19. Attendance problem	+	7	7	0	72	
20. Parent interest and cooperation	—	10	18	4	54	.093
21. Stable home	—	1	3	0	82	
22. Disturbed home environment	+	21	5	1	59	.002
23. Friendly, pleasant	—	11	26	6	43	.011
24. Considerate, fair to others	—	3	13	0	70	.011
25. Aggressive	+	10	4	1	71	.090
26. Resents and rejects authority	+	13	2	0	71	.004
27. Influenced by others	+	4	1	0	81	
28. Active group participation	—	6	13	3	64	.084

TABLE 4.   (Continued)

Teacher Comment Category	D-Score Ratings	Delin- quent Only	Nondelin- quent Only	Both	Neither	Significance Level (if $p<.10$)
29. Well liked, accepted, gets along with peers	—	16	32	12	26	.027
30. Not well accepted, doesn't get along with peers	+	15	5	2	64	.021
31. Attention seeking	+	8	12[a]	0	66	
32. Well-behaved	—	2	4	0	80	
33. Unstable, insecure	+	12	7	2	65	
34. Nervous, restless	+	8	5	0	73	
35. Mature (emotionally)	—	0	4	0	82	
36. Immature (emotionally)	+	6	17[a]	1	62	.017
37. Quiet, shy, tends to withdraw	—	12	11	2	61	
38. Physical defects	+	21	15	11	39	

[a] Not in predicted direction

mean D-score of $+.23$ was found for delinquents and -1.23 for non-delinquents. The difference is clearly significant ($p < .001$).[5]

Among individual D-score items, 29 fell in the predicted direction, while eight fell in the opposite direction (Table 4). Of 26 cases where more than 15 ratings of delinquents and nondelinquents combined were made, *12 discriminated delinquents from nondelinquents at the .10 level or better, of which 8 were significant below the .05 level (sign test).*

Summary of findings.   It appears that even at the third grade level future delinquents and nondelinquents as a group are viewed differently by their teachers. It should be stressed that we are speaking here only of differences above and beyond those which might be due to the effects of such variables as socioeconomic status, intelligence, and ethnic group membership, since the potential effects of these variables have already been controlled through matching. Had these not been controlled, even larger differences would be anticipated, in view of the known relationship between these variables and both personality and delinquency, a relationship confirmed in this research (4).

Nevertheless, even with such controls the differences are impressive,

[5] A nonparametric sign test, based on the number of instances in which delinquent pair members exceeded their nondelinquent matches, yielded similar results ($p = .003$).

particularly at this early age—as evidenced, for example, by the fact that the overall D-score enabled us to discriminate future delinquents and non-delinquents at the .001 level of significance.

In the period from kindergarten through third grade, future delinquent boys already appeared more poorly adapted than their classmates. They appeared to have less regard for the rights and feelings of their peers; less awareness of the need to accept responsibility for their obligations, both as individuals and as members of a group; and poorer attitudes toward authority, including the failure to understand the need for rules and regulations in any well-ordered social group, and to abide by them. They both resented and rejected authority in the school situation. Their overall social behavior was simply less acceptable; they had more difficulty in getting along with peers, both in individual 1-to-1 contacts and in group situations, and were less willing or able to treat others courteously and tactfully and less able to be fair in dealing with them. In return, they were less well liked and accepted by their peers.

In the academic situation itself, they were more easily distracted, daydreamed more, and, in general, had greater difficulty in maintaining attention and sticking to the task at hand until it was completed. They were less likely to display any special ability or interest.

Not surprisingly, these social and academic problems frequently appeared to reflect underlying emotional problems. In the opinion of teachers, as manifested by the ratings and teacher comments, future delinquents more often came from a disturbed home environment and were considered overly aggressive.

Future nondelinquents appeared in many ways as the other side of the coin. Socially, they were rated significantly more cooperative, dependable, friendly, pleasant, considerate, and fair. They were better liked by their peers and more accepted as members of the group.

In the school situation, they showed a considerably greater sense of individual and group responsibility, greater acceptance of constituted authority, and more acceptable social behavior generally.

Their parents appeared more often to show interest in the child's academic and social progress, and to cooperate more readily with school authorities. Emotionally, these boys appeared less aggressive.

Study II: Socioeconomic Status and Intelligence

The question arising in our minds at this juncture was whether or not the general picture described above was equally applicable to all subgroups, or whether the picture might change as we proceeded from one social class-IQ subgroup to another. However, to approach this problem, it was necessary to subdivide our subjects, not only into the two matched groups of delinquents and nondelinquents employed in Study I, but also along the dimensions of socioeconomic status and intelligence.

For reasons which are elaborated elsewhere (4), it appeared most appropriate, both for statistical reasons and because of the socioeconomic and IQ distributions of residents of this predominantly middle-class

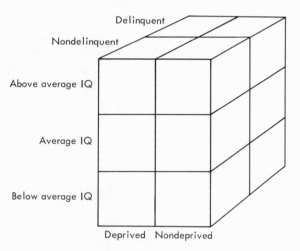

FIG. 2.   The basic 2 x 2 x 3 design.

city, to employ two levels of socioeconomic status ("deprived" and "nondeprived"), and three levels of intelligence (below average, average [90–109 IQ], and above average). As may be seen in Figure 2, this yielded a 2 x 2 x 3 design. The number of subjects falling into each of the cells of this design is shown in Table 5.

TABLE 5.   *Distribution of Subjects According to Socioeconomic Level, IQ, and Delinquency Status (K-3)*

	Delinquents			Nondelinquents		
	Below		Above	Below		Above
Socioeconomic	Average	Average	Average	Average	Average	Average
Level	IQ	IQ	IQ	IQ	IQ	IQ
Deprived	5	20	0	5	20	0
Nondeprived	13	33	15	13	33	15

As statistically oriented readers are aware, the optimal method of analyzing a design of this sort involves a 2 x 2 x 3 analysis of variance. Such an analysis would permit us simultaneously to determine not only if there are differences on a personality measure between delinquents and nondelinquents, between IQ categories, and between deprived and non-deprived subjects, but also whether there are *interaction effects* among two or more of these variables (i.e., in nonstatistical terms, and for present purposes, whether there are variations in the relationship of personality characteristics to delinquency as we proceed from one social class-IQ subgroup to another).

However, use of this one, maximally efficient method of analysis requires a basic minimum number of subjects in all cells of the design. Unfortunately, as Table 5 makes clear, this is not the case in our sample, since no subject fell in the above average-IQ-deprived-delinquent cell. Apparently it is very unusual for a subject to be delinquent, socioeconomically deprived, and still obtain an above average IQ score. (Examination of a *representative sample* of our entire population indicates that the combination of high IQ-deprived-nondelinquent is somewhat more common in the general population, but still relatively rare.)

The absence of above average IQ-deprived cells forced us to modify our methods of analysis. This will become clear as we proceed. *The important fact for the reader (whether statistically oriented or not) to realize at this point is simply that the actual distribution of our subjects made it impossible to include an above average IQ-deprived subgroup in our comparisons of the personality characteristics of delinquents and nondelinquents.*

Teacher Comments and D-score. Breaking down individual teacher comment check list items into social class-IQ subgroups was not feasible, because too few entries would have appeared in the various cells for any one trait to make statistical analysis meaningful. On the other hand, since a fairly large number of children (N-172) had D-scores, it was possible to analyze them further. Figure 3 shows the actual distribution of mean D-scores at this age level for future delinquents and nondelinquents in each of the social class-IQ subgroups, as well as in the group as a whole.

As may be seen, saying that delinquents have a mean D-score of +.23 while nondelinquents average —1.23, may be quite misleading when we come to a consideration of the various subgroups. Thus, for example, in the nondeprived-below average IQ subgroup, nondelinquents are actually closer to the overall delinquent mean than to the nondelin-

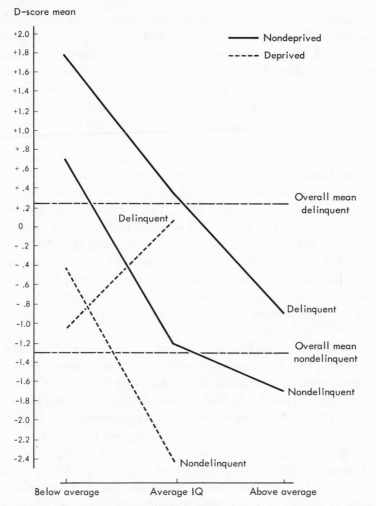

FIG. 3.   Distribution of mean D-scores for delinquents and matched nondelinquents by social class-IQ subgroup. N – 172. K – 3.

quent. Conversely, delinquent youngsters in the nondeprived-above average and the deprived-below average IQ subgroups come much closer to
the overall nondelinquent mean than to the delinquent. Such results appear to lend support to one of the basic tenets of this study, namely, that
*personality factors may be differentially related to delinquency, depend-
ing on the social class and IQ status of the child.*

Analyses of variance.   Are the kinds of differences shown in Figure
3 meaningful, however, or do they simply reflect the effects of chance?

In attempting to determine the statistical significance of the social class-IQ subgroup differences seen in Figure 3, it was not possible, for reasons already stated, to use a straightforward 2 x 2 x 3 analysis of variance. Instead, we were forced to employ three partial analyses of variance in order to achieve as nearly as possible the same degree of information (cf. p. 456). These analyses will be described briefly in this section, although nonstatistically oriented readers may wish to proceed immediately to the next section, *Teacher ratings.*

In the first place, a 2 x 5 analysis of variance was performed. This design involved two independent variables: (1) delinquency-nondelinquency, and (2) five combinations of IQ level and socioeconomic status (e.g., "Deprived-below average IQ"). This analysis yielded significant differences between delinquents and nondelinquents as a group ($p < .001$, as previously noted) and between the various social class-IQ subgroups ($p < .001$). Interpreting these results in terms of Figure 3, it appears that an individual's D-score may be significantly elevated both by delinquency and by lower social class-IQ status, except in the case of deprived delinquents, where D-score actually decreases from average to below average IQ.

However, since this design confounds IQ and social class (each subgroup used in the preceding analysis involved a combination of the two), it did not permit an evaluation of the significance of each of these variables separately. In order to deal, at least partially with this latter problem, two additional analyses of variance were performed. First, a 2 x 2 x 2 analysis of variance was carried out involving two levels of IQ (average, below average), two levels of socioeconomic status (deprived, nondeprived), and two levels of delinquency (delinquent, nondelinquent). This analysis yielded a significant overall difference between delinquents and nondelinquents ($p < .05$ and socioeconomic status ($p < .05$). In addition, there was some suggestion ($p < .20$) of an interaction effect between delinquency and intelligence, with the largest differences between delinquents and nondelinquents occurring in the average IQ range.

This type of analysis (unlike the 2 x 5 analysis) permitted us to consider the effects of intelligence and social class separately from one another at the average and below average IQ levels. However, it did not allow us to include above average IQ subjects. For this reason, one additional 2 x 3 analysis of variance was performed, involving only nondeprived subjects. This permitted us to include the above average IQ subjects and hence to cast additional light on the possible effects of IQ considered separately among nondeprived subjects. After the exclusion of deprived subjects, this analysis yielded a significant overall difference between delinquents and nondelinquents ($p < .025$), as in previous analyses. It also indicated that the D-score was strongly affected by intelligence ($p < .005$).

Teacher ratings. It will be recalled that six items of personal-social behavior were noted fairly frequently by teachers at this age-grade level. These were: *work habits, social acceptability, response to authority, sense of responsibility, regard for persons,* and *leadership.* It has already been shown that three of these traits (*social acceptability, sense of responsibility,* and *regard for persons*) differentiated delinquents from nondelinquents at better than the .05 level.

There was no assurance, however, that each of these traits would discriminate in the same direction or to the same extent as we proceeded from one social class-IQ subgroup to another.

In fact, the findings from the D-score analysis suggested the likelihood that at least some of them would not. It appeared desirable, therefore, to subject each of these traits to the same series of complementary analysis of variance designs that we had employed for D-scores, and this was done. Unfortunately, however, the results (or in some cases, the lack of results) at this age level have to be interpreted more cautiously, and also less fully for the following reason: The total number of pairs involved for each of these traits was consistently smaller than for D-score (ranging between 96 and 104, as contrasted with 172 for D-score). As it turned out, this had its greatest effect in the below average IQ-deprived subgroups, limiting the number of subjects to four in these analyses, as compared to ten in the D-score analysis. Other subgroups, while also reduced in number, still contained reasonable numbers of subjects.

At this age-grade level, therefore, the results of the D-score analysis appear deserving of greater confidence. Nevertheless, despite smaller numbers (both overall and particularly in the below average IQ-deprived subgroup), several traits still showed effects of variables other than delinquency status, and the statistically significant findings on these traits will be summarized briefly. Detailed results of the various analyses of variance supporting these statements are available elsewhere (4).

Regard for persons. Figure 4 shows the distribution of ratings for the five subgroups on this trait. As may be seen, as one progresses from below average to above average IQ among nondeprived subjects, favorableness of rating shows a (statistically significant) increase for both delinquents and nondelinquents, with the greatest increase occurring in the nondelinquent group. This has the effect of placing nondelinquents

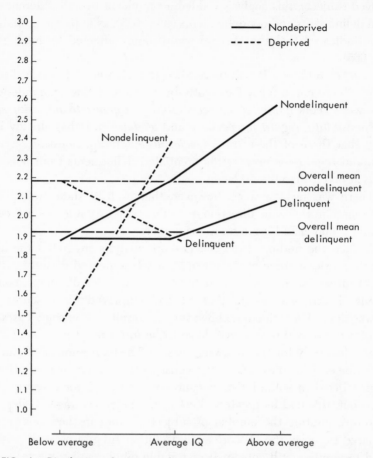

FIG. 4. Distribution of mean teacher ratings of "regard for persons" for delinquents and matched nondelinquents by social class-IQ subgroup. N – 96.
K – 3.

in the below average IQ subgroup closer to the actual delinquent mean,
while placing above average IQ delinquents closer to the overall nondelinquent mean.

It may be observed that in the below average IQ-deprived subgroup, delinquents scored more favorably than nondelinquents. This is
interesting, since it corresponds to the findings for the D-score analysis
and several other teacher ratings. However, in view of the small number
of subjects in this subgroup, this observation must be viewed merely
as suggestive; not surprisingly, it fails to find support in any of the
analyses of variance.

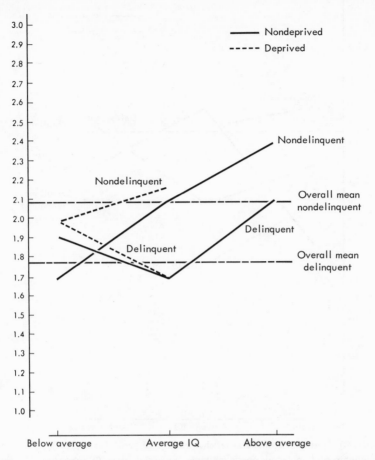

FIG. 5. Distribution of mean teacher ratings of "sense of responsibility" for delinquents and matched nondelinquents by social class-IQ subgroup. N – 104. K – 3.

Sense of responsibility. Figure 5 shows the distribution of ratings on this trait. What appears to be reflected here, according to the various analyses of variance, is a significant tendency for delinquents and nondelinquents (deprived and nondeprived) to show few differences at the below average IQ level, but marked differences at the average IQ level. Furthermore, among nondeprived subjects, there appears to be at least a tendency for favorableness of rating to increase with increases in IQ from below average to above average.

Again, as in the case of *regard for persons,* it would appear presumptuous to conclude that overall delinquent-nondelinquent differences on

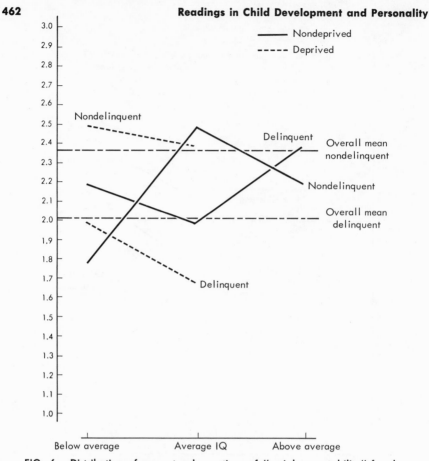

FIG. 6.   Distribution of mean teacher ratings of "social acceptability" for delinquents and matched nondelinquents by social class-IQ subgroup. N – 96.
K – 3.

this trait are likely to be equally applicable to all subgroups. For example,
as may be seen, among nondeprived subjects, *delinquents* of above average IQ fell at the overall *nondelinquent* mean and *nondelinquents* of
below average IQ actually fell below the overall *delinquent* mean. Furthermore, while fairly wide differences separating nondelinquents and delinquents occurred among all subgroups at the average and above average
IQ levels, at the below average IQ level there were either no differences
or the direction of differences was actually reversed (though not significantly so).

Social acceptability.   Figure 6 shows the distribution of teacher
ratings on this trait. In this case, it will be recalled from Study I that the
significance level for overall delinquent-nondelinquent differences fell at

the .025 level. As Figure 6 suggests, the failure to obtain a larger level of significance appears to have been due primarily to reversals in the direction of delinquent-nondelinquent differences among nondeprived subjects at the below average and above average IQ levels. This interpretation finds support in the various analyses of variance conducted for this trait.

Certainly, it would appear incautious, on the basis of these findings, to assume that overall delinquent and nondelinquent means for *social acceptability* could be applied to nondeprived subgroups of below average and above average intelligence, although they appear quite applicable to the other subgroups, both deprived and nondeprived.

Work habits. The distribution of teacher ratings for this trait is shown in Figure 7. It will be recalled that this trait, unlike those discussed above, showed no significant overall mean difference between delinquents and nondelinquents. When one examines Figure 7, these results do not appear surprising. While in a number of subgroups fairly wide delinquent-nondelinquent differences are seen (considerably wider than the *overall* mean difference), in the case of two of the three greatest differences, the delinquents scored more favorably.

These findings would appear to raise a warning of a different sort from those previously suggested. While the numbers of subjects involved in the subgroups showing reversals is quite small, making definitive statements suspect, it is at least possible (as a delinquency-intelligence *interaction effect* suggests) that the failure to obtain a significant overall delinquent-nondelinquent difference may have been due, not to the possibility that there were, in fact, no differences, but that the nature and distribution of these differences varied from one subgroup to another.

Obviously, this may be true of a number of personality characteristics. If so, investigations which confine themselves to studying only *overall* delinquent-nondelinquent differences (and this includes the great majority) may be ruling out as unrelated to delinquency, traits which, in some subgroups at least, and conceivably in all, actually may be strongly related to it.

The remaining two traits, *leadership* and *response to authority,* had originally shown no significant overall mean differences between delinquents and nondelinquents, and also showed no other main or interaction effects in the various analyses of variance.

Summary of Teacher Ratings and D-score Findings

Viewed together, the findings from the D-score analysis, supple-

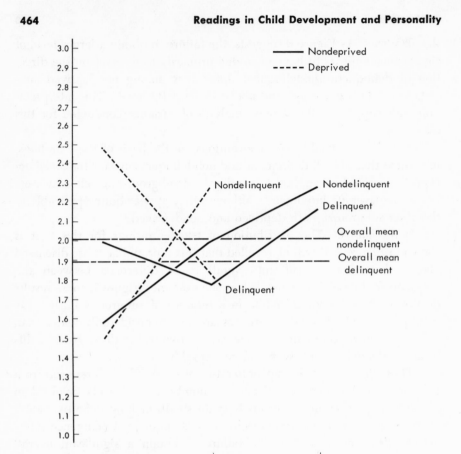

FIG. 7.   Distribution of mean teacher ratings of "work habits" for delinquents and matched nondelinquents by social class-IQ subgroup. N – 98. K – 3.

mented by the more limited findings on individual teacher rating analyses, suggest that:

1.   Personality trait ratings may be differentially related to delinquency, depending on socioeconomic status and IQ. As a result, *overall* means and mean differences between delinquents and nondelinquents may be quite misleading when applied to a particular social class-IQ subgroup. In many instances, delinquents in a particular subgroup scored closer to the overall nondelinquent mean than to the delinquent; conversely, in other subgroups nondelinquents scored closer to the overall delinquent mean than to the nondelinquent. This fact alone would appear to lend support to one of the basic hypotheses of this study; namely, that

personality factors may be differentially related to delinquency, depending on the particular personality factor involved and on the social class and IQ status of the child.

2. On overall D-score, and on most individual traits, nondelinquents obtained more favorable mean ratings than delinquents in most subgroups. This would be expected, in view of the fact that significant overall differences between delinquents and nondelinquents (with nondelinquents scoring more favorably) were obtained for D-score, *social acceptability, sense of responsibility,* and *regard for persons.*

3. The largest mean differences between delinquents and nondelinquents occurred without exception among socioeconomically deprived children, either in the average IQ or below average IQ subgroups.

4. In some instances (e.g., *work habits*) where significant overall differences between delinquents and nondelinquents are *not* found, in this and other investigations, this may be due, at least partly, to variations in the direction of delinquent-nondelinquent differences from one social class-IQ subgroup to another.

5. In the case of boys of below average IQ, future delinquents *tended* to receive *more favorable* ratings than nondelinquents. This was especially likely to be true in the case of socioeconomically deprived subjects, although this observation must be viewed with considerable caution, due to the small number of subjects frequently present in the below average-IQ-deprived subgroups.

It would appear that in those instances where significant interaction effects between delinquency and intelligence were found on either the 2 x 2 x 2 or 2 x 3 analyses of variance, absence of delinquent-nondelinquent differences, or reversals in the direction of these differences, among children of below average IQ were primarily responsible.

It should also be obvious that in *all* instances where delinquent subjects received the same or more favorable scores than nondelinquents, it would be a mistake to consider overall delinquent-nondelinquent differences as applicable to these subgroups, since the latter did not contribute to the size and significance of the overall difference, and in at least some cases (i.e., those where significant interaction effects were found) substantially reduced them.

6. There is some tendency among *nondeprived* subjects for favorableness of rating to increase with increases in IQ. This observation is supported by the fact that a highly significant main effect for intelligence was obtained on the 2 x 3 analysis of variance for D-score. Among individual teacher ratings on the 2 x 3 analysis, considerable variation was

found, with significance levels for main effect for intelligence ranging from .05 to nonsignificance, with most traits showing a *trend* toward significance. No such tendency for favorableness of rating to increase with intelligence could be observed among *deprived* subjects.

7. Except in the case of D-score, there is little *direct* relation between favorableness of teacher ratings and socioeconomic status, and even in the case of D-score, the expected direction of the difference is reversed, with deprived children scoring *more favorably* at both IQ levels, as the accompanying figures indicate. These statements are supported by the absence of a main effect for socioeconomic status in the 2 x 2 x 2 analyses, except in the case of D-score where a significant effect was found.

This finding is of considerable general interest, in view of the contention of many sociologists and psychologists that teachers tend to rate lower-class children more unfavorably than middle-class children on personal-social traits in the school situation as a result of bias stemming from the average teacher's membership in middle-class culture. At least in this age-grade period, the most *favorable* teacher comments and ratings at the average IQ level characteristically were given to *deprived* nondelinquents.

It would appear that the apparent bias of teachers noted by some investigators may be due to a greater incidence of lower IQs (not necessarily lower potential intelligence) and of delinquent trends among socioeconomically deprived children. But where a deprived child, even though he may be identified with lower-class culture, appears capable of average intellectual performance and socially responsible future behavior, he tends to be rated, at least according to this investigation, as or more favorably than his middle-class peer.

SUMMARY

Even in the period from kindergarten through the third grade, future delinquents generally appeared more poorly adapted than nondelinquent peers of the same age, sex, IQ, socioeconomic status, residential background, and ethnic group membership, as measured by teacher ratings and a content analysis of informal teacher comments. As a group, they manifested less acceptable social behavior, more academic difficulty, and a greater incidence of emotional problems.

However, these general findings cannot be applied indiscriminately to all subgroups in the population. There were marked differences in the relationship of various personality traits to delinquency status from one social class-IQ subgroup to another. While in most subgroups non-delinquents received more favorable ratings from teachers on most traits, the size of delinquent-nondelinquent differences and the ranges in which these differences occurred varied considerably.

Furthermore, on some traits even the direction of delinquent-non-delinquent differences changed as one proceeded from one social class-IQ subgroup to another. Thus, on a majority of traits, future delinquents of below average IQ received more favorable teacher ratings than their nondelinquent peers. In short, ratings of personal-social behavior at this age were related, not only to future delinquency status, but also to socio-economic status and intelligence, whether directly or through interaction with delinquency status.

REFERENCES

1. Bandura, A., & Walters, R. H. *Adolescent aggression.* New York: Ronald, 1959.
2. Cloward, R. A., & Ohlin, L. *Delinquency and opportunity: a theory of delinquent groups.* Glencoe, Ill.: Free Press, 1960.
3. Conger, J. J., Miller, W. C., Gaskill, H. S., & Walsmith, C. R. *Progress report.* (Grant no. M–3040) National Institute of Mental Health, U.S.P.H.S., Washington, D.C., 1960.
4. Conger, J. J., & Miller, W. C., *Personality, social class, and delinquency.* New York: Wiley (in press).
5. Glueck, S., & Glueck, E. T. *One thousand juvenile delinquents.* Cambridge: Harvard Univer. Press, 1934.
6. Glueck, S., & Glueck, E. T. *Unraveling juvenile delinquency.* New York: Commonwealth Fund, 1950.
7. Hathaway, S. R., and Monachesi, E. D. (Eds.) *Analyzing and predicting juvenile delinquency with the MMPI.* Minneapolis: Univer. Minnesota Press, 1953.
8. Healy, W., & Bronner, A. F. *New light on delinquency and its treatment.* New Haven: Yale Univer. Press, 1936.
9. Maccoby, Eleanor E., Johnson, J. P., & Church, R. M. Community integration and the social control of juvenile delinquency. *J. soc. Issues,* 1958, **14,** 38–51.
10. Merrill, M. A. *Problems of child delinquency.* Boston: Houghton Mifflin, 1947.
11. Salisbury, H. E. *The shook-up generation.* New York: Harper (Crest Books), 1959.
12. Shaw, C. R. *Delinquency areas.* Chicago: Univer. Chicago Press, 1929.
13. Shaw, C. R., McKay, H. D., *et al. Juvenile delinquency and urban areas.* Chicago: Univer. Chicago Press, 1942.

14. Wattenberg, W. W. *The adolescent years.* New York: Harcourt Brace, 1955.
15. Werner, E. & Gallistel, E. Prediction of outstanding performances, delinquency, and emotional disturbance from childhood evaluations. *Child Develpm.* 1961, **32,** 255–260.
16. Wirt, R. D., & Briggs, P. F. Personality and environmental factors in the development of delinquency. *Psychol. Monogr.,* 1959, **73,** No. 15, 1–47.

INDEXES

INDEX OF NAMES

INDEX OF SUBJECTS